THE THEATRE OF REVOLT

THE THEATRE OF REVOLT

An Approach to the Modern Drama

ROBERT BRUSTEIN

WITH A NEW PREFACE BY THE AUTHOR

Elephant Paperbacks

IVAN R. DEE, PUBLISHER, CHICAGO

THE THEATRE OF REVOLT. Copyright © 1962, 1963, 1964, 1991 by
Robert Brustein. This book was originally published in 1964 and is here
reprinted by arrangement with the author.

First ELEPHANT PAPERBACK edition published 1991 by Ivan R. Dee,
Inc., 1332 North Halsted Street, Chicago 60622. Manufactured in the
United States of America and printed on acid-free paper.

Library of Congress Cataloging-in-Publication Data:
Brustein, Robert Sanford, 1927–
      The theatre of revolt : an approach to the modern drama /
Robert Brustein. — 1st Elephant paperback ed.
            p.   cm.
      Reprint. Originally published: Boston : Little, Brown, 1964.
      Includes bibliographical references and index.
      ISBN 0-929587-53-7
      1. Drama—20th century—History and criticism. I. Title.
PN2189.B7   1991
809.2'04—dc20   90-23644

FOR NORMA: *La bella donna della mia mente*

Foreword

The purposes of this book are threefold: to examine the development of a single consuming idea or attitude in eight modern playwrights; to analyze the work of these writers in depth; and to suggest an approach to the modern drama as a whole. The undertaking is ambitious, and, no doubt, smacks of presumption. How can eight men adequately represent such a large and complicated manifestation as modern dramatic literature? How indeed can one attitude or idea suitably encompass the variety in the work of these eight alone? To justify my claim, I hope to demonstrate, during the course of this study, that the theme of revolt is sufficiently general and inclusive to merit this unusual emphasis: it is the current which runs through the majority of modern plays. Similarly, I hope to show how a playwright's handling of this theme determines his approach to character, plot, diction, and style. If I can persuade the reader of this through reference to the writers I have included, he will then be able to see, I hope, how this method can be fruitfully applied to many playwrights not directly considered in these pages. The modern drama has hitherto been studied largely from the point of view of style — as a manifestation of Realism, Naturalism, Symbolism, Expressionism, etc. By treating the modern drama as an expression of revolt, I intend to illustrate how all these "isms" merely disguise the essential unity of this movement. For a movement it is, the most important modern dramatists being bound together by common assumptions and a common point of attack.

These assertions I must justify in the book. But here I must defend my choice of those eight writers included for special study: Ibsen,

Strindberg, Shaw, Chekhov, Brecht, Pirandello, O'Neill, and (considered together with Artaud) Genet. Most of these names need no justification; but the list is partial; and there may be disappointment over the exclusion of this or that particular playwright. In anticipation of these objections, I should declare that my selection was guided partly by principle, partly by prejudice. I believe these eight dramatists to be the finest, most enduring writers in the field; and I was determined not to include any playwright who would not be read fifty years hence. There are those who may regret the omission of Sean O'Casey; but he has always struck me as an extremely overrated writer with two or three competent Naturalist plays to hi credit, followed by a lot of ideological bloat and embarrassing bom bast. Jean Giraudoux and Jean Anouilh are widely regarded, but i is no doubt a fault in me that I have never been able to respond ver strongly to either: both strike me as gifted stylists with shallow point of view and fragile sensibilities. Albert Camus and Jean Paul Sartr are stimulating minds but indifferent dramatists; I have, therefore exploited their ideas while ignoring their plays. Among Americar playwrights, Thornton Wilder, Arthur Miller, and Tennessee Williams all have enthusiastic partisans: I am not among them. There are a number of newer writers — especially Beckett, Ionesco, and Dürrenmatt — who strike me as very interesting, but none has yet completed a sufficiently various body of writing to be included in this book (though many are discussed in passing). I do regret that I was not able to consider the plays of Synge, Lorca, and Yeats. I admire all three writers excessively; but while I could probably justify their omission on the grounds that their work is not sufficiently ambitious or varied, the simple fact is that I omitted them for lack of space. If the interested reader sees the relevance of their work to the drama of revolt, then I have accomplished a major purpose of this book.

I wish to thank those who gave generously of their time and advice, especially during the early stages in the preparation of this manuscript: Eric Bentley, who prodded me into new areas of thought, George P. Elliott, who provoked me into new areas of feeling, Evert Sprinchorn, who opened up new areas of research, Stanley Burnshaw, who corrected my grammar. Whatever errors the book still contains, of course, are my own; but many errors were avoided with the help of these good men. I also wish to thank my students at Columbia College, who continue to be a source of intellectual stimulation to me, and who unwittingly helped to write this book. And I am indebted to the Guggenheim Foundation for a grant in 1961-1962, and to Columbia's Council for Research in the Humanities for two grants in lieu of summer teaching. Finally, I wish to thank my stepson, Phillip, for permitting me to devote time to writing that otherwise would have been spent with him; and my dear wife, Norma, for her continuing support, encouragement, and love to one who was often morose, and discouraged at his labors.

Preface to the Second Edition

Over a quarter of a century has passed since *The Theatre of Revolt* was first published, years which constitute a period of considerable activity in the drama. Readers and students sometimes ask me if the intervening time has altered my estimation of the playwrights discussed or my perception of the movement they represented. I am asked even more often whom I would have included if the book were to be written today.

My answer to the first question is a qualified no. Revolt in its messianic, social, and existential manifestations still seems to me a highly useful way, though not the only way, to characterize the Romantic movement of modern drama. And virtually all the eight playwrights included have maintained their high status as the strongest influences on the direction of this movement in its form and substance. Samuel Beckett—among those I found it premature to include, having not yet completed "a sufficiently various body of writing"—is a significant omission. He is the great metaphysical playwright of our time and perhaps the most characteristic exponent of what I called existential revolt. I regret my failure to give him a chapter of his own.

I think, too, that if *The Theatre of Revolt* were to be written today, it would have to include a chapter on post-O'Neill American playwrights, notably David Mamet, Sam Shepard, and David Rabe, as well as on the visionary auteur/director Robert Wilson, who is beginning to restore to the drama some of its earlier messianic ambitions. Harold Pinter, David Hare, and Caryl Churchill merit attention as a manifestation of post-Shaw British revolt, though like the Americans none yet deserves a single chapter to him- or herself. The same is true of post-Brecht German drama (Handke, Kroetz, Mueller), post-Pirandello Italian (Dario Fo), and post-Chekhov Russian (Mayakovsky and Bulgakov). No single dramatist separates himself from the national pack in the manner of the eight seminal figures who form the substance of the book.

I think also that any new version of *The Theatre of Revolt* would have to pay considerably more attention to the production aspects of the theatre, especially directing. When I first wrote this book, I was a full-time critic, teacher, and scholar. Since then I have supplemented these interests with a much deeper involvement in practice. I hope that my book has proved helpful not just to students of modern drama in preparing for exams but also to practitioners in preparing for production. Still, plays are meant to be performed rather than read (or read about), and it would have been useful had I included more hints about how these plays can be fulfilled through staging.

It is true that I have discussed this, in desultory fashion, in subsequent writings. But if I ever get the chance to write a sequel to *The Theatre of Revolt,* I am pledged to pay it the attention it deserves.

Cambridge, 1990

Contents

Contents

I

THE THEATRE OF REVOLT

Let us begin with a pair of images.

First, imagine an open temple of classical proportions, surrounded by rising tiers. Gathered on separate levels are artisans, citizens, nobility — divided into classes but forming a unified congregation of spectators. In front of the temple is an altar before which stands a high priest in hieratic robes. Beyond the temple is a city; beyond the city, the celestial spheres, moving steadily in their orbits. The priest conducts a ritual ceremony by miming a myth of heroism and violence. The congregation is startled by the growing frenzy of the action; the atmosphere grows taut and strained. The high priest concludes his service with a ritual sacrifice, and blood pours from the altar. The congregation screams as if it were the victim. Some spectators fall from their seats; the temple cracks; the city begins to crumble; the spheres start wildly from their course. At the point when total dissolution seems imminent, the scene freezes. The spectators file out, their anxiety mingled with an ethereal calm.

Now, imagine a perfectly level plain in a desolate land. In the foreground, an uneasy crowd of citizens huddle together on the ruins of an ancient temple. Beyond them, a broken altar, bristling with artifacts. Beyond that, empty space. An emaciated priest in disreputable garments stands before the ruined altar, level with the crowd, glancing into a distorting mirror. He cavorts grotesquely before it, inspecting his own image in several outlandish positions. The crowd mutters ominously and partially disperses. The priest turns the mirror

[3]

on those who remain to reflect them sitting stupidly on rubble. They gaze at their images for a moment, painfully transfixed; then, horror-struck, they run away, hurling stones at the altar and angry impreca-tions at the priest. The priest, shaking with anger, futility, and irony, turns the mirror on the void. He is alone in the void.

The first is an image for the theatre of communion; the second for the theatre of revolt.

By theatre of communion, I mean the theatre of the past, domi-nated by Sophocles, Shakespeare, and Racine, where traditional myths were enacted before an audience of believers against the back-ground of a shifting but still coherent universe. By theatre of revolt, I mean the theatre of the great insurgent modern dramatists, where myths of rebellion are enacted before a dwindling number of specta-tors in a flux of vacancy, bafflement, and accident. I have described these two theatres metaphorically in order to make two points rapidly: (1) that the traditional and the modern theatres are clearly dis-tinguishable from each other in regard to the function of their drama-tists, the engagement of their audiences, and the nature of the worlds they imply and evoke, and (2) that the playwrights of the modern theatre form a movement just as distinctive as the various schools of the past. Ibsen, Strindberg, Chekhov, Shaw, Brecht, Pirandello, O'Neill, and Genet — to name the dramatists discussed at length in this book — are all highly individualistic artists. Yet they share one thing in common which separates them from their predecessors and links them to each other. This is their attitude of revolt, an attitude which is the product of an essentially Romantic inheritance. It is my purpose in this book to isolate the distinguishing characteristics of modern drama, to demonstrate its unity as a Romantic movement, and to trace the development of Romantic revolt in the works of its eight foremost playwrights.

As a prologue to these discussions, however, it is necessary to examine how dramatic revolt evolved; and for this purpose I must emphasize not the differences between the traditional and modern theatres, but rather their organic connections. For while the theatre of revolt has immediate roots in nineteenth-century Romanticism, it is, in a larger sense, the inevitable consequence of a long preparatory process which begins in the Middle Ages. The ruins in the second image are the remains of the proud monuments of the first. It is atop the broken hierarchies, discredited values, and collapsed institutions of traditional culture that the modern dramatist meditates his revolt.

The theatre of communion, in fact, reaches its historical climax with a premonitory glimpse into the disintegration of the traditional world order. The drama of the Western world, like the drama of the Greeks, describes a trajectory which arches from belief to uncertainty to unbelief, always developing in the direction of greater skepticism towards temporal and spiritual laws. Greek tragedy, for example, moves from the religious piety of Aeschylus to the tragic ambivalence of Sophocles to the angry agnosticism of Euripides, finally dissipating itself in the spiritual indifference of Menander and New Comedy. And Western drama develops from the religious certainty of the medieval playwrights to the doubts and hesitations of the Stuart dramatists, where the characters of Webster and Middleton look up to empty heavens and Shakespeare's tragic heroes peer into a vast abyss. A growing sense of futility and despair infects both Hellenistic culture and the culture of late Renaissance Europe, which is reflected in certain Naturalistic philosophies, calling everything in doubt.

> 'Tis all in pieces, all coherence gone;
> All just supply, and all relation.

In England, John Donne speaks for an age anticipating the imminent collapse of order.

Donne's contemporaries provide these premonitions with theatrical form in myths of defeat, and in images of decay, mutability, and disease. The music of the spheres turns to a discord; the string of degree is untuned; the paragon of animals is also a quintessence of dust. Skulls and skeletons become recurrent props in the theatrical display, and the highest value is courage in the face of death. Comedy grows brutal, tragedy loses its clear definition, and good and evil become confused, as the universal order is rearranged to the accompaniment of loud cracking sounds in the heavens. Before long, the theatre is dominated by purely secular forms. When the Romans took over from the Greeks, they banished God from the stage and plumped the audience down in the area once reserved for the altar. In Western drama, Heroic plays and Restoration comedies accomplish the same ends, providing an atmosphere of fake idealism or brutal cynicism, but little interest in the religious nature of man.

If the theatre of communion climaxes with a sense of spiritual disintegration, the theatre of revolt *begins* with this sense, inheriting from the Western tradition a continuity of decay in an advanced stage. Shakespeare developed, slowly and painfully, a negative view of life, but this is the initial assumption of the modern dramatist; and unlike the Greeks, he can make no restitution for the bitterness of his protest. No plague is purged by the exile of his Oedipus, no Court of the Areopagus founded on the suffering of his Orestes, no Denmark restored by the death of his Hamlet — even though exile, suffering, and death are often the unreasonable fate of his heroes. Similarly, if the theatre of communion incorporated fearful visions and agonizing prophecies, these have all been realized in the theatre of revolt. Lear's eloquent madness has degenerated into the insane babbling of Ibsen's Oswald; Leontes's momentary jealousy has become the pathological obsession of Strindberg's Father. Gloucester mutters against the wanton cruelty of gods which Chekhov's futilitarians do not even grace with curses; Albany foresees a day when men will prey upon each other — it has already arrived in Brecht. Benedict and Beatrice are wilting in Shaw's Heartbreak House; the melancholy of Hamlet quickens into the painful anguish of Pirandello and the black despair of O'Neill; Iago's half-world becomes the whole world of Jean Genet. *No* and *nothing* and *never* — Lear's repeated negatives — are now the modern dramatist's vocabulary of refusal, as he labors to cast off his legacy of dissolution.

This legacy, of course, is not just a literary inheritance; it is the time's bequest; the world which fosters the modern dramatist is growing increasingly circumscribed and limited. When Ibsen leaves Norway in 1864 to begin his great epic dramas in Rome, the scientific

[6]

Naturalism prefigured by Galileo, Bacon, and Descartes has already triumphed; it is now the world view of civilized Europe. Darwin's *Origin of the Species* has appeared in 1859, a mortal blow at the divine origins of man. In the same year, Marx has completed his *Critique of Political Economy*, a mechanistic approach to history which analyzes the development of cultures solely on the basis of class interests. And in 1863, Renan publishes his *Life of Christ*, in which Jesus, denied his divine birth, his miracles, and his resurrection, is characterized less as a supernatural being than as an inspired prophet and rebel.

Naturalism is replacing supernaturalism, the experiment is superseding the apparition. The statistic is being substituted for the insight, prose is supplanting poetry. Religious orthodoxy is still powerful, but the Church has become the prey of pharisees, of hypocritical observances and superficial respectability. Science is growing arrogant and assured, but is providing no magical ideas or metaphysical grace to satisfy mankind's yearning for ritual and sanctity. As for the great social-political revolutions, these have resulted in the consolidation of middle-class power; and the failure of the radical revolutions of 1848 have discouraged hopes that this power will be easily overthrown. Liberty, equality, and fraternity are becoming cant terms, as wage slavery replaces serfdom, justice is corrupted by privilege, and neighbors prey upon each other for gain, while progress pays for its blessings with the evils of industrialism: slag heaps, child labor, blackened cities. The revolutionaries of the early nineteenth century had anticipated the full realization of human freedom. But the deterministic sciences have put limits on man's possibilities, the machine has broken his link with nature and his fellow beings, and the State is beginning to make increasingly greater claims on his person. Modern man is stalked by chaos:

> Things fall apart, the center cannot hold;
> Mere anarchy is loosed upon the world.

Yeats rephrases the premonitions of Donne in even more apocalyptic accents. The image of modern society becomes that of a dungeon —

gray, filthy, squalid, forbidding — where man labors interminably, in the poisoned air, at humiliating tasks.

The modern drama, in short, rides in on the second wave of Romanticism — not the cheerful optimism of Rousseau, with his emphasis on institutional reform, but rather the dark fury of Nietzsche, with his radical demands for a total transformation of man's spiritual life. And Nietzsche remains the most seminal philosophical influence on the theatre of revolt, the intellect against which almost every modern dramatist must measure his own. When Nietzsche declared the death of God, he declared the death of all traditional values as well. Man could create new values only by becoming God: the only alternative to nihilism lay in revolt. Nietzsche's arrogant *I will* was a desperate response to an absurd universe. And all modern revolt, as Albert Camus writes in his monumental study *The Rebel* (*L'Homme Révolté*), is "born of the spectacle of irrationality, confronted with an unjust and incomprehensible condition." Confronted with the same metaphysical absurdity, the modern dramatist takes up Nietzsche's challenge, assuming an attitude of refusal which puts him in conflict with the laws of modern necessity. Rejecting God, church, community, and family — vindicating the rights of the individual against the claims of government, morality, conventions, and rules — he adopts the posture of the rebel, chafing against restraints, determined to make all barriers crack.

The revolt of the dramatist, it is important to add, is more imaginative than practical — imaginative, absolute, and pure. In the earlier phases of the theatre of revolt — in some of the works of Ibsen, for example, and of Shaw — the drama sometimes begins to look like an act of utility; and in the plays of Brecht, it is designed to lead to political revolution. Even in the majority of these works, however, the programmatic element is actually insignificant — or much too radical for any practical application. Dramatic art is not identical with reality, but rather proceeds along a parallel plane; and dramatic revolt, therefore, is always much more *total* than the programs of political agitators or social reformers. The modern dramatist is essentially a metaphysical rebel, not a practical revolutionary; whatever

[8]

his personal political convictions, his art is the expression of a spiritual condition. For he is a militant of the ideal, an anarchic individualist, concerned with the impossible rather than the possible; and his discontent extends to the very roots of existence. The work of art itself becomes a subversive gesture — a more imaginative reconstruction of a chaotic, disordered world.

One consequence of the dramatist's revolt is his estrangement from officialdom, and — since he rejects the conventional pieties — from the official culture. This culture continues to persist, of course, in the theatrical marketplace, where the commercial dramatist, in Strindberg's words, functions as a "lay preacher, peddling the ideas of his time in popular form, popular enough for the middle classes, mainstay of theatre audiences, to grasp the gist of the matter without troubling their brains too much." But the theatre of revolt is not a popular theatre, nor are its dramatists much concerned with instructing the middle classes. Quite the contrary, they have apparently determined, like Théophile Gautier, to be "the terror of the sleek, baldheaded bourgeois" — their common enemy becomes middle-class man himself. From Ibsen, who turned in rage on those "fatted swine-snouts," to Genet, who puts upon the stage the ritual annihilation of the entire white race, every rebel dramatist is incensed by some aspect of this prosperous world; and even Chekhov, the gentlest spirit in the theatre of revolt, is moved to declare about his plays, "All I wanted to say was 'Have a look at yourselves and see how bad and dreary your lives are.' "

Chekhov indicts the bourgeois for his lack of culture and lack of nerve, Ibsen for his mediocrity and compromise, Strindberg for his cowardice, Shaw for his complacency, Brecht for his hypocrisy and greed, Pirandello for his meddling and scandal-mongering, O'Neill for his Philistinism, Genet for his sham. The indictments accumulate, adding fuel to the fire of Nietzsche, who had declared war on "the mediators and mixers" — those "half-and-half ones that have neither learned to bless nor to curse from the heart." The ideal of the golden mean was anathema to Nietzsche ("That is mediocrity," he wrote, "though it be called moderation"); and many of the rebel dramatists share his contempt for the soft virtues of Christianity and the reasonable, humanitarian values of liberal democracy. Detesting middle ways, scorning middle emotions, defying the middle classes, the rebel dramatist begins to celebrate, secretly or openly, the values of the extreme — excess, instinct, emancipation, ecstasy, drunkenness, rapture, revolt. Thus, the "damned compact liberal majority," as Ibsen called it, becomes the dramatist's chief antagonist. And since this majority constitutes the theatre audience, the spectator himself comes under attack, either assailed from the stage directly, or represented on the stage as a satirical figure. No longer the spokesman for the audience, or its paid entertainer, the dramatist becomes its adversary, letting the spectators know, as Shaw lets them know in the preface to his earliest plays, that "my attacks are directed against themselves, not against my stage figures."

Inevitably, the dramatist pays for his revolt by being rejected in turn. Like Joyce, who fled from Ireland refusing to serve what he no longer believed, the modern dramatist spends much of his creative life in exile — a fugitive, outcast, or outlaw. Ibsen, the Norwegian, goes to Rome and, later, to Germany, declaring, "I had to flee the swinishness up there to feel fully cleansed"; the Swedish Strindberg finds refuge from the real and imagined abuse of his countrymen in Paris; Shaw leaves Ireland forever to live in England; Brecht, in retreat from the Nazis, moves to Scandinavia and thence to the United States; Genet spends most of his young manhood in European jails. As a result, the theatre of revolt is a cosmopolitan movement, nourished by international sources. While the dramatist continues to write of his country, even in exile, he no longer exalts it or advances its cause. Nationalistic dramas are rare, while national characteristics stimulate his satire and reproaches.

Even when the rebel dramatist is not in geographical exile, he feels like an outlander, since he has lost his sense of belonging. A stranger to his family, a leper to society, a heretic to the Church, he is also a metaphysical outcast, for he is spiritually destitute as soon as he ceases to believe in God. "Then the time of exile begins," writes Camus, discussing Nietzsche, "the endless search for justification, the aimless nostalgia, 'the most painful, the most heartbreaking question, that of the heart which asks itself: where can I feel at home?' " "Where is — my home?" the inconsolable Nietzsche continually asked. "For it do I ask and seek, and have sought, but have not found it." And Ibsen writes to Georg Brandes, upon his return to Norway: "Up here by the fjords in my native land. But — but — but! Where am I to find my homeland?" *Where am I to find my homeland?* — each rebel dramatist must ask himself the same heartbreaking question. In the theatre of revolt, the note of banishment is repeatedly struck, and the modern drama aches with nostalgia, loneliness, and regret.

In *Thus Spake Zarathustra,* Nietzsche prophesied the end of exile: "Ye lonesome ones, ye seceding ones, ye shall one day be a people: out of ye who have chosen yourselves, shall a chosen people arise. . . ." The dramatist of revolt looks forward to the same consummation, and even tries to realize it through his work. The more isolated and hermetic he becomes, the more his vision of communion intensifies — the alienated spirit begins to seek out those of his kind. Even writing for the theatre suggests these needs, since the theatre audience represents a collective in miniature; but the dramatist wants to convert this collective into a "chosen people" through the transforming power of his art. He is, in short, like a spoiled priest who still wants to exercise his function but cannot believe in the Christian sacraments. In a world without God, he must shape a congregation, invent a liturgy, create a faith. "To kill God and to build a Church," writes Camus, "are the constant and contradictory purposes of rebellion." These contradictory purposes are the foundation of the theatre of revolt, where each dramatist labors to make a new union out of his secession — to make his initial act of revolt the occasion for a new kind of grace.

In *Inferno,* Strindberg speaks of a religion for which the whole world is waiting — not "a compromise with the established religions" but rather "a progress towards the new." This is the demand of the theatre of revolt. Playwrights like Eliot and Claudel may make their peace with "the established religions," but the theatre of revolt is distinctly heterodox, when not downright heretic. And though Strindberg and O'Neill are both temporarily attracted to Christianity, the Church even for them is only a way station on a long Romantic quest for faith. This quest is common to all the rebel dramatists, though it takes various directions. Some are drawn to science, some to politics, some to art, some to Satanism, some to Buddhism, Hinduism, or Confucianism — but each of these creeds is a religious alternative, and even the most materialistic programs are embraced as a form of metaphysical salvation. Ibsen's Darwinism has strong mystical overtones; Shaw's Lamarckism is a branch of his "vital religion"; even Brecht's Communism seems like a substitute for going into a monastery. Needless to say, none of these faiths prove very satisfactory as a means to salvation — the new world religion has yet to arrive. The theatre of revolt fails to build its Church, and records this failure in a growing mood of despair.

And also in a growing mood of withdrawal. The drama begins to assume the characteristics of a private art, even though it has always been the most public of literary expressions. Because of the dramatist's breach with his audience, and his indifference to dramatic rules, modern plays begin to assume epic dimensions — longer, more difficult, and more episodic than plays of the past. This increasing formlessness is accompanied by an increasing discursiveness, as the rebel dramatist becomes an evangelist, proselytizing for his faith. Prefaces, prologues, critical tracts, manifestos, and appendices start to accompany works of drama — the playwright produces not only myths but also commentaries on the myths. Chekhov alone, in the theatre of revolt, remains uninterested in general ideas; the others become obsessed with doctrine and dogma, frequently breaking out of dramatic forms into extradramatic formulations.

The theatre of revolt, in other words, is extremely self-conscious and self-involved, as befits a Romantic movement. And like the other Romantics, the dramatist begins to enter his work to a hitherto unprecedented degree. Strindberg and O'Neill are almost indistinguishable from their heroes; Ibsen and Shaw identify themselves with their heroes to a large extent; Brecht hides his experience in his plays, but speaks out directly through the figure of a third-person narrator; Pirandello and Genet shape their works to an almost solipsistic concept; and even Chekhov hovers about his plays as a moral presence. Whether involved as an idea or a character, the modern dramatist is continually exploring the possibilities of his own personality — not only representing but exhorting, not only dramatizing the others but examining the self. This self-examination, common enough to the other Romantic arts, does not with them constitute such a radical break with tradition. The material of the lyric poet has always been largely personal, and even the autobiographical element in Proust or Joyce does not violate the conventions of a form which, ever since Homer, has permitted the author his part in the narrative. The subjectivity of the rebel dramatist, on the other hand, is unique, since the drama has traditionally been a form of imitation — impersonal, objective, detached — with the author excluded from the work.

Still, the theatre of revolt is only partially subjective; the rebel dramatist continues to observe the requirements of his form. A play proceeds by dialogue, and dialogue implies debate and conflict. Without debate, the drama is propaganda; without conflict, mere fantasizing. The rebel dramatist may desire to live out his revolt in his art, but this desire is disciplined by his objective consciousness. Personal fantasies and abstract ideas enter the modern drama, but concrete action and imitation remain — the self shares the stage with the others. The platform is double-layered because the artist himself is split — split in his attitude towards himself, towards life, towards the world. "Artistic creation," observes Camus, "is a demand for unity and a rejection of the world. But it rejects the world on account of what it lacks and in the name of what it sometimes is." And so it is with dramatic creation. The rebel who wishes to transform the world is also an artist who must accurately represent it; the Romantic who would destroy all boundaries is also a Classicist, accepting limitations in life and art. This ambivalence makes the rebel dramatist vacillate between negation and affirmation, between rebellion and reality. Unable to master his contradictions, he dramatizes them in his plays, grateful for a form in which tensions do not have to be resolved.

[13]

Thus, while each of the rebel dramatists takes revolt as his central theme, he also criticizes revolt in the name of reality; at the same time that he identifies with his rebel characters, he repudiates them too. In Ibsen, especially, revolt is ambiguously treated, being alternately exalted and punished; but this ambiguity pervades all the major dramatists. In Shaw, the rebel is both the hope of the world and a windy orator; in Chekhov, he is torpid and apathetic for all his vigorous speechifying; in Brecht, he embodies the impulse towards change and the impulse towards adaptation; in Strindberg, O'Neill, and Pirandello, he subsides into a melancholy stoicism after the failure of his dreams; in Genet, he develops into the very image of authority he wants to annihilate. The idea of revolt remains pure and absolute, but the act of revolt is usually a source of tension, suffering, or despair. And while the rebel character is usually an extension of the playwright, the playwright is always examining the consequences of his actions.

It is this conflict between idea and action — between conception and execution — which forms the central dialectic of the modern drama. For the rebel dramatist is one who dreams — and puts his dreams to the test. This may suggest why the conflict of illusion and reality is such an important theme in the modern drama: illusion and reality are the twin poles of the dramatist's imagination. All true rebels hate reality and labor ceaselessly to change it; but no true artist can withdraw entirely from the world of matter. The more rebellious the artist, the more he takes refuge in a sphere of fancies and illusions; but even the most subjective artists in the theatre of revolt are pulled irresistibly back to the tangible, material world they would escape. The dream landscapes of Strindberg and Genet are contiguous with the views seen from our own windows; beneath the drama of appearances lies a pattern of solid facts.

This may account for the style of the modern drama — and, especially, its ambiguous realism. The mark of the genius, for that arch-Romantic Jean Jacques Rousseau, was his refusal to imitate; by this remark he intended to express his abhorrence of the real. Pirandello illuminates Rousseau's statement when he observes that "in imitating a preceding model, one denies one's own identity, and remains of necessity behind the pattern" — the more one copies reality, the less one realizes the self. Camus carries this one step further by demonstrating how the most individual style is the sign of the most passionate rebellion, while realism, with its subordination of the self, is the official aesthetic of totalitarianism. Yet many of the most fiercely individualistic modern dramatists write in a relatively realistic style.

It must be understood, however, that modern dramatic realism is usually a subterfuge. For just as the antirealist dramatists are constantly evoking reality, so the realist dramatists are merely sublimating their Romantic individualism in a chastened style. Edmund Wilson tells how Flaubert, with his appetite for "the gorgeous and the untamed," forced himself to write, in corseted prose, of the "pusillanimity and mediocrity of contemporary bourgeois France." This exactly describes the willed development of the modern realist dramatist. Ibsen, considered the father of modern realism, begins his career with extravagant epics, celebrating man in nature, then turns to the most prosaic-seeming forms; but beneath the humdrum surface, his old Romanticism continues to bubble; even his "modern" plays are acts of rebellion in disguise. Ibsen's problem remains one that every modern dramatist must solve for himself — how to find, without spurning reality altogether, that necessary link between the natural and imaginative worlds. And thus while the rebel may wish to withdraw into untamed nature or into a realm of his own invention, his plays are set, more often than not, in a world of sober probability — contemporary citizens in urban drawing rooms, conversing in the flat language of everyday life.

These are hardly ideal terms for those who would, no doubt, prefer to unleash their imaginations, heighten their language, and break out into passionate revolt — but to rebel against the world, one must continue to confront it. And herein lie the paradoxes of the rebel dramatist. He would exalt the ideal, yet he is imprisoned in the real. He would vindicate the self, yet he must also examine the claims of the others. He would sing of ecstasy, wildness, and drunkenness, yet he must cope with the tedious, conditioned world.

[15]

The theatre of revolt, then, is the temple of a priest without a God, without an orthodoxy, without even much of a congregation, who conducts his service within the hideous architecture of the absurd. A missionary of discord, he spreads a gospel of insurrection, trying to substitute his inspired vision for traditional values, trying to improvise a ritual out of anguish and frustration. Instead of myths of communion, he offers myths of dispersal; instead of consoling sermons, painful demands; instead of a liturgy of acceptance, a liturgy of complaint. He is an apostate priest, and one who secretly would be God. Taking as his motto Lucifer's *Non serviam,* he emerges as the spirit of denial, the man who says No, pursuing his Yes down the countless avenues of revolt.

To chart these avenues is the purpose of this book. The process is difficult and complicated, since their direction varies with each dramatist. But, in general, we can distinguish three main highways into which the avenues run. The first is extremely broad, the second more narrow, and the third a one-way street, for the modern drama grows progressively more confined as the exigencies of the time begin to limit the possibilities of revolt. I have called these categories of revolt *messianic, social, existential.* These terms will be more fully elaborated, but I can define them quickly through reference to my initial images. *Messianic revolt* occurs when the dramatist rebels against God and tries to take His place — the priest examines his image in the mirror. *Social revolt* occurs when the dramatist rebels against the conventions, morals, and values of the social organism — the priest turns the mirror on the audience. *Existential revolt* occurs when the dramatist rebels against the conditions of his existence — the priest turns the mirror on the void. Each of the eight dramatists considered in this book — in fact, most of the dramatists in the modern theatre — can be classified as messianic, social, or existential rebels; some fall into one category, some into two, some into all three. To demonstrate this, it is necessary to examine the background, nature, and style of each aspect of dramatic revolt.

Messianic revolt is the initial stage of the modern drama, and the most unashamedly Romantic. It can be found in Ibsen, Strindberg, Shaw, and O'Neill; it crops up again in Genet; and it characterizes minor dramatists like Wagner, D'Annunzio, Sartre, and Camus. The messianic drama is designed as an act of revelation — a Pisgah view of Palestine — for it revolves around the thought and actions of a new Messiah, who thinks himself destined to replace the old God and change the life of man. Messianic revolt is the most subjective, grandiose, and egotistical of all dramatic rebellion — and so persistent in the drama that one is forced to say it is with Ibsen's early messianic epics, and not with his later "modern" plays, that the modern drama properly begins. For it is messianism which detonates the theatre of revolt. And though the explosion is loudest at the beginning of the movement, when the dramatist is bursting with a turbulent Romanticism and everything seems possible, its reverberations can be felt throughout the entire modern theatre.

Messianic drama is a medium of absolute liberation, unrestrained by dramatic rules or human limitations, through which the rebel dramatist indulges his insatiable appetite for the infinite. Conceiving the universe to be a projection of his own personality, which can be altered or manipulated through superhuman will, he imagines himself a Creator superior to God, and destined to transform life into something more ordered than the meaningless botch he sees around him. As Strindberg puts it, through his autobiographical character, the Stranger, in *The Road to Damascus,* Part I:

And I feel my spirit growing, spreading, becoming tenuous, infinite. I am everywhere, in the ocean which is my blood, in the rocks which are my bones, in the trees, in the flowers; and my head reaches up to the heavens. I can survey the whole universe. I *am* the universe. And I feel the power of the creator within me, for I am He! I wish I could grasp the all in my hand and refashion it into something more perfect, more lasting, more beautiful. I want all creation and created beings to be happy, to be born without pain, live without suffering, and die in quiet content.

Here, where Strindberg imagines himself gigantic and transcendent — assuming divine powers and refashioning the world after his own plan — is the very essence of messianic revolt.

Strindberg is the least reticent of the messianic dramatists about his personal urge towards Godhead, but this hungry *I want* — the cry of perpetual dissatisfaction — rings through all the dramas of this type: it is the sound of the will to power. "Dead are all the Gods," wrote Nietzsche, "now do we desire the Superman to live" — the messianic rebel echoes this demand. Ibsen, in *Emperor and Galilean,* foresees a Third Empire of the Will where "the present watchword of revolt will be realized" and "men will not need to die in order to live as gods on earth." Shaw, in *Man and Superman,* envisions a future man "omnipotent, omniscient, infallible, and withal completely, unilludedly self-conscious: in short, a God," and introduces this self-conscious deity into the last play of *Back to Methuselah.* Siegfried, the protagonist of Wagner's *Ring* cycle, breaks the god Wotan's spear with his sword *Nothung,* thus becoming the *seliger Held,* or sanctified hero. Camus's Caligula aims "far above the gods . . . taking over a kingdom where the impossible is king." O'Neill's Lazarus, in *Lazarus Laughed,* announces that "the greatness of Man is that no god can save him — until he becomes a god!" And Genet's Chief of Police, in *The Balcony,* turns his lust for reputation into a rebellious assault on the very heavens.

The messianic hero, in short, is a superman, combining the qualities of malefactor and benefactor — of one who kills God and one who builds a Church. As a malefactor, he is in the tradition of earlier Romantic heroes — Schiller's Karl Moor, Goethe's Goetz, Hugo's Hernani — an outlaw, warring on society and seeking complete gratification beyond conventional laws (the heroines of messianic drama — Ibsen's Solveig and Agnes, Strindberg's Lady, Wagner's Brunhilde, Shaw's Ann Whitefield — are also related to a type from earlier drama, the Romantic *ewig Weibliche*). The struggle of the messianic hero with God, however, makes him more akin to Aeschylus's Prometheus and Goethe's Faust, not to mention Marlowe's Tamburlaine, who desired to "set black streamers in the firmament to signify the slaughter of the gods." Prototypes for the messianic hero, in fact, can be found among all the great insurgents of myth and religion: Lucifer, Mephistopheles, Cain, Judas, Don Juan. Cain and Judas, for

[18]

example, are among the rebels who appear in a vision to Ibsen's Emperor Julian — two "freedmen under necessity," pointing the way to his own rebellion. Strindberg's Stranger announces "I am Cain, you see," and dabbles in the Devil's work. Cain, the "revolted son," is also a prominent character in *Back to Methuselah,* while Don Juan, the "enemy of God," is the hero of *Man and Superman.* Genet identifies himself with "Lucifer, crossing swords with God," and O'Neill's Dion Anthony develops, throughout *The Great God Brown,* into a Faust figure under a pact with the Devil. In short, the messianic hero feels accursed, and draws his defiance and strength from the deepest springs of evil.

As a malefactor, the messianic hero desires to kill God and destroy the old order; as a benefactor, he desires to build an order of his own. Like Prometheus, he defies the heavens for the sake of man — but like Moses, Christ, Buddha, Brahma, and Confucius, he tries to form new laws, representing himself as a savior with the means of salvation in his grasp. Like most saviors, he suffers the fate of the scapegoat at the hands of the multitude; and the betrayal of the messianic hero provides the dramatic climax of the messianic play. But his doctrine provides its intellectual spine. This doctrine, of course, belongs to the author, embodying his personal convictions and commitments. He designs his work, therefore, as creative religion or scriptural writings or wisdom literature — the modern equivalent of the gospels, the Koran, Confucian maxims, the Upanishads.

The messianic drama, in consequence, is tendentious and systematic — a philosophical play on the order of Goethe's *Faust.* It is also rather windy and rhetorical, sometimes spilling over — like the Revolutionist's Handbook which Shaw appended to *Man and Superman* — into discursive, nondramatic prose. Epigrammatic maxims and revolutionary mottos are not unusual: "All or nothing" (*Brand*); "Death to old Death" (*Lazarus Laughed*). And it is notable for a hortatory, admonitory tone. As for its doctrine, this is not usually very impressive when separated from the play proper. For the various messianic creeds — whether Ibsen's philosophy of the will, Wagner's religion of art, Strindberg's Hindu resignation, Shaw's life force, O'Neill's neo-

Dionysianism, or Genet's cult of crime and evil — are neither very comprehensive nor very convincing nor even very original (most of this material is borrowed from other rebel thinkers like Kierkegaard, Schopenhauer, Nietzsche, Dostoyevsky, or D. H. Lawrence). Still, the significant thing about messianic drama is not so much its philosophical content as its posture of revolt — its restless search for coherence in a world of abandoned gods.

The messianic play, in short, is a dramatization of the Romantic quest for faith; as such, it is the most personal mode in the theatre of revolt, and functions as the dramatist's religious testament. This is not to say the material is autobiographical (though it sometimes is), but rather that the messianic dramatist always has strong affinities with his protagonist. The messianic hero, in one way or another, is an extension of the playwright, who thus provides himself with superhuman faculties: the hero is the imaginative realization of the playwright's dreams, the vicarious acting out of his moral imagination. Ibsen admitted that Brand, Peer Gynt, and the Emperor Julian were aspects of himself; Wagner identified with Siegfried, and named his child after him; Strindberg put himself into his Stranger, as O'Neill did with most of his central characters; and Shaw had much (too much) in common with his Ancients.

Each dramatist, on the other hand, preserves his distance from his play as well. The hero's messianic doctrine is almost invariably rejected, and the hero himself never quite achieves divinity, for he is usually abandoned by the playwright by the end of the play. Ibsen's Julian dies, a victim of his own power drive, and Brand is rebuked by the God of Love; Strindberg's Stranger ends up on the threshold of a monastery, befogged by doubts and contradictions; O'Neill's Dion Anthony expires in agonies of self-hatred and uncertainty; Genet's Satanic rebels learn that their revolt cannot succeed, since God is "the final victor." In the last play of *Back to Methuselah,* Shaw projects himself into a world of the future where all his prophecies have been realized — but this is the only instance of Utopian wish-fulfillment in the theatre of revolt. For even in the messianic drama — the most audacious, wishful, and egocentric of all theatrical revolt

— the Romantic urge towards freedom is partly checked. Despite the prominence of subjective ideas, the drama still remains a form of conflict — a clash between the ideal desires of the hero and the insurmountable obstacles of the real world.

Naturally, the messianic drama is conceived on a grand scale. It is almost always very long, and sometimes — a result of the artist's revolt against rules — almost unstageable, though it is obviously shaped by the hand of a dramatist (closet dramas with messianic qualities, like Hardy's *Dynasts,* do not qualify). *Brand* takes at least seven hours to perform; *Emperor and Galilean* is a double drama; *The Road to Damascus* is a trilogy; *Back to Methuselah* is a "metabiological pentateuch"; and the *Ring* cycle must be played on four separate evenings, each of them exhausting. The length of the messianic play suggests its testamental function — and also suggests its epic structure. Such a work rarely enjoys a unified plot, but consists instead of short, episodic scenes with multiple set changes. As for its setting, it takes place either in the past (*Emperor and Galilean*), the future (*Back to Methuselah*), or some unlocalized time and place, like that of a dream (*The Road to Damascus*). When the setting is contemporary (*Man and Superman*), a dream sequence may be introduced at some point (the Don Juan in Hell scene) to distance the play. Despite this remoteness, however, the contemporary relevance of the messianic play is never in doubt. For just as Nietzsche used the old Persian God Zarathustra to express his modern philosophy, so the messianic dramatist employs his characters to enact his revolt and to embody his vision of salvation.

As a literary genre, the messianic drama falls into the category of myth or romance, for its central figure conforms to the definitions supplied by Northrup Frye, in *The Anatomy of Criticism,* of the mythic hero ("superior in *kind* both to other men and to the environment of other men") and of the Romantic hero ("superior in *degree* to other men and to his environment"). His actions are the marvelous doings of a superhuman figure — sometimes a god, sometimes a great hero, sometimes an inspired visionary. Still, his superiority lies not so much in noble birth, physical prowess, or miraculous deeds as in certain lofty moral and spiritual qualities which raise him above the common run of men. Ibsen looked forward to an "aristocracy of character, of will, of mind" — Nietzsche to a "new nobility . . . which shall be the adversary of all populace and potentate rule" — that is the class to which the messianic hero belongs. For, despite the touch of divinity about him, he is still mortal. (Shaw's Ancients live to be over three hundred, and Genet's Chief of Police will reign for two thousand years, but most messianic heroes ultimately face death and disillusionment.)

Finally, the language of messianic drama is lofty and elevated. Some plays are written in verse, some in a heightened prose — but messianic diction is invariably oracular, if not bombastic. For the messianic drama is informed by a powerful prophetic quality. It is the newest testament of the author, who functions as an inspired seer, handing his enlightened revelation to a benighted world.

The second stage of the modern theatre, *social revolt,* is much less ambitious, though much more familiar to modern audiences: it characterizes the best-known plays of the contemporary stage. Social revolt dominates Ibsen's "modern" plays, Strindberg's "Naturalist" dramas, Chekhov's inner actions, most of Shaw, a large part of Brecht, and some of Pirandello — as well as the peasant dramas of Synge and Lorca, the parables of Dürrenmatt, and the entire work of such secondary dramatists as O'Casey, Odets, Miller, Osborne, Wesker, and Frisch. Social revolt, of course, is usually an aspect of messianic drama, but there it is subordinate to other matters; when it dominates a play, it is a relatively modest manifestation. The emphasis of the drama shifts from radical cures to careful diagnoses, with the patient taking the stage and the physician withdrawing behind the scenes. Instead of examining the relationship between man and God, the social dramatist concentrates on man in society, in conflict with community, government, academy, church, or family.

There is a corresponding change in dramatic form. The episodic play gives way to the three- and four-act structure; the drama loses its untidy flamboyance and becomes tight, compact, well-made. Social drama is Classical in the sense of Edmund Wilson's definition of Classicism: "In the domain of politics and morals, a preoccupation with society as a whole; and in art, an ideal of objectivity." Though the social drama is occasionally Expressionistic, it is more frequently written in the realistic or Naturalistic style, through which the objective ideal is best maintained. Messianic voluptuousness and exuberance are replaced by more controlled and modulated feelings, as the playwright absents himself from the proceedings and permits the action to speak for itself. Social, political, moral, and economic questions are aired in an atmosphere of impartiality; sociological and psychological insights grow common; scientific ideas begin to influence the dramatist, particularly Darwin's theory of heredity and environment. Ibsen, Strindberg, Shaw, and Brecht all begin to think of themselves as literary scientists under the influence of Darwin, Lamarck, or Marx, while Chekhov, who claims no intellectual influences, adheres to an ideal of juridical detachment.

As for characters, the social drama puts contemporary society on the stage and draws its *dramatis personae* from the middle class. The protagonist is subject to the same laws as the rest of us, shares the same ambitions (or lack of them), performs the same domestic duties, speaks the same unlovely prose. Human stature shrinks to average height, and man's surroundings close in. Ibsen's Brand makes his way up the heights to die, but Oswald Alving is doomed to stagnation by inherited disease and environmental oppression; Strindberg's Stranger enjoys the freedom of a dream, but his Father is confined in a straitjacket; Shaw's John Tanner is occupied with the future of the race, but his Candida is primarily concerned with domestic problems. The empires of messianic drama have been replaced by crowded, sweating towns; the sun is out of reach; and human possibilities are dwindling. Ibsen's townspeople are degenerating in their "tasteless parlors"; Chekhov's gentry are paralyzed by apathy and inertia; Pirandello's escapists are frozen in illusion; Brecht's oppressed characters cannot even afford personal opinions. The roar of the lion is drowned by the bleating of the lamb; *I want* and *I will* give way to *I accept*. Compromise, adaptation, and survival become the order of the day, as man draws back from his boundaries and begins to tiptoe gingerly through his life.

Under these circumstances, it is a wonder that rebellion continues to function at all. But, as I suggested earlier, the Classical style of the social drama is constructed on a fundamentally Romantic base. Ibsen abandons the messianic play because, being ordered towards the artist rather than the audience, it is inappropriate for the presentation of modern life — but he never abandons his rebellious inclinations. Strindberg's wild prejudices, similarly, make a mockery of his attempts at "Naturalism"; Pirandello's metaphysical anguish permeates his surface realism; and Brecht's anarchistic nature makes his social dramas leap with fury and mockery. Indeed, the rebel dramatist even enters the social drama occasionally, if only in disguise — as Doctor Stockmann in *An Enemy of the People,* as Jean in *Miss Julie,* as Captain Shotover in *Heartbreak House,* as Laudisi in *It Is So! (If You Think So),* as Mackie in *The Threepenny Opera.* And even in the more rigorously objective plays, like those of Chekhov, rebellion is still rumbling in their depths. To write for modern audiences, as Ibsen saw, is to repudiate the subjective heroic mode; but in the social drama, the action itself is a form of rebellion, being an assault on the abuses of the time.

Social drama, in short, represents modern life for the purpose of whipping and scourging it — it is an imitation for essentially satiric purposes. Such revolt, however, is negative. The dramatist may still be trying to kill God (if only through His earthly institutions and delegated figures of authority), but he is no longer much occupied with building a Church: the social rebel rarely suggests any clear-cut alternatives to the things he would like to destroy. It is true that propaganda plays and problem dramas are offshoots of social revolt, but I am excluding such works from this study. When Sean O'Casey writes about a Communist revolution bringing sensuality to Puritan Ireland, or when Arthur Miller evokes our sympathy for the plight of the common man, we are confronted less with works of art than with political acts or social gestures, and it is by utilitarian rather than literary criteria that such acts and gestures should be judged. As for Shaw and Brecht, these writers may also be political revolutionaries, but insofar as a positive ideology informs their work, their work is compromised. And, as a matter of fact, Shaw's Socialism, discussed at length in prefaces and tracts, remains outside his plays, while Brecht's Communism is a matter of implication in all but his explicit agitprop dramas. The major social rebels are philosophical anarchists, whatever their political affiliations, for they display a profound distaste for every form of human organization, if not for humankind itself.

The social rebel can trace his heritage back to Lillo, Steele, Diderot, Beaumarchais, Lessing, and Hebbel, though he differs from these bourgeois dramatists in his satiric animus and his hatred for middle-class life. In place of the virtuous apprentice and the honest merchant, he substitutes the vicious criminal and the venal capitalist. And though Arthur Miller may, like Diderot and Beaumarchais, "seek for tragedy in the heart and spirit of the average man," most social rebels (possibly even Brecht, who always refused to idealize the proletarian) reserve a secret admiration for heroes: "I would have my mob all Caesars," writes Shaw, "instead of Toms, Dicks, and Harrys." Nor do they often "seek for tragedy"; tragedy is no longer possible in this mode. Instead, comic and serious elements begin to jostle each other with an effect of dissonance which grows ever more irritating. The bourgeois dramatists measured their success by the ability to draw tears from the audience, a faculty which their drama possessed, according to Coleridge, in common with the onion. But modern social drama possesses a harsh, condemnatory tone which thwarts and frustrates hypocritical sentimentality, and it draws no tears at all, unless they be tears of exasperation. For while the bourgeois dramatist supported democracy (still a revolutionary creed), the modern social dramatist is more concerned with the degradations of the democratic dogma. He may begin by believing in social progress, but he grows increasingly skeptical about the capacity for human perfectibility.

The drama of social revolt is usually written in what Frye calls the "low mimetic mode," the style of most realistic fiction: "The hero is one of us; we respond to a sense of his common humanity, and demand from the poet the same canons of probability that we find in our experience." This hero is "superior neither to other men nor to his environment" — as Frye proceeds to observe, in fact, the word "hero" no longer retains its full meaning. This degeneration of the hero is evident, in the social drama, in a moral, structural, and sexual sense. The central character disappears from Chekhov's dramas altogether, and the group takes the stage; in Brecht, the protagonist is retained, but is now significant less for heroism than for cowardice and rapacity; in most social dramas, women begin to assume central roles. The setting of the social play is usually contemporary; its structure is compact, and organized towards climaxes of feeling; its language is the prose vernacular of everyday life. In social revolt, the rebel dramatist has suppressed his will to power in order to examine and protest against the institutionalized life of man.

In the last stage of the modern drama, *existential revolt,* the dramatist examines the metaphysical life of man and protests against it; existence itself becomes the source of his rebellion.[1] The drama of existential revolt is a mode of the utmost restriction, a cry of anguish over the insufferable state of being human.

This form of revolt is identical with what Camus calls "metaphysical rebellion . . . the movement by which man protests against his condition and against the whole of creation." Such a definition could be applied, with equal accuracy, to messianic revolt, and, indeed, existential drama embodies the same kind of discontent with the basic structure of life. On the other hand, while messianic revolt is potent and positive, existential revolt is impotent and despairing. The messianic dramatist makes his characters superhuman; the existential dramatist makes them subhuman. The one exaggerates the extent of human freedom; the other, of human bondage. It is significant that the exis-

[1] Unfortunately, the adjective *existential* has recently been monopolized by a fashionable French philosophy, but I am using this late seventeenth-century word in its original, more neutral sense. As the *Oxford English Dictionary* defines "existential," it means simply: "of and pertaining to existence." Existentialism is a highly self-conscious movement; existential revolt is not. And though Sartre and Camus may be existential rebels on occasion, very few existential rebels are formal Existentialists.

tential drama begins to appear with increasing frequency in our own age — an age of totalitarianism. The Gods and supermen of messianic drama have turned into animals and prisoners; the world is a vast concentration camp where social intercourse is strictly forbidden. Alone in a terrifying emptiness, the central figure of existential drama is doomed, as it were, to a life of solitary confinement.

Existential revolt, in short, occurs during the old age of the modern drama, though chronologically it may sometimes appear much earlier. It is the revolt of the fatigued and the hopeless, reflecting — after the disintegration of idealist energies — exhaustion and disillusionment. This explains its close relationship to messianic revolt, for it is actually an inverted development of the messianic impulse. As a matter of fact, a number of modern dramatists, messianic in their youth, conclude their careers as existential rebels, their urge towards Godhead dissipating in anguish and frustration. Typical of this progression is the career of the early nineteenth-century dramatist Georg Büchner — the ancestor of modern existential drama — who, after a short period as a radical messianic rebel, becomes convinced that human action is futile and writes of man crushed under the awful fatalism of history. Büchner is an extraordinary figure in his age, but his development is quite common in ours. Strindberg, for example, turns to existential revolt after the horrors of the Inferno crisis convince him of the vanity of trying to be God; O'Neill, in his last plays, converts his messianic demands into existential appeals; and existential revolt can even be detected under the fixed smile of Shaw. The early plays of Brecht, moreover, have a substructure of existential revolt and so have the plays of Pirandello. And existential revolt is the dominating impulse behind the plays of Williams, Albee, Gelber, and Pinter — not to mention Beckett, Ionesco, and the entire "theatre of the absurd."

Existential revolt represents Romanticism turned in on itself and beginning to rot. Extremely contemptuous of messianic ideals, disbelieving totally in messianic individualism, the existential rebel, nevertheless, shows vestiges of the old radical demands. He is a Neo-Romantic, raging against existence, ashamed of being human, revolted by the body itself. One of the strongest identifying marks of

[27]

the existential drama is its attitude towards the flesh, which is usually described in images of muck, mud, ashes, and fecal matter, in a state of decomposition and decay. Strindberg, obsessed throughout his existential plays with the "dirt of life," identifies the world with garbage pits and dungheaps, and feels imprisoned in Swedenborg's Excremental Hell. Brecht, in *Baal,* calls man "a creature eating on a latrine," while inveighing against "the good god who so distinguished himself by joining the urinary passage with the sex organ." Shaw's amusement at the physical nature of man barely disguises his Swiftian revulsion from it. O'Neill's Edmund, in *A Long Day's Journey into Night,* muses, "We are such stuff as manure is made on," and Samuel Beckett creates a world in which the sexual organs have lost their procreative power and man's functions are now exclusively excretory. As Lucky describes the situation, during his garbled monologue in *Waiting for Godot,* "Man in brief in spite of the strides of alimentation and defecation wastes and pines wastes and pines. . . ." Existential man certainly wastes and pines. The body is no better than a waste product destined for the disposal heap, while the extent of human progress is measured in the bowels and the digestive system.

This Neo-Romantic horror at the physical functions is an aspect of what Lionel Trilling, in his essay "The Fate of Pleasure," calls the "modern spirituality," and attributes to a number of modern writers: Kafka, Joyce, the later Yeats. Antihumanist, sometimes antihuman, these writers are opposed to the "comfortable and consumer-directed" arts (those arts which Brecht is to call "culinary"), and dedicate their work not to luxury and enjoyment but rather to discomfort and unease. The existential dramatist is one with these writers, for he also excludes the principle of pleasure from his work, and shares the same distaste for humanistic affirmations. Gusto, joy, and sensuality give way to dark brooding and longings after death — the ideal of human perfectibility to a vision of human decay. Out of these feelings is created the existential hero — or *anti*hero — a character related to that figure of disgust whom Professor Trilling calls the original of the species (though Büchner's Woyzeck antedates him by about thirty years): Dostoyevsky's Underground Man. The antihero of existential drama is rarely as articulate as Dostoyevsky's character, but he is just as miserable, morbid, and morose — which is to say, just as opposed to idealism and ideals. Where the messianic superman is vigorous, aristocratic, heroic, the existential antihero is disadvantaged, humiliated, perverse, and thoroughly incapable of significant action.

The very opposition of the two types suggests there is a relationship between them, which Nietzsche himself was quick to perceive: "Dostoyevsky's Underman and my Overman," he wrote, "are the same person clawing his way out of the pit into the sunlight." The Underman, however, never clambers out of the pit, and rarely sees the sunshine. Strindberg's characters in *A Dream Play* are losing their color in a quarantine station — in *The Ghost Sonata* they are hardening into mummies. The Brecht menagerie is immobilized by the horrifying implications of the Copernican system. Pirandello's characters are imprisoned in their illusions. O'Neill's derelicts in *The Ice Man Cometh* are lost in pipe dreams, while the blasted family of *A Long Day's Journey* are swallowed up in fog. Under these conditions, the antihero cannot act — partly because of a growing paralysis, partly because of external causes, partly because he will not move those limbs and organs he detests. The central figure of existential drama is sometimes very old — like the solitary character of *Krapp's Last Tape,* or the two figures in Ionesco's *Chairs* — but usually just inert. The best image of existential drama is Winnie, in Beckett's *Happy Days,* buried up to her neck in the earth — or the two tramps in *Waiting for Godot* with their famous "Yes, let's go. (*They do not move.*)"

Without action, there can be no tragedy; yet existential drama is, *in tone and atmosphere,* the most tragic of the modern genres. The messianic rebel may project himself into the heroic exploits of his dramatic characters, but the existential dramatist projects himself into their melancholy and complaint, and often manages to transcend his disgust with genuine feelings of compassion. "Humankind is pitiable," Strindberg's Daughter of Indra intones repeatedly, while the author, recoiling from the abyss of absurdity, forces himself to accept the painful riddles and contradictions of life. Strindberg's stoicism is rather typical of existential drama, which frequently subsides into a kind of resignation — an acceptance of waiting, patience, and ordeals. O'Neill's derelicts wait for death; Beckett's tramps wait for Godot; Gelber's junkies wait for their connection — even Brecht, the most relentless of the existential writers, eventually works his way through to a state of Confucian calm and serenity. Thus, if the existential drama is tragic, it is tragic in its perceptions. It lacks a tragic hero, but it evokes a tragic sense of life, that mood one often finds in Sophocles:

> Never to have lived is best, ancient writers say;
> Never to have drawn the breath of life, never to have
>   looked into the light of day;
> The second best's a gay goodnight and quickly turn away.

Here, as translated by Yeats, in the third stasimon of another drama of old age, *Oedipus at Colonus,* one finds the underlying theme of existential rebellion, a theme restated almost as beautifully in Beckett's *Godot:* "They give birth astride a grave, the light gleams an instant, then it's night once more."

"And a man's life's no more than to say 'One,' " muses Hamlet, while Beckett's Pozzo, three hundred years later, makes the same observations on the awful brevity of life: "One day we were born, one day we shall die, the same day, the same second." But if the gravedigger puts on the forceps, it takes him an eternity — time's winged chariot rushes by a scene of intense boredom and ennui. This sense of double time, alternately swift and tedious, is implicit in most existential drama,[2] and becomes the lament of the existential rebel. Hating the present, fearing the future, he withdraws into the past, and writes his plays on the theme of time and memory. Williams's *Glass Menagerie,* for example, is an existential exploration of memory; O'Neill in

---

[2] It is also implicit in Chekhov. In *The Cherry Orchard,* old Firs concludes a play about apathy and tedium with the remark, "Life has slipped by as though I'd never lived"; and in *The Three Sisters,* Chekhov shows his characters aging while seeming to stand stock-still. Like the existential dramatists, Chekhov often writes of regret for a wasted life, and of paralysis and inertia — but he lacks their rage and disgust. The existential dramatist is in revolt against life; Chekhov seems to be more in revolt against his characters.

A Long Day's Journey moves forward in time and backwards in memory simultaneously; and time is the central subject of Pirandello, who, agonized by the formless flux, conceives of characters escaping into the immobility of history or the timelessness of art. Bergson's philosophical theories, especially his theory of duration, strongly influence the existential drama — from him, the existential dramatist borrows the concept of subjective, as opposed to clock, time. This emphasis on time suggests the reflective, nostalgic quality of this drama; its central figure is a man whose life is spent mournfully meditating on his past. The antihero is no longer a Cartesian *chose qui pense* — he is now the Bergsonian *chose qui dure*.

This melancholy resignation, however, is accompanied by a continuous protest, occasionally expressed through violent outbursts, almost always through a mordant, biting style. If all the more vigorous forms of revolt have now become futile, the rebel can still express his outrage verbally. To the nothingness of life, he responds with the dry mock, even though this irony is sometimes expended on himself. Even in the act of accepting the absurd, in short, he is still caught in an act of negation. And the best personification of this ambivalent mood is Strindberg's Poet, in *A Dream Play*, one who bathes in mud while he continues to scan the heavens:

POET, *ecstatically*. Out of the clay the God Ptah fashioned man on a potter's wheel, a lathe, *mockingly*, or some other damned thing. . . . *Ecstatically*. Out of clay the sculptor fashioned his more or less immortal masterpieces, *mockingly*, which are usually only rubbish. . . . *Ecstatically*. Such is clay! When clay is fluid, it is called mud.

O'Neill's characters alternate in the same manner between yea- and nay-saying, between ecstasy and mockery; and hope and despair, of course, are the vacillating moods of Beckett's tramps. Pirandello also breaks his compassionate mood with loud, mocking laughter; and Brecht's scorching irony is one of the most famous marks of his style.

Irony, in fact, is the mark of the entire existential drama, which is written in what Frye calls the "ironic mode." In the ironic mode, the word "hero" has lost its meaning entirely — the central figure is "inferior in power and intelligence to ourselves, so that we have a sense of looking down on a scene of bondage, frustration, or absurdity." This is the scene of the antihero — usually a tramp, a proletarian, a criminal, an old man, a prisoner, confined in body and spirit, and deteriorating in his confinement. Strindberg imprisons his characters in a nightmare, and Beckett in an undefined world (probably the future) of bareness and infertility. But even when the setting is relatively realistic — as in the plays of Pirandello, Brecht, and O'Neill — the claustrophobic atmosphere is just as oppressive. For in existential drama, nature, society, man no longer exist. In this final phase of the modern drama — in these nightmares, chimeras, hallucinations, and feverish fables — revolt finds its most pessimistic, contracted, and exhausted form.

Existential revolt is the final phase — but it is not the conclusion of the modern drama, even though so many recent plays are permeated by it. For in the radical theory of the French writer Antonin Artaud, the theatre of revolt again begins to develop messianic ambitions, and in the plays of Jean Genet, these ambitions are now being imaginatively realized. Could it be that the drama is about to repeat its cycle? According to Giovanni Battista Vico, civilization itself has a cyclical form, proceeding from divine to heroic to human manifestations — after which a clap of thunder signals the repetition of the process. This theory certainly describes the development of Greece and the West, and the concomitant development of the theatre of communion. Does it describe the development of the theatre of revolt as well? Since Vico, an eighteenth-century philosopher, could not imagine a cycle of civilization lower than the human, or a form of life baser than civic man, his *Scienza Nuova* omits an important stage of the modern experience. But Vico's prophecy is otherwise fulfilling itself in the theatre of revolt, and that clap of thunder is especially ominous. The new messianic writers are consciously striving to re-create the conditions of traditional theatre. Artaud wishes to restore to the drama its primitive function, and Genet's work takes the form of hieroglyphic ritual. But these very efforts become acts of revolt. With

Artaud and Genet, the modern theatre turns apocalyptic once again, and once again Romanticism is in full flower. If the modern theatre is an Eternal Recurrence, and Gods and Heroes are again to take the stage, then the obvious place to start this study is where the theatre of revolt began — in the magnificent messianic mind of Henrik Ibsen.

II

HENRIK IBSEN

In 1869, Henrik Ibsen, then forty-one, paused in his dramatic labors to compose a short poem. He had left his beloved Rome just one year before to settle in Dresden (he was to remain in exile from Norway until 1891), and he had just completed his first mature realistic prose play, *The League of Youth,* after having established his reputation as the author of *Brand* and *Peer Gynt.* Since *The League of Youth* contains strong satire on the hypocritical opportunism of the contemporary Scandinavian Liberal, critics were beginning to charge Ibsen with having joined the Conservative faction. The poem — "To My Friend, the Revolutionary Orator" — is addressed to one of these critics, and is a polemical defense against the current charges. In these verses, Ibsen affirms that he is still a perfervid revolutionary — but he then proceeds to distinguish his own revolt from anything in recorded history. All previous revolutions, he declares, were compromised by their incompleteness — even the Flood, the most radical revolution of all time, left a few survivors aboard Noah's ark. For him, on the other hand, nothing short of total revolution will suffice: "Your changing pawns is a futile plan;/ Make a sweep of the chessboard, and I'm your man." Intoxicated by an uncompromising vision of absolute freedom and purity through a total purge of existing life, he announces what he sees as his own part in this revolution: "With pleasure I will torpedo the Ark!"

Torpedo the Ark! No wonder Georg Brandes — Ibsen's friend, advisor, and best contemporary interpreter — thought him the most radi-

[37]

cal man he had ever met.[1] Discontented with everything but a new beginning, Ibsen finds it impossible to identify with any existing parties, systems, or programs, or even to ally himself with any existing revolutionary principles. His revolt, in short, is so individualistic that it transcends politics entirely. We would do well to remember, should we ever be tempted to regard Ibsen as the champion of such things as women's rights, divorce, euthanasia, or cures for syphilis, how sublimely indifferent he is to social amelioration or political reform. As he writes to Brandes two years later, "Yes, to be sure, it is a benefit to possess the franchise, the right of self-taxation, etc., but for whom is it a benefit? For the citizen, not for the individual." The distinction he makes here is plain, and Ibsen's own sympathies are undisguised. The citizen is domesticated man, the agent of existing institutions, who identifies his needs with the needs of the community as determined by the compact majority: Karsten Bernick, Torvald Helmer, Pastor Manders. The individual is revolutionary man, superior to all confining social, political, or moral imperatives, who finds his purpose in the pursuit of his own personal truth: Pastor Brand, Doctor Stockmann, Master Builder Solness. In Ibsen's mind, these two types are like slave and master, so fundamentally opposed that a victory for one is inevitably a defeat for the other, so that the citizen's rights are always attained at the cost of the individual's freedom. Ibsen may possess, in his drama, a highly ambiguous attitude towards his rebel heroes, but on this question there is no doubt where he *personally* stands: self-realization is the highest value, and if this conflicts with the public welfare, then the public welfare can go hang.[2]

[1] Brandes was not the only one to be impressed by Ibsen's radicalism. Ibsen's angry conversations at Bjørnsen's house, during 1883, so astonished one of the guests that he wrote: "He is an absolute anarchist, wants to make a *tabula rasa,* put a torpedo under the whole Ark; mankind must begin again at the beginning of the world — and begin with the individual. . . . The great task of our time is to blow up all existing institutions — to destroy." This letter was written one year before Ibsen wrote *The Wild Duck.*

[2] Eleven years later, in 1882, Ibsen is still carrying on in a similar vein: "I have not the gifts that go to make a satisfactory citizen. . . ." he writes. "Liberty is the first and highest condition for me. At home, they do not trouble

All his life political parties tried unsuccessfully to claim Ibsen as their own, only to be met with contempt and indifference. And the playwright's response is perfectly explicable in view of his position of revolt: he is hostile to all movements based on a social conception of man. In Ibsen's view, the Conservatives merely preserve a corrupted status quo, affirming exhausted traditions and outworn conventions for their own profit, while the Liberals, manipulating a mindless majority, merely palliate an advanced disease with useless nostrums. As for the Radicals, they would only change the shape of the social system, not the fact of it — the Ark he would torpedo is the very State itself. "Now there is absolutely no reasonable necessity for the individual to be a citizen," he continues in his letter to Brandes. "On the contrary, the state is the curse of the individual. . . . The state must be abolished! In this revolution I will take part!" Such a revolution, of course, could exist only in the fevered fantasies of an Anarchist or a Utopian Marxist, and Ibsen certainly has strong Marxist-Anarchist strains in his nature. But even were such a revolution to become feasible, Ibsen would probably not support it, since it would necessarily become a social revolt rather than the revolt of an individual. Ibsen's revolt, in short, is so personal that it can find common cause with nothing else in existence. For him, all movements are compromised by their collective goals, for all collectives — not only the State, but community, church, and even family — are the enemies of freedom, infringing on the natural liberties of man.

Considering the extreme radicalism of Ibsen's beliefs, it is entirely fitting that he should initiate the theatre of revolt; and we shall not confront another modern dramatist whose revolutionary integrity remains quite so pure. It is this revolt that I intend to illustrate in this essay. In a career marked by multiple contradictions in dramatic philosophy, and persistent changes in dramatic form, Ibsen's turbulent insurgency remains his most important and consistent identifying characteristic from first to last. Ibsen's personal rebelliousness, as we shall see later, is often checked by a corrective counter-impulse which helps both to

very much about liberty, but about liberties — a few more, a few less, according to the standpoint of their party."

discipline and disguise it; but even when his drama finds its most detached and objective form, it still remains the biography of his rebellious spirit. Thus, we shall occasionally find Ibsen's art taking a social and political direction, especially in his middle period, when the author is concerned with smashing hallowed idols, exposing the lies of modern conventions, and ridiculing the various pieties of the Norwegian community. Yet, it is important to remember always that Ibsen's revolt is poetic rather than reformist or propagandist, and that even his specifically polemical activities are subordinate to a larger purpose which changes little throughout his dramatic career. The great danger in Ibsen criticism is the tendency to examine his works in isolation from one another, and not — as Ibsen urgently requested — as a continuous, consistent development. When we study this development, we shall be able to confirm his plaintive remark towards the end of his career that "I have been more of a poet and less of a social philosopher than is commonly believed." We shall also be able to see that Ibsen's revolt, like that of many great contemporary poets, is *total* — which is to say, he is dissatisfied with the whole of Creation and not just certain contemporary aspects of it. For Ibsen's deepest quarrel is probably less with those pillars of church, state, and community who dominate his plays than with the supreme authority figure, God himself. Behind his demand for a new beginning for mankind, one can glimpse his half-hidden desire to fashion a new Creation more in keeping with the logic of his poetic imagination. With this new Creation represented by the body of his art, the basic Ibsenist conflict is frequently messianic — its hero a rebel against God and its issue not superficial changes in the social structure but a complete alteration in the moral nature of man.

Before proceeding to illustrate the strong rebellious strains in Ibsen's plays, we must pause here to parry a more familiar view of Ibsen, and a more popular interpretation of his work, which are just the opposite of what I have described. For despite the efforts of a generation of excellent critics (Hermann Weigand, Francis Fergusson, Eric Bentley, Janko Lavrin), certain misconceptions continue to cloud our understanding of Ibsen's underlying purpose, misconceptions fomented

by critics who obscure the playwright's more significant innovations
while emphasizing his lesser achievements. Basing their views partly
on the external facts of Ibsen's life, and to a larger extent on misconceptions of his less impressive plays, these critics visualize Ibsen as a
bemedaled journeyman-dramatist, equipped with side whiskers, a
portly belly, and an impeccable family life, who becomes — after a
somewhat unstable youth — one of the most respected and respectable
members of the Norwegian community, and is finally buried like a
celebrated State official. It is this comfortable burgher whom H. L.
Mencken describes, in the preface to the only sizable anthology of
Ibsen's works available for years, as

a highly respected member of the middle class, well-barbered, ease-loving,
and careful in mind; a very skilful practitioner of a very exacting and
lucrative trade; a safe and sane exponent of order, efficiency, honesty, and
common sense . . . [who] believed in all the things that the normal, law-
abiding citizen of Christendom believes in, from democracy to romantic
love, and from the obligations of duty to the value of virtue, and [who] always gave them the best of it in his plays.

On the basis of this image, Mencken vigorously denies that Ibsen had
any mystical side to his nature or any "idiotic symbolism" in his plays,
adding that "he gave infinitely more thought to questions of practical
dramaturgy — to getting his characters on and off stage, to building
up climaxes, to calculating effects — than he ever gave to the idea-
tional content of his dramas." Though intended as a tribute, this might
be the description of any Scribean artificer of liberal, rationalistic persuasion; and it is such half-truths and errors that have now become
standard ammunition for attacks on Ibsen by know-nothing journalists.

Ibsen's early English partisans would never have made him the
Philistine that Mencken describes, but, in a way, they contributed the
cornerstones for his edifice of misconceptions. To enthusiasts like William Archer, for whom prose realism was the triumphant climax of all
Western drama, Ibsen's greatness consisted largely in his invention of
a new dramatic method, based on the French well-made play, which

finally banished the aside and the soliloquy from the stage,[3] while to Bernard Shaw, the Norwegian's significance lay in his having introduced social-political discussion into the drama through the agency of a "villain-idealist" and an "unwomanly woman." This Ibsen — the playwright of realistic dramaturgy, extended ethical debates, and the emancipated woman — may have exhilarated Archer, Shaw, and Mencken, but he alienated innumerable readers and, what is worse, infuriated a whole generation of succeeding dramatists. Some of the most impressive artists in the theatre of revolt, in fact, defined their work in direct opposition to these Ibsenite concepts, while showing scant respect for the master himself. To Strindberg, Ibsen was "that Norwegian bluestocking," a mere partisan of women's rights; to Synge, he was only a town artist who imitated reality in "joyless and pallid words"; to Yeats, he was "the chosen author of very clever young journalists"; to Wedekind, he was the breeder of a lethargic menagerie of gray *Haustiere* (domestic animals); and to Brecht, he was simply an extinct bourgeois: "Very good — for [his] own time and [his] own class." It is doubtful if the work of any of these dramatists, excluding that of Yeats, would have been the same without the achievements of Ibsen. Yet the popular misconceptions are so firmly established that even these dramatists were unable to see Ibsen's poetry, vision, and fire.

Actually, the prevalent image of Ibsen has little foundation in fact, for if it is relevant at all (which is doubtful), it is relevant in relation to less than one third of his total work. The emphasis on Ibsen's prose realism and polemicism dates from the time when the Ibsen controversy was raging at its fiercest, and partisans had to make the master's plays support his own cause. Yet, the legend stubbornly persists, still continuing to do more harm to Ibsen's reputation than any other single influence, including the consistently poor production of his plays and the frequent inartistry of Continental, English, and American Ibsenites. It is a legend perpetuated by false emphasis, by isolating certain

---

[3] Archer, however, when he settles down to discussing Ibsen's plays, as he does in the excellent introductions to his English translations, is much more understanding and complex.

of Ibsen's characteristics while ignoring others.[4] In order to avoid the same errors — and to account for them more fully — let us consider Ibsen's drama as a creative unity, examining his career as a whole and excluding from our general consideration only those dramas he wrote during his artistic immaturity. We shall seek for the thread which binds his work together, that figure in the carpet which the author himself hinted at, in conversation with Lorentz Dietrichson, when he observed: "People believe that I have changed my views in the course of time. This is a great mistake. My development has, as a matter of fact, been absolutely consistent. I myself can distinctly follow and indicate the thread of its whole course — the unity of my ideas and their gradual development." When we extricate this thread of thematic consistency, we shall better understand his approach to form; and we shall, I think, discover an artist who was always more a Romantic poet than a prose realist and who never quite managed to suppress his aspiration towards the sublime.

I suggested earlier that Ibsen's basic material is the expression of rebellion, an element which, however muted, disguised, or repressed, is never completely absent from his work. In its purest form, Ibsen's rebellion is messianic, expressed through relatively shapeless, expansive, extravagant epics like *Brand, Peer Gynt,* and *Emperor and Galilean.* But since Ibsen wrote only three masterpieces in this form, it is necessary to demonstrate how Ibsen's revolt functions in plays more conspicuous for discipline, order, and objectivity. Similarly, though one usually finds the dramatist of revolt suggesting his own sympa-

---

[4] It is astonishing to what lengths certain critics will go to make Ibsen conform to their interpretations of him. Mencken, for example, asserts, without a shred of evidence, that Ibsen "lost his mind" while working on *John Gabriel Borkman;* this fantasy he probably invented to account for the mystical-symbolical qualities of that play, and of *When We Dead Awaken* which followed it. William Archer — also disturbed by the overt mysticism of Ibsen's last play — speculated about it in a similar, though more circumspect, manner: "One could almost suppose [Ibsen's] mental breakdown to have preceded instead of followed the writing of the latter play." Ibsen's so-called mental breakdown consisted of a stroke in which he lost control of his motor faculties. It occurred *after* the completion of *When We Dead Awaken,* and was definitely *not* an outbreak of insanity but rather a form of paralysis.

thies with his rebellious heroes, sometimes through lyrical, enthusiastic, and self-adulatory identification, Ibsen — even in his messianic epics — seems at times peculiarly detached, skeptical, and ironic towards such heroes, when he is not downright hostile to them. And it is necessary to explain why Ibsen sometimes denounces his rebel idealists with as much heat as his Philistines and conformists. Brand, for example, whose identification with God is so strong that it becomes a revolt against God, is punished, with the author's obvious approval, by celestial vengeance in the form of an avalanche. And Stensgard, the pompous orator of *The League of Youth* — after revealing that he is guilty of the same presumptuousness ("I tell you the wrath of the Lord is in me. It is His will you are opposing. He has destined me for the light") — is cruelly ejected from the community as a demagogue and an adventurer.

With the single exception of Doctor Stockmann, in fact, all of Ibsen's idealists are subject to partial or complete condemnation — a pattern which probably made Shaw conclude that the idealist was Ibsen's primary villain.[5] This is a mistake, but there is no denying that Ibsen's plays yield substantial support for such an interpretation. When a character professes to urge the "claims of the ideal" or to "hold aloft the banner of the ideal," he is quite frequently dismissed as a hypocrite, a meddler, or a booby. To Ibsen, idealism is sometimes identified with the philosophy of the Devil (an honorific foreign term, as Doctor Relling tells us, for *lies*), while the rebel is, like Gregers Werle, a self-deceiving blunderer whose energies on behalf of the ideal prove a curse to the average man and a danger to the community.

When we find this fanatical individualist defending the safety of the community — this defiant aristocrat of the will worrying over the hap-

---

[5] Shaw also reaches this conclusion by redefining words to suit his whims. For him, the "idealist" is one who worships existing conventions. The man whom we would call the idealist — one who, like himself and Ibsen, would strip the masks from conventions and replace them with unrealized ideals — Shaw calls a "realist." Shaw's whimsical approach to language produces a semantic confusion as bewildering as the medieval boggle over the realist and the nominalist. Shaw anticipated that "I shall be reproached for puzzling people by thus limiting the meaning of the term ideal" — but instead of being reproached, Shaw helped to establish a tradition of misapprehensions about Ibsen.

piness of the average man — we know we are on precarious ground and must tread gently. For Ibsen seems to be denying the very terms of his own rebellion which, in its purest form, is dedicated to torpedoing the community and raising the average man to heroic stature. Surely, it is contradictions like this which brought the charge that he had changed his views. Nor are these the only ones. In *Brand,* Ibsen seems both to approve and disapprove the notion that the rebel must be absolutely true to his calling; in *Ghosts,* he demonstrates both the importance and futility of advanced opinions; in *Rosmersholm,* he expresses both hope and despair over the possibility of mankind's ennoblement from within. In *A Doll's House,* he is radical, attacking the marriage built on a lie; in *The Wild Duck,* he is conservative, showing that domestic falsehoods, under certain conditions, are entirely necessary to survival. He applauds the rebellious Doctor Stockmann for exposing the diseased roots of modern life; he excoriates Stensgard and Gregers Werle for proceeding to the same goal. It is a commonplace of Ibsen criticism that the playwright will often advance a doctrine in one play with heated conviction, only to retract it, with equal conviction, in the next. And the abundance of unsynthesized theses and antitheses in his drama — purpose versus compromise; freedom versus necessity; age versus youth; duty versus the joy of life; truth versus illusion; reality versus ideals; work versus love; emancipation versus guilt; compassion versus severity — has been the frustration and despair of every doctrinaire Ibsenite. If Ibsen is a systematic rebel, then he is a peculiarly evasive one; and anyone seeking philosophical certainty or ideological consistency in his works had better beware.

Yet, despite the author's omnipresent ambiguity, complexity, and elusiveness, a kind of consistency can be adduced if we look below the surface of action and statement to Ibsen's particularized rebellion. To do this, however, we must first understand his method of creation, noting the strong subjective element (an infallible sign of the Romantic temperament) imbedded in each of his plays, and providing both their literary motive and material. It is surprising that this element has not been more remarked upon, since Ibsen left so many hints about its existence. In a verse written in 1877, for example, he writes (after defining life as a battle with internal trolls), "To write poetry means to hold/A judgment day over oneself." This seems to be an open admission that for Ibsen, the very process of creation was a form of self-examination proceeding from an inner struggle of conscience. In a letter, he later confirmed this in somewhat different terms: "Everything I have written has the closest possible relationship with what I have lived through, even if that has not been my personal — or actual — experience," adding, in another note, that the artist "must be extremely careful in discriminating between what one has observed and what one has experienced, because only this last can be the theme for creative work."

Experience, then, was the taproot for Ibsen's themes and characters — but experience of a very special kind. Rejecting that "personal — or actual — experience," which was connected with the outward events of his own life (unlike Strindberg, Ibsen very rarely exploited his personal biography in his plays), Ibsen was inspired instead by the experience of his inner life, the forces molding his intellectual, emotional and spiritual development. It was through analyzing this inner life, by probing his buried self for faults and virtues and exposing his own character to ruthless examination and criticism, that Ibsen drew the outlines for all his major rebels. This technique of character creation can be clearly detected in Ibsen's epic period where his Romanticism is most feverish and his identification with his plays is less successfully disguised; and when Ibsen writes his epic works, he is not reluctant to admit his close relationship with his central characters. "Brand is myself in my best moments," he writes in 1870, "just as it is certain that by self-analysis I brought to light many of both Peer Gynt's and Stensgard's qualities." Self-analysis, it should be noted, also brought to light the undisguised messianism of Ibsen's Emperor Julian: in this rebellious figure, he observes, "as in most of what I have written in my riper years, there is more of my inner life than I care to acknowledge to the public." Ibsen's identification with his rebel heroes, however, is not confined to his epic period. Even after he switches to the realistic mode with its more objective emphasis, he continues to employ this method, though it is less obvious in his first two or three prose plays. He considers himself less "muddleheaded" than Doctor Stockmann but admits that they "agree on many things"; he calls Solness, the renegade master builder, a figure "somewhat related to me"; and we do not need the author's testimony to see his resemblance to characters like Rosmer, Borkman, Allmers, and Rubek, the rebellious *personae* of his last, openly autobiographical plays.

Considering his willingness to share the character of a blackguard like Stensgard, in fact, I think we may even go so far as to suggest that Gregers Werle, the prince of villain-idealists, is a satirical portrait of the artist as well. For while we must be careful not to press these identifications too hard, it is probable that many Ibsen characters — superficially modeled on contemporary figures or general social types — are actually closer to Ibsen's concept of himself than is immediately apparent. What I am trying to suggest is that Ibsen's conflicting attitudes towards similar characters in two different plays, or towards a single character in the same play, are a product of his marked ambivalence towards himself. Yielding to the pull of this ambivalence, Ibsen swings like a pendulum from egoism to humility, from self-exaltation to self-hatred, sometimes unfettering himself, sometimes disciplining himself through the medium of art. Ibsen's apparent contradictions, then, are merely the results of certain dialectical stresses within his own character. His attacks on idealism reflect his temporary ironic feelings towards his own idealism; his strictness towards moralists is the severity of a confirmed moralist; his satire on the rebel figure is an attempt to punish the rebel in himself.

The same thing applies to Ibsen's changing attitudes towards his themes. For while Ibsen's plays may occasionally conclude with an appearance of intellectual certainty, the artist himself is always floundering in doubts and ambiguities. Ibsen is the victim of warring antinomies with which he struggles without cease throughout the whole of his career. Temperamentally disinclined towards the moderate center, where contraries are often resolved, Ibsen examines first one extreme position, then its opposite, toying with dogmas but always forced into an undogmatic dualism. Ibsen, then, is an idealist whose ideals cannot be systematized from his plays. But this lack of system, on the other hand, is merely the inevitable, though paradoxical, result of his peculiar rebelliousness. Singlemindedly devoted to truth, often at the expense of beauty, Ibsen has no illusions about the permanence of truth; for him, all intellectual postulates, no matter how persuasive, are invariably reduced to lifeless conventions in time. For Ibsen, therefore, the ultimate Truth lies only in the perpetual conflict of truths, and even the rebel must be careful not to institutionalize his revolt. Thus, the real quintessence of Ibsenism is total resistance to whatever is established, for his anarchistic iconoclasm extends not only to the current conventions of his time, but even to his own current beliefs and convictions. Unable to challenge any position without anatomizing its equally valid (or equally invalid) opposite,[6] Ibsen emerges as the champion of no ideology other than the ideology of the negative assault. *On the contrary* (*Tvertimot*) — the words on his lips when he died — might very well be the epitaph to his total dramatic work.

All of Ibsen's drama is the product of this ambivalence, precariously balanced between the author's involvement and detachment, between the subjective and the objective, the ethical and the aesthetic, the rebellious and the controlled. This ambivalence provides each of his plays with a double level, in which a drama of ideas coexists with a drama of action, so that Ibsen's characters, functioning both in thought and deed, have a rich intellectual life in addition to their dramatic existence. The drama of ideas is generally the expression of Ibsen's personal rebellion, while the drama of action puts this rebellion into some kind of objective perspective. For while Ibsen will often use a character to advance some rebellious doctrine which he probably holds himself, he is almost never satisfied with mere ventriloquism. At the same time that he advances an abstract idea, he examines the consequences of this idea in the arena of human action, demonstrating both the theoretical power of certain truths and their baleful effect on the lives of others when put into practice. At his best, then, Ibsen will

---

6 Janko Lavrin reports a conversation of Ibsen's in which the playwright remarked that any idea, carried to its conclusion, usually touches on its own contradiction. Clearly, Ibsen is less interested in ideas, as such, than in the conflict of ideas — which is why he is a playwright and not a philosopher.

treat the drama of ideas and the drama of action as two contiguous developments which touch and enrich each other throughout the play, deriving his energy, drive, and excitement from the one, and his detachment, complexity, and thickness from the other. At his worst, Ibsen's manipulation of the strings is unsure or clumsy, so that his endings sometimes seem equivocal or his characters inconsistent: In *A Doll's House,* for example, Nora's abrupt conversion from a protected, almost infantile dependent into an articulate and determined spokesman for individual freedom may serve the drama of ideas but it is totally unconvincing in the drama of action. But when Ibsen perfects this method, it becomes one of his most original contributions to the modern theatre, endowing his work with a double-leveled perspective which cannot be matched by any other modern playwright.

Ibsen, then, is a Romantic rebel with a Classical alter ego which restrains his headier impulses towards total liberation, self-expression, and moral idealism by inhibiting his freedom, restricting his rebellion, and testing his ideals in the world of accommodation and compromise. We have already seen how Ibsen's self-imposed discipline results in certain vertical conflicts within the individual plays. It can be seen, from another angle, in the horizontal development of his art and his changing concepts of dramatic form. The progression of Ibsen's career, in fact, is as dialectical as any of his plays. Works like *Brand, Peer Gynt,* and *Emperor and Galilean,* are relatively overt expressions of the author's early Romanticism in which he creates an architecture of poetry and metaphysics out of huge, irregular blocks of stone. But beginning with *The League of Youth,* and continuing through his "modern" phase (an eleven-year period, ending with *Hedda Gabler* in 1890), Ibsen suppresses his Romanticism — along with his poetry, his mysticism, and his concern with man in nature — to satisfy a pull towards prose, objective reality, and the problems of modern civilization. This Classical counterrhythm gives one the impression that Ibsen's art has been totally transformed. The rebel against God is domesticated into a rebel against society; the scene focusses on the collective as well as on the individual; the humanistic medical doctor becomes an important character, as Darwinist notions of heredity and environment begin to impinge on the action; the language becomes more thin and chastened; the characterization more specific; the themes more contemporary; and the entire drama takes on, first, that manipulated quality we remember from the well-made play, then, that precision of form we associate with Sophoclean tragedy. As if to prove that this spirit has changed much less radically than is first apparent, for, in his realistic plays, he has merely contained his rebellious spirit within a new form. As if to prove that this spirit has remained unsullied, Ibsen returns, in his last great plays, to his early prophetic, autobiographical, and metaphysical concerns, dramatizing them in a way which combines the Romantic freedom of his youth with the Classical restraint of his middle years. To trace Ibsen's artistic development in more precise detail, let us examine works from each of his three major periods, discussing them in relation to the personal circumstances under which they were written.

Any discussion of Ibsen's mature art must start with *Brand*, since this monolithic masterpiece is not only the first play he completed after leaving his native country, but his first, and possibly his greatest, work of enduring power. Nothing in Ibsen's previous writings prepares us for a play of this scope, not even the substantial talent he displays in *The Vikings at Helgeland* and *The Pretenders*, for *Brand* is like a sudden revelation from the depths of an original mind. It is highly probable that Ibsen's achievement in *Brand* was intimately connected with his departure from Norway, for he seemed to find an important source of creative power in his self-imposed exile: "I had to escape the swinishness up there to feel fully cleansed," he wrote to his mother-in-law from Rome. "I could never lead a consistent spiritual life there. I was one man in my work and another outside — and for that reason my work failed in consistency too." Ibsen's desire for creative consistency was certainly fulfilled during his sojourn in Rome. Besides filling him with admiration for the "indescribable harmony" of his new surroundings ("beautiful, wonderful, magical," he called them), Ibsen's *Italienische Reise,* like Goethe's before him, seems to have opened him up to an expansive Romanticism. Ibsen himself was quite conscious of the influence of Rome on his art, for in describing to a friend how *Brand* had come to be written, he said: "Add to this Rome with its ideal peace, association with the carefree artist community, an existence in an atmosphere which can only be compared with that of Shakespeare's *As You Like It* — and you have the conditions productive of *Brand*." It was a period of the most exquisite freedom Ibsen had ever known, and his nostalgia for these years was later to find expression in Oswald's enthusiastic descriptions of the buoyant *livsglaede* (joy of life) to be found in the Paris artist community.

On the surface, *Brand* — an epic of snow and ice with a glacial Northern atmosphere and a forbidding central figure — would seem to have little in common with this warm, sunny Italian world. Yet the sense of abandon which Ibsen was experiencing is reflected in the play's openness of form and richness of inspiration ("May I not . . . point to *Brand* and *Peer Gynt*," wrote Ibsen later, "and say: 'See, the wine cup has done this!' "). Though it was originally conceived as a narrative poem, Ibsen soon reworked *Brand* into a five-act poetic drama, a work so conscientiously long and unstageable that Ibsen was astonished when a Scandinavian company decided to produce it. For Ibsen, exulting in the luxury of pure self-expression, had written the work unmindful of the limiting demands of an audience or the restricting requirements of a theatre. Having finally freed his imagination from its frozen Northern vaults, Ibsen had at last discovered how to make his work an integral part of his spiritual life. The solution was simple enough; he had to be the same person *in* his work as outside it. Although in *The Pretenders* Ibsen had dramatized the conflicts in his own soul through a fictional external action, *Brand* was the most thoroughgoing revelation of his rebellious interior life that Ibsen had yet attempted, an act of total purgation, in which he exorcised the troll battle within his heart and mind by transforming it into art.[7] With *Brand*, Ibsen confronted for the first time and in

---

[7] Ibsen himself considered *Brand* to be a purgative work: "It came into existence," he wrote to Laura Kieler, "as the result of something I have lived *through* — not merely met in life; it was necessary for me to rid myself, through poetic creation, of something I had inwardly finished with." Elsewhere,

combination the great subjects which were to occupy him successively during the course of his career: the state of man in the universe, the state of modern society, and the state of his own feverish, divided soul.

The play, a storage house for all of Ibsen's future themes and conflicts, is constructed like a series of interlocking arches, each ascending higher than the last. The lowest arch is a domestic drama, in which Ibsen examines the relationship of the idealist to his family (the basis for later plays like *The Wild Duck*); the middle arch is a social-political drama, in which he analyzes the effect of the aristocratic individual on a democratic community (the basis for plays like *An Enemy of the People*); and the highest arch is a religious drama, in which he shows the rivalry between the messianic rebel and the nineteenth-century God (the basis for plays like *The Master Builder*). Pastor Brand — a reforming minister of extraordinary zeal (his very name means "sword and fire") — is the hero of all three dramas, and Ibsen's supreme idealist, individualist, and rebel. In the tradition of the Old Testament prophets, and those apostles of religious purification who arise in human history to change the course of the world, Brand is remorselessly dedicated to his cause. Like Luther, he has elected to be the "chastiser of the age," scourging the excesses of individuals and institutions; like Moses, he is determined to bring new codes of spiritual purity to a generation of idlers, appeasers, and dreamers; and like Christ, he is committed to the salvation of all mankind through a complete transformation of human character. Brand, however, is a very peculiar Christian, if indeed he can be called Christian at all. Intensely masculine, patristic, strict, and unyielding, he rejects the compassionate side of Christianity in his determination to close the gap between what is and what should be by making human practice conform to spiritual ideals. Actually, Brand is more extreme than the most apocalyptic Puritan reformers, a Savonarola of the will who brings Protestant individualism to the furthest reaches of its own implications. For, as Brand develops

---

Ibsen wrote: "Creation has been to me like a bath, whence I have felt myself emerge purer, healthier, freer."

[52]

his theology, he demands not only that each man become his own Church, but — so strict are the extremes of his ideal — *even his own God.*

Man becomes a god by imitating God, but Brand's God — not a "gentle wind" but a "storm" — is almost inimitable, being the purest and most uncompromising of celestial beings. He is identified with the Ideal itself, to be attained through the unlimited striving of the human will. Because of his emphasis on will, the mortal sin for Brand is cowardice and half-heartedness. Like Kierkegaard before him, and Nietzsche after,[8] Brand is disposed towards the great saint or the great sinner — the man who lives his life extremely with a purpose either good or evil — but he cannot abide the will-less mediocrities who fail to be anything fully. Brand's Devil, therefore, is the spirit of compromise, while his concept of evil is identified with the middle way of moderation, accommodation, luxury, ease, and moral laziness. Taking "All or nothing" as his rebellious credo, he has resolved to make "heirs of heaven" out of the dull and cloddish inhabitants of the modern world, fashioning a new race of heroes to match the heroic figures of the past.

Brand, who follows his own precepts with uncompromising integrity, is himself one of these heroes — but at a terrific cost. Struggling painfully to conquer any emotions which might lead him from the path of righteousness, he becomes contemptuous of any but the hardest virtues: for him, love is merely a smirch of lies ("Faced by a generation/ Which is lax and slothful, the best love is hate"),[9] while charity and humanitarianism are the encouragement of human weakness ("Was God humane when Jesus died?"). Thus, Brand finally succeeds in suppressing his own human feelings, an ambiguous

[8] Kierkegaard writes, "Let others complain that our times are wicked; *I* complain that they are contemptible, for they are without passion," while Nietzsche complains not that man is bad but that "his baddest is so very small!"

[9] Twenty-five years before Ibsen wrote *Brand,* Emerson was reflecting in a similar vein in his essay "Self-Reliance": "The doctrine of hatred must be preached, as the counteraction of the doctrine of love, when that pules and whines. I shun father and mother and wife and brother when my genius calls me. . . . Let us affront and reprimand the smooth mediocrity and squalid contentment of the times."

victory which makes him at the same time both wholly admirable and wholly impossible. Like most monastic, disciplinary types, he has something forbidding and inhuman in his nature. Ibsen usually associates him with images of cold and hardness (snow, steel, iron, stone); even the conditions of his birth (he was "born by a cold fjord in the shadow of a barren mountain") suggest his icelike qualities. By comparison, the beauty-loving painter Ejnar and his lovely fiancée Agnes are identified with "mountain air, the sunshine, the dew, and the scent of pines," and their pursuit of Southern pleasures is a striking contrast to Brand's singleminded pursuit of the ideal.

Yet, such is Brand's heroic stature, fierce courage, and charismatic power that by the end of Act II Agnes has been converted to his religion of "grayness," leaving Ejnar to take up her duties by Brand's side. It is in the domestic scenes that follow (Acts III and IV) that Brand's defective humanity is most strongly dramatized, for his fanatic ideals of moral purity succeed in destroying his entire family; first his mother, who dies unshriven when Brand refuses to visit her unless she freely gives away her fortune; then his young son Alf, a victim of the Northern cold who has been refused the Southern warmth (an Ibsenist image for love); and finally Agnes herself, forced into dreadful choices and ultimately deprived of even the relics of her mother love. All this while, Brand has been engaged in a terrific struggle with himself, torn between his ideal and his love for Agnes and Alf. Yet his decision to be a god has left him with no real choice; and when Agnes warns him "He dies who sees Jehovah face to face," he can only accept the terrible implications of his Godhead and let her die. When she abdicates her painful life with an ecstatic cry ("I am free, Brand! I am free!"), Brand has achieved a moral victory only through the sacrifice of everything he loved in the world — as Shaw put it, through "having caused more intense suffering by his saintliness than the most talented sinner could possibly have done with twice his opportunities."

Yet it is only in the domestic portions of the play that Brand emerges as a villain-idealist; like all great reformers (even Christ treated his family with scant respect), he has no time or capacity for a happy private life. When he plays a public role, in the social-political scenes, he is a bright contrast to the citizenry he has come to reform. Here, Brand, a typical *Sturm-und-Drang* hero, is the individual at war with society, denouncing its worm-eaten conventions, its limited aspirations, its corrupt institutions. His antagonist, in this drama, is the Mayor, society's elected representative — like Mayor Peter Stockmann and Peter Mortensgard, a "typical man of the people," and therefore Brand's instinctive enemy. The conflict between them arises from their conflicting expectations from their constituents. Brand, appealing to spiritual man, seeks the salvation of the individual through a revolution in his moral consciousness; the Mayor, appealing to social man, seeks the pacification of the community through attention to its material needs. Wishing to make life easier, the Mayor wants to construct public buildings; Brand, wishing to make life harder, wants to construct a new Church. This conflict — in which Brand obviously expresses Ibsen's own predisposition in favor of the individual against the community, the moral against the social, the spiritual against the material, radical revolution against moderation and compromise — is ultimately irreconcilable. But since Brand's following has increased, the Mayor, pulling his sheets to the wind, capitulates, following the desires of the compact majority by helping Brand with his plans. The Mayor, however, has not lost the battle. He has merely made a strategic retreat in order to assimilate his enemy. And, as for Brand, his temporary success has made him unwittingly betray his own ideal.

In Act V, which forms the climax of the religious drama and the heart of the play, Brand becomes what Ibsen really intended him to be — neither a villain-idealist nor a hero-reformer but a tragic sufferer existing independently of moral judgments. At the beginning of the act, Brand is seen as a fashionable preacher, a popular commercial personality like Billy Graham. His new Church is about to open and Brand himself is to be decorated by the State for his services to the community. Multitudes have gathered for the event — vaguely sensing that the destruction of the old Church was some form of sacrilege and trembling with apprehension "as though they had been summoned to elect a new God." Brand himself is very morose; he cannot pray and his soul is full of discords. His mood grows blacker when the Provost — the theological counterpart of the Mayor — begins to inform him that religion is merely an instrument of the State to insure itself against unrest. When he warns Brand to concern himself with the needs of the community rather than the salvation of the individual, Brand suddenly becomes aware that the Church is a lie and that he has become a corrupt institution himself. Ignoring the Provost's contention that "the man who fights alone will never achieve anything of a lasting nature," he tells his enthusiastic followers that the only true Church is the wild and natural world of the fjords and moorlands, not yet tainted by human compromise, hypocrisy, and evil: "God is not here!/ His kingdom is perfect freedom." [10]

Like Moses leading his people towards the beautiful promised land, Brand makes his way upwards to the freedom and purity of the cliffs and mountains. But like Moses' followers, the people begin to slacken and grumble when the way grows hard. The Grand Inquisitor, in Dostoyevsky's *The Brothers Karamazov,* had told the resurrected Christ that the common man seeks not Godhead, but miracle, mystery, and authority. And now it is Brand's turn to learn of human limitation, as his followers clamor for water, bread, prophecies, security, and miracles in place of the spiritual victory he promises. When he offers them no more than "a new will," "a new faith," and "a crown of thorns," they feel betrayed and begin to stone their Messiah. And when the Mayor arrives with the Provost to reclaim the sheeplike flock with a promise of food and safety, they repudiate Brand's salvation altogether, meekly returning to their secular lives below.

[10] Cf. the last verses of Ibsen's early poem "On the Heights" (1859-1860), which also celebrates, in ringing tones, the absolute purity of life in natural surroundings, free from the pollutions of the city:

> Now I am tempered like steel; I follow that call
>   which summons me to wander in the height!
> I have lived out my lowland existence;
>   here on the moor there are freedom and God,
>   down there grope the others.

Brand is left alone on the moorlands, torn and bleeding, to meditate upon his mistakes. In putting vengeance, justice, and retribution
before forgiveness, charity, and compassion; in repudiating the "God
of every dull and earthbound slave," Brand has pursued Godhead
through the pursuit of an incorruptible ideal. But while making him
Godlike, this quest has also made him a rebel against the very Deity
he had tried to serve. Brand's messianism has turned him into
something harder and crueler than God, and it has broken the backs
of his all-too-human followers. Now Brand must learn that man cannot be God; that he must live with the Devil if he is to live at all; and
that even the freedom of the will is limited by the inexorable determinism of inherited sin.[11] Now, like Moses on Mount Nebo, Brand
is denied the promised land, and must await retribution himself. Yet,
still he adheres to his ideal. When a specter appears, in the shape of
Agnes, offering him warmth, love, and forgiveness if he will only
renounce the awful words *"All or nothing,"* Brand refuses; and when
the spirit is transformed into a hawk flying across the moorlands,
Brand recognizes his ancient enemy, the Devil of Compromise.

Still struggling upwards, Brand finally reaches the Ice Church, a
mighty chasm between peaks and summits where "cataract and avalanche sing Mass." It is Brand's true parish, for there, in the ideal
habitat of the extreme Romantic, Brand may preach his gospel of the
absolute, free from the human world and its compromising influences.
When Gerd — the wild gypsy girl who has accompanied him — suddenly has a half-ironic, half-sincere vision of Brand as the incarnation
of Christ and begins worshiping him as a God, Brand, at last, gives
way to human feeling:

[11] Brand reflects on the limitations of the human will when he discovers that
the wild gypsy girl, Gerd, had been born as an indirect result of his mother's
greed (she had rejected a poor wooer who thereupon fathered Gerd on a
gypsy woman). This is an early example of Ibsen's musings on parental guilt,
a subject he will later explore in *Ghosts.* Ibsen's ambivalent feelings about
human freedom date from as early as 1858 where one finds, in *The Vikings at
Helgeland,* this curious passage: "Man's will can do this thing or that; but fate
rules in the deeds that shape our lives." In *Emperor and Galilean* (1873),
Ibsen will try to work out, without too much success, his contradictory beliefs
in both freedom and necessity.

Until today I sought to be a tablet
On which God could write. Now my life
Shall flow rich and warm. The mist is breaking.
I can weep! I can kneel! I can pray!

But it is too late. Shooting at the devil-hawk with her rifle, Gerd has
started an avalanche, and Brand is about to be buried in the snow.
At the last minute, Brand asks a final tortured question of God:
"If not by Will, how can man be redeemed?" And the answer comes
from the heavens in booming tones: *Han er deus caritatis* — "He is
the God of charity, mercy, love."

It is an answer which completes the play, but denies its philosophical basis. For if Brand's severe demands have all been wrong,
and man is redeemed only through love, then the whole intellectual
structure of the work collapses; and Brand's relentless attacks on compromise and accommodation are all superfluous. We must remember,
however, that Ibsen is not rejecting Brand's revolt as an idea; he is
merely rejecting it as a form of action. And since Brand's judge is
a God of love, even Brand, we must assume, is forgiven at the last.
The ending of *Brand,* nevertheless, like the ending of so many of
Ibsen's plays, is inconclusive, an early example of Ibsen's failure to
integrate his drama of ideas with his drama of action — and this
itself is the result of his refusal to adopt a positive synthetic doctrine.
Up until the ending, we can regard Brand *both* as a great hero-saint-
reformer with a redeeming message of salvation *and* as a flawed, repressed, and ice-cold being whose ruthless dedication to an impossible
ideal causes untold suffering and needless deaths. Up until the ending, we can admire Ibsen's extraordinary capacity for keeping two
antithetical attitudes in his mind at the same time, so that he is able
to exalt messianic rebellion as an idea, while condemning it in practice. But the ending demands a synthesis which the author cannot
provide; instead, he chooses to invalidate the intellectual hypothesis
of his play. Still, even in this vaguely unsatisfying ending, one is filled
with admiration for this defeated, yet triumphantly Godlike hero,
whose eternal struggle upwards has somehow enlarged the spiritual
boundaries of man.

We must conclude, then, that both the success and failure of the play stem from the unreconciled conflicts of the playwright. For Ibsen's split attitude towards his hero reflects the clash in his own soul between the twin poles of his temperament — the Romantic idealism of the reforming rebel and the Classical detachment of the objective artist. This dualism — fatal to a man of action but invaluable to a dramatist — is present whenever Ibsen examines the effect of absolute idealism on private happiness, a subject that is to obsess him all his life. But though he will treat this delicate theme again and again in the future, he will never make a presentation of such compelling power and grandeur.

Brand introduced Ibsen into worldwide fame; and exhilarated by his success, he decided to have another try at the episodic poetic play with *Peer Gynt*. If Brand's character reflects Ibsen in his best moments (which is to say, at his most morally elevated), then Peer's reflects Ibsen in his most irresponsible moments (which is to say, at his most morally lax); yet, it is Peer who charms and ingratiates. It is likely that Ibsen, after punishing his own fanatical idealism, is here trying to discipline the more permissive side of his nature, the seeker after pleasure in the Italian sun. The play — with its folk quality, its satirical touches, and its occasionally tropical atmosphere — would seem to be the very obverse of *Brand*. Actually, it is a dramatization of the same themes, treated from a comic-ironic angle. Peer, the embodiment of modern compromise, hypocrisy, irresponsibility, and self-delusion, is very much like those feckless citizens whom Brand had come to reform. And while the play has no rebel or idealist to urge him towards the heights, the playwright himself acts in this capacity, assuming the function of Brand and exposing the extent to which Peer falls short of the ideal. Ibsen is here working out the negative technique he will use in most of his realistic plays, in which not the rebel but the characters rebelled against move to the foreground of the action.

Ibsen is also working out the various implications of nineteenth-century selfhood, a subject he had barely probed in *Brand*. What does it mean to realize yourself? What self represents the true individual? The Hegelian distinction that Ibsen draws in *Peer Gynt* is between character and personality, the one defined by a person's inner reality, the other by the mask he shows to the world. Peer's much-vaunted self, being merely a capricious and unstable public face, suggests he has personality without character, ego without identity. Peer, therefore, emerges as the essential opportunist. Infected with the disease of halfness, he is always prepared to adapt himself to circumstances; and dedicated to pure appearance, he must find beauty in ugliness, courage in cowardice, truth in illusion, nourishment in excrement. Thus, the climax of the drama occurs in the madhouse scene. There Peer unwittingly discovers his most appropriate Kingdom of Self, for there illusion reigns supreme, madness being the triumph of the ego over external reality.

Peer's life, then, has been a tragedy of waste. Unlike the average man, Peer began with a strong potential; he might have been "a shiny button on the coat of the world" — possibly an artist, considering his gifts for fantasy. But he chose to be neither a great saint nor a great sinner, only an opportunistic mediocrity. Now, buried under lost opportunities, he is marked for retribution, destined for the Button Molder's ladle. Yet, Ibsen — remembering the lesson he had forced on Brand — turns compassionate at the end, and gives Peer one last chance for salvation. In the "tranquil love" of Solveig,[12] Peer's self has been preserved. And now, aware that "to be yourself you must slay yourself," he prepares to redeem his soul by a self-sacrificial dedication to some calling higher than his own immediate pleasure or advancement. Presumably, the Button Molder will decide, at the last crossroad, whether Peer has succeeded in his task without sacrificing the happiness of those around him — a dilemma which Brand had totally failed to solve.

It was a dilemma that Ibsen now prepared to face in his own artistic life, for he had decided to go the way of Brand and Peer Gynt,

---

12 This phrase is used by Rebecca West in *Rosmersholm*. In that play, in *Peer Gynt,* and in most of Ibsen's work, love is the one form of redemption that the author never questions, primarily because it is the only ideal which the author thought could ennoble mankind "from without."

suppressing his own personal pleasures for the sake of supreme dedication to his calling. The immediate result of this momentous decision was his move from Rome to Dresden in 1869; soon after came
a more tangible result, *The League of Youth*. In this clumsy play
about political maneuvering in a southern Norwegian town, Ibsen's
decision to embark on a radically new career is immediately apparent. It is a work without a single line of verse — without a trace of
poetic feeling — concerned with the details and problems of contemporary life, and corseted in a tight five-act structure which recalls
the well-made play. Despite its inartistry and banality, *The League of
Youth* is, in many ways, quite typical of the new phase of Ibsen's
art. In later years, he is to find another form of expression for his
poetic impulses, but verse is gone forever.[13] Gone too is the extravagant sweep of his poetic masterpieces, and their self-expressive
freedom. Ibsen has entered a period of extreme self-denial, which is
even signified — considering his affection for Italy and general distaste for the Germans — by his move to Dresden. But it is German
order, clarity, and restraint, rather than Italian ebullience, warmth,
and intoxication which have now become essential to his art.

Before suppressing his Romanticism completely, however, Ibsen
publishes his last great messianic epic, *Emperor and Galilean*,
which finally appears in 1873, nine years after it was begun in Rome.
This monumental double drama in ten acts is obviously designed as
Ibsen's philosophical testament: "The positive world-philosophy

---

[13] See Ibsen's letter to Lucie Wolf (1883): "Verse has been most injurious
to dramatic art. . . . It is improbable that verse will be employed to any extent
worth mentioning in the drama of the immediate future; the aims of the dramatist of the future are almost certain to be incompatible with it. It is therefore
doomed. For art forms become extinct, just as the preposterous animal forms
of prehistoric times become extinct when their day is over. . . . I myself have
for the last seven or eight years hardly written a single verse; I have exclusively
cultivated the very much more difficult art of writing the genuine, plain language spoken in life."

Ibsen, still very much the dramatic poet if no longer the poetic dramatist,
is overstating his position here, as he admits a year later in another letter: "I
still remember that I once expressed myself somewhat disrespectfully about
the art of verse; but that was the result of my own personal connection with
this art form at that particular moment."

which critics have so long demanded from me," he writes, "they will find here." In trying to resolve his own contradictions and assume an affirmative posture, Ibsen borrows freely from Hegel. The play even has a Hegelian subtitle: "A World-Historical Drama" — and Hegel's pattern of thesis-antithesis-synthesis is the pattern of its thematic development. While Ibsen's thesis and antithesis are brilliantly conceived and interpreted, however, his synthesis is much too cloudy to qualify as a "positive world-philosophy." Even when he wants to, Ibsen cannot codify his revolt, and his contradictions remain unresolved. Nevertheless, Ibsen was inordinately fond of this play, and thought it his masterpiece. Written in a luminous prose, modeled on the synoptic gospels, and informed by a strange visionary power, it is offered as a prophetic book for the world of the future.

Ibsen's hero, with whom he is quick to admit his affinities, is the fourth-century Roman Emperor Julian — called the Apostate because of his efforts to overthrow the state religion of Christianity. In the first part of the play, "Caesar's Apostasy," Ibsen traces the early career of Julian, characterized as a disenchanted youth, ardently tasting all varieties of religious experience in a quest after beauty and truth. None of the pagan doctrines satisfy him, however, and, after rejecting them all, he is finally drawn to a Dionysian seer from Ephesus called Maximus the Mystic, who becomes his spiritual adviser for the rest of his life. Julian vacillates between the conflicting empires of Caesar and Christ, the conflicting claims of flesh and spirit, the conflicting demands of freedom and necessity, the conflicting values of self-realization and self-abnegation — both Peer Gynt and Brand inhabit his soul and tear him apart. Julian tries to resolve his conflicts by consulting the supernatural; and, with the aid of Maximus, he visits a symposium of spirits, hoping to find the path to his salvation.

During this seance, Julian sees apparitions of "three great freedmen under necessity": Cain, Judas, and one "who is not yet among the shades." This last visitor, we later learn, is called "Messiah," an Emperor-God who is both ruler and redeemer — "Emperor in the kingdom of the spirit — and god in that of the flesh." Julian immediately assumes this Messiah to be himself, and, filled with messianic fervor, he determines to found the Third Empire of which the oracle goes on to speak — an empire to be achieved only through the mystical exercise of the will. Like the Messiah, the Third Empire is a synthesis of two opposing claims. "Founded on the tree of knowledge and the tree of the cross together, because it hates and loves them both," it will combine "Logos in Pan — and Pan in Logos," fleshly joy and the spiritual word. This paradox is never adequately explained — but one thing about Ibsen's vision of the future is certain: "In that empire, the present watchword of revolt will be realized."

In *The Emperor Julian,* the second part of the drama, Ibsen reveals Julian to be a false Messiah. Having misunderstood the oracle and pursued his will-to-power, Julian is persecuting Christians and declaring himself the only God, at the same time reviving the rites of Apollo and Dionysus. Julian's apostasy, and his war against Christ, however, have only strengthened Christianity: miracles are once again abounding, and the faithful are embracing martyrdom with the old joy. Julian even helps, unwittingly, to fulfill an ancient Christian prophecy when, having rebuilt the temple of Apollo, which Christ once threatened to destroy, he sees it annihilated by a whirlwind. Cursed by the bishops, resisted by the people, Julian is learning what has hitherto been obscure: "Jesus Christ was the greatest rebel that ever lived. . . . He lives in the rebellious minds of men; he lives in their scorn and defiance of all visible authority."[14]

Maximus had prophesied to Julian: "Both Emperor and Galilean shall succumb" — but he did not mean that either would perish. Rather, Caesar and Christ would both be assimilated in the new Messiah, as a child succumbs to the youth and the youth to the man. Now, Julian must pay for his misreading of Maximus's prophecy. After attempting, and failing, to establish his Godhead by conquering the

---

[14] Ibsen's interpretation of Jesus here is very close indeed to that of Ernest Renan, whose *Life of Jesus,* published in 1863, he had almost certainly read. See especially Chapter VII of Renan's book, where Jesus is characterized as an absolute rebel, dedicated to civic anarchy and perfect idealism.

world, Julian is finally wounded in Persia. And like a later Ibsen hero (Solness in *The Master Builder*) who will also attempt the "impossible," Julian dies to the accompaniment of "singing in the air." Maximus speaks his epitaph. Julian had been misled — like Cain and Judas — by a prodigal God who is spendthrift of souls; but his death has moved mankind closer to its goal. Although Julian was not, as Maximus had thought, the mediator between the two empires, nevertheless Maximus is certain that "The third empire shall come! The spirit of man shall once more enter into its heritage — and then shall the smoke of incense arise to thee, and to thy two guests in the symposium." Men still await "the Mighty One" — "self-begotten in the man who wills" — the Messiah who will turn them into gods on earth.

Emperor and Galilean contains many stunning dramatic passages, as well as being an extraordinary anticipation of Nietzsche's later attitudes towards Christianity, Dionysus, and the Superman. But the play does not succeed in formulating that "positive world-philosophy" that the author promised: the Third Empire remains a vague and misty dream. Nevertheless, *Emperor and Galilean* is a fine illustration of Ibsen's messianic demands, and the religious strain which always lies at the bottom of his thought. Furthermore, in the conflicting empires of Caesar and Christ, Ibsen has embodied his own irreconcilable conflicts — between flesh and spirit, free will and necessity, realism and idealism — contradictions which will always be present, in one way or another, in his mind. In a speech made in Stockholm in 1887, Ibsen said:

I have been charged on various occasions with being a pessimist. And that is what I am, in so far as I do not believe in the absoluteness of human ideals. But I am at the same time an optimist in so far as I believe fully and steadfastly in the ability of ideals to propagate and develop. Particularly and specifically do I believe that the ideals of our age, in passing away, are tending towards that which in my drama *Emperor and Galilean* I have tentatively called the Third Empire.

The rest of his plays still strive, however quietly, to bring that messianic dream about.

[64]

But after *Emperor and Galilean,* Ibsen has finished with the messianic drama. Having cast his lot with "the art of the future," he has decided to create not sprawling epics about man on the top of the world but rather well-constructed realistic prose works about man in the depths of the community. Accompanying this discovery is his conversion to the Classical objective mode. It is the presentation of modern life that now concerns him, a subject for which the poetic Romanticism of his youth is inappropriate; and so he purposely limits his resources, developing a chastened and disciplined style. Whatever the ultimate rewards of this decision, the immediate sacrifices must have been tremendous. For Ibsen has decided to give up the natural settings of the fjords and mountains for the cluttered appointments of decorated drawing rooms; the religious-philosophical drama for the drama of everyday life; the unrestricted freedom of epic heroes for the petty limitations of contemporary husbands and housewives; the soaring image and suggestive metaphor for flat conversations in the parlor over cigars and Tokay. Since it took Ibsen some time to master the new experimental forms, his repudiation of the confident techniques of his youth must have filled him with uncertainty and apprehension. But although he regretted his decision for the rest of his life (his last plays ache with his remorse), he never once turned back to the epic poetic form. Probably remembering his own aphorism, he had determined to slay himself in order to become himself, killing his Romantic desire for self-expression for the sake of a selfless seeking after truth.

It is undoubtedly one of the most heroic decisions in the whole of modern art, the act of a man who was clearly — to use Edmund Wilson's striking phrase about Mallarmé — "a true saint of literature." Yet, despite his desire for a more rigorously detached attitude towards his art, Ibsen's conversion to Classicism was far from absolute, and his desire for objectivity was never quite fulfilled. Formally, there is no question that Ibsen's art has changed; and he is extremely preoccupied, during this period, with the careful organization of "reality." But it must be emphasized that Ibsen was attracted to realism for highly unconventional reasons — not because it afforded the dramatist an opportunity to document the surface of life, but because it permitted him to penetrate that surface to the hidden truth beneath. It is, in short, Ibsen's revolt — his desire to probe the appearance of things to expose the true motives of mankind — that distinguishes him from many of his lesser contemporaries and followers, most of whom were either pamphleteers or photographers. In this period, Ibsen's spleen is aroused principally by modern hypocrisy — the gap between what is and what should be, the distance between what is practiced and what is affirmed — and his assaults are aimed at the lies that form the basis of modern institutions. In short, while Ibsen's formal approach has changed, his themes remain substantially the same; and while his style is now more objective, his drama remains essentially the history of his revolt.

Ibsen's prose realism, then, is primarily a new surface manner beneath which the old thematic obsessions still obtrude. In transforming his art, Ibsen has not been able to destroy his Romantic rebellion; he has simply found another way to express it. He has turned his attention to the life of the community not to affirm it but to scourge and purify it,[15] vindicating the rights of the individual against its compromising claims; and he has adapted the language of prose in order to discover a modern stage poetry, expressible through means other than speech. Even now, Ibsen's art is far from fixed. From this point on, he will be restlessly experimenting, devel-

[15] "Zola goes to bathe in the sewer," wrote Ibsen, "I go to cleanse it." This scouring of the social life could be construed as a positive act, and Ibsen, in a letter of 1886, did assign a social purpose to his work: "Each of us must strive to make the world's social order better; this I am doing to the best of my powers." Ibsen's satire, however, usually approaches this end from a negative direction; only in *Little Eyolf,* which concludes with its central characters dedicating themselves to humanitarian ideals, does a positive purpose manifest itself. Shaw, nevertheless, takes this play as typical, and attributes to Ibsen ideological political opinions: "Thus we see that in Ibsen's mind," he writes in *The Quintessence of Ibsenism,* "the way to Communism lies through the most resolute and uncompromising Individualism." This is nonsense; even in his most benevolent moods, Ibsen could never bear the idea of a planned society. Shaw's inability or unwillingness to understand the anarchistic strain in Ibsen's nature accounts, in part, for his insistent misrepresentations of the playwright.

oping, evolving — trying to create a form which will satisfy both sides of his dualistic nature. Since his rebellion is now more disciplined and controlled by form, Ibsen's art no longer expresses his emotional life so freely. But his aspiration towards the ideal continues unabated. Even when the bourgeois upholstery is piled up to the windows, Ibsen's beloved fjords — the symbols of Romantic freedom — can still be glimpsed outside. Though he proceeds now by different and more circuitous routes, he is always trying to find his way back up the mountains to the pure, free air above.

In *Ghosts,* the culminating work of Ibsen's "realistic" period, the fjords and mountains are out of reach, but they can just be seen through the conservatory windows, providing a healthy contrast to the fetid atmosphere within. With *Ghosts,* Ibsen has at last gained control over his new drama, after the experimental bungles of *The League of Youth, Pillars of Society,* and *A Doll's House,* for he has finally achieved a perfect wedding of form and subject matter. His success is the result of substantial technical experimentation; after careful study of the Greeks, he has junked the techniques of the well-made play[16] in favor of the more integrated structure of Sophoclean tragedy. As a result, one is no longer bothered by the noise of Scribean machinery in the wings. Plotted without sensational reversals and unconvincing conversions, *Ghosts* contains no surprise marriages (as in *The League of Youth*), no death ships prevented from sailing at the last minute (as in *Pillars of Society*), no incriminating letters rattling around in the mailbox (as in *A Doll's House*). Instead, as Francis Fergusson has observed, the work is constructed on the pattern of *Oedipus,* beginning at a point right before the catastrophe, and proceeding, like a detective story, by digging up evi-

[16] Ibsen's attitude towards the well-made play, like all his attitudes, is ambiguous. He used the French techniques — and he also despised them. Speaking of his own well-made dramas, he wrote: "These works have mostly a perfected technique, and therefore they please the public; they have nothing to do with poetry and therefore perhaps they please the public still more." He was no more admiring of what he called "Scribe and Co.'s dramatic sweetmeats," though he learned a good deal from the Scribean play. For an extended discussion of the influence of the well-made play on Ibsen's structure, see Maurice Valency's *The Flower and the Castle.*

dence from the past, to a terrible and inevitable conclusion. Because of this perfection of form, one no longer senses a structural incompatibility between the drama of ideas and the drama of action — as one does, for example, in *A Doll's House,* where a long discussion follows after the play has, for all intents and purposes, concluded. Idea and action are perfectly unified in the central image of the work.

The importance of this image is suggested by the fact that it is embodied in the title: Ghosts haunt the atmosphere — ghosts, as Mrs. Alving indicates, in a crucial passage, of two distinct kinds:

I am half inclined to think we are all ghosts, Mr. Manders. It is not only what we have inherited from our fathers and mothers that exists in us, but all sorts of old dead ideas and all kinds of dead beliefs and things of that kind. . . . And we are so miserably afraid of the light.

Mrs. Alving's ghosts, then, are (1) *an intellectual inheritance* — the specters of beliefs which continue to prevail long after they have lost their meaning, and (2) *a spiritual inheritance* — the spirits of the dead which inhabit the bodies of the living, controlling their lives and destinies. The dead ideas of the past are examined, and exploded, during Mrs. Alving's conversations with various members of the household, especially Pastor Manders. By defending emancipated opinions, Mrs. Alving combats, for Ibsen, the hypocrisy and conventionality of such respectable pillars as the stodgy Pastor, opening up such "forbidden" subjects as incestuous marriages, premarital intercourse, intelligent child rearing, and female equality. This play of ideas — suffering the fate that Ibsen prophesied for all ideas — has now become a little ghostly too, while the conflict between Mrs. Alving and Pastor Manders seems a little too easy and simplistic.

But Ibsen is much less interested in specific ideas than in a generalized insight. And Mrs. Alving, like Brand, emerges not only as a *raisonneur,* but as a tragic sufferer with serious flaws herself. It is in the drama of action that her basic flaws — a weakness of will coupled with a limitation in understanding — are exposed. For while she possesses all the right ideas, she lacks the Right Idea: a healthy skepticism about the power of ideas when not backed with some form of radical action. Well-intentioned, liberal-minded, intellectually wise, Mrs. Alving is nevertheless unable to forge an effective practice out of her theories, lacking the courage to act upon her convictions. Thus, despite the fact that she is devoted to enlightenment (Ibsen usually associates her with a lamp, lighting up dark places), she is herself benighted. And like Pastor Manders and his Dickensian shadow, Jacob Engstrand, she is a hypocrite, her actions determined by the pressure of public opinion and the fear of scandal.

Mrs. Alving's moral hypocrisy is centered in the Orphanage, which, like Engstrand's Sailor's Home, is a respectable-looking monument built on a rotten foundation. By pouring Captain Alving's fortune into this building, Mrs. Alving hopes to satisfy opinion, ease her guilty conscience, hide her husband's past, throw off the Alving inheritance and preserve Oswald's pure memories of his father; but it is too much for that delicate structure to bear. When the Orphanage burns up, it is as if all the lies of the past are burning with it (appropriately enough, Captain Alving's name will now be perpetuated in Engstrand's brothel). And Oswald, suffering from the last stages of inherited syphilis, is burning up too. Her awareness of Oswald's disease signals the beginning of Mrs. Alving's education, a process which will not conclude until the play is over. She had always looked on Oswald as an extension of herself, someone allowed the freedom which she had been denied, but now she learns that Oswald is himself a ghost, an extension of his dead father, carrying the family's inheritance in his diseased veins. Trying to find the origin of the curse on the house of Alving, Mrs. Alving continues to exhume the past — and like Oedipus, discovers that she herself is the culprit.

The process, however, is gradual. Having been converted to Oswald's vision of the joy of life, Mrs. Alving is finally able to admit to herself that she killed the sensual life of her husband, and compounded her guilt by remaining with him after he had turned profligate. Yet her education is still not complete. She still believes that she can set the crooked straight through an effort of understanding, and determines to save Oswald by enlightening him about the truth of his family background. But when all the murk has cleared, the sun of "enlightenment" comes up, and Oswald is finally able to "see your home properly," he very appropriately goes mad. His disease has been inaccessible to emancipated opinions or advanced ideas, because — like Greek necessity and Christian original sin — it had determined his fate long before the action began. Mrs. Alving's tragic education is now over. Like Oedipus, she has discovered that the past is unredeemable, for, like Oedipus's killing of Laius at the crossroads, her decision to remain with her husband (a modern form of *hamartia* or tragic error) had started inexorable destructive engines in motion which the human will could no longer control. Dogged by Nemesis, pressed to an act of euthanasia, and screaming with characteristic indecision, she watches Oswald idiotically groping towards the sun, while the pure fjord landscape looms up beyond, as if rebuking the folly and futility of the entire modern world.

"The whole of mankind is on the wrong track," wrote Ibsen in his notes to the play, thus indicating that *Ghosts* was not simply the tragedy of the Alving household, but the tragedy of nineteenth-century bourgeois Europe. For his underlying purpose here was to demonstrate how a series of withered conventions, unthinkingly perpetuated, could result in the annihilation not only of a conventional family but, by extension, the whole modern world. Thus, Mrs. Alving's weakness, Oswald's disease, Captain Alving's profligacy, Engstrand's hypocrisy, and Pastor Mander's stupidity are all merely cankered buds sent up by the dying roots of modern society. For while Mrs. Alving believes in free will, she is nevertheless the victim of outmoded standards of behavior which were bound to result in ruin. *Ghosts,* therefore, while closely patterned on Sophoclean tragedy, lacks one Sophoclean essential: a fatalistic acceptance of human doom. Sophocles ascribes the destruction of his heroes to the will of the gods; Ibsen ascribes it to the stupidity and inhumanity of generation after generation of men. And so the implications of Ibsen's position are the very opposite of Greek fatalism: even his belief in determinism implies a belief in will. For behind his conviction that mankind is on the wrong track is hidden his secret desire for a moral revolution through which mankind can once again be redeemed. Ibsen's task, in these realistic plays, is not to

champion this revolution but rather to show the need for it by exposing the corpse that infects the cargo of modern life. Thus, even in this
detached and coldly objective work,[17] Ibsen's rebellion still continues
to function, seething under the surface of his art.

In *An Enemy of the People,* which followed quite uncharacteristi-
cally within a year, Ibsen's rebellion has once more broken through
the realistic surface, propelled by his fury over the hostile reception
tendered to *Ghosts.* Since he published the play before he had an opportunity to cool his anger or complicate his theme, *An Enemy of the
People* is the most straightforwardly polemical work Ibsen ever wrote.
He had said of *Ghosts,* with much pride and some accuracy, that "in
the whole book there is not a single opinion, not a single remark to be
found that is there on the dramatist's account," but all of *An Enemy
of the People* is there "on the dramatist's account." His self-discipline
momentarily weakened by his hurt pride, Ibsen has invested this play
with the quality of a revolutionary pamphlet; and Stockmann, despite
some perfunctory gestures towards giving him a life of his own, is very
much like an author's sounding board, echoing Ibsen's private convictions about the filth and disease of modern municipal life, the tyranny
of the compact majority, the mediocrity of parliamentary democracy,
the cupidity of the Conservatives, and the hypocrisy of the Liberal
press.

As a result, *An Enemy of the People* is both an inferior work of art
and an invaluable example of Ibsen's naked rebellion. Unlike Brand,
who begins as a messianic rebel, Stockmann is converted to messianism through his growing awareness of the imperfections of modern
humanity. And at the end of the play, his family gathered admiringly
about him, he is preparing to reform the world through selective
breeding, identifying himself with Luther and Christ.[18] Because of
Stockmann's late development, the drama of action is almost com-

[17] "In none of my plays," Ibsen wrote in the course of denying his kinship
with any of the characters of *Ghosts,* "is the author so extrinsic, so completely
absent, as in this last one."

[18] "I shall hurl my ink-pot at their heads!" shouts Stockmann, in an excess
of rage, and determines, a little later, to gather twelve ragamuffins about him
as disciples to whom he will pass on the legacy of revolt.

pletely subordinated to the drama of ideas; and Stockmann emerges as the only rebel in Ibsen's drama whose defiant idealism is never tested in its effect on the happiness of others. The play shows Ibsen with his guard down, permitting his reformist tendencies to triumph momentarily over his self-critical dualism; and thus exposing his aristocratic idealism,[19] the messianic quality which always lies at the bottom of his art.

Despite the crudeness, the vague hysteria, and the hollow posturing that sometimes characterize *An Enemy of the People*, it possesses a dynamism and energy which no other Ibsen prose work can boast, as if the author, unshackled by artistic complexity, were once more breathing the heady, exhilarating air of freedom. Actually, the play is a transitional work, which anticipates Ibsen's later development. Apparently having grown dissatisfied with the restricting pseudo-impartiality of the objective mode, Ibsen is already preparing to forge a more personal, vigorous, and direct expression of his revolt. As it is, Stockmann is probably the first really positive hero that Ibsen has created since Julian the Apostate — but he is too simplistically heroic to satisfy the author's dualism. In *The Wild Duck*, Ibsen pauses to punish himself severely for this self-indulgence by launching a murderous satirical attack on the messianic idealist. But after this, Ibsen is finished

19 "Zola is a democrat," wrote Ibsen, "I am an aristocrat," meaning, of course, that he believed in an aristocracy of character. It is interesting to note what happens to this aristocrat when he falls into the hands of a democratic disciple like Arthur Miller, who bowdlerized *An Enemy of the People* for the Broadway stage. The antisocial elements of the play are called "fascistic," and cut; its apocalyptic quality is tempered with moderateness and reason; and its posture of defiant individualism is watered down into a plea for the protection of minority groups. In his preface, Miller says that the play handles the "question of whether the democratic guarantees protecting political minorities ought to be set aside at a time when the mass of men condemn it [*sic!*] as a dangerous and devilish lie." Of course, the play does no such thing. But in order to fit the work to his liberal-democratic Procrustean bed, Miller proceeds to lop off its more radical limbs (Ibsen's line "The strongest man in the world is he who stands alone," for example, becomes, in Miller's adaptation "We are the strongest people in the world and the strong must learn to be lonely" — a mere copybook maxim). We can all agree with Miller that unpopular political groups should be protected from governmental interference, but Ibsen's polemic cuts a good deal deeper than that.

with the drama of the community. *Hedda Gabler* and *Rosmersholm* follow, each dominated by a strong central character; and then comes the last phase of his career, in which the messianism of Brand is adapted to the realism of *Ghosts,* and the works are centered once again on the divided, semi-autobiographical hero.

Even *The Wild Duck* can probably be considered as a semi-autobiographical work, though it contains the harshest criticism Ibsen ever directed against himself, and is almost a repudiation of everything he had written thus far. In its more open form, its harshly satirical tone, and its unresolved conclusion, *The Wild Duck* bears out Ibsen's contention that "in some ways this new play occupies a position by itself among my dramatic works." But its novelty is especially clear in its intellectual stance, for it is the only play in which Ibsen completely denies the validity of revolt. Stockmann had declared, obviously with the author's approval, that "all who live on lies must be exterminated like vermin." Yet Gregers Werle — a fanatical Ibsenite, whose metaphors, attitudes, and symbol-mongering suggest he has carefully read each of the master's works — exposes the lies of the Ekdal family, and succeeds only in mutilating everybody in it. In trying to follow Ibsenite principles, Gregers is, furthermore, excoriated so mercilessly that he almost seems a scapegoat. To use Ibsen's angry descriptive images, he is a "quacksalver," "mad, demented, crackbrained," a neurotic busybody suffering from "an acute attack of integrity," "morbid, overstrained," a superfluity seeking a mission, "thirteenth at table" — in short, an ugly, unwanted, unattractive man.

Yet *The Wild Duck* must be interpreted less as a repudiation of Ibsenism than a corrective to it. For while Gregers seems to be a typical Ibsenite, he is actually a sadly unbalanced one — almost a caricature of Stockmann or Brand. His commitment to the ideal, for example, comes from without, not from within, since it is the consequence of his conscience pangs over his father's sordid behavior; and he tries to realize the ideal not through his own heroic striving but through urging exemplary behavior on others. It is a sign of Gregers's intellectual inadequacy that he should mistake that latter-day Peer Gynt, Hjalmar Ekdal, for a superior being; but it is also a sign that he is a very incomplete rebel. For while Gregers may possess Brand's destructive fanaticism (his deadly effect on the Ekdals recalls Brand's effect on his family), he lacks Brand's heroic virtues, particularly his individualism and aristocratic will; Gregers is not a hero but a hero-worshiper. Ibsen is attacking the negative side of rebellion without bothering to affirm its positive side — an imbalance probably designed to correct the reverse imbalance in *An Enemy of the People.* Thus, Ibsen — who has suggested before, with much indignation, that the average man feeds on illusions — treats this insight now with a good deal more equanimity — not because he has grown more tolerant of the average man, but because he is more interested in attacking the inadequate idealist. It is doubtful that Ibsen has grown indifferent to the heroic claims of idealism and rebellion, since he continues to treat these with his usual respect in all his later plays. He is simply refusing to be institutionalized by slavish followers.[20] Most important, in satirizing the Ibsenite who tries to codify his principles into rigid formulae, Ibsen is satirizing the ideologist in himself — that indignant moralist who would smash human happiness for the sake of ennobling mankind.

In *Hedda Gabler* and *Rosmersholm,* Ibsen returns to the Classical form of *Ghosts.* Once again, a dead person determines the actions and characters of the play (General Gabler in *Hedda;* Beata in *Rosmersholm*); and once again, the rebel is treated with equivocal sympathy. Hedda is even more morbid and neurotic than Gregers, and almost as destructive; but having recovered his sense of dialectic, Ibsen puts Hedda in Romantic contrast to the bourgeois mediocrities whose lives she helps destroy. This contrast is even more striking in *Rosmersholm.* The action centers on isolated heroes rather than the conformist community, and the development of the play follows Rebecca's gradual transformation under the influence of a harsh but heroic way of life ("The Rosmer view of life ennobles. But . . . it kills happiness").

---

20 In a letter to Brandes (1883), Ibsen wrote: "I maintain that an intellectual fighter in the outpost-line can never collect a majority. . . . Quite a compact crowd now stands where I stood when I wrote my various books, but I am no longer there myself; I am somewhere else — I hope, farther on."

After these transitional plays, Ibsen leaves off scourging the community, turning again to the tumult in the soul of the hero and becoming more and more subjective until he finally leaves realism behind altogether. It is the last phase of his career, coincident with his return to Norway after an exile, broken only by short visits, of twenty-seven years. The note of banishment is still struck; yet his last plays stand as a monument to an almost completed mission.

In the best play of this final period, *The Master Builder*, the religious, mystical, and poetic strains in Ibsen's nature, repressed through a gigantic exertion of will, have burst forth again, now contained within a domestic but strongly symbolic framework and communicated through a prose heavily charged with ambiguity. Bygmester Solness is the most compelling of Ibsen's later, brooding self-portraits, a messianic hero pulled down from the heights to reside in the community of men, and now painfully laboring to drag himself up again. This is, of course, pure autobiography; and, as has been often observed, the play contains many such elements, culled from Ibsen's emotional, and sometimes even his "actual," experience. The character of Hilda Wangel, for example — that voracious, beautifully plumed bird of prey who urges Solness towards a fatal demonstration of his will, virility, and potency — is based on an eighteen-year-old girl whom the sixty-four-year-old playwright had recently met (he called her "a May sun in a September life"). Solness's fear that the younger generation will rise up and smite him suggests Ibsen's fear of being eclipsed by rising young playwrights like Strindberg, Knut Hamsun, and Hauptmann. Solness's sense that his unremitting dedication to his calling has destroyed his happiness is a reflection of Ibsen's doubts and regrets, further expressed in *John Gabriel Borkman, Little Eyolf,* and *When We Dead Awaken,* about his own dedication as an artist. And Solness's development as a builder, proceeding from towered churches to "homes for human beings" to towered houses, parallels Ibsen's development from his epic poetic plays to his realistic prose works to the symbolic, poetic realism of his last period.

The most interesting biographical element in *The Master Builder*, for our purposes, is its strong messianic theme, which deserves special emphasis because it is so often overlooked.[21] In this aspect of the play (which dominates the last act), Solness emerges as another Promethean rebel, similar in many ways to Emperor Julian, who is defined by his ambiguous relation to God. Long before the action begins, Solness had been a pious and reverent man, and had tried to express his devotion to God by building churches to His great glory. In return, Solness believes, God had rewarded him with certain superhuman powers — "helpers and servers" — which account for his fabulous luck and his tremendous will. Though this interpretation seems rather farfetched, Solness is not demented. His will — now somewhat diseased through remorse and fear — is indeed an almost supernatural instrument, providing him with a hypnotic power over his employees. And all through his career, Solness — somewhat like Haakon in *The Pretenders* — has been unusually favored by circumstances; even his career was initiated by a lucky catastrophe, for after his wife's ancestral home had burned down, he had constructed a successful project on the ruins.

Yet, ever since that conflagration, Solness has been in revolt against God. When his children died as an indirect result of the fire, Solness blamed God for trying to rob him of his worldly happiness for the sake of a more complete dedication to his divine calling. Refusing to be the instrument of a celestial purpose, Solness repudiated God when hanging the wreath on the church tower at Lysanger, a negation which Hilda Wangel — who was present — somehow heard as the vibrations of "harps in the air." At that moment, Solness dedicated his career not to religious monuments to the greater glory of God but to secular dwelling places for the greater comfort of human beings. But even as a "Free builder" he has felt no joy. Aline, his wife — consumed with self-reproach over the death of her children — has become a frigid Death-in-Life. And since the community has no real use for the homes he has built for it, Solness (like Ibsen) is himself con-

[21] It is not overlooked, however, by Hermann Weigand, who gives a penetrating analysis of this "mystery play," as he calls it, in his book *The Modern Ibsen*.

sumed with remorse for having suppressed his aspiration towards the heights.

Now Solness fears Nemesis — the punishment of God — which he suspects will come in the shape of the younger generation battering down his door. And so it does, though not from the direction he expects. It is Hilda Wangel, his youthful admirer — and not his rival, the young apprentice Ragnar — who knocks ominously on his door, unwittingly becoming the Angel of the Lord. Hilda sees Solness through the idealizing distance of her childhood memories, and now she wants her ideal realized. Determined to whet his blunted spirit, she urges him "to do the impossible once again"; and Solness responds, basking in the warmth of her youth, hero worship, and Viking amorality. His will becomes more strong and certain; his conscience more robust; and his rebellion more defiant and dangerous. Convinced by Hilda that he is a superhuman being, beyond the good and evil of ordinary mortals, he determines to run away with her to build "castles in the air" — though he is still cautious enough to want a "firm foundation."

But first he must earn her love, transcending his age and decline through a display of masculine potency. The opportunity arrives when he builds a tower on his new home (a religious pinnacle on a secular structure), and is persuaded by Hilda to hang a wreath on it, despite his attacks of vertigo. In terms of the religious aspect of the play, this is not only an act of *hybris,* but an act of blasphemy, since it is tantamount to a declaration of Godhead. And when he climbs up to the top, retribution speedily follows. Dizzied by the heights, and confused by Hilda's enthusiastic waving of her shawl, Solness plummets to the earth; Hilda, applauding the achievement of the impossible ideal, continues to wave her shawl aloft, fixed on the hero but mindless of the broken human being at her feet. As the younger generation breaks into the garden she cries, "My — my Master Builder."

It is a great cathedral of a play, with dark, mystical strains which boom like the chords of an organ. Since Ibsen is once again concerned with a powerful central hero who wills his fate, rather than a victim of a circumstantial process, the work has a feeling of loftiness and grandeur which has been missing from his art since the early days. As a heroic rebel, Solness is in a class with Ibsen's epic heroes. Unlike Brand or Julian or Stockmann, he has no organized messianic doctrine with which to revolutionize the world, but his audacity and daring give him the stature that Mrs. Alving, Gregers, and Nora Helmer totally lacked. He is, in fact, one of the strongest in Ibsen's gallery of individualists. Warring with God, he is finally conquered through overweening pride; but his defeat is a partial victory — he has also conquered God by attempting the deeds he feared most to do. Ibsen's treatment of Solness shows that his interest in objective rebellion is now over for good. *The Master Builder* is free from all considerations of biology, determinism, and Darwinism (even the humanistic doctor is now assigned a secondary role), and the play cannot even be comprehended in a purely realistic reading. Ibsen's symbolism has begun to dominate the action, making it suggestive and metaphorical rather than specific and concrete. For after building homes for human beings and finding little satisfaction in the task, Ibsen has now returned to the great towering structures of his early years — building them now, to be sure, on a "firm foundation" of disciplined form. Somewhat dizzied by the heights, fearful that his own powers are failing, he has apparently resolved to put a wreath on his career by returning to the free expression of his interior life which, for so many years, he had partially abandoned. In his next two plays, *John Gabriel Borkman* and *Little Eyolf,* the fjords, the mountains, and the sea have come into his work again, and in his last, *When We Dead Awaken,* he finally makes his way up to the heights to die.

Ibsen wrote *When We Dead Awaken* in 1899, when he was seventy-one. Subtitled "A Dramatic Epilogue," it is clearly designed as the playwright's final statement, even though he is to speak, right before his stroke, of entering the battlefield again "with new weapons and in new armor." The weapons and armor of this play were novel enough to have shocked a number of usually sympathetic partisans, notably William Archer, who called it "wholly impossible," "purely pathological," "an exaggeration of manner to the pitch of mannerism."

Archer's dislike for the play — based on his conviction that Ibsen had sacrificed "surface reality to underlying meaning" — can be quickly dismissed if we remember his own peculiar prejudices; it was Archer who rejected Elizabethan drama because of its "unrealistic" asides and soliloquies. When we cease regarding Ibsen purely as a prose realist, we will be able to see that *When We Dead Awaken* is not so much a new departure as a continuation and intensification of all his old themes, in which his mysticism, no longer concealed under an authenticated surface, has become more rampant and overt. In many ways, the play can be compared with Shakespeare's late romances or Beethoven's last quartets: the experimentation of an artist who is prepared to fall into excesses in order to expand the possibilities of his art. Like *The Winter's Tale,* for example, the play is full of minor flaws, and often inconsistent in plot and character. But it shows no falling off at all in dramatic power. Quite the contrary, it is one of the most valuable testaments we have to Ibsen's extraordinary mind and vision. And it suggests that, had he lived, Ibsen might have developed in the same direction as Strindberg or Maeterlinck, creating a drama of the soul to which the physical events of everyday life have been completely subordinated.

Ibsen's last work concludes the series of autobiographical dramas begun with *The Master Builder* which deal with the aging rebel, despairing of life and racked with guilt, who experiences an ambiguous victory at the moment of death. Like Solness the architect, Rubek the sculptor is an artist whose work no longer satisfies him; like Solness, he is stimulated by a woman to acts of great daring, mortally straining himself in the process. Rubek, however, begins at a later point of development than any of Ibsen's other heroes. Instead of realizing the incompatability of dedicated work and consuming love at the end of his life, he begins with this awareness; and throughout the action, therefore, he is trying to weld the two opposites into a synthesized whole. Actually, Rubek has chosen the joy of life over his calling before the play even begins. For after a life of hard work, he elected to spend his old age in semi-retirement — living with Maia, his wife, in a sunny Italian villa and turning out facile portrait busts of prominent men. Rubek, however, soon grew tired of this aimless happiness; and Maia began to bore him, too. Now, misanthropic, sullen, and indifferent to his wife, Rubek has returned North to a health resort, to sip seltzer and read newspapers near the fjords and mountains. At the same time that Maia chides him for his broken promises (he had offered to show her "all the glory of the world" from a high mountain), Rubek chides himself for his lost opportunities, still yearning for a great driving passion which will give his old age some meaning.

When he comes upon a mysterious lady in white, attended by a Sister of Mercy, Rubek thinks he has found what he has been seeking, for the lady turns out to be Irene, a former model and the inspiration for his earlier masterpiece, "Resurrection Day." At that time, his work had been inspired by love; and now Rubek realizes that in Irene his warring conflicts were once resolved. The realization, however, comes too late. When Irene had offered to serve him "in frank, utter nakedness . . . with all the pulsing blood of my youth," Rubek had rejected her. Fearing that his art would suffer if he permitted the materials to use the master, he merely thanked her for a "priceless episode" and went his way. The conflict between the artist-man and the mother-woman (a conflict Shaw is later to exploit) had resulted in Irene's spiritual annihilation. Served too late, the God of Love becomes the God of Death, and she is now a frozen image from a world beyond the grave. Consumed with a desire for revenge, she plots to kill Rubek with a small stiletto which she carries with her. Regarded by realistic standards, she looks like a homicidal maniac, but realism is rather alien to the play; she is more like a symbolic figure — an allegorical spirit of Nemesis.[22]

While Rubek seeks his resurrection in Irene, Maia seeks hers in

[22] The similarity of Ibsen's Irene to Dürrenmatt's Claire Zachanassian in *The Visit of the Old Lady* is too striking to be overlooked. They not only display the same nonhuman, allegorical attributes, but also share a number of specific qualities: Irene, like Claire, has been married many times (to a Russian, a South American, etc.), was forced into a life of prostitution after the conclusion of her love affair, and has now dedicated herself to achieve revenge on the man who ruined her life. Dürrenmatt makes explicit what is already implicit in Ibsen's play — the similarity between his heroine and certain figures of vengeance in Greek tragedy (Medea, Clytemnestra, the Furies).

Ulfheim, the bear hunter. In the crisscross structure of this play, the husband and wife switch partners as in an unearthly minuet. As the embodiment of sensuality, joy, warmth, and life (note the significance of her name), Maia is ideally suited to Ulfheim, about whom she notes, with a huge sense of relief, "There's not a bit of the artist. . . ." [23] Both are healthy young animals with no desires beyond the satisfaction of their own immediate physical pleasures. Ulfheim, in fact, is a kind of satyr figure ("goatish and lecherous"); and his association with the hunt — with bears, dogs, red blood, and red meat — carries over into his love life: he regards all women as "game." Nevertheless, it is this Scandinavian Stanley Kowalski who offers to fulfill Rubek's forgotten promise to Maia; he will take her away from the "brackish ditchwater" and show her all the glories of the world, unsullied by "the trail and taint of men." Uflheim and Maia, possessed with buoyant, Philistine joy, are from a totally different world from Rubek and Irene — the world of the living as opposed to the world of the dead — and even their mundane chitchat contrasts strongly with the charged mystical language of the sculptor and his model.

Rubek, too, has found his ideal mate, though for less exhilarating reasons. While trying to recapture his lost intensity through Irene, he discovers that, like her, he is dead, and "for the life you and I led," as Irene tells him, "there is no resurrection." Rubek's growing awareness of his own deadness is further illustrated in his stone masterpieces. For this work — "our child," as Irene calls it — is the main symbol of the "resurrection" theme of the play. Like Solness's art (and like Ibsen's), the sculpture has actually gone through three stages of development. The first, an image of transcendent hope and expectation, shows the figure of a young girl (Irene) rising from the dead and caught in an eternal moment. The second adds a series of contemporary figures. Like Rubek's portrait busts, they have an externally respectable appearance, but are really "pompous horse-faces,

---

[23] This phase stuck in the head of Ibsen's great admirer, James Joyce, who used it, positively, to describe Leopold Bloom in *Ulysses*. Joyce's own play, *Exiles*, is, furthermore, very closely modeled on *When We Dead Awaken* in its structure, theme, and characters.

and self-opinionated donkey muzzles, low-browed dog skulls, and fatted swine-snouts" — those "dear domestic animals" suggest what Ibsen now thinks of the characters in his realistic plays (not to mention the public that attends them). In the third stage, paralleling Ibsen's last autobiographical period, the artist himself is in the foreground, weighed down with guilt, imprisoned in his "private hell," suffering "remorse for a forfeited life."

Despite this artistic insight into the futility of his hopes ("Never again in all eternity," Rubek says of the artist-figure in the statuary, "will he attain to freedom and the new life"), Rubek still anticipates both transfiguration and resurrection through Irene. And it is her role to disillusion him, to kill his hopes, to show him the vanity of his striving: "When we dead awaken," she reveals, "we see that we have never lived." Nevertheless, despite Irene's spectral despair, despite Rubek's sin against the spirit of life, both are given a final opportunity to scale the heights to freedom. The two couples, newly paired, have spent the night on the mountainside. Irene, taunting Rubek, urges him "higher, higher — always higher." Fearless of the storm which is about to break (the winds whirl about him, sounding like "the prelude to Resurrection Day"), Rubek is now determined to fulfill all his broken promises by ascending to the uttermost peak. His will grows so powerful, in fact, that Irene, forgetting her intention to kill him, follows Rubek joyfully — "up in the light, and in all the glittering glory! Up to the Peak of Promise." As Ulfheim and Maia remain safely below, Rubek and Irene scale the mountain together to hold their marriage feast. But their climbing aspiration, like that of Brand, is finally climaxed by an avalanche; and the doomed couple are swallowed up by the snow. As they find an ambiguous fulfillment in death, the orgasm of the spirit which no other climax can exceed, Maia sings her song of liberation from below, "I am free as a bird! I am free!"

"I am free as a bird! I am free!" It could be Rubek's epitaph as well. For, in this strange and tortured play, so reminiscent of *Oedipus at Colonus,* the sculptor finds his final release, after a life of errors, on the mountain of aspiration where only the gods can tread. Ibsen too was expressing his sense of release in this final testament of his art.

For after a life of messianic striving, he is imaginatively feeling his way up the mountain, by Rubek's side, to the wide, expansive area above. It had been thirty years since Brand's prophetic cry that "Man must struggle till he dies," and Ibsen had spent them all in heroic combat with the trolls in his heart and mind, rebelling against the human and divine forces which would limit individual freedom. His struggle had taken him up and down Europe, seeking a homeland, exiled in spirit from the modern world, always exposing its disease and corruption. And struggling to find truthful expressions for his double vision which would mirror both his own subjective rebellion and the conformity of modern society, he had wandered from the fjords and moorlands to the civilized plateau below, longing for the heights and raging against the depths. At the last, Ibsen had found his way back to the mountains where, free from the "taint" of man, liberation and revolt were pure and absolute. To a restless nature like his, always dissatisfied, always moving on, there could be no peace until death; and the total revolution he had envisioned in his youth could be realized only in apocalypse, in the pure, cold avalanche from the Northern skies. In *When We Dead Awaken,* the spiritual exile has found his homeland; the messianic prophet has found his ultimate truth; the tired artist has found his resting place. And Ibsen, the rebel, has found his release, after a lifetime of ceaseless aspiration.

III

AUGUST STRINDBERG

To all appearances, August Strindberg would seem to be the most revolutionary spirit in the theatre of revolt. Actually, that distinction must go to Ibsen, but Strindberg is certainly the most restless and experimental. Perpetually dissatisfied, perpetually reaching after shifting truths, he seems like a latter-day Faust with the unconscious as his laboratory — seeking the miracle of transmutation in the crucible of his tormented intellect. The metaphor is precise, for transmutation — the conversion of existing material into something higher — is the goal of all his activity, whether he works in science, turning base metals into gold, or religious philosophy, turning matter into spirit, or in drama, turning literature into music. His entire career, in fact, is a search for the philosophers' stone of ultimate truth through the testing of varied commitments. In his theatre, where almost every new work is a new departure, he experiments with Byronic poetic plays, Naturalistic tragedies, Boulevard comedies, Maeterlinckian fairy plays, Shakespearean chronicles, Expressionistic dream plays, and Chamber works in sonata form. In his religious and political attitudes, he covers the entire spectrum of belief and unbelief, skirting positivism, atheism, Socialism, Pietism, Catholicism, Hinduism, Buddhism, and Swedenborgian mysticism. In his scientific studies, he ranges from Darwin to the occult, from Naturalism to Supernaturalism, from physics to metaphysics, from chemistry to alchemy. His literary work is one long autobiography, whether it takes the form of confessional novels, misogynistic short stories, revolutionary verses, anguished letters, scientific treatises, theatrical manifestoes, or short plays, full-length works, double dramas, and trilogies. More than any other dramatist who ever lived, Strindberg writes *himself,* and the self he continually exposes is that of alienated modern man, crawling between heaven and earth, desperately trying to pluck some absolutes from a forsaken universe.

Because of his restless Romanticism, and particularly because he initiated an alternative "anti-realistic" theatre in opposition to Ibsenist "realism," Strindberg has generally been regarded as Ibsen's anti-mask, the nonconformist Bohemian in contrast with the stolid, practical bourgeois. At first sight, indeed, the two Scandinavians do seem separated by a much wider gulf than the boundary that divides their two countries. Compare *Pillars of Society* with *A Dream Play.* The one, tightly structured and carefully detailed, proceeds from the daylight world of domestic problems, casual discourse, and social awareness; the other, shadowy in outline and fluid in form, emerges out of a chimerical world of fantasy, delusion, and nightmare. Yet, these two plays are extreme examples of each man's art; and the contrast between the two playwrights, while unquestionably strong, has been somewhat overemphasized at the expense of their similarities. As a matter of fact, both are part of the same dramatic movement, sharing certain general traits which have rarely been explored.

Undoubtedly, Strindberg himself is largely to blame for this unfair emphasis, since he had a tendency to define himself *against* Ibsen, and spent most of his career directly or indirectly attacking what he thought to be the older man's themes and forms.[1] His hostility is understandable. When Strindberg came to artistic maturity, Ibsen was considered the master dramatist of Europe — and like all figures of authority to Strindberg, he was therefore ripe for attack. Yet, Strindberg never understood Ibsen very well, and his antagonism often seems to be based on rather willful misconstructions of the Norwe-

[1] Ibsen was perfectly aware of Strindberg's antagonism towards him, and kept a portrait of Strindberg on his wall: "I cannot write a line," he remarked, "without that madman standing and staring down at me with his mad eyes." Later, he told an American writer about the source of his interest in Strindberg: "The man fascinates me because he is so subtly, so delicately mad."

gian's work. It is clear, for example, that while Strindberg was obsessed with the conflict between the sexes, this subject hardly interested Ibsen, except as a metaphor for a wider conflict between man and society. But since Strindberg had come to regard art (and life) as a battleground in which there was no room for subtlety or neutrality, he became convinced that Ibsen was the fervent champion of his hated enemy, the emancipated woman.

The play that convinced him was, of course, *A Doll's House*. For in spite of the fact that, in early years, Strindberg had identified deeply with Ibsen's *Brand*, he always preferred to couple Ibsen with this more domesticated work, which he called "sick like its author." Here he found the seedbed for that "Nora-cult" of feminism which he saw infecting Scandinavia like a loathsome pestilence; and ignoring the complexity, ambiguity, and essentially nonsexual character of *A Doll's House*, he simply concluded that Ibsen was the leader of the other side, fomenting plots to undermine masculine domination. As a result of this initial misunderstanding, he mistakenly interpreted *Ghosts* as a treacherous attack on Captain Alving, a dead man no longer able to defend himself against character defamation;[2] he assumed that *The Wild Duck* was a libel on his family life, thinking that Ekdal's doubtful paternity of Hedwig was meant to suggest that he, Strindberg, was not the father of his own child; and he found in *Hedda Gabler* and *The Master Builder* (two plays which did not support his convictions about Ibsen's feminism) conclusive evidence that Ibsen had fallen under his spell and changed his views. Throughout his life, Strindberg was subject to severe paranoiac symptoms, in which fears of persecution alternated with delusions of grandeur; and while his ability to transform these symptoms into art constitutes one of the most thrilling triumphs of modern drama, his paranoiac tendencies hardly qual-

---

[2] See *The Father*, Act I, where the Doctor says: "And I should like you to know, Captain, that when I heard Mrs. Alving blackening her late husband's memory, I thought what a damned shame it was that the fellow should be dead." Either the Doctor or Strindberg did not attend to *Ghosts* very carefully, because, before the end of the play, Captain Alving's blackened memory has been partially whitewashed again.

ify him for objective evaluations of other people's work and motives. Yet, it is Strindberg's view of Ibsen's subject matter, coupled with that tiresome characterization of Ibsen as a mouthpiece for social problems in realistic form, which dominates most comparisons of the two dramatists.[3]

If these assumptions are correct, and Ibsen is merely the champion of bourgeois realism and the emancipated woman, then the gap between the two men is unbreachable. Since the assumptions are quite wrong, let us attempt to close the gap a little. Where do Ibsen and Strindberg join hands in the theatre of revolt? Quite clearly, in their basic artistic attack. Both are essentially autobiographical writers, exorcising their furies by dramatizing their spiritual conflicts; both are subject to a powerful dualism which determines the changing direction of their themes and forms; and both are attracted to the more elemental aspects of human nature. But above all, both are Romantic rebels whose art is the unrelieved expression of their revolt.

In the beginning of his career, in fact, Strindberg's point of departure is almost indistinguishable from Ibsen's. "I am Jean-Jacques's *intime* when it comes to a return to nature," he writes to a friend in 1880. "I should like to join him and turn everything upside down to see what lies at bottom; I think we are so much entangled, so terribly much regulated that things can't be put right, but must be burnt up, blasted, and then begun afresh." Two years later, at the age of thirty-three, Strindberg puts these sentiments into verse form. In a poem called "Esplanadsystemet" (The Building Program), he envisions the young razing everything to the ground, while a respectable pillar of society looks on with disapproval:

[3] Pär Lagerkvist's comments are typical. In order to praise Strindberg, Lagerkvist has to attack Ibsen, exploding all the rusty artillery of anti-Ibsenist criticism: "Ibsen, who was long the modern writer *par préférence* because he exhaustively plodded through all the social, sexual, and mental-hygienic ideas and ideals which happened to come up for discussion, merely weighs us down with his perfectly consummated and fixed form, impossible of further development. . . ." ("Modern Theatre: Points of View and Attack," *Tulane Drama Review*, Winter 1961, p. 22.) At this point, it grows tiresome to repeat that Ibsen's forms are far from fixed, and his basic subject matter has very little to do with social, sexual, or mental-hygienic "ideas."

"What! This is the spirit of the times! Demolishing houses!
Dreadful! Dreadful! What about constructive activity?" —
"We're tearing down to let in light and air;
Don't you think that constructive enough!" [4]

Even as late as 1898, in *The Road to Damascus,* Part II, Strindberg
— through the mouth of the Stranger — is still expressing his determination to "paralyze the present order, to disrupt it," envisioning
himself as "the destroyer, the dissolver, the world incendiary."

In these images of demolition, the destructive fantasies of a total
revolutionist, Strindberg joins Ibsen in his uncompromising revolt
against modern life. Finding common roots in Rousseau and the Romantics, each hopes to redeem mankind from spiritual emptiness
through desperate remedies: Strindberg by clearing away rotten buildings, Ibsen by torpedoing the Ark — both by unremitting warfare on
all existing social, political, and religious institutions. The negative,
individualistic, and essentially antisocial quality of these attacks exposes their metaphysical sources. Both playwrights begin as messianic
rebels, animated by strong religious needs, and determined to war on
the God of the old while advancing towards something new. Strindberg's early plays — works like *The Freethinker, The Outlaw,* and
Master Olof — are often strongly reminiscent of Ibsen's *Brand* and
Emperor and Galilean in their rebellion against God, sometimes even
embodying open attacks on God as the author of madness and the
father of evil. In the epilogue to *Master Olof,* for example, it is God
who maliciously introduces misery into the world ("The creatures
who live [on Earth]," He declares, "will believe themselves gods
like ourselves, and it will be our pleasure to watch their struggles
and vanities"), while it is Lucifer, the rebellious son who, Prometheus-
like, tries to bring good to man, and is outlawed for his pains.

Strindberg's identification with Lucifer, rebelling against a mad,
merciless, mechanical Will, is quite clear throughout the first phase of

[4] I am indebted to Evert Sprinchorn for calling my attention to this untrans-
lated poem. The translations I have used in this chapter are those of Elizabeth
Sprigge, except for that of *Miss Julie,* which is by Professor Sprinchorn, and
The Road to Damascus by Graham Rawson. I have rendered the *Inferno* passages myself from the original French.

his career. In his opposition to established authority, Strindberg also identifies with related figures like Cain, Prometheus, and Ishmael — all rebels against God — willingly, and sometimes rather theatrically, embracing their pain and torment as well. Like Ibsen voluntarily exiled from his native land, Strindberg wandered over Europe, alienated from the world of men even when most honored there. "Born with nostalgia for heaven," he writes in *Inferno*, "I cried even as a child over the filthiness of existence, finding myself homeless among my parents and society." He often describes himself as a pariah — "a beggar, a marked man, an outcast from society" (*Inferno*) — outlawed from paradise, his brow marked with the sign of the rebellious son. Strindberg's admiration for religious rebels presses him well beyond the usual revolutionary postures to an embrace of Satanism, under the spell of which he practices black arts, worships the occult, and studies the transmigration of souls, pursuits which he considers dangerous and diabolical. As the Confessor says, in *The Road to Damascus:* "This man is a demon, who must be kept confined. He belongs to the dangerous race of rebels; he'd misuse his gifts, if he could, to do evil." Strindberg's flair for self-dramatization leads him to exaggerate his demonic activities, for they were really harmful to nobody but himself (he suffered severely from sulphur burns). But there is no doubt that he thought himself pledged to Lucifer by a kind of Mephistophelian pact.

This seems like a much more radical form of rebellion than anything found in Ibsen. But as Strindberg implies in *Inferno* ("Ever since childhood," he writes, "I have looked for God and found the devil"), his revolt against authority is really the reverse of his desire for authority, just as his Satanism is actually an inverted form of Christianity. In consequence of this shaky posture, Strindberg's revolt is always a little nervous and uncertain, rather like the act of a man in constant dread of retribution. And while Ibsen's messianism remains consistent, Strindberg's is gradually tempered by his fears of divine revenge from an omnipotent power. Even when he considers himself a freethinking atheist, these fears are never far from the surface. He became an unbeliever, as he declares in *Inferno,* when "the unknown

powers let slip their hold on the world, and gave no more sign of life."
But when these "unknown powers" do begin to appear to him in the
'nineties, his messianism becomes less and less defiant, until he finally
becomes convinced that the powers are personally guiding his destiny,
and revealing themselves to him in every material object.

Even then, however, vestiges of his messianic defiance remain. He
wishes to do the will of these nameless authorities, but even in his moments of submission he "feels rebellious and challenges heaven with
doubts." Reflecting on the wayward history of his beliefs, he even begins to blame the powers for his own spiritual uncertainty:

You have directed my destiny badly; you have brought me up to chastise,
to overthrow idols, to stir up revolt, and then you withdraw your protection from me, and deliver me over to a ridiculous recantation! . . . When
young I was sincerely pious, and you made me a free-thinker. Out of the
free-thinker you made an atheist, and out of the atheist a religious man.
Inspired by humanitarians, I advocated socialism. Five years later, you
showed me the absurdity of socialism; you have made all my enthusiasms
seem futile. And supposing that I again become religious, I am certain
that in another ten years, you will reduce religion to absurdity.
Do not the gods play games with us poor mortals . . . !

(Inferno)

These tones reveal the equivocal nature of his surrender. He would
like to be obedient; yet he cannot suppress the suspicion that the powers are malevolent humorists who kill men for their sport. Thus, even
when Strindberg seems to have repudiated his revolt, he is still rebelling against the authorities he both hates and fears.

On the other hand, his surrender has made him modify the *form*
of his revolt. For just as Ibsen, trying to discipline the messianic tendencies of *Brand*, disguises his rebellion in the objective social mode
of *Ghosts*, so Strindberg adapts his messianic rebellion, later in his career, to conform with his new desire to submit. The cry of pain one
hears in the passage above, in fact, is to become Strindberg's most
characteristic tone in such later plays as *Easter, A Dream Play*, and
The Ghost Sonata — for there his revolt is existential, directed against
the meaninglessness and contradictions of human existence. Thus,

while Strindberg and Ibsen both begin at the same point of departure, they soon develop in different directions. Ibsen, continuing to believe in the importance of the will, begins to measure his rebellious ideals against the social reality: he seeks a spiritual and moral revolution which will transform the soul of man. Strindberg, coming to believe in a strict determinism (the higher powers), loses faith in his rebellious ideals: he seeks deeper spiritual insights in order to resolve his own painful dilemmas. Ibsen continues to reject God; Strindberg wavers between affirmation and negation, finally giving way to a melancholy fatalism which one never finds in Ibsen. For while Ibsen works through to a Greek tragic *form,* his rebellion remains strong and constant. Strindberg finally works through to a Greek tragic *mood,* his rebellion partially dissipated by his effort to accept and understand.

On the other hand, while Ibsen is the more faithful rebel, Strindberg is the more faithful Romantic, for he will make fewer concessions to the world beyond his imagination. It is here, in the comparative degree of their involvement in the world of others, that the essential difference between the two playwrights is exposed, for Ibsen offers a superficial deference to external reality which Strindberg totally refuses. This is not to say that one is objective and the other subjective — both are essentially subjective writers, insofar as each makes his own internal conflicts the subject of his art. But since Ibsen's resistance to the demands of his unconscious is stronger than Strindberg's, and more disciplined by the real world, he is willing to disguise his spiritual autobiography in the conflicts of semiobjectified characters, while Strindberg remains the unashamed hero of his work, endorsing his psychic, marital, and religious attitudes through the medium of his art. Consequently, while Ibsen will measure the consequences of rebellion on the happiness of others, Strindberg concentrates almost exclusively on the conflicts in the rebel's own soul.

In other words, Classicism is a mode totally alien to Strindberg, even when he seems to be exploiting it. For even the techniques of "Naturalism" are, for him, a springboard for his unabashed Romanticism. Unlike Ibsen, he is unable to test his subjective responses on the

objective world because, also unlike Ibsen, he doesn't much believe
in the objective world. Anticipating Pirandello, Strindberg works on
the assumption that the world beyond his imagination has no fixed
form or truth. It becomes "real" only when observed through the subjective eyes of the beholder, and (here he differs somewhat from
Pirandello) especially "real" when the beholder has poetic, clairvoy-
ant, or visionary powers. Strindberg's subjective relativism explains
why his art always turns inexorably in on himself and his own responses; in a world of elusive truth, only the self has any real validity.
Thus, if Ibsen is primarily concerned with self-realization — or blast-
ing avenues of personal freedom through the cramped quarters of
modern society — Strindberg is primarily concerned with *self-expression* — or justifying the superiority of the poet's vision in a world
without meaning or coherence. Both are Romantic goals and closely
allied. But since Strindberg lacks even Ibsen's grudging respect for external reality, he is by far the more self-involved Romantic, one who
worships the "cult of the self" (as he puts it in *Inferno*) as "the supreme and ultimate end of existence." In his personal life, this ego-
worship often takes the form of severe psychotic delusions in which
Strindberg loses his grip on reality altogether; and it robs his art of
such Ibsenist virtues as self-discipline, detachment, and dialectical
power. But it provides Strindberg with a Dionysian vitality which carries us along in spurts of ecstasy, lyricism, irrationality, cruelty, and
despair — and a dramatic technique which, in his early plays, is almost totally free from the need for balance or moderation, and, in
his later ones, has almost totally burst the bonds of restraining rules.

Because of his commitment to a subjective art, it is impossible to
analyze Strindberg's work without some reference to his life, especially to that dualism which, like Ibsen's, plagued him throughout his
career. In Strindberg's case, this dualism was psychological rather
than philosophical, and began at the moment of his birth. The child of
a tailor's daughter who had seen domestic service, and a *déclassé* ship-
ping agent who claimed to have noble blood, Strindberg was inclined
to regard these circumstances as the source of all his later troubles,
interpreting them in a manner which is always psychologically reveal-

ing, if not always psychologically accurate. In *The Son of a Servant,*
for example, Strindberg expressed his conviction that — since he was
conceived against his parents' will (i.e., illegitimately) — he was
born without a will (i.e., essentially passive and feminine). And since
he identified his father and mother with the highest and lowest classes
of society, he concluded that this inheritance accounted for his vacil-
lation between peasant servility and aristocratic arrogance.

On top of this, Strindberg's childhood followed an almost Classical
Oedipal pattern. He adored his mother with a passion he was later
to call (with astonishing frankness) "an incest of the soul," and he
hated his father as a powerful and threatening rival. Like Strindberg's
feelings throughout his life, however, these early emotions were confused and contradictory. Since his mother had rejected him in favor
of his brother Axel, he sometimes detested her as well — feeling at
times that she was the dearest creature on earth, at other times that
she was depriving him of love and nourishment.[5] And since he generally measured his own weakness by his father's strength, he tempered
his hatred of the older man with a kind of cringing fear and respect.

The consequences of Strindberg's ambivalence towards his father
were later to be realized in his ambivalence towards all male authority, notably in his alternating rebellion against and submission to the
higher powers. His ambivalence towards his mother had a different
effect, determining the shape of his love life and his general attitudes
towards women. Like those Romantics described by Mario Praz in
The Romantic Agony, Strindberg had split his mother in two — the
chaste Madonna and the erotic Belle Dame Sans Merci — and, unconsciously recapitulating his early feelings later in life, he vacillated

[5] Love and nourishment are always closely related in Strindberg's mind. His
striking image of the Vampire Cook in *The Ghost Sonata* — who "boils the
nourishment out of the meat and gives fibre and water, while she drinks the
stock herself" — probably derives from his childhood feeling of love-starvation;
the Milkmaid of the same play, on the other hand, is (reflecting the other side
of Strindberg's ambivalence) a symbol of female generosity and mammary
abundance. The miserly Mother in Strindberg's Chamber play, *The Pelican*
(1907), who starves the household of food and love — thus murdering her
husband and weakening her children — is another example of the ungiving,
motherly Vampire.

between an intense worship of the female and an even more intense misogyny. Strindberg was himself aware, in more lucid moments, that his misogyny was "only the reverse side of my fearful attraction towards the other sex" (in his early years he had even been a partisan of free love, companionate marriages, and feminism!). Yet, caught in a tight neurotic web, he was never able to transcend his ambivalence, and alternated between regarding women as evil vampires, sucking out his manhood, and virtuous maternal types who gave him the comfort he so sorely craved.

Sometimes he revealed this ambivalence by dividing women into two distinct classes: (1) the "third sex" — composed of emancipated females — whom he detested for their masculinity, infidelity, competitiveness, and unmaternal attitudes, and (2) older, more motherly women (generally sexless) — such as Mamma Uhl, his mother-in-law, and the Mother Superior of the hospital of St. Louis[6] — whom he adored for their kindness and compassion. More often he tried to combine the two types in one person — and when he succeeded, he usually married her. For he was always attracted to women he could love for their maternal qualities and hate for their masculinity, reacting to them with bewildering changeability.[7] Consider his violent feelings towards his first wife, Siri Von Essen, as described by Strindberg in *Confessions of a Fool.* So long as she was married to another man,

[6] "The nun is affectionate," writes Strindberg in *Inferno,* "treats me like a baby, and calls me *mon enfant,* while I call her *ma mère.* How good it is to speak the word mother which I have not uttered for thirty years." As he writes about the Matron to Frida Uhl, "The mere presence of this *mère* comforts and soothes me. *La douce chaleur du sein maternel,* as Baudelaire calls it (I think it was he), does me good." Elizabeth Sprigge, in her sensitive biography *The Strange Life of August Strindberg,* has called attention to the soothing influence of this gentle woman on the ailing dramatist. Needless to say, I am indebted to Miss Sprigge's scholarship throughout this chapter.

[7] Strindberg writes to a friend about two letters he sent to Siri in the same day: "In one I told her to go to Hell; in the other, to come to Runmarö. Well! What of it? Moods that shift between love and hate are not madness!" All his wives remarked upon these continual alterations in feeling. Harriet Bosse, more sympathetic than the others, put it this way: "I have a feeling that Strindberg revelled in meeting with opposition. One moment his wife had to be an angel. The next the very opposite. He was as changeable as a chameleon." (*Letters of Strindberg to Harriet Bosse,* ed. and trans. by Arvid Paulson, p. 87).

and their union remained "spiritual," Strindberg worshiped her as a superior being — idealizing her aristocratic bearing, "white skin," and ethereal purity ("frigidity," according to her unromantic first husband, Baron Wrangel). It was Strindberg, too, who encouraged her to go on the stage, but as soon as they were married, he began to accuse her of careerism and competitiveness, not to mention lesbianism, infidelity, drunkenness, coquetry, uncleanliness, bearing him another man's child, doubting his sanity, trying to dominate him, and not keeping the accounts! In his next two marriages — to Frida Uhl, an ambitious journalist, and Harriet Bosse, a lovely young actress almost thirty years his junior — the pattern repeated itself, though with diminishing intensity, as Strindberg gradually realized that his ambivalent feelings stemmed from his own psychotic disorder.

Strindberg's tendency to find a comforting mother and an evil wanton in every woman he loved accounts for his curious attitude towards erotic relations. He expects to have his spirit elevated through romantic love, only to find he has been dragged down into the mud:

In woman I sought an angel, who could lend me wings, and I fell into the arms of an earth-spirit, who suffocated me under mattresses stuffed with feathers of wings! I sought an Ariel and I found a Caliban; when I wanted to rise she dragged me down; and continually reminded me of the fall. . . .

(The Road to Damascus, Part III)

What he is describing here is the sexual experience; and what he implies is a profound distaste for the sexual act. This distaste — accompanied throughout his life by a pronounced revulsion to all physical functions and secret fears for his virility — provides some clue to Strindberg's vacillating feelings. For his hatred of the flesh was probably the consequence of his nostalgia for the spiritual purity he enjoyed during childhood, when he was permitted to love his mother with a love beyond the body. When he matured, however, and began seeking his mother in the women he married, he had to deal not only with the divided love-hate feelings he inherited from that early relationship, but also with the incest taboo. It was this taboo that caused him to transform the mother-woman into a spider-woman — he had to justify his attraction to her — and when this transformation failed, he became impotent as an unconscious defense against his own guilts.[8] As for his obsession with female domination, Strindberg's desire for a mother reduced him to a weak and passive dependent, while his intellect rebelled against his childlike state. In short, Strindberg wished to have the purity and passivity of the child and the masculine aggressiveness of the adult. Desiring to dominate and be dominated, seeking *eros* and *agape* in the same woman, he was the victim of contradictory needs which left him in perpetual turmoil and confusion.

I must apologize for this bare Freudian treatment of Strindberg's dualism; but so much of it has been established, or at least suggested, by Strindberg himself [9] that the analysis is essential, especially since the roots of Strindberg's art are so clearly sexual and pathological. In Strindberg's dualism, moreover, we will be able to see the nucleus not only of his sexual problems, but of his various artistic, scientific, religious, and philosophical attitudes as well. For the struggle in Strindberg's mind between the male and the female, the father and the mother, the aristocrat and the servant, spirit and matter, aggressiveness and passivity, is the conflict which determines the direction of his career. If we project Strindberg's dualism onto the whole of his drama, we shall be able to understand his development from Naturalism to Expressionism, from scientific materialism to religion and the supernatural, from a convinced misogynist to a resigned Stoic with compassion for all living things. We shall also understand the changing na-

[8] Strindberg's uncertainty about his virility is clear throughout his letters; one of his greatest fears is that he will be considered inadequate as a lover. Writing to Harriet he remarks: "The day after we wed, you declared that I was not a man. A week later you were eager to let the world know that you were not yet the wife of August Strindberg, and that your sisters considered you 'unmarried'. . . . We did have a child together, didn't we?" (*Letters to Harriet*, pp. 52-58). Strindberg was also convinced that "where sensual pleasure is sought, there will be no children." In view of his need to keep the sex act pure, it is remarkable that he was able to make love at all.

[9] Strindberg eventually grew quite lucid about the origins of his feelings towards women; and though he could never cure himself entirely of his neurosis, he knew himself to be imprisoned in a cycle of eternal repetition, dating from his childhood.

ture of Strindberg's revolt, for his conversion from messianic prophet to an existential visionary is directly connected with the resolution of Strindberg's conflicts after years of horrible suffering.

The mature writings of Strindberg fall into two well-defined periods, separated by the *Inferno* crisis — a dark night of the soul lasting five or six years, during which Strindberg wrote no dramatic works at all. To his first period (1884–1892) belong works like *The Father, Miss Julie, Creditors, Comrades,* and about nine one-act plays, in which the recurring subject — treated further in the essays, stories, and autobiographical novels written during this period — is the battle between men and women. Almost all of these works are conceived in a Naturalistic style, which is contradicted in execution by a number of non-Naturalistic elements — especially the author's undisguised partisanship of the male character and the masculine position. Strindberg's control of the Naturalistic method is further weakened by his tendency to strip away all extraneous surface details, and sometimes even to sacrifice character consistency and logical action, for the sake of his concentration on the sex war.[10] Still, there is no doubt that Strindberg thinks of himself as a Naturalist during this period — not only in his approach to playwriting but in his approach to science and metaphysics as well. Having abandoned the religion of his youth, he is now a freethinker, with inclinations towards atheism; and having been converted to Darwinism, he tends to conceive of characters in terms of the survival of the fittest, natural selection, heredity, and environment. Buckle's relativistic approach to history has taught him to doubt all absolute truths; and his interest in empirical science has encouraged him not only to experiment with the chemical qualities of matter, but

[10] Strindberg's concept of Naturalism is not at all conventional. He rejects the typical Naturalist play as mere "photography," insisting instead on a special form of conflict: "This is the misunderstood Naturalism which holds that art merely consists of drawing a piece of nature in a natural way; it is not the great Naturalism which seeks out the points where the great battles are fought, which loves to see what you do not see every day, which delights in the struggle between natural forces, whether these forces are called love or hate, rebellious or social instincts, which finds the beautiful or ugly unimportant if only it is great." ("On Modern Drama and Modern Theatre," 1889.)

even to regard human beings as objects of scientific curiosity, to be examined without pity or sentiment.

Strindberg's conception of the war between the sexes was undoubtedly influenced primarily by the emotional crisis he was experiencing with Siri Von Essen; but his convictions about sexual relations were supported by certain philosophical sources as well, which Strindberg (like the Captain in *The Father*) consulted in order to find support for his attitudes. It is highly probable, for example, that Strindberg read Schopenhauer's *Metaphysics of the Love of the Sexes,* which affirms that sexual attraction is a diabolical invention for the propagation of the race by the "will of the species . . . ready relentlessly to destroy personal happiness in order to carry out its ends" — and that the satisfaction of this will leaves the lover with "a detested companion for life." Strindberg's readings in Nietzsche must also have confirmed him in his sexual attitudes, for the philosopher shared many of Strindberg's prejudices — not only against Ibsen (whom Nietzsche called "that typical old maid") but against the emancipated woman ("Thou goest to women?" Zarathustra asks. "Do not forget thy whip!") When Strindberg sent *The Father* to Nietzsche, in fact, the German philosopher replied that he was highly pleased to see "my own conception of love — with war as its means and the deathly hate of the sexes as its fundamental law . . . expressed in such a splendid fashion."

In the next few years, a good many more Nietzschean conceptions appeared in Strindberg's work, for he becomes the single most important influence on Strindberg in this period. Under this influence (which lasted until the philosopher went mad, and sent Strindberg a letter signed *Nietzsche Caesar!*), Strindberg continues to develop a rigorously masculine program, which consists in despising weakness, worshiping the superhuman, and regarding life as a war to the death between master and slave, strong and weak, possessed and dispossessed. Strindberg also shares with Nietzsche an overwhelming contempt for Christianity, a religion he declares is fit only for "women, eunuchs, children, and savages." And since he finds Christianity to be a weak and female religion, he begins to reject the softer Christian virtues —

like compassion, sympathy, pity, and tenderness — as also suitable only for women.

In their place, Strindberg exalts the hard masculine virtues. The most admirable quality for Strindberg, at this time, is strength — strength of will, strength of intellect, strength of body. Thus, his male characters are often conceived as Nietzschean Supermen, endowed with the courage to live beyond the pale of commonplace bourgeois morality. For Strindberg professes to find a grim pleasure in the tragic quality of human existence and the tough, predatory character of human nature. It is this Nietzschean ecstasy, in fact, that Strindberg opposes to Ibsen's tamer *livsglaede* when, in the preface to *Miss Julie,* he declares: "I myself find the joy of life in its strong and cruel struggles." In his discipleship to Nietszche, as in his discipleship to Darwin, Strindberg sometimes vulgarizes, exaggerates, or distorts the master's ideas. Nevertheless, his attraction to Nietzsche is unusually strong — so strong, in fact, that he describes the philosopher's influence on him in the imagery of marriage: "My spirit has received in its uterus a tremendous outpouring of seed from Frederick Nietzsche, so that I feel as full as a pregnant bitch. He was my husband." [11]

We would not pause to find any significance in such metaphors were it not that Strindberg's life and work also suggest his feminine passivity. For there is abundant evidence that Strindberg's defiant masculinity is more an impersonation than an actuality, designed to conceal the weaker, more womanish aspects of his nature. Strindberg was sometimes perfectly conscious of this — he often expressed the thought that he should have been born a woman — but, at this time at least, he is at great pains to hide it. It is clear, however, from his fears for his virility and his fears of being dominated, that, even when he seems to be blustering most, his masculine identification is highly uncertain. As for the Strindberg hero, he may look like a Nietzschean strong man, but he is quite often in danger of being symbolically cas-

[11] Strindberg is very fond of this image. He uses it again, after reading *Hedda Gabler,* to describe his imagined influence on Ibsen — though now the husband-wife roles are reversed: "See now how my seed has fallen in Ibsen's brain-pan — and germinated. Now he carries my semen and is my uterus. This is *Wille zur Macht* and my desire to set others' brains in molecular motion."

trated. For while the author, in his paranoiac fantasies, will identify with the robust heroes of antiquity, his artistic honesty makes him put these fantasies in perspective: his Hercules is often robbed of his club and set to do women's tasks at the distaff.

Strindberg himself is aware of the ambiguous manliness of his male characters, though not of the reasons for it. In discussing the hero of *The Father* with Lundegard, he writes: "To me personally, he represents a masculinity which people have tried to undervalue, deprive us of, and transfer to a third sex. It is only in front of women that he appears unmanly, because she wants him to, and the laws of the game compel a man to play the part that his lady commands." We may safely question whether "the laws of the game" are responsible for the Captain's passivity; but *something* unmans him, as it unmans almost every male character Strindberg creates in this period. For the typical development of his "Naturalist" hero is from a position of aggressiveness to a position of helplessness: in *The Father,* the Captain ends up in a straitjacket; in *Creditors,* Adolph collapses into an epileptic fit; and even in *Miss Julie,* where the male triumphs, Jean becomes a sniveling coward at the end, shivering at the sound of the Count's bell.[12]

In all these plays, the antagonist is a woman — more accurately, an emancipated woman — an Omphale who will not rest until she has

[12] It should be noted that in two of these plays, the male figure is reduced to impotency by the connivance, direct or indirect, of an older man related to the female antagonist: Julie's father, the Count, in *Miss Julie;* and Tekla's first husband, Gustav, in *Creditors.* Under a Freudian analysis, the older man appears as a father figure, punishing the son, by means of a symbolic emasculation, for his incestuous relations with the mother. This submerged theme — as Denis de Rougemont has noted in *Love in the Western World* — is common to European love literature: its literary source is the Tristan myth, but its psychological source is the family romance. Strindberg's tendency to dramatize the family romance is especially clear in *Creditors,* a play which evokes Strindberg's feelings towards Siri and towards her first husband, Baron Wrangel. As Strindberg half understood ("I loved you both," he writes to Wrangel. "I could never separate you in my thoughts, I always saw you together in my dreams"), Siri and Wrangel are unconsciously identified with his own parents. In *Creditors,* Gustav (Wrangel) revenges himself on Adolph (Strindberg) for stealing away his wife, Tekla (Siri) — father punishes son for his incestuous feelings towards mother. Thus, Adolph's epileptic fit, at the end of that play, is really a symbolic castration.

reversed roles with her Hercules, and assumed his position of authority. The conflict of these plays, therefore, is provided by the opposition of male and female, and the issue is not resolved until one of them has conquered. As a member of the "third sex," the typical Strindberg heroine (Laura, Miss Julie, Berta, Tekla) has a strong masculine streak in her nature too — sometimes even stronger than the man's, for while he occasionally expresses a childlike desire for tenderness, she remains adamant until she feels herself invulnerable. The paradox of this struggle, therefore, is that while the male is physically, and often intellectually, superior to the woman, he frequently falls victim to her "treacherous weakness"; for, in all plays but *Miss Julie,* the heroine lacks honor and decency, pursuing her ends by subtle, invidious, and generally "unconscious" means. Yet, even when Strindberg permits the woman her victory, he feels compelled to demonstrate her basic inferiority. When she competes with the man in a worldly career, as in *Comrades* and *Creditors,* it is only through his help that she succeeds at all; and the man must be brought to realize, as Strindberg was brought to realize, that the sexes cannot coexist on equal terms.

The Father (1887), though by far the most aggressive work Strindberg ever wrote, is typical of the plays of this period. The work has a contemporary domestic setting, and contains a few hints about the importance of heredity and environment, so Strindberg sent it to Zola as an example of the New Naturalism (Zola admired it, but criticized its obscure social milieu and its incomplete characterization). Yet, it is incredible that *The Father* could ever have been taken for a Naturalistic document. It is more like a feverish and violent nightmare — so irrational, illogical, and one-sided that it seems to have been dredged up, uncensored, from the depths of the author's unconscious.[13] Furthermore, Strindberg's identification with his central character is so explicit that it is sometimes difficult to determine whether the author or the character is speaking; and Laura is such a highly colored portrait of Siri Von Essen that the character is almost totally malevolent

---

[13] Carl E. W. L. Dahlström very properly treats *The Father* as a form of hallucination in his book, *Strindberg's Dramatic Expressionism.*

— and sometimes quite incomprehensible without some understanding of Strindberg's confused attitudes towards his marriage. Strindberg himself was perfectly conscious, at the time he wrote it, of the subjective nature of his play: "I don't know if *The Father* is an invention or if my life has been so," he wrote to Lundegard, "but I feel that at a given moment, not far off, this will be revealed to me, and I shall crash into insanity from agony of conscience or suicide." Strindberg was actually to do neither, though for a long while he was very close to both. But in *The Father,* he was clearly "acting a poem of desperation," hoping to placate his furies by giving his personal history full dramatic expression.

He was also endeavoring to pay off an old score. For Strindberg partially designed *The Father* as a reply to Ibsen's *A Doll's House,* using Laura as a diabolical contrast to Nora Helmer. One might say that both plays attack conventional sexual attitudes, Ibsen dramatizing the woman's revolt against the tyrannizing male, and Strindberg the male's revolt against the tyrannical woman. But despite the superficial neatness of the parallel, it is not very accurate. For while Strindberg had a personal stake in the "woman question," Ibsen was completely indifferent to it except as a metaphor for individual freedom. Nora's real antagonist is not Torvald, but society itself, insofar as it restricts her desire (shared by most of Ibsen's heroes) for self-realization. The Captain's antagonist, however, is Woman, and he is opposed only to those social conventions which grow from a misunderstanding of the venomous female nature. With the issue reduced to a struggle between the sexes rather than a conflict of ideas, Strindberg's work differs from Ibsen's even in its use of props. In *A Doll's House,* for example, the lamp is an instrument of enlightenment, underscoring significant revelations — but in *The Father,* it is purely an instrument of aggression: the Captain throws it at his wife after a particularly trying interview.

For while *A Doll's House* uses the techniques of the well-made play, hinging on tortuous twists of plot and reversals of character, *The Father* has a positively relentless power which carries it through, without psychological complexity or manipulated action, to a violent and furious conclusion. Compare Ibsen's elaborate stage directions with Strindberg's peremptory notes. The setting of *A Doll's House* is so carefully documented that the Helmer household is as tangible and solid as the real world, but the walls of the Captain's house seem flimsy and penetrable, as if incapable of containing the explosive forces within. Actually, the setting of *The Father* is less a bourgeois household than an African jungle where two wild animals, eyeing each other's jugular, mercilessly claw at each other until one of them falls. It is not to Zola's Naturalism that we must turn for precedents, but to works like Kleist's *Penthesilea* and Shakespeare's *Othello* — and to Aeschylean tragedy, for, like Agamemnon and Clytemnestra, the Captain and Laura are monolithic figures hewn out of granite, and stripped of all character details extraneous to their warring natures.[14]

Because of the intensely subjective nature of the play, it is somewhat difficult to separate Strindberg's conscious artistic design from the distortions unconsciously introduced by his sense of personal grievance. On the basis of its bare plot, *The Father* seems to have been conceived as the tragedy of a freethinker. The Captain, a vigorous cavalry officer,[15] who combines a military career with scientific work, has lost his belief in God and the afterlife. Consequently, he must — somewhat like D'Amville in Tourneur's Jacobean play *The Atheist's Tragedy* — seek his immortality almost exclusively through his child Bertha. He therefore attempts to educate her mind and mold her will in strict accordance with his own views, so as to leave a piece of himself on earth after his mortal remains have decayed. This brings

14 If *The Father* suggests parallels with Aeschylus's *Agamemnon*, *The Pelican* is very definitely a modern version of *Choephori*. Frederick and Gerda, the two dispossessed children, are Orestes and Electra, swearing vengeance on their mother for the "murder" of their father. The Aegisthus of the piece is Axel, the mother's second husband and coconspirator.

15 It is interesting that the masculine profession which Strindberg gives his hero belongs to Baron Wrangel, who was also a Captain in the Guards — in Strindberg's one-act play, *The Bond*, the hero is actually a Baron. Strindberg regarded Siri's first husband in much the same manner as he regarded his father — as a figure of superior virility — and often tries to overcome his own weakness by identifying with Wrangel's strength. Even in *Creditors* this partial identification is clear — for if Gustav is the father revenging himself on the son, he is also Strindberg revenging himself on Siri.

him into conflict with his wife. For while the Captain wishes to rear Bertha as a freethinker, preparing her to be a teacher and eventually a wife, Laura wants her to have religious training, and to follow an artistic career. In order to achieve ascendancy, Laura proceeds to destroy her husband. Having learned from the Captain's adjudication of a paternity suit against a subordinate that no man can be sure he is the father of a child, she proceeds to pour the henbane of doubt in his ear about the true paternity of Bertha. His growing jealousy and suspicions, aggravated by his wife's success in frustrating his career, eventually goad him to acts of violence for which he is declared insane. At the end, when he is immobilized and impotent, Laura proclaims her victory and seizes the prize: "*My* child! *My own* child!" (Emphasis mine)

But Strindberg, who had a deeper intention than this in mind, proceeds to universalize the action. When the Captain, writhing in a straitjacket, turns to the audience and cries, "Wake, Hercules, before they take away your club," his words ring with all the activistic force of Marx's call to the workers to shake off their chains. Clearly, *The Father* is designed as a kind of allegory, with the Captain as Everyman and Laura as Everywoman, an object lesson to sanguine husbands, urging them to revolt against their domineering wives. The play, then, is really about a struggle for power which began long before the dispute over Bertha's education. Considered thus, it is not only the tragedy of a freethinker but the tragedy of a Romantic as well, for it is intended to mirror the strife which rages beneath the surface of all modern Romantic marriages.

In this sphere of action, the Captain is portrayed as a clumsy giant who, having learned too late the true nature of women, is brought to suffer the consequences of his early innocence. When he first married Laura, he had worshiped her as a superior being, attempting like most Romantics to find salvation through his love. But, like most Romantics, he had failed to reconcile his desire for a mistress with his need for a mother. The two desires were, in fact, irreconcilable, for as Laura tells him: "The mother was your friend, you see, but the woman was your enemy." Yet, it is to the mother in Laura that the

Captain turns in his moment of greatest suffering, even though it was the woman in Laura who is the cause of it: "Can't you see I'm helpless as a child? Can't you hear me crying to my mother that I'm hurt? Forget I'm a man, a soldier whose word men — and even beasts — obey. I am nothing but a sick creature in need of pity." If the Captain were willing to remain in a state of childlike dependency, there would be no strife, for Laura can accept him as a child; but since the Captain feels compelled to assert his masculine power, she hates him "as a man." [16] The two faces that Laura shows the Captain lead him to act with alternating tenderness and hostility towards her, an ambivalence reflected in the mood of the play where the energy of battle is occasionally broken by nostalgic interludes, during which the two antagonists pause to reflect, in tones of gentle poetic melancholy, on the mother-child relationship which was their only ground for mutual affection.

It is in these contemplative scenes that the origin of the struggle is revealed. When his romantic expectations of marriage had failed, the Captain — resenting his slavery to a woman he had offered himself to as a slave — began to sublimate through intellectual activity; and his life with Laura turned into "seventeen years of penal servitude," presided over by a ruthless, competitive warder. For Laura, who could respond to her husband only when he came to her as a helpless child, was repelled by his sexual embraces ("The mother became the mistress — horrible"), and determined to avenge herself by dominating the marriage. Though Strindberg only faintly suggests this, it is likely — considering his filial relation to Laura — that the Captain shared her revulsion for physical contact. But his recurring doubts about his manhood made him misconstrue her reaction and become even more aggressively ardent: "I thought you despised my lack of virility, so I tried to win you as a woman by proving myself as a man." This fatal mistake resulted in total warfare between them, to which the dispute over Bertha provides only the catalystic climax.

[16] Considering that the Captain is so willing to act the part of the passive infant, in fact, he seems rather obtuse when, in Act I, he asks, "Why do you women treat a grown man as if he were a child?"

The struggle is the substance of the play, and it turns the entire household into an armed camp. Its outcome, however, is foreordained, since the house is crawling with women, and most of the men in the area are too conventional or too gentlemanly to accept the Captain's interpretation of the female character. As the Captain looks desperately about him for allies, determining who is "in league against me" or "going over to the enemy," the sides divide; and Strindberg's personal stake in this war leads him to divide his characters as well, judging them wholly on the basis of their attitude towards the Captain's position. *The Father* includes, among its *dramatis personae,* an Ibsenist Doctor and Pastor, but they are judged by standards quite different from Ibsen's. Doctor Ostermark, for example, acceptable enough when Strindberg sees him as a humanist, a scientist, and a male, is condemned when he becomes a muddleheaded tool of Laura's; and the Pastor, while occasionally satirized for his religious beliefs is tolerated because of his masculine sympathy for the Captain.

As for the women, Strindberg marks the deck by identifying all his female characters — those onstage and off — with some form of quackery. And since he associates women, at this time, with religion and superstition, their quackery invariably takes a supernatural form. As the Captain notes:

The house is full of women, all trying to mold this child of mine. My mother-in-law wants to turn her into a spiritualist; Laura wants her to be an artist; the governess would have her a Methodist, old Margaret a Baptist, and the servant girls a Salvation Army lass.

Bertha herself believes in ghosts, and practices automatic writing upstairs with Laura's mother; and even the Captain's old nurse, Margaret — the most sympathetic woman in the play, since she is the most maternal — is called hard and hateful in her religious convictions. It is Margaret, too, who deals the Captain his death blow by tricking him into the straitjacket (she pretends that she is the mother and he the child, and she is fitting on his woolen tunic). For sweet as she may be, her female nature instinctively aligns her with the Captain's enemies. Since the Captain, like Strindberg at this time, is a rationalist, a materialist, and a misogynist, the lines are drawn between intellectual freethinking men and irrational, superstitious, and malevolent women. And on this sexual battlefield, almost everybody seems to act in rather mechanical conformity with his or her unconscious alliance.

This sounds dangerously like paranoia; and it is certain that the Captain's persecution complex is one of the major factors in his mental breakdown. But since Strindberg shares his hero's paranoiac distemper, he is clearly undecided about the state of the Captain's mental health. We are as befuddled as the Doctor, for example, as to whether the Captain's acts of violence are to be construed as "an outbreak of temper or insanity." Is he a healthy man driven insane by Laura's poisonous insinuations or are the seeds of madness present in his mind before the play begins? Strindberg hedges. On the one hand, he sees the Captain as a relatively stable man on the verge of an important scientific discovery[17] who, infuriated by the false rumors his wife has spread about his mental condition, the frustrations she has put in his way, and, most of all, the doubts she has sown about the paternity of his child, is goaded into madness ("All steam-boilers explode when the pressure-gauge reaches the limit"). In this view, the Captain's sense of persecution is perfectly understandable since he *is* being persecuted — not only by Laura but by every woman in the house. On the other hand, Strindberg suggests that the Captain's will has been diseased since birth, that he fears for his sanity before the action begins, and that Laura's stratagem merely exacerbates a dangerous existing condition: it is in cases of *instability,* as the Doctor tells Laura, that "ideas can sometimes take hold and grow into an obsession — or even monomania." Thus we have a character who fears for his reason, yet believes his reason to be "unaffected"; who declares himself, by turns, both weak and strong of will; who is subject

[17] The ability to function as a scientist was always a proof of sanity to Strindberg, though it would not make much of an impression on a psychiatrist. In Act I, the Doctor is astonished to think that the Captain's mind might be affected, because "his learned treatise on mineralogy . . . shows a clear and powerful intellect." Strindberg alludes to his scientific experiments again in *Inferno* as proof that he could not be insane.

to persecution mania, yet actually being persecuted. In short, Strindberg, unable to objectify his own difficulties, hesitates between writing a balanced play about a paranoiac character and a paranoiac play about a balanced character — illogically introducing elements of both.[18] Before ambiguity of this kind, we must simply fold our hands, admitting the futility of trying to extract any logical consistency from this intensely subjective nightmare.

Yet, like a nightmare, *The Father* does possess a kind of internal logic, which makes all its external contradictions seem rather minor; and it maintains this dreamlike logic right up to its shattering climax. For it assumes total warfare between men and women, in which unconscious thoughts are as blameworthy as explicit actions, and every woman in the world is either adulterous or treacherous, and, therefore, the natural enemy of man:

My mother did not want me to come into the world because my birth would give her pain. She was my enemy. She robbed my embryo of nourishment, so I was born incomplete. My sister was my enemy when she made me knuckle under to her. The first woman I took in my arms was my enemy. She gave me ten years of sickness in return for the love I gave her. When my daughter had to choose between you and me, she became my enemy. And you, you, my wife, have been my mortal enemy, for you have not let go until there is no life left in me.

---

[18] Strindberg's hesitation is also evident in his conception of Laura's character. Is she consciously evil, an Iago pouring doubt into Othello's ear, a predatory animal who fights with everybody who thwarts her will? Or is she *unconsciously* wicked, the perpetrator, as the Pastor describes it, of "a little innocent murder that the law cannot touch. An unconscious crime." Just as the Captain wavers between his love of the mother and his hatred of the wife, so Strindberg wavers between these two contradictory interpretations of Laura. When there is no more need to lie, Laura tells her husband, "I didn't mean this to happen. I never really thought it out. I must have had some vague desire to get rid of you — you were in my way — and perhaps, if you see some plan in my actions, there was one, but I was unconscious of it." To this, the Captain replies, "Very plausible" — but the plausibility of this explanation is exploded when we remember Laura's other speeches to her husband, her cunning insinuations to the Doctor, and her conscious decision to proceed with her plan right after she has been informed that an insane man loses his family and civil rights.

In the weird logic of the play, the Captain's conclusions are perfectly correct, for just as he was defeated by the evil Laura, so is he finally led into the trap by the maternal Margaret. Caught in a net like Agamemnon, roaring like a wounded warrior, he can shout that "rude strength has fallen before treacherous weakness." But though he remains defiant, it is perfectly clear that it is his own weakness which has betrayed him — for over the straitjacket lies the soft, vanilla-scented shawl of the mother. Even at the last moment, his fatal ambivalence is clear, for after spitting his curses on the whole female sex, he lays his head upon Margaret's lap, declaring: "Oh how sweet it is to sleep upon a woman's breast, be she mother or mistress! But sweetest of all a mother's." And blessing Margaret, he falls into a paralytic swoon. But though the Captain has ceased to struggle, Strindberg's revolt against women continues to the end. For the "blessed" Margaret has betrayed this freethinker once again — falsely claiming that "with his last breath he prayed to God."

Slanderous, prejudiced, one-sided, these are certainly accurate descriptions of the play. Having dramatized the hostility which accompanies all romantic love, and having discovered some of the psychological reasons for it, Strindberg would seem to have invalidated all his insights through his exaggerated misogyny; yet these very exaggerations provide the play with its impact, and the very unfairness with which it is executed provides its momentum. Fourteen years later, in *The Dance of Death*, Strindberg will take up similar characters in a similar situation, treating them with much greater balance, detachment, and cogency; but the tortured, consuming, inflammatory power of this play is something he will never equal again.

In *Miss Julie*, written a year later (1888), Strindberg seems to have gained a good deal more control over himself and his material. The play is a decided advance in objectivity, generally free from the author's paranoiac symptoms. And while the subject of the work is still the mortal conflict of the sexes, it is, significantly, the male who conquers here, and the female who goes down to destruction. The victory of Jean, the valet, is assured by the fact that he has nothing feminine in his nature at all. Compared with the hero of *The Father,* in fact, he seems to be pure brute, for he shares neither the Captain's sense of honor, nor his need for motherly comfort, nor his lacerating doubts about his manhood. As Strindberg describes Jean, he possesses "both the coarseness of the slave and the toughmindedness of the born ruler, he can look at blood without fainting, shake off bad luck like water, and take calamity by the horns." Strindberg, attracted as usual to masculine strength, identifies deeply with Jean in many ways, and is exhilarated by his brutishness, though he is too fastidious to make a complete identification with this ambitious servant. Nevertheless, as his conception of his hero suggests, Strindberg is feeling much more security in his own masculinity at this time. And the play embodies, in abundance, those qualities which Strindberg associates exclusively with the male: discipline, control, self-sufficiency, cruelty, independence, and strength.

In the fine preface he has appended to the work — obviously composed in a mood of brashness, confidence, and high spirits — Strindberg documents his achievement, giving these male virtues their aesthetic and philosophical equivalents. For here he expounds his theory of Naturalism. Beginning by ridiculing the debased ideas found in the commercial theatre, Strindberg goes on to repudiate, as well, all drama with an ethical motive, where the spectator is induced to take sides or pass judgments. We do not know if he would include *The Father* in that category, though it certainly belongs there. But *Miss Julie,* at least, is offered as a work without tendency, moralizing, or subjective prejudices: a simple scientific demonstration of the survival of the fittest. Strindberg concedes that the fall of his heroine may arouse pity, but he attributes this response to the spectator's "weakness," and looks forward to a time when, through the progress of science, audiences will be strong enough to view such things with indifference, having dispensed with those "inferior and unreliable instruments of thought called feelings." Echoes like these of Darwin and Nietzsche, Strindberg's scientific and philosophical authorities during his "male" period, resound throughout the preface, and so do echoes of Zola, Strindberg's masculine dramatic theoretician. For *Miss Julie* is undoubtedly the closest thing to a Naturalist drama that Strindberg is ever to write. The hero and heroine — as "characterless" as real people — have been provided with an elaborate social-psychological history, and are controlled by their heredity and environment; the action is loose, natural, and compact without being plotty; the dialogue has the aimlessness of real speech; and the acting style, makeup, costumes, settings, and lights have all been designed for a minimum of artificiality.

Yet, despite all these unusual concessions to the "real," *Miss Julie* is not, strictly speaking, a Naturalistic work — partly because of the ballet, mime, and musical interlude Strindberg introduces into the work in the middle, but mostly because the author is constitutionally incapable of Naturalist impartiality.[19] It is true that Julie is much more objectively conceived than Laura and that Jean is a much more complicated character than the Captain. But if the play has an appearance of detachment, this is because an entirely new element has been introduced which balances Strindberg's sympathies. For if, formerly, Strindberg was mainly concerned with the sexual war between men and women, he is now examining a social conflict as well, between a servant and an aristocrat. And while he is still identifying with the male as a Hercules in combat with Omphale, he is also identifying with the female as a Don Quixote in conflict with an unscrupulous thrall. In short, Strindberg has not suspended his partialities, he has merely *divided* them. Both Jean and Julie are projections of the splits in the author's nature — the male versus the female, and the aristocrat versus the servant — and, in each case, he is defending himself against the side that he fears more.

Strindberg's split sympathies can be detected even in the preface, though in disguised form. Despite his pretense at scientific imparti-

19 It is doubtful if such a thing as Naturalist impartiality can ever be absolute, since the need for some principle of selection ultimately invalidates the fiction of artistic detachment. Yet, even a casual comparison of *Miss Julie* with, say, any work of Chekhov's, will show how far short Strindberg falls of objectivity. Actually, Strindberg's anger against emancipated women, his attraction to aristocratic Supermen, and his revulsion to dirt are attitudes which suggest he does not really share the Naturalist temper — a temper usually democratic, egalitarian, "advanced" on such social questions as female rights, and rather obsessed with the more sordid aspects of life.

ality, for example, his misogyny is still perfectly clear, for he characterizes Julie as a "man-hating woman," a type that "forces itself on others, selling itself for power, medals, recognition, diplomas, as formerly, it sold itself for money." [20] Similarly, though he affects a Darwinian indifference to the supersession of the "old warrior nobility" by the "new nobility of nerve and brain," he admits that the aristocrat's code of honor was "a very beautiful thing," and that the new man rises in the world only through base and ignoble tactics. Strindberg's admiration for the sexual aristocracy of Jean, in fact, is qualified by his sense of the servant's inherent vulgarity: "He is polished on the outside, but coarse underneath. He wears his frock coat with elegance but gives no assurance that he keeps his body clean." Jean's lack of cleanliness is not something designed to endear him to Strindberg, who throughout his life had an intense revulsion to dirt; but it signifies that if Jean is the sexual aristocrat, he is the social slave, just as Julie is the sexual slave but the social aristocrat. In each case, Strindberg's sympathies, despite his protestations of neutrality, are enlisted firmly on the side of the aristocracy.

The dramatic design of *Miss Julie* is like two intersecting lines going in opposite directions: Jean reaches up and Julie falls down, both meeting on equal grounds only at the moment of seduction, in the arms of the great democratizer, sex. Both are motivated by strong internal (in Julie's case, almost unconscious) forces which propel them towards their fate — underscored by social-sexual images of rising and falling, cleanliness and dirt, life and death. These images inform the entire play but are unified in two contrasting poetic metaphors: the recurring dreams of Jean and Julie. In Julie's dream, she is looking down from the height of a great pillar, anxious to fall to the dirt beneath, yet aware that the fall would mean her death; in Jean's, he is lying on the ground beneath a great tree, anxious to pull himself up from the dirt to a golden nest above.

---

[20] Actually, Julie — with her white skin, aristocratic bearing, and emancipated opinions — is another, more lucidly executed portrait of Siri Von Essen. And so there may be a touch of self-hatred in Strindberg's remark that "degenerate men unconsciously select their mates from among these half-women."

The crossover is the crux of the action: Jean seduces Julie during the Midsummer Eve festivities, and then induces her to cut her throat in fear that their impossible liaison will be discovered. Julie's descent, therefore, is a movement from spirit to flesh, motivated by her attraction to dirt and death. She unconsciously desires to degrade herself, to be soiled and trampled on, and when she falls, she ruins her entire house. Born, like Strindberg, of an aristocratic father and a common woman (her mother is associated with dirt through her fondness for the kitchen, the stables, and the cowsheds), Julie finds in her parentage the source of her problems. Her father's weakness has taught her to despise men, and the influence of her mother, an emancipated woman, has encouraged her to dominate and victimize them. Jean has seen her with her weakling fiancé, forcing him to jump over her riding crop like a trained dog; and in the torrent of abuse which pours from her after she has been seduced, her hatred of men is further underlined. On the other hand, neither her class arrogance nor her sex hatred is total. Her fiancé has filled her with egalitarian ideas, so that she tempers her aristocratic impudence with democratic condescension ("Tonight we're all just happy people at a party," she says to Jean. "There's no question of rank"). And her natural sexuality, heightened by suggestions of masochism, weakens her masculine resolve ("But when that weakness comes, oh . . . the shame!"). Like Diana, her wayward bitch, she is a thoroughbred who consorts with the local mongrels, since her unconscious impulses lead her, against her will, to roll herself in dirt.

By contrast, Jean's ascent is associated with cleanliness and life, and is a movement from the flesh to the spirit. He wishes to be proprietor of a Swiss hotel; and his highest ambition is to be a Rumanian count. Like Julie, he is trying to escape the conditioning of his childhood — a childhood in which filth, muck, and excrement played a large part. As we learn from his story of the Turkish outhouse, his strongest childhood memory is of himself on the ground yearning towards cleanliness. Having escaped from the Turkish pavilion through its sewer, he looked up at Julie in "a pink dress and a pair of white stockings" from the vantage point of weeds, thistles, and "wet dirt that stank to high heaven." At that time, he went home to wash himself all over with soap and warm water. Now he is still washing himself, in a metaphorical sense, by trying to rise above his lowly position and aping the fastidious manners of the aristocracy. For just as Julie is attracted to his class, so is he impelled towards her. He has become a lower-class snob through his association with his betters, wavering between an aristocratic affectation of French manners and tastes, and a slavish servility amidst the Count's boots.

The contrast between the two characters is further emphasized by their conflicting views of the sexual act and the concept of "honor." Despite her mother's influence, Julie believes rather strongly in Romantic love and Platonic ideals, while Jean, despite his rather pronounced prudishness, regards love merely as an honorific term for a purely animal act — as Iago would put it, as "a lust of the blood and a permission of the will." Jean, indeed, is the Elizabethan Naturalist come to life in the modern world, though, unlike the Elizabethan dramatists, Strindberg does not make the Naturalist a villain. Jean is superstitious, and pays lip service to God (a sign, Strindberg tells us, of his "slave mentality"), but, in effect, he is a complete materialist, for whom Platonic ideals have no real meaning whatsoever. Though he admires Julie's honor, he knows it is only a breath; truth, like honesty, is wholly at the service of his ambition, for he will lie, cheat, and steal to advance himself; and as for conscience, he might say, had he Richard III's eloquence, "It is a word that cowards use." It is because of his pragmatic materialism that Jean so values reputation, whereas Julie, the idealist, seems to scorn it. For like the Elizabethan Machiavel, Jean knows that it is external appearances rather than personal integrity that determines one's success in the world. Strindberg undoubtedly views this unscrupulous valet as a link in the evolution of the Superman.[21] And though he secretly disapproves of all his

[21] F. L. Lucas, discussing the play in his book *Ibsen and Strindberg*, calls Jean a "lout" and Julie a "trollop," while calling Strindberg himself a "cad." Lucas's moralistic malice makes his criticism of Strindberg distorted, narrow-minded, and cranky. And though he will occasionally confess that, "My dislike of drunkenness, literal and artistic, may be morbidly excessive," he does not realize how much these prejudices affect his understanding of Strindberg. Here

values, he is willing to countenance Jean, in spite of his baseness, because of his effective masculine power.

Jean, therefore, differs from the Captain in his toughness, self-sufficiency, and total lack of scruples; but Strindberg has apparently decided that Iago's ruthlessness, rather than Othello's romantic gullibility, is the necessary element in achieving victory over the female. Yet, if Jean is no Othello, then Julie is no Desdemona either; and just as Julie learns that Jean is not a shoe-kissing cavalier, so Jean is disillusioned in his expectations of Julie. Jean's disenchantment is signified by his growing realization that the aristocracy is also tainted. For, in getting a close look at Julie, he sees that she, too, has "dirt on your face," and that the inaccessible golden nest is not what he had hoped:

I can't deny that, in one way, it was good to find out that what I saw glittering above was only fool's gold . . . and that there could be dirt under the manicured nails, that the handkerchief was soiled even though it smelled of perfume. But, in another way, it hurt me to find that everything I was striving for wasn't very high above me after all, wasn't even real. It hurts me to see you sink far lower than your own cook. Hurts, like seeing the last flowers cut to pieces by the autumn rains and turned to muck.

Julie, in short, has achieved her unconscious desire. She has turned to muck, and been cut to pieces by the rain. And now there is nothing left for her but to die.

In this act of expiation, Jean serves as Julie's judge and executioner; but it is in her death that she proves her social superiority to Jean, even though she has been sexually defeated by him. In the most obvious sense, of course, her suicide signifies his victory; just as he chopped off the head of Julie's pet songbird, so he must chop off hers, lest she decapitate him (the sermon in church that morning, significantly, concerned the beheading of John the Baptist). But if Jean triumphs as a male, he is defeated as a servant, for her honorable su-

is an example of an eighteenth-century mind confronting a modern mind, and recoiling in disgust.

icide, a gesture he is incapable of, makes his survival look base.[22] Strindberg dramatizes Jean's ignobility by his servile cringing at the sound of the Count's bell. Slobbering with uncontrollable fear, he hypnotizes Julie into going into the barn with his razor. But despite this display of will, it is Julie, not Jean, who is finally redeemed. Hitherto convinced of her own damnation because of the biblical injunction that the last shall be first and the first last, Julie discovers that she has unwittingly attained a place in paradise through her fall. For she learns that "I'm among the last. I *am* the last" — not only because she is last on the ladder of human degradation, but because she is also the last of her doomed and blighted house. As she walks resolutely to her death, and Jean shivers abjectly near the Count's boots, the doubleness of the play is clarified in the conclusion. She has remained an aristocrat and died; Jean has remained a servant and lived; and Strindberg — dramatizing for the first time his own ambiguities about nobility and baseness, spirit and matter, masculine and feminine, purity and dirt — has remained with them both to the very end.

The Father and *Miss Julie,* twin prayers in Strindberg's worship of the masculine and the finest works of his first phase, are followed within a few years by a profound spiritual crisis, during which Strindberg's last resistance to the feminine and religious aspects of his nature is broken, and after which his art undergoes an emphatic change. Strindberg's harrowing diary of this crisis, *Inferno* — along with *The Road to Damascus,* an autobiographical trilogy written after the crisis was over — documents the history of his artistic, sexual, and religious "conversion." Strindberg, after divorcing Siri in 1892, has separated from Frida Uhl in 1894, a year after their marriage. Living like a derelict in Paris, he has repudiated the drama and given himself over entirely to scientific experiments; his literary output during a five-year period consists primarily of three technical treatises. Despite his apparent dedication to science, however, Strindberg is becoming increasingly interested in the supernatural, as he grows

[22] Martin Lamm reports that, in Strindberg's original conception, Julie was to snatch the razor from Jean's hand with the taunt, "You see, servant, you cannot die."

more and more convinced that there are unknown powers guiding his destiny. Actually, Strindberg is preparing to renounce what he calls the "antiquated, degenerate science" of the nineteenth century as limited and unimaginative. "Familiar with the natural sciences since my youth," he writes in 1895, "and later on a disciple of Darwin, I had discovered the inadequacy of a scientific method which recognized the mechanization of the universe without recognizing a divine Mechanic." Strindberg's quest for this "divine Mechanic" is a sign of his growing need for a religious view of life — a need he first expresses, inversely, by his worship of Luciferian evil, his Satanic appearance (he had adopted, at this time, a cape and beard), and his occult experiments. Nevertheless, Strindberg's revolt continues unabated. Even when he gives up his Satanism, he remains too rebellious to commit himself to any creed or institution for long. Sometimes he is attracted to Catholicism, primarily because of its motherworship in the cult of Mary; sometimes to Buddhism, because "I am, like Buddha and his three great disciples, a woman hater, just as I hate the earth which binds my spirit because I love it." These shortlived commitments, themselves so ambivalent, indicate Strindberg's continuing dualism. Searching for absolutes, Strindberg is perpetually pressed back into relatives, still too proud to bend his spirit to any higher authority.

It is this "devilish spirit of rebellion," as Strindberg puts it in *The Road to Damascus*, that "must be broken like a reed." And it is partially broken, after a prolonged period of unrelieved physical and spiritual torment. For Strindberg, his persecution mania growing, becomes convinced that he is being hounded by invisible enemies who are discharging poisonous gases into his room, and trying to electrocute him by means of an infernal electrical apparatus. Fearing for his sanity, he flees Paris to consult a number of baffled doctors, only to be afflicted with electrical shocks in every European city he visits. In the home of Mamma Uhl, his mother-in-law and a Swedenborgian Catholic, however, he does find some relief — under her consoling influence, Strindberg relaxes like an unhappy child awakening from a dreadful nightmare. Yet, even with her, Strindberg's old ambivalence manifests itself. Believing that the feminists have laid a morbid plot against his life, he begins to suspect even his mother-in-law of complicity: "I had forgotten that a female saint is still a woman, i.e., the enemy of man."

Under the sway of this maternal woman, though, Strindberg continues his readings in Swedenborg, in whose mystical visions he finally discovers what he thinks to be the explanation for his months of agony. He has been suffering from a religious state called *Devestatio* — God has been seeking him, and he has been too proud to let himself be found. Freed from his torment after this insight, Strindberg determines to live a life of repentance. And, indeed, he gives up both his occult and scientific studies, begins to wear a habit of monkish penitential cut, and even considers entering a monastery after the publication of *Inferno*. As for his philosophical position, this, we learn from a crucial passage in *The Road to Damascus*, Part III, has progressed from a harsh one-sidedness to a compassionate doubleness in his acceptance of life's contradictions:

Thesis: affirmation; Antithesis: negation; Synthesis: comprehension! . . . You began life by accepting everything, and then went on to denying everything on principle. Now end your life by comprehending everything. Be exclusive no longer. Do not say: either — or, but: not only — but also! In a word, or two words, rather, Humanity and Resignation.

Humanity, Resignation, and the melancholy understanding of two conflicting positions — these are to be the tones struck in Strindberg's drama from this point until the end of his career.

For Strindberg, at last accepting the ambivalence which had been in him since birth, has finally permitted himself to accept those elements in his nature which he had always feared the most and fought the hardest. Freudians might say that, after a long period of trying to identify with his father, he is now permitting himself to identify with his mother as well; theologians might say that he has finally found his way to God after a long period of resisting Him. Strindberg himself is inclined to interpret his experience religiously, envisioning himself as Paul of Tarsus, claimed by the Lord on the road to Damascus. But whatever interpretation one chooses, it is certain that Strindberg is now confirming those attitudes and accepting those influences which he used to reject as too passive, weak, or feminine. His new concern with the unconscious, for example, is evidence of his change — for he used to consider the unconscious the exclusive province of women; and his endorsement of religion, and even Christianity (fit for "women, eunuchs, children, and savages"), shows that he is no longer afraid of female spirituality. Instead of masculine mentors like Darwin, Nietzsche, and Zola — those theoreticians of a tough, ruthless view of life — Strindberg is seeking out more compassionate teachers, generally those with a spiritual or supernatural vision. Swedenborg is a crucial influence at this time, along with Buddhist theologians and Hindu philosophers; and Symbolist writers such as Maeterlinck, formerly too ethereal for Strindberg, are now his primary literary models. No longer defying the universe or trying to become God, Strindberg is now yielding to the unknown and seeking to do its will. Looking for correspondences rather than causes, he has replaced his former Naturalism and atheism with a new concern for the supernal forces behind material things.

The effect of Strindberg's conversion is, of course, especially evident in his plays, where in this second phase of his career (1898–1909) it has profoundly influenced his conception of theme, subject matter, character, and form. Strindberg is still inclined to view the relations between the sexes as strife; but he is much more willing now to regard this struggle from the woman's point of view. For, influenced by Balzac's *Séraphita* — "he-she . . . *l'époux et l'épouse de l'humanité*" — Strindberg has at last determined to affirm the male-female split in himself. As a result, women begin to play a much more central, and sympathetic, role in his plays: The Lady in *The Road to Damascus,* Jeanne in *Crimes and Crimes,* Eleanora in *Easter,* the title character in *Swanwhite,* Indra's Daughter in *A Dream Play,* the Milkmaid in *Ghost Sonata* — some of these are surrogates for the author, and all have that maternal quality which Strindberg so admired without any of the wantonness which used to accompany it. In addition, the religious piety of these women, formerly a stimulus for

Strindberg's scorn, is now a sign of tenderness, warmth, and virtue. In his new veneration for the religious life, Strindberg is anxious to exalt the worshiper — as he is anxious to exalt the priest (compare the sympathetic Abbé in *Crimes and Crimes* with the rather simple-minded Pastor in *The Father*). The frequent subject of his satire now, in fact, is his old impious self — the rationalistic, blasphemous male with aspirations towards the superhuman, like Maurice in *Crimes and Crimes*. For, in this second phase of his career, many of Strindberg's plays are designed as acts of penance, in which he tries to expiate his sense of guilt, and scourge his desire for worldly vanities.

As for Strindberg's dramatic techniques, the change in these can also be attributed to his conversion. In repudiating philosophical Naturalism, Strindberg repudiated dramatic Naturalism as well, scornfully classifying this genre as a symptom of "the contemporary materialistic striving after faithfulness to reality" (*Notes to the Intimate Theatre*). Gone is the compact form and psychological detail of *Miss Julie*. In their place has come a flowing, formless, fluid series of episodes — so feminine in their feeling of flux — in which Strindberg imaginatively uses lights, music, visual symbols, and atmospheric effects to cut through the materiality of life to the spiritual truths beneath. The Chamber play, a short episodic work in which Strindberg tries to approximate the condition of music, becomes an important experimental mode at this time, but even when his plays are longer, they tend to assume a musical form. Many of these works belong to that genre which we now call Expressionism. The term is apt only in suggesting that they are expressions of Strindberg's unconscious. Such plays as *The Road to Damascus, A Dream Play, The Ghost Sonata,* and *The Great Highway* are more accurately described, in Strindberg's own phrase, as "dream plays." For they are alike in their use of free form, so close to the form of a dream, and in their languid abstractness: locations are vague; space is relative; chronological time is broken; and characters possess allegorical names like the Stranger, the Student, the Poet, the Hunter, and the Dreamer. The dream plays are, of course, only a sampling of the works that Strindberg wrote during his second phase. Yet, even in his Shakespearean chronicle plays (*Gustavus Vasa, Eric XIV*), and his more realistic Chamber plays (*The Pelican, The Storm*), we are never too far from the author's unconscious mind where the supernatural dominates and subjective fantasies are given full play: "I write best," he remarks at this time, "in hallucination."

On the other hand, it is important to realize that the change in Strindberg is just a question of emphasis: the qualities he is now openly admitting into his drama were always there, though forcibly suppressed. The unconscious source of his inspiration was perfectly clear, for example, in *The Father,* and so was the essentially passive nature of his sexual, emotional, and intellectual responses. In this later period, Strindberg, understanding his dualistic conflicts better, is no longer resisting them so vigorously. Yet, he has still not been able to resolve them. His short-lived marriage to his third wife, Harriet Bosse, for example, indicates that his sexual problems have remained fairly constant. And while the tone of his plays is more saintly and forgiving, his thematic concerns have also remained essentially the same. Even his new religious humility is modified by traces of the old skeptical arrogance: in *Crimes and Crimes,* Maurice agrees to go to the Abbé's church to repent, but he will go to the theatre the next evening; and in *The Road to Damascus,* the Stranger — brought to the door of the Church in Part I — is still afflicted with doubts at the end of Part III, even though he is being initiated into a monastery. Like these characters, Strindberg remains in a state of suspension. If he is no longer fighting God, he is still questioning Him, for he is still a rebel, raging against the awful limitations of his humanity. He has tried to escape from life into a realm of pure spirit, but he cannot resist the pulls of the body which drag him back into the filth, muck, and flesh of the material world.

Strindberg, in fact, is becoming more and more obsessed with human grossness at this time. In *Black Banners* (1904), he writes of his nausea at the sound of men sucking their soup (eating was always a source of repugnance to him), at sweating and stinking human bodies, and at garbage heaps, toilets, and spittoons. Strindberg's revulsion at dirt was inferentially suggested in *Miss Julie;* in his later works, his disgust is even more openly expressed. In *The Ghost Sonata*, for example, it is the task of "keeping the dirt of life at a distance" which weighs down the characters, for there Strindberg even seems to be revolted by such simple household chores as cleaning ink off the fingers and fixing a smoking chimney. The "dirt of life" is, of course, life itself, and especially the life of the flesh. For Strindberg's hatred of dirt is intimately bound up with his lifelong disgust at the physical functions of man, especially the physical expression of love which he sees as a base animal act degrading a lofty spiritual feeling.

In the light of his attitude towards the body, Strindberg's commitment to a life of spirit becomes a little clearer, for he tends to regard the physical world, to borrow John Marston's imagery, as "the very muckhill on which the sublunarie orbes cast their excrement." It was Freud who observed that to attempt to rise above the body is to treat the body as an excremental object; and there is no question that Strindberg possesses what Norman O. Brown has called the "excremental vision":[23] he equates the human body with dung. Lesser writers with similar feelings (Maeterlinck is one) generally respond to their hatred of the flesh by turning away from reality altogether, creating a never-never land of airy fantasy. But the superior genius of Strindberg lies in his ability to confront his feelings courageously. It is, in fact, the inescapable interdependence of body and spirit, lust and love, dirt and flowers, which forms the major theme of these later plays, where he tries to explore, in dramatic terms, the melancholy Yeatsian paradox: "Love has pitched his mansion in the place of excrement." He cannot affirm this paradox; he will no longer try to deny it. He will only, in accordance with the Hegelian synthesis he

---

[23] See Brown's fascinating study, *Life Against Death*. The excrementalist is appalled by the sexual act because it is consummated so near the excretory organs. Jonathan Swift, a writer obsessed with excremental horror, writes: "Should I the Queen of Love refuse/ Because she rose from stinking ooze?" Writing to Siri, Strindberg uses much the same imagery: "You're walking in filth — you, the queen with the sunlit forehead." Even the act of writing often seems dirty to Strindberg. To Siri, he says, "I can get poetry out of filth if I must," and he tells Harriet, "To put things into words is to degrade — to turn poetry into prose!" After a while, Strindberg came to believe that the very act of living was filthy, and the only thing clean and pure was death.

has adopted, try to understand it. But in this desperate effort at understanding, where Strindberg projects his tortured dualism onto the whole of life, his existential rebellion finds its greatest expression.

Of all the works that Strindberg wrote during this period, *A Dream Play* is probably the most typical and the most powerful. To judge from the parallel dreams of Jean and Julie, Strindberg always believed in the significance of the dream life; but here he has converted this conviction into a stunning dramatic technique. Though the "dream play," as a genre, is probably not Strindberg's invention — Calderón, and possibly even Shakespeare in *The Tempest,* anticipated his notion that "life is a dream," while Maeterlinck certainly stimulated his interest in the vague, spiritual forces "behind" life — the form is certainly his own, in which time and space dissolve at the author's bidding and plot is almost totally subordinate to theme. The Dreamer, whose "single consciousness holds sway" over the split, doubled, and multiplied characters is, of course, Strindberg himself, who is also present as the Officer, the Lawyer, and the Poet, and, possibly, as Indra's Daughter. As he describes the Dreamer in his preface, "For him there are no secrets, no incongruities, no scruples and no law. He neither condemns nor acquits, but only relates, and since on the whole, there is more pain than pleasure in the dream, a tone of melancholy, and of compassion for all living things, runs through the swaying narrative."

Because of the absence of "secrets," *A Dream Play* is even more self-exploratory than *The Father;* but although a direct revelation of Strindberg's unconscious mind, it is almost entirely free from any personal grievance. For Strindberg, the drama is no longer an act of revenge, but rather a medium for expressing "compassion for all living things." In *A Dream Play* the world is a pestilent congregation of vapors; the miseries of mankind far exceed its pleasures; but, for these very reasons, humans must be pitied and forgiven. The prevailing mood of woe in the work stems from the author's sense of the contradictions of life, some of which are suggested by the Poet in the Fingal's Cave section. After chancing upon the sunken wrecks of ships called

Justice, Friendship, Golden Peace, and *Hope,* this Poet offers a petition to God in the form of anguished questions:

> Why are we born like animals?
> We who stem from God and man,
> whose souls are longing to be clothed
> in other than this blood and filth.
> Must God's image cut its teeth?

Indra's Daughter quickly silences this rebellious questioning — "No more. The work may not condemn the master! Life's riddle still remains unsolved" — but it is the unraveling of this painful enigma of existence which is the purpose of the play. Consequently, the work is structured on similar contrasts, conflicts, and contradictions: Body versus Spirit, Fairhaven versus Foulstrand, Winter versus Summer, North versus South, Beauty versus Ugliness, Fortune versus Misfortune, Love versus Hate. Even the sounds of the play communicate Strindberg's sense of the dissonance of life: a Bach toccata in four-four time is played concurrently with a waltz; a bell buoy booms in chords of fourths and fifths. For, in this work, life itself is no more than a disordered and chaotic struggle between opposites, and the movement of the play is towards explaining the cause of these divisions.

Like *Faust,* the play begins with a prologue in Heaven, a celestial colloquy over the lot of mortals. The god Indra explains to his Daughter that the earth is both fair and heavy because "revolt followed by crime" destroyed its almost perfect beauty. Listening to the wail of human voices rising from below, he determines to send the Daughter through the foul vapors to determine if human lamentation is justified. Indra's Daughter, descending, becomes the central character of the play. Indicating how far Strindberg has come from his old misogyny, she is — like Eleanora in *Easter* — a "female Christ," expressing the author's sympathy for the fate of humanity and his readiness to redeem man by sharing in man's sufferings. She is also Strindberg's Eternal Feminine; each man finds in her sweet, forgiving nature the realization of his own particular ideal. To the Officer, the first of Strindberg's dream surrogates, the Daughter is Agnes, "a child of heaven," and in her encounter with this embittered character, the Daughter is already beginning to see some motive for human complaint. He is imprisoned in a Castle which grows, throughout the action, out of manure and stable muck. Likened to the flowers (they "don't like dirt, so they shoot up fast as they can into the light — to blossom and to die"), the Castle is an image of life itself: the human spirit, trying to escape from the excremental body, aspires upwards towards the Heaven, but is always rooted in filth.[24]

Against this paradox of life, the Officer strongly protests, striking his sword on the table in his "quarrel with God." For despite his urge to aspire, he, too, is mired in filth. Like the Captain in *The Father,* he is another Hercules, doomed to an unpleasant labor: he must "groom horses, clean stables, and have the muck removed." Imprisoned in eternal adolescence, he is being punished for a childhood sin, for he once permitted his brother to be blamed for the theft of a book which he himself had torn to pieces and hidden in a cupboard. When the Daughter offers to set him free from the Castle (i.e., from his neurotic fears and guilts), he is, however, equally dubious: "Either way I'll suffer!" And when time and space dissolve back to the Officer's childhood, we see why adulthood is just as painful as adolescence. In this scene, the Officer's Father has given his Mother a silk shawl — still a symbol of maternal compassion for Strindberg. But she gives it away to a needy servant, and the Father feels insulted. In this life of shifting sands, what seems a generous act to one is an evil act to another; all of existence is suffering; and, as the Daughter observes now and throughout the play, "Humankind is to be pitied."

But the Daughter, still believing in worldly redemption, exclaims, "Love conquers all"; and the scene dissolves again for the first demonstration that she is wrong. The setting is a stage door, much

24 In *The Ghost Sonata,* Strindberg uses the image of the Hyacinth in the same manner. The bulb is the earth; the stalk is the axis of the world; and the six-pointed flowers are the stars. Buddha is waiting for the Earth to become Heaven: i.e., for the Hyacinth to blossom, aspiring above its mired roots. Both the Castle and the Hyacinth, of course, are also phallic images — the sexual organ is pitched in the place of excrement.

like the place where Strindberg used to wait for Harriet to finish at the theatre, and the motif of the scene is — waiting. Waiting for Victoria, his heart's desire, with a bunch of flowers is the Officer, now freed from the Castle. But Victoria never comes. Time passes, with an accelerated whirring of lights; the Officer grows older and shabbier; the roses wither. The Daughter sits with the Doorkeeper, having taken from her the shawl (once the Mother's), now grown gray from its absorption of human misery. For nobody is contented except a Bill-sticker who, after fifty years of waiting, has attained *his* heart's desire: a net and a green fishbox. Yet, even he grows unhappy after a time: the net was "not quite what I had in mind," the fishbox not quite as green as he had expected. Suffering the twin tragedies of getting and not getting what one wants, everybody in the world is afflicted with unhappiness. But behind a cloverleaf door (the Officer, poking at it, has an *intermittence du coeur,* recalling the guilty cupboard of his youth) lies the explanation of human misery and the secret of life. Yet, the Law forbids the opening of it.

The scene dissolves once again to the Lawyer's office, where the Daughter and the Officer hope to get the door opened. Everyone there has grown ugly from "unspeakable suffering." And the Lawyer's face, like the Mother's shawl, is marred by the absorption of human crime and evil. The second of Strindberg's dream surrogates, the Lawyer shares with the Daughter some of the qualities of Christ. Like Jesus, he has taken on himself all the sins of the world; and like Jesus, he is in conflict with the righteous, who condemn him for defending the poor and easing the burdens of the guilty. When he is denied his Law degree during an academic procession, the Daughter's shawl turns white, and she fits him with a crown of thorns. But since he too is a rebel, quarreling with God, she must explain to him the reasons for injustice: Life is a phantasm, an illusion, an upside-down copy of the original.[25] And the four Faculties (Theology, Philosophy, Medi-

---

[25] This idea, like so many others, Strindberg probably found in Nietzsche, who writes in *Zarathustra:* "This world, the eternally imperfect, an eternal contradiction and imperfect image — an intoxicating joy to its imperfect creator. . . ."

cine, and Law) are merely voices in the madhouse, each claiming wisdom for itself while scourging the sane and the virtuous.

Determined to put her theory of redemption through love to the test, the Daughter marries the Lawyer. But it is in this familiar Strindberg domestic scene that the irreconcilable conflicts of life are most agonizingly dramatized. While Kristin, the Maid, pastes all the air out of the apartment, the couple engage in sharp quarrels over their conflicting tastes in food, furnishings, and religious beliefs. Neither is right or wrong. It is simply a condition of life that one's sympathies are the other's antipathies, "one's pleasure is the other's pain." [26] The Daughter, stifling in the house, tied to her husband by their child, and revolted by the dirty surroundings, feels herself "dying in this air." And when the Officer — now at the top of the seesaw of fortune — enters seeking his Agnes, the Daughter and the Lawyer decide to part. The Lawyer dissolves their marriage, comparing it to a hairpin. Like a hairpin, a married couple remain one, no matter how they are bent — until they are broken in two.

The Officer has decided to take the Daughter to Fairhaven, the land of youthful summer love, but through some miscalculation, they find themselves in Foulstrand, an ugly burnt-out hell, dominated by a Quarantine Station.[27] In this land, where life itself is a form of prolonged quarantine, young people are robbed of their color, hopes, and ideals, fortune turns to misfortune, youth becomes age. Strindberg's third dream surrogate enters, a visionary Poet who embodies the theme of opposition. Alternating between ecstasy and cynicism, he carries a pail of mud in which he bathes. The Quarantine Officer ex-

---

[26] This, like everything else in the play, is a perception which Strindberg achieved through personal suffering. As he writes in *Inferno:* "Earth, Earth is hell, the prison constructed by a superior intelligence in such a way that I cannot take a step without affecting the happiness of others, and others cannot be happy without giving me pain."

[27] The Quarantine Station is closely modeled on Swedenborg's Excremental Hell. Describing this Hell in *Inferno,* Strindberg recognizes it "as the country of Klam, the country of my zinc basin, drawn as if from life. The hollow valley, the pine knolls, the dark forests, the gorge with a creek, the village, the church, the poor house, the dunghills, the streams of muck, the pigsty, all are there."

plains that "he lives so much in the higher spheres he gets homesick for the mud," leading the Officer to comment, "What a strange world of contradictions." Yet, even in Fairhaven, the heavenly paradise, contradictions mar the holiday atmosphere. The pleasure of the rich is attained only through the suffering of the poor; the fulfilled love of beautiful Alice leaves the passions of ugly Edith unrequited; the "most envied mortal in the place" is blind. Even in this place, in short, happiness is fleeting and ephemeral; and the only way to sustain pleasure is to die at the moment of achieving it, as a newlywed couple proceed to do, drowning themselves in the sea.

It is, to be sure, a grim vision that informs this work, combining the woeful sense of vanity in Ecclesiastes with the Sophoclean plaint that it is better never to have been born. Despite his conviction that life is universal suffering, however, Strindberg seems to have exonerated human beings from responsibility for it. It is not mankind but the system which is evil — not human character but the immutable conditions of existence. For, as we learn in the Schoolmaster scene, where the Officer, once again imprisoned in adolescence, is forced to learn his lessons over and over like a child, life takes the form of an eternal recurrence, a cycle of return which defeats all efforts at progress, change, or development.[28] "The worst thing of all," as the Lawyer tells the Daughter, is "repetitions, reiterations. Going back. Doing one's lessons again." Caught in his own repetition compulsion, locked in the pattern of his neurosis, Strindberg has found in his personal torment the universal agony of mankind, where one is forced to repeat mistakes, despite the consciousness of error. Thus, when the cloverleaf door is finally opened, the secret of life is discovered to be — nothing. The area behind the door is a vast emptiness.

Condemned by the righteous for bringing man the truth,[29] the

---

[28] Evert Sprinchorn, in his interesting article, "The Logic of *A Dream Play*," *Modern Drama*, December 1962, demonstrates how Strindberg invests the very structure of the play with this cyclical development — something he had already done with Part I of *The Road to Damascus*.

[29] Another Nietzschean idea, that the righteous are those who crucified Christ: "And be on thy guard against the good and the just!" he affirms in

Daughter has had enough. She has suffered with all humanity —
more extremely than others because of her sensitive nature — and
now she knows that human complaint *is* justified. Shuffling off her
earthly bonds, as her companions cast their sorrows into the purifying
flames, the Daughter prepares to leave the world behind. But first she
must provide the answer to the Poet's riddle, explaining the origin of
the conflicts she has seen. Her interpretation, expressed in images of
Buddhist and Hindu philosophy, is the perfect symbolization of
Strindberg's dualism. In the dawn of time, she says, when Brahma, the
"divine primal force," let himself be seduced by Maya, the "world
Mother," the issue was the world — compounded ever since of elements both spiritual and fleshly, male and female, sacred and pro-
fane. Trying to escape from female matter, the descendants of
Brahma sought "renunciation and suffering," but this, in turn, con-
flicted with their need for sexual love. Torn in two directions at once,
pulled towards Heaven and dragged down to Earth, man became the
victim of "conflict, discord, and uncertainty"— the "human heart is
split in two"— and that is why the immortal soul is clothed in "blood
and filth." Having given her answer, the Daughter blesses the Poet for
his prophetic wisdom, and ascends to Indra, as the Castle blossoms
into a giant chrysanthemum. It is the end of the dream, for the
Dreamer has awakened; it is the orgiastic vision of the Poet, his mind
dressed in its visionary Sunday clothes; but it is also the continual aspiration of the soul after the body has died.[30] In death only, Strindberg seems to be saying, is there redemption — for only in death are
contradictions resolved, and the fleshly recoil finally stilled.

It was only through death, too, that Strindberg was able to resolve
his own contradictions. When he succumbed to cancer in 1912, hug-
ging a Bible to his breast and muttering, "Everything is atoned for,"
he had at last found his way to that peace which, half in love with

---

Zarathustra. "They would fain crucify those who devise their own virtue —
they hate the lonesome ones."

[30] The image of the bursting Castle, as Professor Sprinchorn has suggested,
is clearly sexual; and it is significant that Strindberg, like most Romantics,
identifies sex with death.

death, he had been seeking all his waking life. The conflicts within him had almost torn him in two; but his art is witness to the fact that he had never surrendered to his own despair. Always ashamed of being human, Strindberg rejected the external world so completely that he often bordered on insanity. But except for his most disordered years, he was usually able to convert pathology into a penetrating, powerful, and profound drama. This transformation was perhaps his most impressive achievement, for his art was in a constant state of flux, always yielding to the pressures from his unconscious. When he learned to control his misogyny in later years, and soften his resistance to the female principle, he faced life with the quietism of a Buddhist saint, sacrificing his defiant masculinity to the need for waiting, patience, ordeals, and expiation. But though his mood had changed and his spirit was chastened, his quarrel with God was never far from the surface. His rebellious discontent, expressed through a drama of perpetual opposition, had simply found its way into a dissatisfaction with the essence of life itself. Strindberg left instructions before he died that his tomb be inscribed with the motto of *Crimes and Crimes:* AVE CRUX SPES UNICA. But in view of his lifelong unrest and uncertainty, and his inability to commit himself to any particular creed, a more appropriate epitaph might have been the final lines from his last play, *The Great Highway:*

> Here Ishmael rests, the son of Hagar
> whose name was once called Israel,
> because he fought a fight with God,
> and did not cease to fight until laid low,
> defeated by His almighty goodness.
> O Eternal One! I'll not let go Thy hand,
> Thy hard hand, except Thou bless me.
> Bless me, Your creature, who suffers,
> Suffers Your sundering gift of life!
> Me first, who suffers most —
> Whose most painful torment was this —
> I could not be the one I longed to be!

With his work in our hands, it is perfectly clear that this rebel's eternal struggle with God is the key to his greatness. And it is the glory of his art that, despite his perpetual dissatisfaction with himself, few could wish him to be anyone other than who he was.

IV

ANTON CHEKHOV

Since Anton Chekhov is the gentlest, the subtlest, and the most dispassionate of all the great modern dramatists, it is open to argument whether he properly belongs in this discussion at all. I believe that his title as a rebel playwright can be effectually — if only partially — established; even this, however, remains to be proved. Certainly, the surface of Chekhov's art is not promising evidence of his rebellious inclinations. A seemingly arbitrary arrangement of landscape, character details, aimless dialogue, silences, shifting rhythms, and poetic mood, this surface constitutes the most convincing attempt at dramatic verisimilitude in the entire modern theatre; and rather than being ruffled by the energies of dissent, it strikes many observers as singularly smooth and placid. On the other hand, the Chekhovian surface is deceptive, and for all its thickness and texture, it is not impenetrable. Beneath lie depths of theatricality, moral fervor, and revolt; and between the surface and this substratum there is a constant ironic tension. This does not mean, however, that the Chekhovian surface can be ignored; it is much too essential to the wholeness and harmony of his art to be considered a mere subterfuge. In seeking to understand Chekhov's inner motives and intentions, we must be careful not to slight his more obvious aesthetic achievements; in trying to unearth the sources of his revolt, we must dig gently lest we unsettle that delicate balance where reality and rebellion coexist in perfect poise and equilibrium.

For Chekhov's revolt takes an entirely different form than anything we have yet considered. It is revolt by indirection — muted, objectified, dispassionate. Ibsen and Strindberg, both nourished on a revolutionary Romanticism, were occupied with the friction between their *personal* rebelliousness and the opposing forces of the social, religious, and metaphysical reality. But Chekhov, excluding personal affirmations entirely, is totally uninterested in an even indirectly auto-biographical art. As well as being the most modest and unassuming of men ("Forgive me," he begs Suvorin in a characteristic tone, "for forcing my personality on you"), Chekhov is the most impersonal of playwrights. And rather than quarreling with the reality principle, he is content to make reality the sum and substance of his art. Thus, Chekhov uses the drama neither as a vehicle for individualistic self-realization (Ibsen) nor as a means of exorcistic self-expression (Strindberg) but rather as a form for depicting that fluid world beyond the self, with the author functioning only as an impartial witness.

This sounds like Naturalism, and, indeed, Chekhov (in the early part of his career at least) usually defines his aims according to Naturalistic principles. "Literature is called artistic," he writes in 1887, "when it depicts life as it actually is. Its aim is absolute and honest truth." Elsewhere, he declares that the writer must be "as objective as a chemist," renouncing "every subjective attitude" in recapturing the quality of "life as it is." In his resistance to subjective Romanticism, Chekhov goes even further. He asserts that fictional characters must have an existence completely independent of an author's personal judgments and opinions. As he writes in 1888:

The artist should not be a judge of his characters or of what they say, but only an objective observer. I heard a confused, indecisive talk by two Russians on pessimism and so must convey this conversation in the same form in which I heard it, but it is up to the jury, i.e., the readers, to give it an evaluation. My job is only to be talented, i.e., to be able to throw light upon some figures and speak their language.

The job of being talented, then, consists in being an ideal eavesdropper — a neutral court reporter who communicates facts to a "jury" without distortion or comment: "Let the jury pass judgment on them," he adds, two years later, "it is my business solely to show them as they are." This is the language of the literary scientist (Strindberg and Ibsen each made similar scientific claims in the course of their careers), and Chekhov certainly earns his right to consider himself a scientific writer. Whatever modifications occur in his aesthetic creed, he never abandons his selfless devotion to the natural nor his commitment to "absolute and honest truth."

Yet, Chekhov is not really a Naturalist at all. Despite his detachment — despite his extraordinary capacity for imitating reality — he cannot entirely suppress his personal attitudes or refrain from judging his characters. His plays reflect both his sympathy for human suffering and his outrage at human absurdity, alternating between moods of wistful pathos and flashes of ironic humor which disqualify them from being mere slices of life. For if Chekhov is a detached realist, permitting life to proceed according to its own rules, he is also an engaged moralist, arranging reality in a particular way in order to evoke some comment on it: "When I write," he affirms in 1890, "I count upon my reader fully, assuming that he himself will add the subjective elements that are lacking in the telling." Chekhov the moralist hovers in the depths of his plays, expressing himself through a hidden action which sometimes breaks into melodrama and a satiric attack which sometimes bursts into farce. But however subterranean he may be, the moralist is always dictating character, action, and theme, while the realist is reworking these so as to exclude whatever seems mannered, subjective, or unnaturally theatrical. As David Magarshack has correctly observed, even Chekhov's Naturalist aesthetic changes later in his career, for his concern with "life as it is" is eventually modified by his growing conviction that "life as it is" is life as it should *not* be.[1]

[1] Actually, Magarshack asserts that Chekhov developed a concept of "life as it should be," but this suggests a more concrete attitude towards the future than Chekhov ever displayed. Chekhov never formulated a program for social, political, or religious change, and it was against his principles to introduce such a program into his plays. Magarshack tries to support his argument by quoting the following letter which Chekhov wrote to Suvorin in 1892: "The best

This conviction, as we shall see later, is the basis for Chekhov's revolt. But before examining the particulars of this revolt, it might be wise to investigate wherein Chekhov differs from the rebel tradition, as represented by Ibsen and Strindberg. For it is largely Chekhov's resistance to the Romantic drama that determines the unique form of his own, and that gives his own rebellion its special poignancy and originality.

It is clear, first of all, that Chekhov's antipathy to subjective rebellion strongly affects his attitudes towards dramatic form. Ibsen and Strindberg, occupied with finding new postures by which to dramatize their changing relations to the outside world, are both singular for their formal experimentation. But Chekhov's forms are fixed. Shunning self-dramatization, he seems more concerned with refining an unchanging vision of objective reality — generally embodied in the same class of characters, the same kind of plot, and the same homogeneous structure; the four-act realistic play. Magarshack distinguishes Chekhov's work into "direct action" plays (*Platonov, Ivanov, The Wood Demon*) and "indirect action" plays (*The Seagull, Uncle Vanya, The Three Sisters, The Cherry Orchard*), but although this distinction is extremely valuable in suggesting how Chekhov made his conflicts more and more recessive, it indicates a refinement of technique rather than a radical revision of form. As a matter of fact, Chekhov's first and last full-length plays show more formal consist-

---

[Classical writers] are realists and depict life as it is, but because every line is permeated, as with a juice, by a consciousness of an aim, you feel in addition to life as it is, also life as it should be. . . . But what about us? We depict life as it is, but we refuse to go a step further. We have neither near nor remote aims and our souls are as flat and bare as a billiard table. We have no politics, we do not believe in revolution, we deny the existence of God, we are not afraid of ghosts. . . . But he who wants nothing, hopes for nothing, and fears nothing cannot be an artist." This passage shows Chekhov's desire for a higher artistic purpose than mere representation, but it hardly proves that he possessed any idea of "life as it should be." Quite the contrary, it indicates Chekhov's awareness that his modern skepticism has destroyed, for him, the possibility of any political or religious idealism. I disagree with Magarshack on this and related issues, but I am deeply indebted to his perceptive study, *Chekhov the Dramatist*.

ency than any two successive works of Ibsen or Strindberg: his tools get sharper, but his materials remain essentially the same. In trying to weave a convincing illusion of reality, Chekhov applies his technical resources to the ruthless excision of the false and the melodramatic rather than to the discovery of new modes of dramatic art. After writing *The Cherry Orchard,* he boasts — significantly — not that the play is a formal breakthrough but that there is "not a single pistol shot in it."

Though it is dangerous to seek his opinions in his work, it is possible that Chekhov's attitudes towards formal experimentation are expressed in *The Seagull* — a play which deals, to a large extent, with the function of the creative artist. In the dream play of Treplev — a budding Symbolist playwright who travels "a picturesque route without a definite goal" — Chekhov may be satirizing the fashionable experiments of the Maeterlinckian avant-garde who "depict life not as it is, and not as it ought to be, but as we see it in our dreams." This, at least, is Treplev's artistic credo, and one of the purposes of the play is to bring him to some realization of the vanity of his experiments: "I come more and more to realize that it is not a question of new and old forms, but that what matters is that a man should write without thinking of forms at all, write because it springs freely from his soul." We may safely assume that Chekhov approached the drama this way: trusting that by expressing his vision honestly, the proper form would evolve of itself. Technically, of course, such an approach created tremendous problems. For the drama, by its very nature, demands compactness and emotional climaxes, and Chekhov had to learn how to recreate life on the stage in a natural, yet ordered and interesting manner. Chekhov's solution for this dilemma, one of the great technical achievements of the modern stage, was to achieve a synthesis between theatricality and reality, guiding events which seem to have no visible means of propulsion, and developing a form which seems to be no form at all. Through conspicuous theatrical experimentation, the author becomes more important than his materials, and Chekhov was determined to avoid even such indirect manifestations of his personality.

Reluctant to signal his presence through the manipulation of form, Chekhov is even more reluctant to do so through his characters. All his plays proceed without *raisonneurs* or author's surrogates, and his mature work even lacks clear-cut central characters: the four major dramas are group portraits of rural middle-class life from which individuals occasionally detach themselves for solos, duets and trios without ever assuming the prominence of a protagonist. Chekhov, for obvious reasons, cannot identify with any character enough to make him central; but even if he could, the character would undoubtedly remain firmly unheroic. For unlike Ibsen — who also tried to create ensemble plays about average contemporary types, but who could never quite do without a protagonist — Chekhov has no secret admiration for heroic behavior. In fact, he finds conventional dramatic heroes to be inflated, romantic, and melodramatic, which is to say, out of keeping with observable behavior:

The demand is made that the hero and heroine should be dramatically effective [he writes]. But in life people do not shoot themselves, or hang themselves, or fall in love, or deliver themselves of clever sayings every minute. They spend most of their time eating, drinking, running after women or men, talking nonsense. It is therefore necessary that this should be shown on the stage. A play ought to be written in which the people should come and go, dine, talk of the weather, or play cards, not because the author wants it but because that is what happens in real life. Life on the stage should be as it really is, and the people, too, should be as they are and not on stilts.

Chekhov, therefore, removes the "stilts," observing his characters in the trivial and commonplace routine of everyday life, and seeking the ordinary gesture even in the lives of the most gifted men.[2]

---

[2] Chekhov, like so many modern dramatists, was attacked for refusing to idealize his characters. His reply is instructive: "I've often been blamed, even by Tolstoi, for writing about trifles, for not having any positive heroes — revolutionists, Alexanders of Macedon. . . . But where am I to get them? I would be happy to have them! Our life is provincial, the cities are unpaved, the villages poor, the masses abused. In our youth, we all chirp rapturously like sparrows on a dung heap, but when we are forty, we are already old and begin to think about death. Fine heroes we are!"

He also dispenses with villains. Chekhov's plays are not without malevolent figures, but the author invariably emphasizes their more commonplace characteristics. This assault on conventional character categories is a conscious intention, and he expresses pride whenever he achieves it. After writing *Ivanov,* for example, he boasts: "There is not a single villain or angel in my play (though I did not resist the temptation of putting in a few buffoons)." For while buffoons are perfectly compatible with Chekhov's ironic sense of life, heroes and villains are the stereotypes of melodrama, a genre he particularly detested. Chekhov, in fact, often ridicules the hero-villain mystique which he had inherited from the traditional stage, primarily by contrasting stereotyped concepts of character with more natural and human ones. In *Ivanov,* for example, the play revolves around the various factitious interpretations of Ivanov's behavior. Sasha, an impressionable young girl, and Dr. Lvov, a narrow uncompromising man, both classify him according to literary conventions: Sasha sees Ivanov as a Hamlet, a superior man to be worshiped and redeemed, while Dr. Lvov regards him as an inhumane and selfish Tartuffe, to be punished and exposed. Chekhov's point, however, is that Ivanov is neither a hero nor a villain but simply an ordinary weak man, consumed with self-pity and subject to neurotic impulses beyond his control.[3]

This suggests another reason for Chekhov's antagonism to heroes and villains: his more sophisticated and inward conception of character. Ibsen and Strindberg, influenced by the dualistic Christian tradition, sometimes conceive an action in terms of good and evil, and divide their characters accordingly: Brand vs. the Mayor; Doctor Stockmann vs. Peter Stockmann; the Captain vs. Laura. Chekhov, scorning conventional moral categories, is more in the tradition of the Greeks as Westernized by Racine, because he envisions a world where neither good nor evil exist as external forces but rather manifest themselves in confused internal struggles. In consequence, Che-

---

[3] In a letter to Korelenko, Chekhov describes Ivanov in this way: "There are thousands of Ivanovs. He is a most ordinary man, not a hero at all. . . ." And in a letter to Suvorin around the same time, he ridicules the characters in the play who try to interpret Ivanov according to prejudices or stereotypes.

khov's characters — like Racine's Phèdre (and Turgenyev's Natalia in *A Month in the Country*) — often seem in conflict less with some other character than with their own weak wills; and like the characters of many Russian novels and plays, they are so self-involved that they often appear not to be listening to each other. (The common Russian interpretation of Hamlet as a victim of his own indecisive nature suggests a national tendency towards the internalizing of conflicts.) Actually, Chekhov has not abandoned the external conflict; it is proceeding relentlessly in the depths of his plays. But on the surface, he seems to be analyzing the psychological feelings of his characters, as they vacillate between hysteria and fatigue, and struggle with uncontrollable unconscious impulses.

Another sign of Chekhov's antipathy to subjective rebellion is his reluctance to introduce his own discursive ideas or philosophical concepts into his plays. Ibsen and Strindberg can occasionally be accused of dramatic ventriloquism — Chekhov almost never. For while Chekhov may, indeed, support some of the opinions reiterated from play to play (those, for example, on the therapeutic power of work),[4] these opinions never seem like personal utterances; they are the exclusive property of the persons who hold them, and serve primarily to reveal character. As for the characters themselves, Chekhov is scrupulous in keeping them separate from himself. They are born, as he tells Suvorin in a famous letter, "not out of ocean spray, or preconceived ideas, not out of 'intellectuality,' and not by sheer accident. They are the result of observation and the study of life."

Thus, it is a dangerous practice to try to pry loose Chekhov's intellectual position from his plays, for he is totally unconcerned with conceptual ideas. As the perceptive Professor Kovalevsky wrote after a meeting with the playwright: "He has not a trace of so-called philosophical training. . . . As for his own philosophy, I wouldn't say he had any. His attitude towards those things in Russia called *burning*

---

4 Chekhov's letters are full of observations on the importance of keeping busy. He occasionally reflects, however, on the pleasures of idleness, too: "Life disagrees with philosophy, there is no pleasure without idleness; only the useless is pleasurable." The conflicting claims of work and idleness — of use and beauty — are, of course, one of the central conflicts in his plays.

questions was indefinite." Ibsen has his Kierkegaard and Strindberg his Nietzsche, but Chekhov cries "To hell with the philosophy of the great of this world!" — and locates his own intelligence in the fact that "I don't lie to myself and don't cover my own emptiness with other people's intellectual rags. . . ." Always trying to defend his work against those "who look for tendencies between the lines," he dissociates himself from all ideologies except the "ideology" of art: "I am not a liberal and not a conservative, not an evolutionist, nor a monk, nor indifferent to the world. I would like to be a free artist — and that is all. . . ." [5]

As a free artist, Chekhov will introduce political, social, and philosophical discussions into his work, because these are threads in the fabric of reality. But he is careful neither to take sides nor to hint at solutions. "It is the duty of the judge to put the questions to the jury correctly," he observes, employing his favorite courtroom metaphor, "and it is for members of the jury to make up their minds, each according to his taste." Even these unanswered questions, however, are subordinate to Chekhov's careful presentation of objective reality. For just as he tries to protect his characters from conventional moralistic interpretations of their behavior, so he tries to preserve their integrity as complicated human beings against narrow ideological definitions of them as political animals.[6] Thus, Chekhov will provide his characters with class roles, political convictions, and philosophic atti-

[5] Gorky — as Ernest J. Simmons notes in his scholarly biography *Chekhov* — observed these qualities in Chekhov after his initial meeting with him: "You are, I believe, the first free man I've ever met, one who does not worship anything. How fine it is that you regard literature as your first and primary business in life." Though Gorky found Chekhov's dedication "fine," however, he was himself a much more political writer, and Chekhov often chided him for his tendentiousness.

[6] Simmons writes that, politically, Chekhov was "a gradualist with a pronounced sense of measure" — one who sympathized with the revolutionary ferment in Russia but who was profoundly suspicious of organized revolutionary movements. Chekhov believed in change not through parties but rather through gifted individuals: "I believe in individuals," he writes in 1899. "I see salvation in individual personalities scattered over all Russia — they may be intellectuals, or peasants — for although they may be few, they have strength." In this, Chekhov is rather like Ibsen.

tudes, but he will never completely define them by these elements, even when they so wish to define themselves. Much of Chekhov's humor, in fact, proceeds from the ironical contrast between a character's opinions and his behavior, as if the political animal and the human being were somehow mutually incompatible.

Chekhov is equally adverse to religious affirmations: he is, perhaps, the most secular playwright in the entire theatre of revolt. "Long ago I lost my faith," he writes to Diaghilev. "It is with perplexity that I look upon religious people among the intelligentsia." Having lost God, Ibsen and Strindberg sought something to take His place; but in Chekhov the messianic impulse seems never to have awakened. Instead of dramatizing the death of God, Chekhov is content merely to suggest the metaphysical void and to analyze its consequences on human character. In his plays, therefore, one feels a vast emptiness, expressed through the melancholy aimlessness of his characters, but no sense of transcendence whatever. Because he is a medical man, Chekhov seems to have little belief in radical cures. Writing in 1892, he affirms that he is a "true physician," and, therefore, "fully, almost cynically, convinced that from this life one can expect only the worst." This pessimism does not reflect back on the author, since Chekhov, excluding himself from his plays, does not number himself among his sick patients. But this doctor, nevertheless, is very helpless — as helpless as the doctors in his fiction. Confronted with an incurable disease — a disease proceeding from loss of faith, of hope, of value — he is unable to prescribe anything more effective than valerian drops. Thus, he will lecture the patient about his responsibility for his present state of health, but he can only suggest a few nostrums as preventatives against despair. For while Chekhov's profound humanity makes him sympathetic, his tough intelligence tells him there is little hope.

In all these ways, then — the modesty of form, the sophistication of character, the subordination of idea — Chekhov diverges from the modern tradition of dramatic revolt. And in each case, we find his disciplined impersonality in sharp contrast with the engaged, subjective dissent of Ibsen and Strindberg. As suggested earlier, though,

Chekhov's impersonality is a surface characteristic; and beneath this surface is a satiric, admonitory moralist, shaping, selecting, and even judging in much the same way as the other rebel dramatists. Chekhov the realist pretends to have no other aim than the faithful representation of reality; but Chekhov the moralist is always conscious of a higher purpose than mere imitation. In the same year, in fact, that he writes "The artist should not be a judge of his characters," he amends this to "The artist . . . must pass judgment *only on what he understands.*" And defending himself against the charge of purposelessness, he adds:

The artist observes, chooses, guesses, combines — these acts in themselves presuppose a problem. . . . If one denies problem and purpose in creative work, then one must concede that the artist is creating undesignedly, without intention, temporarily deranged. . . .

You are right to require a conscious attitude from the artist towards his work, but you mix up two ideas: *the solution of the problem and the correct presentation of the problem.* Only the latter is obligatory for the artist.

(Letter to Suvorin, 1888)

Chekhov, in short, "observes, chooses, guesses, combines" for a special purpose — not to remedy particular evils but to represent them accurately — and it is through this representation that he exercises, indirectly, the moral function of his art.

Chekhov prefers always to keep his moralism underground; but he admits it openly, at least once, when he breaks out to the writer, Alexander Tikhonov:

All I wanted was to say honestly to people: "Have a look at yourselves and see how bad and dreary your lives are!" The important thing is that people should realize that, for when they do, they will most certainly create another and better life for themselves. I will not live to see it, but I know that it will be quite different, quite unlike our present life. And so long as this different life does not exist, I shall go on saying to people again and again: "Please, understand that your life is bad and dreary!"

Despite the fact that an admission like this is rather uncharacteristic of Chekhov, what he states here is implicit in all his major plays. Russian life is "bad and dreary." It can lead only to decay, dissolution, and destruction. And if it is not reformed through some effort of the will, an avalanche will come to clear it all away.

Thus, Chekhov's revolt is directed against the quality of contemporary Russian life. But it is double, taking two, seemingly contrary directions. First, and most obviously, he is in rebellion against the indolence, vacuity, irresponsibility, and moral inertia of his characters — and, since these characters are typical of provincial upper-class society, also against the social stratum that they represent. Chekhov's judgment on these characters is often suggested by his extra-dramatic comments on them. Ivanov is a "whining hero" who lacks "iron in the blood"; Treplev "has no definite aims and that has led to his destruction." In his *Notebooks,* he observes: "It seems to me that we — worn-out, stereotyped, banal people — have grown quite moldy. . . . There is a life of which we know nothing. Great events will take us unawares, like sleeping fairies." Here Chekhov includes himself in his indictment, and Princess Toumanova has emphasized, in her biography (*Anton Chekhov: The Voice of Twilight Russia*), how much Chekhov suffered from the laziness, the sense of drift, and, especially, the boredom that afflict his dramatic characters. Yet, Chekhov was appalled by these feelings ("I despise laziness," he wrote, "just as I despise weakness and sluggishness of the emotions"), and successfully overcame them through meaningful work. Not so his provincial aristocrats, however, who have become idle and useless — charming aesthetes with no aim in life beyond their own satisfaction — whose directionless careers have broken their wills.

In one sense, though, Chekhov does align himself on the side of his characters: that is, insofar as they constitute the last stronghold of the enlightenment against the spreading mediocrity, vulgarity, and illiteracy of Russian life. And it is against these forces of darkness — the environment of his plays — that Chekhov directs his most vigorous revolt.[7] Chekhov himself was passionately addicted to "culture"

---

[7] Simmons observes that the "sentiment of revolt" began to grow in Chekhov around 1898, when it is expressed in a group of stories dealing with "the aspiration for freedom, freedom from all the stuffy conventions of life, from the regi-

— by which he meant not intellectuality (he finds the intelligentsia "hypocritical, false, hysterical, poorly educated, and indolent"), but rather a mystical, indefinable compound of humanity, decency, intelligence, education, accomplishment, and will. And it is by these standards that he usually measures the value of human beings. In a long letter to his brother Nikolai, Chekhov begins by accusing him of an "utter lack of culture," and then proceeds to define the characteristics of truly cultured people in a very significant manner. Among other things, he notes, such people "respect the human personality and are therefore always forebearing, gentle, courteous, and compliant. They will overlook noise, and cold, and overdone meat, and witticisms, and the presence of strangers in their house. . . . They are sincere and fear untruth like the very devil. . . . They do not make fools of themselves in order to arouse sympathy. . . . They are not vain. . . . They develop an aesthetic sense." Cautioning Nikolai "not to fall below the level of your environment," Chekhov counsels him: "What you need is constant work, day and night, eternal reading, study, will power."

Chekhov, who had peasant blood himself, foresaw that cultured individuals might arise from any class of society, however humble, but he did not (like Tolstoi) idealize the peasantry, and the crude utilitarianism of the middle class filled him with disgust. If he is aggrieved by any general fact of Russian life it is the cancerous growth of slovenliness, filth, stupidity, and cruelty among the mass of men; and if he despises the sluggishness and indolence of his upper-class characters, then this is because they, too, are gradually being overwhelmed by the tide, lacking the will to stem it. For if the Russian gentry represents beauty without use, the Russian environment is characterized by use without beauty; and those with the necessary will power are often utterly without the necessary culture cr education. The conflict between the cultured upper classes and their stupefying environment — between the forces of light and the forces of

---

mentation of authority, the imbecility of functionaries, from everything that tyrannizes and debases the human spirit . . ." (*Chekhov*, p. 425).

darkness — provides the basic substance of most of Chekhov's plays, as he alternates between the two sides of his double revolt.

Thus, while David Magarshack somewhat overstates the case by saying that Chekhov's mature plays are dramas of "courage and hope," he is perfectly right to emphasize the moral purpose behind Checkhov's imitation of reality. Chekhov never developed any program for "life as it should be." Like most great artists, his revolt is mainly negative. And it is a mistake to interpret the occasional expressions of visionary optimism which conclude his plays as evidence of "courage and hope" (they are more like desperate defenses against nihilism and despair). Yet, it is also wrong to assume that Chekhov shares the pessimism which pervades his plays or the despondency of his defeated characters. Everyone who knew him testifies to his gaiety, humor, and buoyancy, and if he always expected the worst, he always hoped for the best. Chekhov the realist was required to transcribe accurately the appalling conditions of provincial life without false affirmations or baseless optimism; but Chekhov the moralist has a sneaking belief in change. In short, Chekhov expresses his revolt not by depicting the ideal, which would have violated his sense of reality, and not by merely imitating the real, which would have violated his sense of moral purpose, but by criticizing the real at the same time that he is representing it. He will not comment on reality; he will permit reality to comment on itself. And so it is that while the surface of his plays seems drenched with *tedium vitae* and spiritual vapors, the depths are charged with energy and dissent.

I have already described some of the characteristics of the top layer of Chekhov's art; now let us look at the deeper layers, for it is there that Chekhov's revolt can be most clearly detected. As I have already suggested, this revolt takes two forms. It is directed 1) against the characters, and 2) against the environment, or the forces that are dragging the characters under. For the first type of revolt, Chekhov generally uses farce; for the second, melodrama.

Both farce and melodrama are highly theatrical modes of the kind Chekhov deplores as unnatural; nevertheless, he secretly uses them as much as any of his contemporaries, though they are generally carefully disguised. Both David Magarshack and Eric Bentley have drawn our attention to the farce element in Chekhov's drama, generally ignored by Stanislavsky in production and overlooked by inattentive readers too much occupied with Chekhovian pathos. A superb vaudevillian, Chekhov uses farce freely and openly in his one-act sketches: "In one act things," he advises Suvorin, "you must write absolute nonsense — there lies their strength." In his full-length work, however, farce functions less for its nonsense value than for ironic effect. Chekhov's plays, of course, are teeming with buffoons. In fact, with the exception of his innocent young heroines (Nina, Sonia, Irina, Anya), almost all of Chekhov's characters have their clownish side. Treplev's stammering confusion after his quarrels with his mother; Vanya's hopelessly bungled attempt at murder; Trofimov's tumble down the stairs after his outraged departure from Madame Ranevsky — these are only a few examples of how Chekhov will deflate his characters in order to render a comic judgment on them. For Chekhov uses farce as a satiric device, to alienate us from a character so that we will not become too sympathetically involved with his spurious self-pity or melancholy posturing.

More interesting, because more subtly hidden, is Chekhov's use of melodrama. And I refer not only to melodramatic devices. (Many observers have already commented on Chekhov's weakness for effective act curtains, often brought down after a pistol shot: a killing, a suicide, or an attempted murder occurs in every play except *The Cherry Orchard,* where a sound like a broken harp string and the noise of an axe replace the zing of bullets.)[8] I refer, rather, to Chekhov's use of the melodramatic formula. For each of his mature plays, and especially *The Cherry Orchard,* is constructed on the same melodramatic pattern: the conflict between a despoiler and his

[8] Magarshack elaborates on this and related theatrical techniques, such as the Scribean love triangle which is central to every Chekhovian play except *The Cherry Orchard* (and even there it appears in the comic underplot involving Yasha, Dunyasha, and Epihodov). We should also note Chekhov's persistent use of the interrupted love scene — a device he borrowed from Turgenyev. Only the most delicate handling of this device prevents it from seeming stagey (in *Ivanov,* it *is* stagey).

victims — while the action of each follows the same melodramatic development: the gradual dispossession of the victims from their rightful inheritance.

This external conflict can be more easily observed if we strip away everything extraneous to the (hidden) plot, ignoring for a moment Chekhov's explorations of motive and character. In *The Seagull*, Trigorin seduces and ruins Nina; Madame Arkadina spiritually dispossesses Treplev, her Hamlet-like son. In *Uncle Vanya*, Yelena steals Sonia's secret love, Astrov, while Serebryakov robs Sonia of her inheritance and produces in Vanya a soul-killing disillusionment. In *The Three Sisters*, Natasha gradually evicts the Prozorov family from their provincial house. And in *The Cherry Orchard*, Lopahin evicts Madame Ranevsky and Gaev, taking over their orchard and turning it into summer estates. In each case, the central act of dispossession is symbolized through some central image, representing what is being ravished, stolen, or destroyed. In *The Seagull*, it is the bird which Treplev kills, identified with Nina who is also destroyed by a man with "nothing better to do." In *Uncle Vanya*, it is the forest, "a picture of gradual and unmistakable degeneration," associated with the lives of the family, degenerating through sheer inertia. In *The Three Sisters*, it is the Prozorov house, eventually hollowed out by Natasha as though by a nest of termites. And in *The Cherry Orchard*, of course, it is the famous orchard, hacked to pieces by the commercial axe. With the possible exception of *The Seagull*, each play dramatizes the triumph of the forces of darkness over the forces of enlightenment, the degeneration of culture in the crude modern world.

What prevents us from seeing these melodramatic configurations is the extraordinary way in which they have been concealed. Technically, Chekhov's most effective masking device is to bury the plot (Magarshack's concept of the "indirect action"), so that violent acts and emotional climaxes occur offstage or between the acts. In this way, Chekhov manages to avoid the melodramatic crisis and to obscure the external conflict, ducking the event and concentrating on the dénouement. Secondly, Chekhov concludes the action before the conventional melodramatic reversal — the triumphant victory of virtue over vice; in its place, he substitutes a reversal of his own invention, in which the defeated characters, shuffling off the old life, begin to look forward to the new. Most important, however, he refuses, as we have already noted, to cast his characters in conventional hero-villain roles. In the buried plot, Chekhov's despoilers act while his victims suffer; but by subordinating plot to characterization, Chekhov diverts our attention from process to motive, and makes us suspend our judgment of the action. Thus, while Trigorin's impregnation and desertion of Nina are the familiar tricks of the dastardly Victorian seducer, he is too flabby and submissive to qualify as a villain,[9] and, anyway, his rejection of Nina takes place between the acts. Similarly, Serebryakov seems more like a harmless, cranky hypochondriac than a malevolent figure; and Lopahin is firmly characterized as a helpful, purposeful, sympathetic friend of the family. Only Natasha, in *The Three Sisters,* can be accused of deliberate villainy; but Chekhov has carefully buried her more repulsive qualities under other character traits in order to obscure her baleful influence on the Prozorovs.

Chekhov also dilutes the melodramatic pathos by qualifying our sympathy for the victims. In most cases, they seem largely responsible for whatever happens to them. This is not to say, as some have said, that we do not sympathize with their unhappy lot, but since Chekhov highlights their inertia, irresponsibility, and waste, we also deplore their helpless inability to resist their fate. Thus, we remember not only Trigorin's bored amorousness and Arkadina's selfishness, but Nina's naïveté and Treplev's aimlessness; not only Serebryakov's fraudulent pomposity and Yelena's indolence, but Vanya's dependency and Astrov's alcoholism; not only Natasha's vulgarity and greed but the Prozorovs' futile illusions about Moscow; not only Lopahin's triumph but Madame Ranevsky's ineffectuality and extravagance. In each case, Chekhov — carefully balancing pathos with irony —

---

[9] In *My Life in Art,* Stanislavsky makes reference to this character as "the scoundrelly Lovelace Trigorin" — which suggests that he misinterpreted the role when he played it for the Moscow Art Theatre. Chekhov, at any rate, was dissatisfied with his performance, writing that "it sickened me to watch him."

avoids the stock responses of conventional theatre by deflecting the emphasis from the melodramatic to the natural and the atmospheric, wrapping layers of commonplace detail around extremely climactic events.

And this is precisely the effect that Chekhov aimed to achieve: "Let the things that happen on stage," he writes, "be just as complex and yet just as simple as they are in life. For instance, people are having a meal at the table, just having a meal, but at the same time their happiness is being created, or their lives are being smashed up." The placid surface of existence, then, is to be a masking device for his controlled manipulation of human fatality; the trivial course of the daily routine is to disguise his sense of process, development, and crisis. Chekhov is so successful in achieving these goals that Anglo-Saxon critics often condemn his plays as vague, actionless, and formless. Walter Kerr, in America, for example, finds them moody, nerveless, untheatrical, while Desmond MacCarthy, in England, complains that they "have no theme except disillusionment and an atmosphere of sighs, yawns, self reproaches, vodka, endless tea, and endless discussions." The stimulus for these superficial observations, of course, is Chekhov's extraordinary atmospheric power; and though producers, following Stanislavsky,[10] have tended to exaggerate Chekhov's use of rhythmic sound effects (scratching pens, guitar music, sneezes, songs, etc.), there is no question that Chekhov evokes, through these means, a poetic illusion of fluid reality.

On the other hand, as recent critics have emphasized, Chekhov's work has the tensile strength of a steel girder, the construction

[10] Stanislavsky's fondness for sound effects was always an amusing source of disagreement between him and the playwright. After Stanislavsky had introduced his usual noises into *The Cherry Orchard*, Chekhov remarked one day during a lull in rehearsal: "What fine quiet. How wonderful. We hear no birds, no dogs, no cuckoos, no owls, no clocks, no sleigh bells, no crickets." Stanislavsky thought these sound effects to be "realistic," but as Chekhov once remarked to Meyerhold, "The stage is art. There is a canvas of Kramskoi in which he wonderfully depicts human faces. Suppose he eliminated the nose of one of these faces and substituted a real one. The nose will be 'realistic,' but the picture will be spoiled." It is a pity that so many modern realists have followed Stanislavsky's approach to reality and not Chekhov's.

being so subtle that it is almost invisible. Thus, while his characters seem to exist in isolated pockets of vacancy, they are all integral parts of a close network of interlocking motives and effects. And thus, while the dialogue seems to wander aimlessly into discussions of cold samovars, the situation in Moscow, and the temperature of the earth, it is economically performing a great number of essential dramatic functions: revealing character, furthering the action, uncovering the theme, evoking in the spectators a mood identical with that of the characters, and diverting attention from the melodramatic events which are erupting under the smooth surface of life. Through this completely original and inimitable technique, Chekhov manages to exercise his function both as realist and moralist, and to express his resistance to modern life in enduring aesthetic form.

To illustrate the foregoing remarks, let us now examine two plays in some detail, each of which illuminates a different aspect of Chekhov's revolt. All four of Chekhov's mature works, of course, are masterpieces, but *The Three Sisters* and *The Cherry Orchard* are considered, by consensus, his highest achievements, from a thematic and technical point of view. And while they differ enough from each other to form an interesting contrast, they are both similar enough to his other plays to give us a comprehensive, if not thoroughly exhaustive, idea of Chekhov's dramatic approach.

The Three Sisters was completed at the beginning of 1901, four years after *Uncle Vanya*. It was written mostly in the Crimea, where Chekhov had retired to recuperate from the tuberculosis which was soon to prove fatal to him. One year before, he had published "In the Ravine," a short story with enough similarities to the play to suggest it might have been a preparatory sketch. The location of the story is a provincial village called Ukleyevo, so ordinary and banal that it is identified to visitors as the place "where the deacon ate all the caviare at the funeral" — nothing more stimulating has ever happened there. Yet, as usual with Chekhov, extraordinary events take place in this commonplace setting. The most important development, for our purposes, is the progress of the woman, Aksinya — married to one of the two sons of Tsybukin, an elderly, generous shopkeeper. Aksinya, contemptuous of the family, parades wantonly about the town in low-necked dresses, and is openly conducting an affair with a rich factory owner. When Tsybukin's unmarried son weds a girl named Lipa — a quiet, frightened, gentle peasant woman — Aksinya becomes intensely jealous; and when Lipa gives birth to a boy child, Aksinya scalds it with a ladle of boiling water, killing both the infant and the hopes of the family. Instead of being punished, however, Aksinya continues to flourish in the town, finally turning her father-in-law and his family out of their own house.

From this story, Chekhov apparently derived his idea for Natalya Ivanovna, the lustful, ambitious, and predatory woman who eventually disinherits the gentle Prozorovs — an action played out against the background of a provincial town so petty, vulgar, and boring that it has the power to degrade its most cultured inhabitants. *The Three Sisters* is richer, more complex, and more ambiguous than "In the Ravine." Chekhov smooths the melodramatic wrinkles of the story by toning down the adulterous villainy of Natasha-Aksinya; and he enriches the story by adding a military background and transforming the petty bourgeois Tsybukins into the leisured upper-class Prozorovs. But the basic outline is the same; and so is Chekhov's careful balancing of the internal and external influences on character, an element of all his mature work. In *Ivanov,* the decline of the hero was mostly determined from within, and Borkin's theory that "it's your environment that's killing you" was rejected as a thoughtless cliché. But in *The Three Sisters,* environment plays a crucial role in the gradual defeat of the central characters, while their own psychological failings are kept relatively muted.

The forces of evil, in fact, are quite inexorable in this work, making the Chekhovian pathos more dominant than usual. Chekhov, according to Stanislavsky, was amazed at the first reading of the play by the Art Theatre, because, in the producer's words, "he had written a happy comedy and all of us considered the play a tragedy and even wept over it." Stanislavsky is probably exaggerating Chekhov's response. Rather than considering it a "happy comedy," he was very careful to call *The Three Sisters* a "drama," the only such classification, as Magarshack notes, among his works. The play is certainly no tragedy, but it is the gloomiest Chekhov ever wrote. Certainly, the author introduces very little of his customary buffoonery. Though the play has its pantaloons, they are too implicated in the events of the house to evoke from us more than occasional smiles: Kuligin, for example, with his genial pedantry and maddening insensitivity to sorrow, is nevertheless a rather pathetic cuckold; and the alcoholic Tchebutykin, for all his absurdity, eventually develops into a withdrawn and nihilistic figure. Furthermore, an atmosphere of doom seems to permeate the household, lifted only during brief festive moments; and even these are quickly brought to an end by the ominous Natasha. Despite Magarshack's desire to read the play as "a *gay* affirmation of life," there is little that is gay or affirmative about it. Chekhov displays his usual impatience with the delusions of his central characters, but they are more clearly victims than most such figures. And while they undoubtedly are partially responsible for their fates (which explains why Chekhov did not want Stanislavsky's actors to grow maudlin over them), much of the responsibility belongs to Natasha, who represents the dark forces eating away at their lives.

For Natasha is the most malevolent figure Chekhov ever created — a pretentious bourgeois *arriviste* without a single redeeming trait. Everyone emphasizes her vulgarity, vengefulness, and lack of culture, and even Andrey, who leans over backwards to be fair, sees "something in her which makes her no better than some petty, blind, hairy animal. Anyway she is not a human being." Women, to be sure, often play a destructive role in Chekhov's plays. But while Madame Arkadina could easily have turned into a Strindberg heroine (she has the same desire to dominate men), and Yelena, that "charming bird of prey," bears a surface resemblance to Ibsen's Hilda Wangel, Chekhov usually resists the temptation to characterize them so baldly. Natasha, on the other hand, is unique in the blackness of her motives. She might be a member of the Hummel family of vampires: sucking up people's nourishment, breaking foundations, speculating in houses. She is a malignant growth in a benevolent organism and her final triumph, no matter how Chekhov tries to disguise it, is the triumph of pure evil. Despite the thick texture of the play, then, neatly woven into the tapestry is an almost invisible thread of action: the destruction of the Prozorovs by Natasha. From the moment she enters the house, at the end of Act I, to accept Andrey's proposal of marriage, until she has secured her control at the end of the play, the process of dispossession continues with relentless motion.

It takes place, however, by steady degrees. The dispossession begins when Andrey mortgages the house to the bank in order to pay his gambling debts, but Natasha, a much more dangerous adversary than a bank, takes over from there. Not only has she "grabbed all the money" (presumably the mortgage money), but she is engaged, throughout the play, in shifting the family from room to room, until she has finally shifted them out of the house entirely. Natasha's ambitions proceed under the guise of maternal solicitude and love of order; and never have such qualities seemed so thoroughly repellent. In the second act, she prepares to move Irina into Olga's room so that little Bobik will have a warmer nursery; in the third act, she prepares to evict Anfisa, the old family servant, because she has outlived her usefulness (Natasha's unfeeling utilitarianism is among her most inhuman traits); and in the last act — with Olga and Anfisa installed in a government flat and Irina having moved to a furnished room — she is preparing to move Andrey out of his room to make way for baby Sophie. Since Sophie is probably the child of Protopopov, Natasha's lover, the dispossession has been symbolically completed. It will not be long before it is literally completed, and Andrey, the last of the Prozorovs, is ejected from the house altogether.

Chekhov illustrates this process through a careful manipulation of the setting. The first three acts take place in interiors which grow progressively more confined; the third act being laid in the room of Olga and Irina, cramped with people, screens, and furniture. But the last act is laid outdoors. The exterior setting tells the story visually: the family is now out of their own home; Andrey pushes the pram around the house in widening circles; and Protopopov (never

seen) is comfortably installed *inside,* in the drawing room with
Natasha. Natasha, however, has not yet finished, for she is determined to violate the outdoors as well. Popping out of the house for
a moment, she expresses her determination to cut down the fir and
maple trees that Tusenbach admires so much, an act of despoliation
that foreshadows a similar act in *The Cherry Orchard.*

The contrast between Natasha and the Prozorovs is demon-
strated, as Magarshack has noted, in the episode of the green sash,
where Natasha revenges herself for an imaginary slight by critiz-
ing Irina's sash over three years later; and her vulgarity is amply
documented by her French affectations and her abuse of the servants.
An even better contrast is provided during the fire that is raging in
town at the beginning of the third act. In this scene, Chekhov sets
off Natasha's *parvenu* pretensions against the instinctive humanity
of the Prozorovs by comparing their attitudes towards the victims
of the conflagration. In accordance with Chekhov's description of
the cultured in his letter to Nikolai ("They will overlook . . . the
presence of strangers in the house"), the sisters generously offer
their hospitality to those without homes, but Natasha is more occupied
with fears that her children will catch some disease. When she considers the homeless, she thinks of them as objects to be patronized —
"One ought always to be ready to help the poor, it's the duty of the
rich" — and begins chattering about joining a committee for the
assistance of the victims, that impersonal, dehumanized approach
to charity invented by the middle class less out of generosity than
out of status-seeking and guilt.

Since the fire is an external crisis introduced to heighten (and at
the same time draw attention from) the crisis occurring within, it
also illustrates Natasha's destructive tendencies. The fire, as Magarshack has noted, is closely identified with that conflagration which
is destroying the Prozorov household; the fate of the victims anticipates that of the family (they are out on the street); and Natasha
symbolically links the two events. As Natasha marches through her
room with a candle, Masha suggests this link by saying: "She walks
about as though it were she had set fire to the town." But at the same

time that Natasha is a symbolic arsonist, she is also a symbolic fire extinguisher. "Always . . . on the lookout for fear something goes wrong," she stalks through the house, snuffing out candles — snuffing, too, all laughter and pleasure in the family. Pleading baby Bobik's health, she puts an end to the Carnival party; for like Serebryakov (who similarly throws cold water on the musical interlude planned by Yelena and Sonia in *Uncle Vanya*), she functions to extinguish joy, and to spread gloom and despair.

The conflict between Natasha and the Prozorovs, needless to say, is always kept very indistinct. Andrey and the sisters are either too polite or too deeply involved in their own problems to comment much on Natasha's activities, and while she and the family brush each other frequently throughout the play, they never break into open argument. Instead of dramatizing the Prozorovs' relations with Natasha, Chekhov defines them against the background of their surroundings, concentrating on the wasting away of this potentially superior family in a coarse and sordid environment. On the other hand, Natasha is really the personification of this environment — a native of the town who lives in the house — and so both she and the environment are actually related forces converging on the same objects. Thus, the surface and the depths of *The Three Sisters* follow parallel lines of development. The gradual dispossession of the Prozorovs by Natasha is the buried action, while their gradual deterioration in their surroundings proceeds above. In each case, the conflict between culture and vulgarity provides the basic theme.

This conflict is clear from the opening lines of the play, when the three sisters — a doleful portrait in blue, black, and white — first reveal their dissatisfaction with the present by reflecting, nostalgically, on the life of the past. A highly educated Moscow family, the Prozorovs were geographically transplanted eleven years before when their father, a brigadier general, took command of an artillery unit in the provinces. As the action proceeds, Chekhov shows how the family, following the father's death, has tried to adapt to their new surroundings: Olga by teaching school, Masha by marrying the local schoolmaster, Irina by working in a variety of civil jobs,

Andrey by marrying Natasha and joining the Rural Board. All these attempts at assimilation are, however, unsuccessful. And regarding their present life as a kind of involuntary banishment, they are now uncomfortably suspended between their idealization of the past and resentment over their depressing provincial existence.

The past, of course, is closely identified with Moscow, seen through a haze of memory as a city of sun, flowers, refinement, and sensibility — in short, of *culture* — as opposed to the cold, stupidity, and dreariness of their town. Their vision of Moscow, like their hopes of returning, is, of course, delusionary — an idle dream with which we are meant to have little patience — and their endless complaining is neither courageous nor attractive. Still, their shared apprehension of the pettiness, drabness, and conformity of their provincial district is terrifyingly accurate. As Andrey describes it (Act IV):

Our town has been going on for two hundred years — there are a hundred thousand people living in it; and there is not one who is not like the rest, not one saint in the past, or the present, nor one man of learning, not one artist, not one man in the least remarkable who could inspire envy or a passionate desire to imitate him. . . . And an overwhelmingly vulgar influence weighs upon the children, and the divine spark is quenched in them and they become the same sort of pitiful dead creatures, all exactly alike, as their fathers and mothers. . . .

In this speech — which may have been intended as an attack on the audience (Chekhov stipulated that Andrey, while speaking it, "must almost threaten the audience with his fists") — Andrey is clearly expressing Chekhov's revolt against the appalling conditions of the provincial town.[11] It is a place in which any man of sensibility is

---

[11] Chekhov had already expressed these views about provincial life in his story "My Life" (1897), where his protagonist has a speech very much like Andrey's: "How is it that in not one of these houses has there been anyone from whom I might have learned to live? . . . Our town has existed for hundreds of years, and all that time it has not produced one man of service to the country — not one. . . . It's a useless, unnecessary town, which not one soul would regret if it suddenly sank through the earth." Chekhov's dislike of the provinces probably stemmed from his feelings towards his birthplace, Tagonrog, which he described as "dirty, drab, empty, lazy, and illiterate."

bound to feel "a stranger, and lonely"; for it is without culture, without art, without humanity, without excellence; and its "overwhelmingly vulgar influence" has the power to brutalize all who live within its circumference. The influence of the town, in its most extreme state, is shown on Tchebutykin, who takes refuge from his disillusionment in alcohol and newspapers and from his professional incompetence in a profound nihilism: "Perhaps it only seems to us that we exist, but really we are not here at all." For just as the Prozorovs respond to their surroundings by weaving the illusion of Moscow, so Tchebutykin responds by declaring that nothing in the world is real, and that "it doesn't matter."

The Prozorovs are aware that the town is brutalizing them, too, which accounts for their growing despair. Masha — dressed in black to illustrate her depression — is perpetually bored; Irina is perpetually tired; and Olga suffers from perpetual headaches. As for Andrey, their gifted brother, he trails his life along with no apparent aim, followed by the senile Ferrapont, as by an ignominious Nemesis. In this lifeless atmosphere, they are drying up, their culture falling from them like shreds of dead skin — each, in turn, will ask, "Where has it all gone?" For whatever might have made them seem unusual in Moscow is here merely a superfluous layer — useless, unnecessary, and gradually being forgotten. Andrey, carefully trained for a distinguished university career, holds a position in which his education is meaningless. Masha, once an accomplished pianist, now "has forgotten" how to play — just as Tchebutykin has "forgotten" his medical training — just as the entire family is forgetting the accomplishments of their hopeful youth. Thus, the Prozorovs alternate between hysteria and despair, their hopes disintegrating in an environment where everything is reduced to zero:

IRINA (*sobbing*): Where? Where has it all gone? Where is it? Oh, my God, my God! I have forgotten everything, everything . . . everything is in a tangle in my mind. . . . I don't remember the Italian for window or ceiling. . . . I am forgetting everything; every day I forget something more and life is slipping away and will never come back, we shall never, never go to Moscow. . . . I see that we shan't go. . . .

Life is slipping by, and time, like a cormorant, is devouring hopes, illusions, expectations, consuming their minds, souls, and bodies in its tedious-rapid progress towards death.[12]

While their culture is being forgotten, however, the Prozorovs do try to preserve a pocket of civilization in this dreary wasteland; and their house is open to limited forms of intellectual discussion and artistic activity. Generally, the discussions at the Prozorovs' reflect the banality of the surrounding area (Solyony's and Tchebutykin's heated argument over *tchehartma* and *tcheremsha* is typical); but occasionally, genuine ideas seem to come out of these soirées. Attending the discussions are the Prozorovs' cultural allies, the military officers stationed in town. Chekhov, according to Stanislavsky, looked on the military as "the bearers of a cultural mission, since, coming into the farthest corners of the provinces, they brought with them new demands on life, knowledge, art, happiness, and joy." Masha suggests Chekhov's attitudes when she observes the difference between the crude townspeople and the more refined soldiers: "among civilians generally there are so many rude, ill-mannered, badly-brought up people," but "in our town the most decent, honourable, and well-bred people are all in the army." Her attraction to Colonel Vershinin is partially explained by his superior refinement, for he is associated in her mind with the old Muscovite charm and glamor. In part, he probably reminds her of her father (also identified with culture), for he lived on the same street, was an officer in her father's brigade, and has now taken command of her father's old battery. Attracted to educated men (she married Kuligin because she mistakenly thought him "the cleverest of men"), Masha unquestionably finds a suitable intellectual companion in Vershinin;

[12] Chekhov heightens this effect by using a technique which Samuel Beckett will later imitate: he makes time pass while giving the impression that time is standing still. The action of the play covers three and a half years; yet, each act seems to follow the other as if no time had elapsed at all. There is another interesting parallel between Chekhov and Beckett, for Chekhov once planned a play with similarities to *Waiting for Godot*. As Simmons describes this unwritten drama, "During the first three acts the characters discuss the life of the hero and await his coming with great expectation. But in the last act they receive a telegram announcing the hero's death."

even their courtship reveals their cultural affinities — he hums a tune to which she hums a reply. Magarshack calls this "the most original love declaration in the whole history of the stage" — actually, Congreve's Mirabel and Millamant employ much the same device, when he completes a Waller verse which she begins — but in both cases, the couples signify their instinctual rapport, and their superior sophistication to other suitors.

While Masha tries to find expression through an extramarital affair which is doomed to failure, Irina tries to discover a substitute commitment in her work. In this, her spiritual partner, though she doesn't love him, is Tusenbach, because he too seeks salvation in work, finally, in a Tolstoyan gesture, resigning his commission for a job in a brickyard. Irina's faith in the dignity of labor, however, is gradually destroyed by depressing jobs in a telegraph office and on the town council — in this district, work can have no essential meaning or purpose. In the last act, Irina looks forward to "a new life" as a schoolteacher; but we have Olga's enervating academic career as evidence that this "new life" will be just as unfulfilling as the old. And when Tusenbach is killed in a duel with Solyony (*his* despoiler), even the minor consolations of a loveless marriage are denied her.

Everything, in fact, fails the family in *The Three Sisters*. And as their culture fades and their lives grow grayer, the forces of darkness and illiteracy move in like carrion crows, ready to pick the last bones. There is some doubt, however, whether this condition is permanent. And the question the play finally asks is whether the defeat of the Prozorovs has any ultimate meaning; will their suffering eventually influence their surroundings in any positive way? The question is never resolved in the play, but it is endlessly debated by Vershinin and Tusenbach, whose opinions contrast as sharply as their characters. Vershinin — an extremely unhappy soul — holds to optimistic theories, while Tusenbach — inexplicably merry — is more profoundly pessimistic.[13] This conflict, though usually

13 Chekhov is probably dramatizing a paradox here, which he once expounded to Lydia Avilova in the course of explaining the alleged gloominess

couched in general terms, is secretly connected with the fate of the Prozorovs. When Masha, for example, declares, "We know a great deal that is unnecessary," Vershinin takes the opportunity to expound his views:

What next? . . . I don't think there can be a town so dull and dismal that intelligent and educated people are unnecessary in it. Let us suppose that of the hundred thousand people living in the town, which is, of course, un-cultured and behind the times, there are only three of your sort. It goes without saying that you cannot conquer the mass of darkness round you; little by little as you go on living, you will be lost in the crowd. Life will get the better of you, but still you will not disappear without a trace. After you there may appear perhaps six like you, then twelve and so on until such as you form a majority. In two or three hundred years life on earth will be unimaginably beautiful, marvelous.

Vershinin, in short — anticipating the eventual transformation of the surrounding area by people like the Prozorovs — believes in the progressive march of civilization towards perfection. And this perfection will be based on the future interrelationship of the benighted mass and the cultured elite ("You know, if work were united with culture, and culture with work") — a synthesis of beauty and utility.

Tusenbach, on the other hand, is more skeptical. Seeing no special providence in the fall of a sparrow or the flight of migratory cranes, he doubts the ability of anyone to influence anything:

Not only in two or three hundred years but in a million years life will be just the same; it does not change, it remains stationary, following its own laws which we have nothing to do with or which, anyway, we shall never find out.

Vershinin's view awakens hope that there is some ultimate meaning to life; Tusenbach's leads to stoicism and tragic resignation. It is the

---

of his themes and characters: "It has been pointed out to me that somber, melancholy people always write gaily, while the works of cheerful souls are always depressing." Chekhov, like Tusenbach, is a cheerful soul with a gloomy point of view.

recurrent conflict between the progressive and the static interpretation of history, and its outcome is as insoluble as life itself.[14]

In the last act, in fact, both views are recapitulated without being reconciled. The military is leaving the town — a sad departure, because it signifies not only the end of Masha's affair with Vershinin, but also the disintegration of the last cultural rampart. Tusenbach anticipates that "dreadful boredom" will descend upon the town, and Andrey notes (reminding us of Natasha's symbolic role), "It's as though someone put an extinguisher over it." The end of the Prozorov way of life has almost come. Masha has turned obsessive and hysterical; Olga is installed in a position she loathes; Andrey, likened to an expensive bell that has fallen and smashed, has become hag-ridden and mediocre. Only Irina preserves some hope, but even these hopes are soon to be dashed. The entire family is finally facing the truth: "Nothing turns out as we would have it" — the dream of Moscow will never be realized, the mass of darkness has overwhelmed them. In the requiem which concludes the play, the three sisters meditate on the future, just as, in the beginning of the play, they reflected on the past, while Andrey pushes the pram, Kuligin bustles, and Tchebutykin hums softly to himself.

Their affirmations, showing the strong influence of Vershinin's view of life, are inexplicably hopeful and expectant. Masha expresses her determination to endure; Irina has faith that a "time will come when everyone will know what all this is for"; and Olga affirms that "our sufferings will pass into joy for those who live after us, happiness and peace will be established on earth, and they will remember kindly and bless those who have lived before." The gay band music played by the military evokes in the three sisters the will to live. But the music slowly fades away. Will hope fade away as well? Olga's anxious questioning of life ("If we only knew — if

---

14 Chekhov's letters occasionally suggest that he agrees more with Vershinin than with Tusenbach on the question of progress: "Modern culture," he writes to Diaghilev, in 1902, "is only the beginning of an effort in the name of a great future, an effort that will continue perhaps for tens of thousands of years. . . ." Chekhov, however, is careful, as always, not to urge his own opinions on his dramatic characters.

we only knew!") is — as if to suggest this — antiphonally answered by Tchebutykin's muttered denials ("It doesn't matter, it doesn't matter!"), the skepticism of Tusenbach reduced to its most nihilistic form. And on this double note — the dialectic of hope and despair in a situation of defeat — Chekhov's darkest play draws to its close.

In *The Three Sisters*, Chekhov depicts the prostration of the cultured elite before the forces of darkness; in *The Cherry Orchard*, he examines the same problem from a comic-ironic point of view. Written while he was dying and with great difficulty, *The Cherry Orchard* is the most farcical of Chekhov's full-length works, and so it was intended. In 1901, when the play was just beginning to take shape in his mind, he wrote to Olga Knipper: "The next play I write for the Art Theatre will definitely be funny, very funny — at least in intention." The last phrase was probably a sally aimed at Stanislavsky (Chekhov deplored his tendency to turn "my characters into crybabies"), and though Stanislasvky did, in fact, eventually misinterpret *The Cherry Orchard* as a somber study of Russian life, Chekhov always insisted on calling it "not a drama but a comedy; in places almost a farce."

The importance of the comic element in the play suggests that Chekhov is emphasizing the other side of his revolt. Instead of merely evoking sympathy for the victims of the social conflict, he is now satirizing them as well; and instead of blackening the character of the despoiler, he is drawing him with a great deal more depth and balance. The change is one of degree — Chekhov has not reversed his earlier position, he has merely modified it — and the dispossession of the victims still evokes strains of pathos which we should not ignore. Nevertheless, in *The Cherry Orchard*, Chekhov is more impatient with his cultured idlers; and their eventual fate seems more fitting and more just.

Chekhov's irony is operative not only against his characters but against the situation in which they find themselves. The play functions, partly, as a satire on conventional melodrama, achieved through the reversal of melodramatic conventions. To illustrate this, let us contrast *The Cherry Orchard* with a work to which it bears surprising

surface resemblances: Dion Boucicault's *The Octoroon* (1859). Boucicault's melodrama is located in the antebellum American South, a
setting which permits the author to combine traditional stereotypes
with a topical antislavery motif. Just as some of the perfunctory Abo-
litionist speeches in *The Octoroon* occasionally remind us of Trofimov's harangues against Russian serfdom, so the Southern setting of
the play is reminiscent of the feudal background of *The Cherry Orchard*. More important, for our purposes, are certain interesting
parallels in plot and character. For like *The Cherry Orchard*, *The
Octoroon* revolves around the sale, on mortgage, of an old ancestral
estate — here called Terrebone. It is the property of Mrs. Peyton —
a genial Southern aristocrat who recalls Madame Ranevsky in her
identification with the culture and leisure of a dying caste. Also like
Madame Ranevsky, Mrs. Peyton has an adopted daughter — Zoe, the
octoroon — who, like Varya, acts as housekeeper to the family; a
family friend — the cracker-barrel Yankee, Salem Scudder — who
hangs around the house like Semyonov-Pishtchik; and even an old re-
tainer — a Negro called Old Pete — who serves the family with the
same doglike fidelity as old Firs. The development of the plot estab-
lishes an even stronger parallel between the two plays, for it concerns
the efforts of Jacob McCloskey, a villainous overseer, to seduce the
octoroon, and to gain control of Terrebone when it comes up for auction. Only the resolution of the Boucicault drama breaks the parallel:
McCloskey is eventually foiled in his villainy, and the family is rees-
tablished in its hereditary rights.

I am not suggesting that Chekhov was familiar with Boucicault's
play. But the materials are conventional enough, and Chekhov certainly knew the popular French "mortgage" melodramas which Boucicault used as his models, for they were the staples of the commercial
Russian stage. Whether or not one believes literary parody to be one
of Chekhov's purposes in *The Cherry Orchard*, however, his departure
from the melodramatic formula is still very instructive. The gentle
victim (Mrs. Peyton) becomes the irresponsible and self-destructive
Lyuba Ranevsky; the virtuous low-born ingenue (Zoe) becomes the
weepy, nunlike Varya; the humorous friend (Salem Scudder) be-

comes the indigent buffoon, Pishtchik; the pathetic old servant (Pete) becomes the comically senile Firs; and the moustache-twirling villain (McCloskey) becomes the generous and warmhearted Lopahin. In each case, Chekhov succeeds in surprising the spectator by reversing the expected stereotype: neutralizing the victims, complicating the victimizer. Instead of the bald ravisher-ravished relationship of Mc-Closkey and Zoe, Chekhov substitutes the pitifully bungled courtship of Lopahin and Varya, where the man is more passive than the woman. And the sale of the ancestral estate occurs not as the consequence of evil external forces (McCloskey's theft of the mortgage money) but rather through the inertia and inadequacy of the family itself. Finally, of course, the expected melodramatic reversal is omitted entirely: the "villain" is not foiled; the estate is not returned.

Chekhov introduces additional surprise, however, by providing a parallel plot in which the expected reversal *does* take place — but in a totally trivial way. For just as Madame Ranevsky tried to pay the mortgage on her estate by borrowing money from the Countess, so Semyonov-Pishtchik borrows frantically from the family to pay the mortgage on *his* — the difference being that Pishtchik's property is, temporarily, saved. "Some Englishman" has discovered "some sort of white clay" on his land, and Pishtchik has sold him the rights to dig it! Chekhov compounds the irony by having Pishtchik pay back part of the money he has borrowed — not, of course, enough to save the cherry orchard, and too late to do so if it were. What Chekhov seems to be saying is that in real life the unusual rarely happens; when it does, its effect is meaningless. For just as the suicide attempts of Vershinin's wife are rendered trivial by the frequency with which they occur, so Pishtchik's good fortune is too meager and ephemeral to save either him or the family. Thus, Chekhov works a brilliant convolution on the melodramatic formula: by introducing Pishtchik's unexpected success, he manages to highlight the unexpected failure of the family.

Chekhov's unique approach can be further illustrated by comparing *The Cherry Orchard* with another group of plays to which it bears some resemblance. For the social background of the work — the transfer of power from the feudal aristocracy to the rising bourgeoisie —

relates it to a drama of social conflict and social change. In most plays of this type, the artist's sympathies are enlisted on the side of the old order, while the rising class is generally criticized for disrupting degree and tradition. Shakespeare, for example, cruelly satirizes the efforts of the upstart Malvolio to climb beyond his station; Molière anatomizes with more sympathy for the middle class — but no less animus against the upstart — the aristocratic pretensions of Monsieur Jourdain; and the Restoration conflict between the truewit and the falsewit is really a defense of traditional aristocratic style against the vulgarities of middle-class imitators. In the nineteenth century, when the ascendancy of the bourgeoisie was almost established, and no amount of ridicule could stem the tide, the artist ceases to treat this subject satirically. Strindberg, in *Miss Julie,* views the war between the classes as a tragic struggle, barely concealing under a pretense of impartiality his sympathy for the fallen warrior nobility; and similar attitudes towards this conflict are later to be implicit in such movies as Renoir's *Grand Illusion,* such novels as Faulkner's *The Hamlet,* and such plays as Williams's *Streetcar Named Desire.*

Chekhov, to be sure, shares some of the class sympathies of these artists, for even when he is exposing the cruelty and indifference of the old order, he is evoking nostalgia for it — partly because his aristocratic characters are so charming, partly because the past is seen through a filmy mist of memory and regret. To Firs — for whom the emancipation of the serfs was "the calamity" — the past was a time of grace, style, order, "horses all the way," while the present is decayed, confused, gone to seed: "In the old days, we used to have generals, barons, and admirals dancing at our balls, and now we send for the post-office clerk and the station master and even they're not overanxious to come." In the old days, by his account, "the peasants knew their place and the masters knew theirs; but now they're all at sixes and sevens, there's no making it out." The disorder perceived by Firs — where, to use Hamlet's phrase, "the toe of the peasant comes so near the heel of the courtier, he galls his kibe" — is richly illustrated in the play. Dunyasha is a "spoilt, soft" maidservant pretending to be a lady, so presumptuous in her affectation of upper-class dress and manners that even Lopahin is provoked to admonish her ("One must know one's place"), while the sinister insolence of the mincing valet, Yasha, is an inevitable concommitant of his vulgar, pseudoaristocratic tastes, so similar to those of the valet, Jean, in *Miss Julie*. Everything, indeed, is at "sixes and sevens." The house is run down; everyone sleeps too late; the servants have been permitting tramps to spend the night; and it is the clumsy clerk, Epihodov, who discourses, in the circumlocutory language of the autodidact, on culture, history, and literature.

The confusion of class roles is most pointedly dramatized in the central action of the play, for Lopahin, the son of a serf, also achieves his success by breaking out of a traditional social relationship. Though he is totally free from any pretensions ("A peasant I was, and a peasant I am"), he has come a long way since the beatings of his childhood; and though he is extremely sympathetic towards the family, he is, in effect, its executioner, inadvertently completing the destruction of the old way of life. Despite his generous character, in fact, he cannot restrain his class-conscious sense of triumph when he finally acquires the estate: "I have bought the estate where my father and grandfather were slaves, where they weren't even admitted into the kitchen." He is, by his own account, "a pig in a pastry shop," smashing the fragile possessions of the house with his characteristic flailing of his arms: in the third act, drunk with power and cognac, he knocks over a table and almost upsets a candelabra, and in the last, of course, he chops down the cherry orchard, the very symbol of the cultured tradition he has concluded.

On the other hand, though Lopahin assumes the function of the Chekhovian despoiler, his character is inconsistent with his role. Gaev, who calls him a "lowborn knave" and a "money grubber," and Trofimov, who compares him with a "wild beast" devouring "everything that comes in his way," are both entirely wrong: both, like the insensitive Dr. Lvov in *Ivanov*, evaluate people by false and stereotyped standards. For unlike Natasha, Lopahin is utterly free from malice, spite, pretentiousness, or vulgarity; if his effect is destructive, his motives are completely innocent. Chekhov is careful to emphasize

Lopahin's excellent qualities in a letter to Stanislavsky: "Lopahin, of course, is only a merchant, but he is a decent person in every sense, should conduct himself with complete decorum, like a cultivated man, without pettiness or trickery. . . ." He is a "cultivated man," because he has successfully risen above his environment, despite his lowly origins. And rather than being an enemy of culture and sensibility, he has excellent possibilities in that direction himself: even Trofimov, in a more generous moment, remarks on his "fine, delicate soul."

Lopahin, in fact, is the most positive character in the play. It is he who labors, with ever-increasing frustration, to bring the befuddled family to its senses; and it is he alone who seems to possess energy, purpose, and dedication. One of the many ironies of *The Cherry Orchard*, in fact, is that while Trofimov theorizes about work ("One must give up glorification of self. One should work, and nothing else"), Lopahin quietly, and untheoretically, performs it. For despite Trofimov's glorious affirmations about humanity and progress, generally delivered as if he were making a stump speech, he is the embodiment of sloth. Asleep when we first hear of him, he is a kind of intellectual somnambulist — a "perpetual student" who lacks the energy to obtain his degree. And though he inveighs against the "filth and vulgarity and Asiatic apathy" of the Russian intelligentsia, he is extremely unkempt and apathetic himself. Lopahin, on the other hand, gets up "at five o'clock in the morning" and works "from morning to night." It is work that provides his identity, and it is work — not money or status or power — which is his life's goal. Thus, he seems less like the sinister Natasha than like the genial Astrov, for like Astrov, he has been wasting his energies among aimless and vacuous people.

Chekhov, in short, softens the act of dispossession by complicating the character of the despoiler; he does so also by qualifying our sympathy for the victims. Certainly, Lyuba and Gaev are a good deal less pathetic than their predecessors, the Prozorovs. Both brother and sister are full of charm and sweetness. But Lyuba's negligence is a determining factor in their present condition (it may even have been the cause of her child's death by drowning), and her uncontrollable extravagance has brought the house tumbling down about their ears. As for Gaev, he is merely an artifact of the old aristocracy — nobility in decay. His orations to the bookcase suggest his pomposity and irrelevance; his relationship with Firs (who treats him like an eleven-year-old) suggests his childish dependence; his obsession with caramels suggests his wasteful self-indulgence; and the imaginary billiard game which always proceeds inside his brain suggests his inability to face reality. Although Chekhov is clearly sympathetic to the aristocracy, he is always careful to balance this sympathy with ironic glimpses into its less appealing side, just as he is careful to modify our nostalgia for the old life with some hard facts about its actual nature. ("Those were fine old times," Lopahin ironically reminds Firs. "There was flogging anyway.")

We may conclude, then, that despite certain similarities to the literary works mentioned above, *The Cherry Orchard* preserves a strict neutrality towards the class struggle, if, indeed, it deals with this struggle at all. Chekhov achieves his neutrality not by remaining aloof from controversy, but by alternating between the two sides. He believes both in the old way of life and the new — both in order and in change — and he disbelieves in them both as well. More than this, however, he documents the surface of his play so painstakingly that no struggle seems to be occurring. For just as he handles a melodramatic formula from an unmelodramatic point of view, so he writes a political play in a totally unpolitical manner. If one were to regard the characters of *The Cherry Orchard* exclusively as class symbols, as some critics have done, it would be necessary to see Madame Ranevsky and Gaev as the aristocracy that is going out; Lopahin as the capitalist bourgeoisie that is taking its place; Trofimov as the revolutionary intelligentsia, preparing for an even more violent class struggle in future;[15] and possibly even Yasha as the new class which will eventually betray Trofimov's revolution to bureaucracy, power politics, and

[15] Trofimov, as a matter of fact, *is* a revolutionary intellectual, sent down from the university for political agitation. Student strikes had occurred at Petersburg University a few years before *The Cherry Orchard* was written, and in 1901, a number of students had been expelled under the government's arbitrary "Provisional Rules."

self-interest. Yet, quite obviously, Chekhov is more concerned with humanity than with the symbols of humanity, and each character transcends his class role to assume a complex life of his own, baffling one's efforts to classify him. Thus, while there are certainly social-political overtones in *The Cherry Orchard,* Chekhov is constantly discouraging any reduction of his characters to purely social-political categories.

I think we can now understand Chekhov's remark to the effect that "great writers and artists must occupy themselves with politics only insofar as it is necessary to put up a defense against politics." Chekhov occupies himself with politics by choosing a traditionally political situation as his subject matter; he defends himself against politics by demonstrating the inadequacy of narrow political interpretations. Modifying the general with the concrete, action with character, consequence with motive, he permits humanity to be seen in all its doubleness and ambiguity. On the surface, the basic material of *The Cherry Orchard* is less a war for dominance between two classes of society than a peaceful interlude during which some property changes hands after repeated warnings have been ignored. The dispossession of the upper-class characters is so pivotal that we are certain it has a more general significance; yet, Chekhov has so minimized conflict that the cherry orchard goes under the axe without evoking any feelings of class hatred. With the surface and the depths of the play following separate lines of development, the event seems both cruel and just, both significant and insignificant, both an end and a beginning.

Chekhov's double attitudes are best illustrated through the resonant image of the cherry orchard itself — the central image of the play, embodying the play's implicit theme. The importance of this image is suggested by its multivariousness: like Ibsen's wild duck, it represents something different to all the leading characters. To Madame Ranevsky and her family, of course, it is the emblem of the culture, grace, and style of the old, leisured manor nobility, a dramatic contrast to the illiteracy, mediocrity, and vulgarity of the surrounding area: "If there is one thing interesting — remarkable indeed — in the whole province, it is our cherry orchard." Lyuba's affection for the orchard, however, has a more personal source than the fact that it is mentioned in the encyclopedia, for she associates it with her childhood among the Russian gentry. Always identified with the color white ("All, all white . . . the white trees . . . the white masses of blossoms"), the orchard reminds her of "my life, my youth, my happiness . . . my childhood, my innocence," and also of "my mother," whom she imagines walking "all in white down the avenue" of trees. But just as Lyuba's innocence and childhood have yielded to adulthood, adultery, and experience, so the virility of the old aristocracy has now given way to weakness, effeminacy, and inertia. The cherry orchard, therefore, is the vestigial symbol of a once vigorous way of life — an aesthetic pleasure in a crude environment — but it also represents the deterioration which has now overtaken that life.

While Lyuba is reminded of innocence, Trofimov is reminded of guilt. For him, the orchard is merely a memento of slavery. Unwilling to idealize a way of life which was based on human suffering, he tells Anya of the apparitions which lodge in the white, ghostlike trees:

Think only, Anya, your grandfather, and great-grandfather, and all your ancestors were slaveowners — the owners of living souls — and from every cherry in the orchard, from every leaf, from every trunk there are human creatures looking at you. . . . Your orchard is a fearful thing, and when in the evening or at night one walks about the orchard, the old bark on the trees glimmers dimly in the dusk, and the old cherry trees seem to be dreaming of centuries gone by and tortured by fearful visions.

The "fearful visions" that Trofimov ascribes to the trees are, of course, the guilty dreams of the decaying aristocracy — Chekhov suggests these guilts through Lyuba's conscience-stricken reaction to the ominous drunken tramp in Act II — for Trofimov sees the orchard in purely political and moral terms. Since his responses are general and abstract ("All Russia," he tells Anya, "is our garden"), the singular possession of Madame Ranevsky is to him merely a symbolic extension of a cruel and exploitative aristocracy, now required to redeem the time.

To Lopahin, on the other hand, the orchard has neither political,

THE THEATRE OF REVOLT

moral, sentimental nor aesthetic significance. A practical man of the utilitarian middle class, for him the most important measure is *use,* and by this measure the orchard is no more than an object which has outlived its purpose: "The only remarkable thing about the orchard is that it's a very large one. There's a crop of cherries every alternate year, and then there's nothing to be done with them, no one buys them." The memory of the ancient Firs, however, extends to a time when the orchard was once a practical and a profitable proposition:

FIRS: In the old days, forty or fifty years ago, they used to dry the cherries, soak them, pickle them, make jam too, and they used —
GAEV: Be quiet, Firs.
FIRS: And they used to send the preserved cherries to Moscow and to Harkov by the wagonload. That brought the money in. And the preserved cherries in those days were soft and juicy, sweet and fragrant. . . . They knew the way to do them then. . . .
LYUBA: And where is the recipe now?
FIRS: It's forgotten. Nobody remembers it.

The recipe is "forgotten" — forgotten like the culture of the Prozorovs — forgotten like the purpose and passion of the decaying Russian gentry. Once valuable both for beauty and utility, the justification for the existence of the orchard has now passed out of memory, and it must go the way of all useless things.[16]

Thus, both the orchard and the way of life it represents are cut down by the utilitarian axe, a process as inexorable as the progress of the seasons which, by the end of the play, have killed the blossoms with a chilling frost (the action begins in May, concludes in October). Yet, for all its inevitability, the event signifies the loss of something irreplaceable in life. What is coming to supplant such things is sug-

[16] Stanislavsky tells of Chekhov's glee when he decided to change the title of his play from *Vìshneviy Sad* to *Vishnéviy Sad.* The movement of the accent introduces a subtle alteration in meaning, for while *Vìshneviy Sad* is "a commercial orchard which brings in profit," *Vishnéviy Sad* is an orchard which "brings no profits [but] grows for the sake of beauty, for the eyes of spoiled aesthetes." This suggests Chekhov's demand that beautiful things must also have some function.

gested in the second-act setting where beyond "an old shrine, long abandoned and fallen out of the perpendicular" are seen "in the distance a row of telegraph poles and far, far away on the horizon . . . faintly outlined a great town." The urbanization and uglification of the countryside are the price which Russia will pay for its growing utilitarianism; and the hideous panorama of modern industrial life will hardly be beautified by the summer villas that Lopahin is preparing to build on the site of the orchard. Nor will the bustling middle class that is moving in have any culture to substitute for the old aristocratic civilization, now "fallen out of the perpendicular" as well.

On the other hand, if Lopahin is at all an accurate representative, the new class will, at least, be energetic, vigorous, and purposeful. And there is a vague chance that the new villas may even develop some compensations too. As Lopahin visualizes it, overoptimistically: "At present the summer visitor only drinks tea in his verandah, but maybe he'll take to working his bit of land too, and then your cherry orchard would become happy, rich, and prosperous. . . ." Whatever the more general significance of their departure, moreover, Madame Ranevsky and her family have not been vitally affected, personally, by their eviction from the house. Lyuba is returning to her Paris lover; Gaev will work in a bank (until his inefficiency becomes too obvious); Varya will take another housekeeping job; and Anya will become a schoolteacher. None is really worse off than he was at the beginning; and though we must, as always, be skeptical about the "new life" that Anya anticipates, she, at least, has successfully sloughed off the debilitating inheritance of her class.[17]

To discourage sentimentality towards this departure, in fact, Chekhov concludes the play by reemphasizing the family's indifference and irresponsibility. Lopahin — still worrying about time (train time

---

[17] The relationship between Anya and Trofimov is very close to the relationship between Nadya and Sasha in Chekhov's story, "The Betrothed" (1903). Nadya, a vital young creature, is taught — by her revolutionary relative, Sasha — to question the values of her dreary provincial existence. She finally breaks off an engagement to start a new and more meaningful life in St. Petersburg. It is one of the most hopeful conclusions Chekhov ever wrote, and may suggest that Anya's expectations of the future are not without basis.

now, not auction time) — has hurried the family out of the house, and the stage is empty for the entrance of Firs. He has been left behind, another victim of Madame Ranevsky's habit of delegating authority to undependable individuals; and ill and failing, though still anxious to discharge his duties, he lies on the sofa to reflect upon the meaninglessness of his existence: "Life has slipped by as though I hadn't lived. . . . There's no strength in you, nothing left you — all gone! Ech! I'm good for nothing." And thus having characterized not only himself but the whole household, he lies motionless as that ominous sound comes from the sky, like the breaking of a harp string, through the noise of the chopping, signifying the end of this useless and superfluous, though charming and civilized class.

Thus, despite the thickness of the play, despite its complexity and ambiguity, Chekhov's revolt still manages to find expression in his indictment of these cultured aristocrats, too will-less to resist their own liquidation — just as, in *The Three Sisters*, it is aimed against the dark environment which drags them under. In each play, Chekhov's revolt remains two-edged, changing in emphasis and attack, but fixed always on the fate of the cultured classes in the modern world. This is the great "problem" of his plays — and it is a problem which, in keeping with his artistic creed, he undertakes not to solve but simply to present correctly. Confronting the same world as the other great dramatists of revolt — a world without God and, therefore, without meaning — Chekhov has no remedy for the disease of modern life. Ibsen speaks of the importance of one's calling, and Strindberg of resignation. But even Chekhov's panacea of work is ultimately ineffectual before the insupportable fact of death.

Still, despite the bleakness of his vision, Chekhov possesses a deeper humanity than any other modern dramatist. For while he never fails to examine the desperate absurdity of his characters, he never loses sight of the qualities that make them fully alive: "My holy of holies," he writes, "are the human body, health, intelligence, talent, inspiration, love, and the most absolute freedom — freedom from despotism and lies." Chekhov himself embodies these qualities so perfectly that no one has even been able to write of him without the most profound affection and love; and he, the author, remains the most positive character in his fiction. Because of his hatred of untruth, Chekhov will not arouse false hopes about the future of mankind — but because he is humane to the marrow of his bones, he manages to increase our expectations of the human race. Coupling sweetness of temper with toughness of mind, Chekhov makes his work an extraordinary compound of morality and reality, rebellion and acceptance, irony and sympathy — evoking a singular affirmation even in the darkest despair. There are more powerful playwrights in the theatre of revolt — artists with greater range, wider variety, more intellectual power — but there are none more warm and generous, and none who bring the drama to a higher realization of its human role.

V

BERNARD SHAW

There is no difficulty in proving Bernard Shaw's debt to the tradition of revolt; the difficulty lies in proving his resistance to it. One of the first to define the new "world movement," [1] and to recognize its rebellious character, Shaw is at once a full-fledged member of this movement and its most enthusiastic partisan. But although he is certainly one of the most dedicated rebel artists of the modern period, he is also a revolutionary journalist, agitating for political, moral, artistic, and religious reform. Since the literary rebel is double-minded and the reforming journalist is single-minded, Shaw's two functions are not really compatible. And since Shaw's reformist propaganda is often more noisy and vehement than his dramatic art, there are times when his artistic achievements are less conspicuous than his active proselytizing for Utopian ideals.

Those who dislike Shaw's work generally dislike it on these grounds, and the author's attitudes make him hard to defend. Standing as an irritating presence between his imaginative creations and the reader, apparently unable to let a work exist in isolation from his comments about it, he is forever weaving the thread of his art into a skein of verbose argument — prattling, theorizing, exhorting, tire-

[1] In a footnote later attached to *The Quintessence of Ibsenism*, Shaw declares that "I attach great importance to the evidence that the movement voiced by Schopenhauer, Wagner, Ibsen, Nietzsche, and Strindberg, was a world movement. . . . The movement is alive today in the philosophy of Bergson and the plays of Gorki, Tchekhov, and the post-Ibsen drama." What he is describing is the modern tradition of revolt.

lessly loquacious. One does not simply experience a play by Shaw. One is also pelted by a hailstorm of prefaces, postscripts, disquisitions, chatty stage directions, and other prose addenda, advising him how to regard the play, the cast of characters, even the playwright who created them, in addition to how to lead his life, rule the state, and advance the race. And as if this were not enough, Shaw provides innumerable tracts, pamphlets, manifestoes, and full-length books on every conceivable subject from anarchism to municipal trading to elaborate his points more discursively. One wishes that at some time in his life, Shaw had learned the virtue of silence.

For whenever he opens his mouth for an extradramatic utterance, he invariably manages to diminish his stature as a dialectical artist by reducing his complex perceptions to uniformitarian dogma. And if this misleads some into believing that Shaw is less an artist than a very clever journalist who uses the drama for purposes of ventriloquism, then Shaw is often quite content to leave this impression. Certainly, Shaw is very uneasy with the name of artist. Preferring compound titles like "artist-philosopher" or "artist-prophet," he tries to emphasize his commitment to a higher purpose than "mere" (his favorite depreciatory adjective) creation. For him, the work of art should extend beyond itself to become an act of ethical reform, influencing "public opinion, public action, and public contribution as ratepayers." Based on this dynamic, his own writings (he insists) are instruments of social utility, not of pleasure — even his comic approach has a didactic justification ("to chastise morals with ridicule") — and though he recognizes that "I must tell my story entertainingly," he feels compelled to add soon after, " 'for art's sake' alone, I would not face the toil of writing a single sentence."

If "the artist-philosophers are the only sorts of artists I take quite seriously," Shaw cannot take the "mere artist" seriously at all, since, playing on the senses of the reader, he feels no animating impulse to change the shape of the world. In Shaw's lexicon, the word "poet" is almost invariably a playful term of abuse. And though he is capable of creating a wide variety of artist types in his drama — from the poet genius Marchbanks to the poetaster Octavius — in Shaw's discursive writings, the poet often appears as a Bohemian aesthete who passes the time of day inventing false ideals, composing sonnets to his mistress's eyebrow, or weaving a beautiful veil of "illusion" over "the unbearable face of truth." Shaw's conviction that the poet-artist is a liar or an idle dreamer is something he inherits from Plato, who put a similar emphasis on the importance of ethical reform; and his Platonic infatuation with the salvation of the community leads him to slight those who are not similarly occupied with socially useful ideas. In such a theory, *utile* precedes *dulce;* beauty is a snare which draws men from the truth. Thus, by Shaw's testimony, his own artistic gifts — his wit, style, insight into character and invention of plot — are merely a "literary knack," which help to entertain the spectator while communicating Shaw's revolt in the most direct and vigorous manner.

Shaw would have us believe, then, that his drama serves the same function as his journalism, being a medium of prophecy, an agency of philosophy, and an expression of his revolutionary aims. While his drama may seem to be objectified, therefore, it is actually an urgent communication from the author to his audience, a discourse rather than a dialogue. Shaw supports a "frankly doctrinal theatre" to replace the "romantic" tradition of "mere artists" like Shakespeare: instead of a theatre of fanciful fictions, a theatre of preachment, indictment, and revolt. Such a theatre will naturally emphasize the element of "discussion" — first introduced (Shaw tells us) by Ibsen, and now the distinguishing mark of the modern drama. As he writes in the preface to *Mrs. Warren's Profession:* "The drama of pure feeling is no longer in the hands of the playwright; it has been conquered by the musician . . . and there is, flatly, no future now for any drama except the drama of thought." No future — and no past either. At his most extreme, Shaw is inclined to reject *all* drama not dedicated to the advancement of ideas, which is why he continually undervalues the Elizabethans while calling Brieux the greatest Western dramatist after Ibsen.[2]

[2] "*A Doll's House,*" writes Shaw, "will be as flat as ditchwater when *A Midsummer Night's Dream* will still be as fresh as paint; but it will have done more

Shaw's Platonism undoubtedly dictates his opinions in these matters, but he is much less simplistic than he appears. T. S. Eliot, in a
famous dialogue, has written, "Shaw *was* a poet — until he was born,
and the poet in Shaw was stillborn." It is more accurate to say that the
poet in Shaw is forcibly suppressed. Actually, Shaw's aesthetic sense
is substantial, though he does his best to bury it. And just as he is perfectly capable of understanding, and even approving, the poet's indifference to community welfare,[3] so is he perfectly capable of re-
sponding to the nondidactic aspects of art. Shaw's passion for absolute
music signifies his strong instinct for beauty; and his eager utilitarianism is probably an attempt to chasten his early aestheticism, when
he allowed himself to be swallowed up in a blind worship of art. As
Eric Bentley notes, in his probing study of the playwright, *Bernard
Shaw,* "the puritanism which warns of the dangers of sensuousness is
but the negative side of a philosophy which makes a great deal — perhaps too much — of the arts."

Still, Shaw's Puritanism must be reckoned with, since, like his
Platonism, it dominates his critical attitudes. At his most conscious,
Shaw is thoroughly determined to adhere to his own moral prin-

---

work in the world; and that is enough for the highest genius, which is always
intensely utilitarian." Shaw's utilitarian aesthetic theory is, of course, anti-
Aristotelian, since Aristotle considered ethical motivation (*ethos*) and dramatic
thought (*dianoia*) to be less important than plot (*mythos*). For Shaw, the
drama is not so much an imitation of an action as a communication of an idea,
its function less to purge the audience of its emotions than to arouse the audience's moral passion. The differences between Aristotelian and Shavian theory
are the differences between tragedy and comedy (or the problem play), and
stem from two irreconcilable views of the function of art.

[3] Explaining why he withheld *Heartbreak House* from the public until the
conclusion of World War I, Shaw writes: "The art of the dramatic poet knows
no patriotism; recognizes no obligation but truth to natural history; cares not
whether Germany or England perish; is ready to cry with Brynhild: *Lass uns
verderben, lachend zu grunde geh'n* sooner than deceive or be deceived; and
thus becomes in time of a war a greater military danger than poison, steel, or
trinotrotoluene." Still, if Shaw the "natural historian" and "dramatic poet" was
capable of writing these lines and formulating this thought, then Shaw the social
philosopher was also capable of suppressing the play until after the armistice,
lest the war effort be damaged.

ciples and ethical formulations. In his antiaestheticism, in fact, he sometimes reminds us (though he lacks their fanaticism) of those dogged Puritan reformers whom Sidney tried to refute in his *Defense of Poesy;* for his Puritan temper makes him censorious of all moral laxness and sensual delight. As he tells Arthur Bingham Walkley in the Epistle Dedicatory of *Man and Superman:*

My conscience is the genuine pulpit article; it annoys me to see people comfortable when they ought to be uncomfortable; and I insist on making them think in order to bring them to conviction of sin. If you don't like my preaching you must lump it. I really cannot help it.

It is this active conscience which makes Shaw overemphasize the philosophical side of his art — and of the art of others, too, since, as a critic, he is inclined to put aside "mere literary criticism" for the sake of unearthing usable moral truths. Thus, in *The Quintessence of Ibsenism*, Shaw sets out to write "not a critical essay on the poetic beauties of Ibsen, but simply an exposition of Ibsenism," and so squeezes Ibsen's devious and complicated rebel art into the narrow confines of polemical social doctrine.

If Shaw were really indifferent to "poetic beauties," he would not waste his time looking for doctrine in the works of artists, when there are much more powerful, comprehensive, and coherent thinkers closer at hand who would serve his ends much better. Still, if Shaw's secret aestheticism attracts him to art in the first place, his Puritan conscience and Platonic purpose are responsible for awkward misrepresentations of this art. The Ibsen who tried so hard to dissociate himself from any consistent position would not have recognized himself in the "social pioneer" of *The Quintessence,* whose "gospel" is designed to save the human race,[4] any more than the archsensualist Wagner would have recognized himself in the "social reformer" and economic theorist of *The Perfect Wagnerite.* Unlike Plato, who ban-

---

[4] See the preface to the third edition (1922) where Shaw declares that the adoption of "Ibsenism" would possibly have prevented World War I: "Had the gospel of Ibsen been understood and heeded, these fifteen millions might have been alive today; for the war was a war of ideals."

ished the artist from his ideal commonwealth, Shaw is very eager to keep the artist in[5] — so eager, in fact, that he is willing to distort his work in order to make him look like a socially useful member of the community. Shaw's search for utilitarian doctrines in the work of nonutilitarian artists, like his impulse to find ethical and religious affirmations in absolute music, suggests his need to adopt his instinctive aesthetic preferences to his conscious sense of purpose — to rationalize art into social ideology.

Such devices make his dramatic criticism lively and controversial, but utterly undependable. The question arises whether he misrepresents his own work as well. Should we regard Shaw as a Platonic thinker, whose art is merely the medium through which he communicates his ideas? Or is he an Aristotelian maker, whose ideas are only one element — and not always the most important — in a total representation? Is he to be evaluated on the basis of his philosophy — its truthfulness, usefulness, and effectiveness in bringing the ideal republic closer to realization? Or is his value intrinsic, resting in the depth and power of his dramatic actions? Is Shaw, in short, to be considered a revolutionary reformer, who has contributed a significant program for the advancement of the human race? Or is he rather a rebel artist, who dramatizes the irreconcilable conflict between subjective revolt and the mitigating restraints of objective reality?

It is quite clear that Shaw is both — both ideologist and artist, both social philosopher and literary rebel, both Platonic thinker and Aristotelian maker. *Both . . . and,* in fact, is the comprehensive formula which Eric Bentley uses to describe the complicated dualism of

---

[5] It is Shaw who defends the artist in *The Sanity of Art* (1895) against Max Nordau's ridiculous charges of degeneracy — and defends him for aesthetic as well as utilitarian reasons: "The worthy artist or craftsman is he who serves the physical and moral senses by feeding them with pictures, musical compositions, pleasant houses and gardens, good clothes and fine implements, fiction, essays, and dramas which call the heightened senses and ennobled faculties into pleasurable activity. The great artist is he who goes a step beyond the demand, and, by supplying works of a higher beauty and a higher interest than have yet been perceived, succeeds . . . in adding this fresh extension of sense to the heritage of the race."

Shaw's total personality. Yet, the question remains whether Shaw handles these disparate functions with equal confidence, and whether they are always effectively combined. Bentley, admittedly writing a polemic in support of Shaw, is inclined to defend all aspects of the author's endeavors, first outlining, approvingly, Shaw's political-economic-philosophical system, and then demonstrating how this system is illustrated, deepened, and qualified in the plays. Edmund Wilson, in his essay "Bernard Shaw at Eighty," on the other hand, is much less respectful of Shaw's intellect, though he finds value in his art: "It always used to be said of Shaw that he was not primarily an artist but a promulgator of certain ideas. The truth is, I think, that he is a considerable artist, but that his ideas — that is, his social philosophy proper — has always been confused and uncertain."

Despite their differing estimates of Shaw's abilities, therefore, both critics suggest that Shaw must be approached in two separate ways — as a systematic philosopher, and as an artist who uses ideas as motifs in the structure of his plays. To this, however, we must add the testimony of Shaw himself, who is inclined to harp on a purely philosophical purpose: "I am, by profession," he writes, "what is called an original thinker." If Shaw, like Ibsen, is suspended between the ethical idealism of the revolutionary reformer and the aesthetic detachment of the objective artist, he is generally less willing to admit such irresolution; if Shaw might say, with almost as much justification as his Norwegian mentor, "I have been more of a poet and less of a social philosopher than is commonly believed," he is, nevertheless, temperamentally incapable of permitting such an admission to pass his lips. Thus, Shaw is a writer who produces works of art almost against his own choice. And though his dramatic writings frequently display that same conflict between the ethical and the aesthetic which dominates the entire theatre of revolt, Shaw's extradramatic writings are devoted to burying the aesthetic entirely, forcing ideological consistency, by a conscious act of will, onto his fundamentally unconscious dualism.

What is worse, he often succeeds. There may be no such thing as Ibsenism, but there is certainly a thing called Shavianism; and a considerable portion of Shaw's work, including some of his plays, is a contribution not to art but to systematic thought. Through Shavianism, Shaw hoped to transform the world; and on this expectation of change, he staked everything, including his natural artistic gifts. As Eric Bentley describes it:

Shaw had artistic genius and knew it. Only he was not primarily interested in artistic genius and artistic reputation. He wanted his pen to be a sword in a struggle that was more ethical than aesthetic. Wishing to change the world, he wished to speak to the public at large, not merely to his literary confreres. . . . He knew that this was to risk sacrificing a high literary reputation (like, say, Henry James's); and the fact that his name is so often linked with the publicist Wells indicates that, for a time at least, Shaw has foregone that kind of reputation.

By Bentley's account, Shaw failed to achieve either the worldly influence he desired or the high reputation he deserved. Excluded from the company of artists like Lawrence, Eliot, and Yeats, each of whom were rather contemptuous of Shaw — scorned even by that more authentic Ibsenite, James Joyce — he eventually achieved astonishing fame as a middle-class idol and theatrical clown, but was never able to claim that he had had very much effect upon the minds of men. He could bear the contempt of his fellow artists, most of whom were consigning him to the oblivion reserved for outmoded Victorians, but his inability to change the direction of a world rapidly moving towards destruction plunged him into despair. Taking note of Shaw's bitter melancholy towards the end of his life, Bentley cites Shaw's mournful observation: "I have solved practically all the pressing problems of our time, but . . . they keep on being propounded as if I had never existed." In this portrait of a serious man whom nobody would take seriously, Shaw emerges as one who had made a vain sacrifice for a world unable to accept its saviors as it is unable to accept its saints. With Saint Joan, Shaw might well ask: "How long, O Lord, how long?"

Bentley's description of Shaw's personal disillusionment is excellent. But he is not quite skeptical enough about the validity of Shaw's claims. Edmund Wilson's conviction that Shaw's social philosophy is

"confused and uncertain" seems more apt, because Shavianism —
taken as a solution to "all the pressing problems of our time" — is as
implausible as its analysis of the problems is inadequate. As a revolutionary doctrine, Shaw's ideology is unoriginal, unconvincing, and
even rather timid; and if the world has remained indifferent to it as a
program for salvation, then this, for once, has been for good and
sufficient reasons. In his art, to be sure, Shaw often displays the
wisdom, skepticism, and doubleness that is missing from his philosophy. But when Shavianism runs rampant in his plays, as it occasionally does, his art degenerates as well. In order to salvage the more
enduring aspects of Shaw's work, let us first try to clear away the
murk of Shavianism, separating his negative artistic rebellion from his
affirmative philosophical doctrine. Then we can go on to show how he
uses this rebellion, dialectically, in his more complicated dramatic
works.

At first glance, Shaw's revolt seems to have much in common
with that of the most extreme rebels of the nineteenth century, for it
is animated by strong messianic tendencies. Fiercely discontented
with the actualities of our time, Shaw is dedicated to working a radical
revolution in the modern consciousness — indeed, in the whole of
modern life. Like Nietzsche, Shaw is repelled by the abjectness,
sloth, and mediocrity of contemporary man; like Rousseau, he is
keenly aware of the corruption in contemporary social and political
institutions; like Ibsen, he is enraged by the falsehood and deception
in contemporary conventions. Though he shares the rebel's hatred of
reality, however, Shaw is more sanguine about his ability to change
it, which is why he offers a detailed program of reform, aimed at
moral, political, and religious salvation. Still, if the gospel of Shavianism is optimistic, social, and progressive, the implications of Shaw's
revolt are negative, individualistic, and disintegrative. The doctrine of
the Superman, while adapted to a benevolent vision of Utopian community life, arises out of Shaw's dissatisfaction with the basic nature
of man and his society; and the doctrine of Creative Evolution, while
it assumes the eventual development of a new type of life, suggests
Shaw's disillusionment with conventional notions of progress through

education.[6] In his determination to destroy existing conventions, to annihilate existing institutions, to change human nature, and to purify modern life, Shaw looks like an extreme form of Romantic idealist, despite his unsparing attacks on "romantics" and "idealists" throughout his works.[7]

What Shaw has in common with Nietzsche, Ibsen, and Rousseau, however, is often weakened by what he has in common with Plato, Jeremy Bentham, Edward Bellamy and the Webbs. For the radical individualism which animates his revolt is usually modified by a social utilitarianism which domesticates and even contradicts it; accompanying his Romantic rebellion against society is a Classical concern with the needs and problems of modern industrial democracy. As a messianic prophet, Shaw is dissatisfied with any social organization manipulated by fallible human beings; but as a Fabian Socialist, Shaw is committed to a realistic and attainable kind of social order, and even writes pamphlets discussing its sociology, politics, biology, medicine, and economics.

As soon as Shaw begins to contemplate positive programs to supplement his negative revolt, he is forced into contradictions. For the Ibsenite rebel who will tolerate no compromise with his ideals must adjust to a Victorian pragmatist who is willing to trim, ameliorate, and flirt with power politics. The Nietzschean individualist who looks forward to the Super*man* must make room for a Platonic republican

[6] Shaw is no crude progressivist or educationist. In the preface to *Man and Superman*, he writes: "Progress can do nothing but make the most of us all as we are, and that most would clearly not be enough even if those who are already raised out of the lowest abysses would allow the others a chance. The bubble of Heredity has been pricked: the certainty that acquirements are negligible as elements in practical heredity has demolished the hopes of the educationists as well as the terrors of the degeneracy mongers. . . ." Having dismissed these liberal illusions about bettering the minds of the masses, Shaw can only contemplate radical solutions: "We must either breed political capacity or be ruined by Democracy. . . ."

[7] I have already commented, in my chapter on Ibsen, on Shaw's playful abuse of these terms. By redefining the "realist" and the "idealist" to suit himself, he is able to pass off his own rebellion against reality as a love of reality, and his Utopian idealism as a passionate pursuit of "truth." See the chapter "Ideals and Idealists" in *The Quintessence of Ibsenism*.

who looks forward to a collective of Super*men.* The Rousseau Romantic who questions the very *essence* of society must accommodate a Fabian Socialist who questions only certain *forms* of society. Shaw is a political impossiblist who cannot appreciate an impossiblism of the imagination; he is always laboring to translate imaginative revolt into social action. But art and politics are not identical activities; and when the chips are down, Shaw is more apt to betray the imagination than sacrifice his belief in human control and state planning, which is why today he often looks less like an artist than like an oracle of the welfare state. For unlike Ibsen, who wanted to torpedo the Ark and begin anew, Shaw — for all his radical theorizing and dangerous moods — is generally more temperate and cautious when contemplating change: "Neither must we undertake a new world as catastrophic Utopians," he warns, "and wreck our civilization in our hurry to mend it." As a fact of life, this is, of course, obvious. As a fact of art, it is restrictive and banal.

Shaw himself is perfectly conscious of the contradictions in his position — "the dilemma," as he puts it, "that civilization means stabilization; and creative evolution means change." There is wistfulness in his observation that "the revolutionist of twenty-five, who sees nothing for it but a clean sweep of all our institutions, finds himself, at forty, accepting and even clinging to them on condition of a few forms to bring them up to date." Sometimes, he attempts to preserve the purity of youthful revolt by dividing his program into short-range and long-range functions — the one, ameliorative and social, the other radical, imaginative, and "religious." Sometimes, however, he tries to correlate the two functions, as when he offers to prove that Ibsen was really a benefactor of society: "The advantage of the work of destruction," he writes in *The Quintessence of Ibsenism,* "is that every new ideal is less of an illusion than the one it has supplanted, so that the destroyer of ideals, though denounced as an enemy of society, is in fact sweeping the world clear of lies." Here, again, Shaw tries to find a practical application for an artistic office, to socialize an essentially nonsocial activity. Ibsen would have found no social "advantage" in his works of destruction, since, for him, society was founded on lies; but Shaw cannot accept the anarchical implications of Ibsen's position.[8] This is even clearer in his discussion of *Little Eyolf* where he tries to adapt Ibsen's anarchism to his own Socialism through much the same kind of contorted reasoning: "Thus we see that in Ibsen's mind, as in the actual history of the nineteenth century, the way to Communism lies through the most resolute and uncompromising Individualism. . . . When a man is at last brought face to face with himself by a brave Individualism, he finds himself face to face, not with an Individual, but with a species, and knows that to save himself, he must save the race. He can have no life except a share in the life of the community. . . ."

The rhetoric is powerful, and the sentiments still are able to stir the blood. But Shaw's remarks have little relevance to Ibsen, who was neither a Socialist nor a Salvationist; and they have even less application to the other great rebel thinkers of the nineteenth century. For while Rousseau, Ibsen, and Nietzsche all anticipate Shaw's dissatisfaction with reality, none of them are moved to "save the race" through wholehearted identification with the community, perhaps because they realize that the state which promises life has served, through mass culture, mass conformity, and mass wars, to degrade, dehumanize, and take life away. As an artist, Shaw undoubtedly experiences his own kind of alienation; and when he is warring on the cant and humbug of contemporary society, his rebellion, if rarely fierce, is generally pure. Still, his sense of purpose makes him subordinate his discontent to affirmative programs of reform; and his com-

---

[8] Shaw's dislike of anarchism becomes almost an obsession. And throughout the nineties, he combats the Anarchist position vigorously in at least three prose works: *The Impossibilities of Anarchism* (1893), *The Sanity of Art* (1895), and *The Perfect Wagnerite* (1898). Shaw believes that without government man's alliance against inhospitable nature would be dissolved, and that anarchism "must always reduce itself speedily to absurdity" when applied "to the industrial or political machinery of modern society." Shaw's position is sound enough, but he does not sufficiently distinguish between philosophical anarchism (the imaginative individualism of the rebel artist) and political anarchism. Ibsen, like so many modern artists, is a philosophical anarchist, which is to say, not a political activist at all.

mitment to salvation through the social unit is too powerful to let him escape into an antisocial individualism.[9] Thus, if Shaw is a rebel, he is a rebel in search of a community, his personal revolt frequently swallowed up by a desperate need to affirm a union of all mankind.

Plagued by such contradictions, Shaw is sometimes pressed away from the perceptions of his art to the earnest Utopianism of his evangelical visions, where, seven degrees removed from the real world, insoluble dilemmas can be resolved in wishful fantasies. Certainly, Shavianism has always looked like a peculiarly eccentric social philosophy which, instead of "sweeping the world clear of lies," merely pushes the dust around a little more. When in the grip of Shavianism, in fact, Shaw is often guilty of the same sin for which he castigates the "mere artist" — weaving a beautiful web of "illusion" over "the unbearable face of truth."

This is certainly true in *Back to Methuselah* (1921), a five-play epic with an extensive preface, and a postscript added in 1945. Shaw was excessively fond of this work (he regarded it as his masterpiece), probably because it is the most systematic introduction to Shavianism he ever compiled. But though it renders Shaw's doctrine in a relatively ordered manner, the work is, significantly, vapid and tedious as art. Here conflict has been subordinated to argument and exposition; and Shaw's acute apprehension of reality has been submerged beneath the weight of Utopian ideals. Usually, the Shavian preface and the Shavian drama perform separate and distinct functions, but here they seem to be continuous — the Idea, elaborated in discursive prose, is merely extended into dramatic dialogue. As a result, the play lacks such redeeming qualities as wit, style, dialectic, subtle characterization, or amusing fable. Bending reality to the shape of his wishes — trying to achieve in fantasy what he cannot achieve in fact — Shaw,

[9] Chesterton calls Shaw a "republican" in the literal Latin sense: "He cares more for the Public thing than for any private thing." Aristophanes also cared primarily for *res publica,* and, in this sense alone, Shaw's comedy is Aristophanic. But Shaw's public interests made his work seem detached from the movement of modern art which is, on the whole, a personal, private, and poetic mode of expression.

in *Back to Methuselah,* looks less like a vigorous artist than like the kind of visionary whom Nietzsche contemptuously called "the play-actor of his own ideal."

The design of the work is simple: the preface advances the theory of Creative Evolution; the five playlets illustrate the theory in semi-dramatic form; and the postscript exhorts the reader to embrace the theory or perish. The preface is, for our purposes, the most interesting part of *Back to Methuselah,* since it best illustrates the messianic character of Shaw's rebellion. Here, Shaw claims a kind of divine authority for his writings. Following Nietzsche, who created *Thus Spake Zarathustra* in the form of the synoptic Gospels, Shaw suggests that *Back to Methuselah* is inspired scripture — significantly, the work is subtitled "A Metabiological Pentateuch." Shaw has already elevated Ibsen, in *The Quintessence,* to "canonical rank" as "one of the major prophets of the modern Bible." Here he seems to aspire towards the same rank himself: "I have written *Back to Methuselah,*" he declares, "as a contribution to the modern Bible," adding that "a new Reformation" is "the whole purpose of this book." Shaw's presumptuous claims are more the result of his desperation than of his arrogance. Having watched man bring upon himself a catastrophic war — a war he attributes largely to the ruthless survival theories of the "Neo-Darwinists" — Shaw has now become more urgent and apocalyptic in his thinking, convinced that "If man is to be saved, Man must save himself." The means of salvation Shaw contributes in the form of a new redemptive system, calling it that "genuinely scientific religion for which all wise men are anxiously seeking."

Shaw's "scientific religion" is actually a hodgepodge of ideas from the various nineteenth-century philosophers, artists, and scientists of whom Shaw approves, but primarily, it combines Bergson's "religion" of Creative Evolution with Lamarck's "science" of Functional Adaptation, both adapted to Shaw's visionary optimism. Familiar enough by now to be described briefly,[10] the Shavian system holds that man has evolved, not through accident (as the Darwinists "mistakenly"

[10] For a more extended description of Shaw's "religious" ideas, see the chapter "Vital Economy" in Bentley's *Bernard Shaw.*

assume), but through the exercise of a universal will — somewhat like Schopenhauer's *Wille* except that it is intelligent and benign rather than cruel and blind. Shaw, finding a rough English equivalent for Bergson's phase *élan vital*, calls this the Life Force. To Shaw, the Life Force is both immanent and transcendent — both in man and outside him — but its central purpose is the determination of man's evolutionary career. For just as the Life Force has made human beings superior to animals, so it will eventually create a being superior to humans. Following Nietzsche, who believed that "man is a bridge and not a goal," Shaw awaits the coming of the Superman. This creature represents to Shaw the last step in man's revolt against God. For with the advent of the Superman, Man will become God, and all social, moral, and metaphysical problems will be solved.

After discussing evolution in the realm of human affairs, Shaw proceeds to discuss its probable effect on art. Still trying to find a positive function for the artist in a reconciled society, Shaw declares: "The revival of religion on a scientific basis does not mean the death of art, but a glorious rebirth of it. Indeed art has never been great when it was not providing an iconography for a live religion." Shaw has to qualify this when he turns his attention to the theatre, since he must admit that the great Western dramatists, appearing during the decline of religion, have usually not had anything "fundamentally positive to say." He adds, however, that comedy — as a "destructive, derisory, critical, negative art" — has, at least, the virtue of being in revolt against "falsehood and imposture," a function which he has already identified as a social and religious good. Shaw has a little more difficulty justifying Shakespearean tragedy, which he finds populated with "pessimists and railers" — but he concludes that Shakespeare "would really not be great at all if it were not that he had religion enough to be aware that his religionless condition was one of despair." [11]

---

[11] In the preface to *Man and Superman*, Shaw had already remarked that writers such as Shakespeare "have no constructive ideas; they regard those who have them as dangerous fanatics" — such writers, therefore, are distinguished from the "artist-philosophers" of whom Shaw approves.

As for the modern dramatists, they have had to wrestle with an even deeper despair:

The giants of the theatre of our time, Ibsen and Strindberg, had no greater comfort for the world than we; indeed much less; for they refused us even the Shakespearean-Dickensian consolation of laughter at mischief, accurately called comic relief. . . . Ibsen was Darwinized to the extent of exploiting heredity on the stage much as the ancient Athenian playwrights exploited the Eumenides; but there is no trace in his plays of any faith in or knowledge of Creative Evolution as a modern scientific fact. True, the poetic aspiration is plain enough in his Emperor or Galilean; but it is one of Ibsen's distinctions that nothing was valid for him but science; and he left that vision of the future which his Roman seer calls "the third Empire" behind him as a Utopian dream when he settled down to his serious grapple with realities. . . .

Aside from the dubious assertion that "nothing was valid for [Ibsen] but science," [12] Shaw's insights into the negative aspects of the modern drama are penetrating and sound. Despite the messianic impulses they both share, neither Ibsen nor Strindberg does offer any "comfort" for the world, other than the metaphysical comfort of art. Shaw, on the other hand, is now preparing to provide that comfort. Where Ibsen merely outlined the *need* for a new religion, stemming from a synthesis of paganism and Christianity, Shaw has already found his faith: Creative Evolution. Where Strindberg wrestled unsuccessfully with God in order to assert the supremacy of man, Shaw has already pinned the old God and is now occupying himself with the new: the Life Force as embodied in the Superman. Having thus solved, to his own satisfaction, the problems that plagued his predecessors, Shaw has decided to top their essentially negative insights with something "fundamentally positive." Declaring his "natural function as an artist" to serve as "iconographer of the religion of my time," Shaw proceeds to turn their messianic expectations into messianic

[12] As a matter of fact, Ibsen's feeling for religion is much more profound, and much less secular, than Shaw's. Shaw seems to acknowledge Ibsen's religious strain when he says, "Ibsen's attack on morality is a symptom of the revival of religion, not its extinction" — but Ibsen is not only interested in religious ethics, but also in religious mysticism.

fantasies, imagining the Life Force operating through a series of "consoling myths."

In the plays which follow this prefatory declaration, Shaw creates five of these "consoling myths," based on the religion of the Life Force. The first, "In the Beginning," is Shaw's revision of the Book of Genesis, now interpreted according to Creative Evolution. The action revolves around Adam and Eve — and later Cain — confronted with the post-lapsarian problem of death. Mortality spells the end of man's hopes, making human aspiration ultimately futile; but the secret which the Serpent insinuates into the ear of Eve is the method by which man can transcend this obstacle — procreation and birth. The suggestion makes Eve recoil in disgust — it is, presumably, too clumsy and ugly, and, in the last play of the sequence, Shaw will suggest a more antiseptic process. Nevertheless, by the second part of the playlet, Eve has heeded the Serpent's advice and brought forth Cain. Shaw's attitude towards Cain exposes his ambivalence towards the rebel. As "the revolted son," Cain is a heroic figure to Shaw, as he was to Strindberg, since his rebellion is an expression of discontent with an intolerable reality. But while it is Cain who visualizes something higher than man ("There is hero and Superman"), he is too antisocial to satisfy Shaw's community-mindedness.[13] As Eve tells Cain, "You are no superman; you are Anti-Man" — an enemy of the Life Force. For if Adam has invented death, Cain has invented murder, pillage, and conquest. The introduction of crime into the world has shortened life even more; the introduction of revenge has turned brother against brother, community against community.

The second play in the sequence — "The Gospel of the Brothers Barnabas" — suggests a way out of the dilemma of death: voluntary longevity. By willing himself a longer term of life (three centuries is the required span), Man will become like God, having achieved omnipotence and omniscience — "greater power and greater knowledge." Shaw's assumption is that man grows both wiser and more

[13] Shaw remarks, in the postscript to this play, "My hero in fiction was the rebel, not the goodygoody citizen whom I despised." Nevertheless, Shaw cannot tolerate any rebellion which does not inevitably lead to good citizenship.

benevolent as he grows older, and more gifted, too, since he is able to outlive those sensual pulls which lure him from perfection.[14] To affirm this theory, Shaw must deny the validity of the whole scientific and religious tradition which opposes it; and he dispatches the opposition in a rather perfunctory manner. Determinism stands in his way, so Shaw imagines that the twentieth-century scientists have rejected Darwin, and that "all scientific opinion worth counting has been converging rapidly on Creative Evolution." The only "scientific opposition" that he mentions holds that "the human race is a failure, and that a new form of life, better adapted to high civilization, will supersede us as we have superseded the ape and the elephant" — in short, even the "scientific opposition" seems to believe in Creative Evolution. As for the religious opposition, with its notion of original sin, the biologist Conrad Barnabas declares, "The Fall is outside Science," while his more theologically-minded brother, Franklyn, explains it away as the consequence of the briefness of life: Adam "let the thistles grow" because "life was so short that it was no longer worth his while to do anything thoroughly well." The thistles in the soul of man, presumably, will be cropped when he is able to achieve his three-hundredth birthday.

In the third myth of the pentateuch, "The Thing Happens," Shaw's fantasy is being realized. An archbishop has lived to be 283, and other human beings are also increasing their life spans. It is A.D. 2170 and the English government is now staffed with Chinese; "Saint Henrik Ibsen" has been canonized; and family bonds are beginning to dissolve. So are all other bonds, for man is now outliving his "childish passions," losing interest in anything but moral and intellectual objects. One character decides against a love affair with a Negress when he discovers that life is too valuable to be wasted; another

[14] In "The Thing Happens," Mrs. Lutestring affirms that her artist-husband only became great when he finished painting "all the foolish pictures" of his youth, but by that time, he was ready to die. Shaw's progressive theory of art, however, is invalidated by Shaw himself, who hardly became a better writer with advancing age. Even in his preface to *Back to Methuselah,* in fact, he admits that his "powers are waning," and that "the exuberance of 1901 has aged into the garrulity of 1920."

discovers that wisdom comes "not by recollections of our past, but by the responsibilities of our future." In the fourth playlet, "The Tragedy of an Elderly Gentleman," we are even further into this responsible future, where human beings are now divided into two classes: the short- and the long-lived. Part of the play is taken up with Shaw's usual Britain-baiting; part with a witless conversation between Napoleon (the resurrected Cain) and an oracle. But the purpose of the playlet is to point up the great intellectual disparity between the short-livers and the long-livers; the tragedy of the short-lived elderly gentleman is that, having sojourned in the land of the long-lived with their deeper sense of reality, he can no longer live "among people to whom nothing is real."

In the last and most famous playlet in the sequence, "As Far as Thought Can Reach," the prophecy of Creative Evolution has been fulfilled — the Superman has evolved. The time is 31,920; the setting is Arcadian; and romping about in Grecian costumes are a group of Youths with pastoral names. Hatched from eggs, fully grown at the age of seventeen, the Youths indulge themselves, for periods of four years, in all the adolescent amusements of mankind: love, sex, music, art, and the dance. Then — like one Maiden who wants "to get away from our eternal dancing and music and just sit down by myself and think about numbers" — they experience a metamorphosis into Ancients. The Ancients are the Shavian Supermen — ageless, hairless beings, thoroughly devoid of charm, beauty, or sexual appetite — who devote themselves to the work of pure contemplation, presumably meditating on the rhythms of the universe. Yet, even this is not the culmination of man's future; one more stage of evolution has yet to be completed, when mind has conquered matter altogether. Lilith, Adam's first wife, concludes the play with such a prophecy. Peering into the vast and endless void, she envisions the ultimate freedom of man after centuries of enslavement to the body: "Now I shall see the slaves free and the enemy reconciled, the whirlpool become all life and no matter." Or, as another character puts it: "The day will come when there will be no more people, only thought."

It is a fitting idea with which to conclude such a dry, dreary, and artless work; no other play of Shaw's so thoroughly estranges one from the man who wrote it. For although the Devil had warned, in *Man and Superman*, "Beware of the pursuit of the Superhuman; it leads to an indiscriminate contempt for the Human," Shaw's contempt now seems so powerful that he has left humanity behind altogether, turning to those "ideal or social or political entities, fleshless, bloodless, and cold" against which D. H. Lawrence (with particular reference to "Bernard Shaw's creatures") was always wont to inveigh. Certainly, the Shavian Superman — stripped of instincts and emotions, and reduced to disembodied mind — is a far cry from the Nietzschean *Übermensch,* that wild, ecstatic immoralist whom Nietzsche hoped would galvanize the feeble emotional core of modern life. And though Shaw considers himself a Nietzschean, one of Zarathustra's admonitions seems to have escaped him: "I go not your way, ye despisers of the body! Ye are no bridges from me to the Superman." It is likely, in fact, had Nietzsche known Shaw's works, that he would have included him, along with Euripides, in his gallery of "Socratic" writers — those overintellectualized enemies of the lofty Dionysian art.[15] It is likely also that most of Shaw's other "influences" — Ibsen, Strindberg, Carlyle, Bergson, Blake, Schopenhauer, Wagner[16] — would have repudiated him too. For Shaw has an incorrigible tendency to mentalize, socialize, and domesticate the more

[15] Nietzsche's Zarathustra, waiting for the "higher man," announces that "there is one that must first come. One who will make you laugh once more, a good jovial buffoon, a dancer, a wind, a wild romp, some old fool —" This sounds like Shaw — but only in part. As Chesterton put it: "Nietzsche might really have done some good if he had taught Bernard Shaw to draw the sword, to drink wine, or even to dance." Shaw's politics, moreover, would probably have depressed Nietzsche, who considered Socialism to be merely a further degeneration of Christianity, and who considered the State to be "the coldest of all cold monsters."

[16] Shaw proclaims his affinities with these writers, but denies that they influenced him, declaring that he formed his ideas independently of philosophy or literature: "Whenever my view strikes [English critics] as being at all outside the range of, say, an ordinary suburban churchwarden," he writes in the preface to *Major Barbara*, "they conclude that I am echoing Schopenhauer, Nietzsche, Ibsen, Strindberg, Tolstoy, or some other heresiarch in northern or eastern Europe." Despite his disclaimers, however, Shaw's debt to other writers is unusually large.

dangerous insights of rebel artists and philosophers. And for all his humanitarianism, he is dedicated not to recovering man's fading humanity, but rather to inventing something altogether new: in the doctrine of Shavianism, man becomes free only by ceasing to be man.

What this suggests is that behind Shaw's concern with the Superhuman — the whole complex of messianic Shavianism — is a profound and bitter existential revolt, more painful, perhaps, than anything we have yet confronted. For Shaw is not simply dissatisfied with certain human activities; he sometimes seems to be in rebellion against the very nature of human existence. The bodiless character of Shaw's Superman — not to mention Shaw's own vegetarianism, teetotalism, and abstention from sexual intercourse after his marriage — indicates a kind of Swiftian disgust at the human body and its functions. And though, like most comic writers, Shaw is often able to transform these personal feelings into ironic amusement at the dualistic nature of man, he is, as a Utopian philosopher, apparently unable to accept man's animality as a permanent fact of life. Strindberg, finally coming to terms with the same feelings, was able to universalize his revulsion at "the dirt of life" in the excremental vision of his art. But Shaw, concerned with a "higher purpose" than this, will neither explore his existential rebellion nor even acknowledge it. Nevertheless, it probably determines the shape of his Utopia in *Back to Methuselah;* and his outrage at human limitation undoubtedly determines the characteristics of his Superman. Thus, despite his pretense at destroying illusions, Shaw cannot accept the reality of his own feelings. And thus, he refuses to see what Arnold called "the object as in itself it really is."

He is, in fact, subject to the granddaddy of all illusions — one, ironically, that he had already described in *The Quintessence of Ibsenism:*

The king of terrors, Death, was the Arch-Inexorable: Man could not bear the dread of that. He must persuade himself that Death can be propitiated, circumvented, abolished. How he fixed the mask of personal immortality on the face of death for this purpose we know. . . . Thus he became an idealist, and remained so until he dared to begin pulling the masks off and looking the spectres in the face — dared, that is, to be more and more a realist.

If Shaw is too much of a "realist" to don the mask of personal immortality, he is too much of an "idealist" to face the "dread" of the "Arch-Inexorable." And so he tries to propitiate, circumvent, and abolish death through a mask of his own invention — voluntary longevity. Philosophy, according to Montaigne, consists in learning how to die; but death has no place in Shaw's philosophy, since it calls an end to progress, and mocks all human aspiration. The ageless Ancient proceeds from the imagination of a man unable to look his "spectres in the face," lest he be forced back into existential despair.

Shaw admits as much by the imperative nature of his phrasing. "We can and *must* live longer." "Professional science *must* cease to mean the nonsense of Weismann and the atrocities of Pavlov." We *"must* renounce magic and yet accept miracle." Such imperatives suggest how Shaw continually reverts to the consoling and the necessary, rather than to the true. If he *must* believe that all the theories, opinions, and facts which contradict his doctrine are "delusions," he cannot prove that the delusions are not his own. Temperamentally unable to contemplate a permanent state of imperfectability, Shaw is finally forced back into simple expressions of faith:

We must either embrace Creative Evolution or fall into the bottomless pit of an utterly destroying pessimism. . . . Discouragement does in fact mean death; and it is better to cling to the hoariest of the old savage-creators than to abandon all hope in a world of "angry apes," and perish in despair like Shakespear's Timon.

This is as close to an admission of emotional desperation as Shaw is likely to come. Confronted with the Arch-Inexorable (Shaw, significantly, identifies discouragement with death), he must turn away his face and seek out utilitarian illusions by which to survive.

Shaw's determination to keep his mask firmly fixed over his anguished features can be clearly observed in his remarks about *Too True to Be Good* (1932). In all other respects a pleasant light comedy, this work is intermittently suffused with the author's almost nihilistic bitterness on the subjects of the cruelty and madness of World War I, the futility of the Geneva negotiations, the aimlessness of the young, and the spiritual dislocation caused by Einstein's universe ("All is caprice; the calculable world has become incalculable"). And the last speech of the play, the concluding sermon of Shaw's protagonist, Aubrey, is a moving confession of messianic bankruptcy:

I am by nature and destiny a preacher. I am the new Ecclesiastes. But I have no Bible, no creed: the war has shot both out of my hands. . . . I must have affirmations to preach. Without them the young will not listen to me; for even the young grow tired of denials. . . . I am ignorant; I have lost my nerve and am intimidated; all I know is that I must find the way of life, for myself and all of us, or we shall surely perish. And meanwhile my gift has possession of me: I must preach and preach and preach no matter how late the hour and how short the day, no matter whether I have nothing to say —

The tone of personal disillusionment is strong, and the autobiographical note is unmistakable; but when critics made the obvious connections, Shaw vigorously repudiated them, declaring that Aubrey's despair "is not my despair," and that he had never lost his messianic beliefs: "I affirm, on the contrary, that never during my lifetime has the lot of mankind seemed more hopeful, and the beginnings of a new civilization more advanced." Shaw can look for a moment into the bottomless pit, but it is not long before he is whistling up his spirits again. His messianic rebellion is his last refuge, his Utopian idealism his last escape, from the tragic impasse of modern existence.

It is for the same reason that Shaw ignores the more depressing implications of nineteenth-century thought. His embrace of Creative Evolution seems like the last desperate gamble of a Victorian rationalist confronted with a mechanical and determined world. Since Shavianism assumes an ordered, reasoned, and coherent universe, Shaw must adopt mystical and irrational principles in order to maintain his assumptions; and despite his affectation of a "scientific method," Creative Evolution is neither scientific nor methodical. Thus, he rejects Darwin not on empirical evidence, but on the grounds that Darwinism inspires pessimism: "What damns Darwinian Natural

Selection as a creed," he declares, "is that it takes hope out of evolution and substitutes a paralysing fatalism which is utterly discouraging. As Butler put it, it 'banishes mind from the universe.'" Still fleeing from discouragement, Shaw puts mind back in the universe in the form of the Life Force — that amiable fiction which seems to be occupied exclusively with human betterment and social perfection, and which resembles nothing so much as the smiling God of Voltaire's Doctor Pangloss.

Shaw is just as unable to accept the concept of a malevolent or determined man as to accept the concept of a determined and mindless universe. Though he follows Ibsen in twitting the liberals and ridiculing their sentimental ideals, Shavianism is itself based on a familiar Liberal illusion: "It is quite useless," Shaw declares, using his characteristic utilitarian phrasing, "to declare that men are born free if you deny that they are born good." Ibsen was forced to modify his subjective faith in the will, and acknowledge the power of fate. But Shaw, still riding the first crest of Romanticism, can tolerate no limitation on human possibility — which is why he repudiates the religious concepts of imperfectibility and predestination, and the scientific concepts of aggression and determinism. Thus, in the century of Darwin, Shaw's characters are never victimized by their biological inheritance. And thus, in the century of Freud, they are totally free from any real anguish, suffering, or neurosis. The Shavian soul is generally a sunlight soul — empty of menace, without fatality. If the unconscious exists in Shaw's writings, it exists largely as a subject for discussion. Made self-conscious — reduced to analytical terms — it loses all its darkness and its threat.

This is not to say that Shaw completely ignores the aggressive side of man. It is one of the major subjects under discussion in the Hell sequence of *Man and Superman;* and the Devil's descriptions of human greed, ruthlessness, and cruelty are among the most eloquent in literature. Still, like his protagonist, Don Juan, Shaw is inclined to attribute such things not to human evil, but to human cowardice, stupidity, or prejudice; and he almost never shows them in action. "Crime, like disease, is not interesting," he affirms in the preface to

Saint Joan, proceeding to dramatize (through the repentance of "mad-dog" De Stogumber) his conviction that whatever passes for human cruelty is really the consequence of ignorance. Shaw's kindness is one of his most appealing qualities, but it makes him incapable of appreciating human defect, while his need to believe in limitless possibilities for mankind continually binds him to the darker, more unredeemable side of human character.

Thus, as late as 1944, during the most terrible war in the history of man, Shaw is still insisting that the "pessimism" of Ecclesiastes, Shakespeare, and Swift is based on a misreading of the human soul:

[Reformers] all agree that you cannot have a new sort of world without a new sort of Man. A change in heart they call it. But the Bible tells us that the heart of Man is deceitful above all things and desperately wicked. . . .

Nevertheless if this book is to be worth writing or reading, I must assume that all this pessimism and cynicism is a delusion caused, not only by ignorance of contemporary facts but, in so far as they are known, by drawing wrong conclusions from them. It is not true that all the atrocities of Capitalism are the expression of human vice and evil will; on the contrary, they are largely the product of domestic virtue, of patriotism, of philanthropy, of enterprise, of progressiveness, of all sorts of socially valuable qualities. . . . With such human material, we can produce a dozen new worlds when we learn both the facts and the lessons in political science the facts can teach.

(*Everybody's Political What's What*)

Here, again, we can observe how Shaw's ideas are motivated by a utilitarian imperative ("if this book *is to be worth* writing or reading, *I must assume*"), and how this imperative forces him into wishful thinking. For the "contemporary facts" which Shaw would have us understand would now have to include the Nazi extermination centers, saturation bombing, and Soviet slave labor camps (Hiroshima and the spectacle of two mass powers threatening each other with nuclear extinction are still to come); yet, he is still affirming the essentially philanthropic nature of man. One can see why Leon Trotsky expressed the wish that "the Fabian fluid that ran in [Shaw's] veins might have been strengthened by even so much as five per cent of the blood of Jonathan Swift." Despite his Marxist orientation, Shaw cannot accept Marx's analysis of the darker human motives behind capitalism. For although he is wont to expend considerable indignation against the "system," he invariably exempts the system-makers from his indictment,[17] providing them with the same "socially valuable qualities" which he hopes to utilize in his new world. In short, Shaw *must* believe in human decency. Without this belief, his hope in the future is misplaced; and all he can look forward to is apocalypse.

We can sympathize with Shaw's dilemma, since we share it. If Shaw has illusions, they are the illusions of mankind in an appalling world; and, as a social philosopher, they permit him to function in a productive manner. Yet, the function of the social philosopher is quite different from the function of the artist, since the *modus vivendi* of the one is often a form of dishonesty to the other. Shaw's need to believe in the possibilities of redemption rob his drama of an essential artistic office: the ruthless examination of all illusions, no matter how unpleasant. Eric Bentley, defending Shaw's optimism, asserts that no other philosophical attitude is possible: "If man is not a moral animal, let us all shoot ourselves. If he *is* a moral animal, then pessimism is an irresponsible pose" — but this is to adopt Shaw's utilitarian posture. The function of the artist is not to console, not to adopt a "responsible" pose, not to support "optimism" or "pessimism" — but to reveal, relentlessly, the truth that lies in the heart of man and in the heart of the universe. Some of the greatest works of art, in fact, have achieved greatness by exposing things which *might* tempt

[17] Although Shaw attacks prostitution, slum-landlordism, professional imposture, and capitalism, he very rarely attacks prostitutes, slum landlords, professional impostors, or capitalists — probably because the only motives he seems to accept as valid are economic ones. In *Mrs. Warren's Profession*, for example, Mrs. Warren is a brothel madam purely out of financial need. And in *Getting Married*, Shaw declares that prostitution has no other source than "the underpayment and ill-treatment of women who try to earn an honest living." This is in direct conflict with all studies of prostitutes and prostitution. In Shaw's world, however, there are very few psychological or emotional determinants, which is why he can continue to believe that an equal distribution of wealth will automatically eradicate all such social evils.

us to shoot ourselves, while elevating us with the prospect of human courage and nobility in the face of a terrible reality.

Such works — *Oedipus, King Lear, Rosmersholm, The Dream Play, The Ice Man Cometh* — are generally tragic dramas, and it would seem that I am chiding Shaw for failing to be a tragic artist. I am not. But I am suggesting that Shaw's failure to penetrate his own existential rebellion has robbed him of a tragic vision, without which his philosophy is trivial and even his comedy seems too narrow and restricted. Without a "sense of horror," as Bentley concedes, Shaw is excluded from the company of such great comic dramatists as Ben Jonson and Molière, neither of whom ignored the less consoling aspects of human character. And his insensitivity to the metaphysical side of man even excludes him from the company of the great modern dramatists of revolt. Too often, Shaw's reformist impulses and imperative needs dull his apprehension of Necessity, so that, like Arthur Miller, he sometimes tends to identify tragedy with social exploitation.[18] For like Arthur Miller, Shaw envisions a reconciled society in which there will *be* no more tragedy — or mystery either, since all human problems will be already solved. Looking forward to what will be, Shavianism can neither understand nor come to terms with what already is.

Thus, while Shaw exalts, exploits, and publicizes the rebel movement, he is totally unable to accept its darker side. The gospel of Shavianism channels the energies of revolt into social-political-philosophical uplift. The irony of Shaw's sense of "higher purpose" is that it imposes crucial restrictions on his art, since it usually prevents him from examining the bitter rebellion in his own heart. Although he finds "the true joy of life" in being "a force of Nature in-

---

[18] "True tragedy," Shaw declares, is "being used by personally-minded men for purposes which you recognize as base" — in short, tragedy is the result of social exploitation. Compare Miller, who writes: "I think the tragic feeling is evoked in us when we are in the presence of a character who is ready to lay down his life, if need be, to secure one thing — his sense of human dignity. From Orestes to Hamlet, Medea to Macbeth, the underlying struggle is that of an individual attempting to regain his 'rightful' position in society." Miller's sociological definition is much more simpleminded than Shaw's, and Shaw never falls into Miller's sentimentalization of common humanity — but neither writer is able to understand the metaphysical basis of tragedy.

stead of a feverish selfish little clod of ailments and grievances complaining that the world will not devote itself to making you happy," it is just this note of personal discontent that we miss in his work — for through this, we could better understand the unhappiness of all men. Shaw's perpetual cheer and optimism do not come easily to him, but they have become, in recent years, his most irritating qualities. If, at the same time that his fame is rising in commercial circles, he seems to be receding from our consciousness, this is perhaps because his buoyant mood is no longer a suitable response to the actualities of our time. In Shavianism, we can see — just as clearly as in the technological vision of H. G. Wells — the utter bankruptcy of the progressive Victorian temper in an age of confusion, upheaval, and ominous threat.

Shaw's messianic philosophy has alienated him from us; the myths of Shavianism neither console nor convince; his "scientific religion" has come to look neither like science nor religion; and his own illusions seem just as pronounced as the ones he sets out to expose — but there are still areas of Shaw's work which remain perfectly valid. Shavianism may seem just as quackish as Swedenborgianism — but like Swedenborgianism, it can sometimes be turned to imaginative use. If we regard Shavianism as a source for Shaw's dramatic metaphors (somewhat like the theosophical concepts of Yeats), then its quackeries seem less important; and if we regard it as a technique for demonstrating the spiritual and moral inadequacy of traditional creeds, then it even serves a valuable illustrative function. Actually, Shaw handles his hatred of reality in two distinct ways. As a revolutionary reformer, he registers his revolt against the real by pursuing the ideal in politics (Socialism) and philosophy (Creative Evolution). But, as an artist, he registers this revolt by recreating reality in the ideal form of art. Shaw may disapprove of those dramatists whose rebellion does not work towards positive goals, but his own rebellion is most compelling when it is least constructive. As Shaw himself understands, "Construction cumbers the ground with institutions made by busybodies. Destruction clears it and gives us breathing space and liberty." Like most artists who construct redemptive systems (Lawrence, for example), Shaw is convincing only in the act of denial. Behind the affirmative yea-sayer is a man who knows how to say no; behind the evangelical quacksalver stands a gifted diagnostician of modern maladies.

As a matter of fact, only a small part of Shaw's creative energies are channeled into Shavianism; one can hardly say that the bulk of his drama is dominated by a philosophical purpose. Accounting for the absence of ideology in his early plays, Shaw says: "Like Shakespear I had to write potboilers until I was rich enough to satisfy my evolutionary appetite (or, as they say, give way to my inspiration)," and he includes among such "shameless potboilers" *Pygmalion, Fanny's First Play,* and *You Never Can Tell* (he might have added *The Philanderer, Arms and the Man, The Devil's Disciple,* and *Overruled*). For a messianic prophet with such serious intentions, Shaw certainly enjoys a large number of holidays in his work; and one begins to suspect that his Puritan disapproval of the "mere artist" may reflect his self-disapproval as a writer of frivolous light comedies. Most of these comedies are still quite delightful; but they are generally free from any radical questioning, since their form is not hardy enough to support much philosophy. Like Oscar Wilde and W. S. Gilbert, Shaw bases his comic technique on the inversion of Victorian conventions, but while he is often outrageous, he is seldom much more: nothing in his work will bring a blush to the cheek of the young person.[19] Similarly, while Shaw is relentless in his ridicule of "Sardoodledom," the great majority of his comedies revolve around a

[19] Richard M. Ohmann, in *Shaw: The Style and the Man,* demonstrates, through a study of Shavian style, that the author often cultivates outrage for its own sake, and owes much of "his enormous popularity" to this ritualized unconventionality: "His denunciations of the old social order burned the ears of the pre-World War I generation, but they stirred the blood, too, and offered forbidden amusement to the more adventurous Victorians and Edwardians. . . . He was still crying the same blasphemies twenty, thirty, forty years later, though, and unconventionality is a garment that can wear thin." Ohmann's book, though primarily a semantic analysis, is one of the most intelligent of recent books on Shaw.

love plot borrowed from the well-made play — usually resolved conventionally, if for unconventional reasons. The artist in Shaw is sometimes so far from being a revolutionary that he seems to be a "mere" entertainer, creating works which are rescued from Boulevard conventionality only by a dazzling style and lively ideas.

Shaw's more serious plays, on the other hand, do embody Shavian principles; but these are usually treated in a highly ambiguous manner. Politically, for example, his dramas are surprisingly neutral. As Eric Bentley observes: "The fact is that while Shaw is a socialist in his treatises, and perhaps chiefly a socialist, he realizes . . . that neither socialism, nor capitalism, nor feudalism, nor any other ism can be the basis of an art, even so social an art as comedy. . . ." [20] Shaw may believe that his plays are written to "influence public opinion," but these works are usually too complicated to evoke a simple response, for like the plays of all the better rebel dramatists, they involve the author's revolt in a shifting dialectic of attitudes. In a letter to the Marxist, Hyndman, Shaw clearly defines this dialectic:

You are an economic revolutionary on a medieval basis of chivalry — Bayard educated by Marx. I am a moral revolutionary, interested, not in the class war, but in the struggle between human vitality and the artificial system of morality, and distinguishing, not between capitalist and proletarian, but between moralist and natural historian.

In another place, Shaw affirms that, as a dramatist, he deals "in the tragi-comic irony of the conflict between real life and the romantic imagination." In both cases, he is partly describing the clash between his own rebellion and reality. If we assume that the "romantic imagination" he speaks of is his own Utopianism — and the "artificial system of morality" he refers to is the system of Shavianism — then we can see that he is usually dramatizing his own inner conflicts: the Platonist versus the Aristotelian, the revolutionary idealist versus the

[20] Contributing to a symposium on the problem play, Shaw observes: "To this day your great dramatic poet is never a socialist, nor an individualist, nor a positivist, nor a materialist, nor any other sort of 'ist,' though he comprehends all 'isms,' and is generally quoted and claimed by all the sections as an adherent."

pragmatic realist, the Socialist versus the Vitalist, the Romantic versus the Classicist. Shaw once told Stephen Winsten that he would never have written plays if he had not been "a chaos of contradictions," for these contradictions, bothersome to an ideologist, are made to order for the drama. In consequence, no matter how wishful, fantastic, or visionary Shavianism may be, Shaw, in his drama, usually disciplines his "romantic imagination," confronting it with an unchanging, and sometimes unchangeable social order.

Take *Man and Superman*. Surrounded by an extensive preface on one side and a full-length revolutionary manifesto on the other — embodying a long "Shavio-Socratic dialogue" in the midst of the play, and a good deal of polemicizing throughout — the work would seem to be a shotgun blast of pure Shavianism, scattering ideology in all directions. Yet, unlike *Back to Methuselah*, where Shaw's "romantic imagination" is unfettered and unrestrained, *Man and Superman* brings his rebellion in conflict with flesh-and-blood reality, balancing the idealism of the philosophical moralist against the neutrality of the "natural historian."

The Epistle Dedicatory lays down the line that the play is *supposed* to follow. Dared by the aesthete-critic, Arthur Bingham Walkley, to write a Don Juan play, Shaw has decided to take up this mischievous suggestion, but he will turn it to his own ends; characteristically, he is preparing to invert (and domesticate) the traditional Don Juan character. From the Tirso de Molina *Burlador de Sevilla* to the Mozart–Da Ponte *Don Giovanni*, Don Juan has always been represented as a libertine and seducer who is finally punished by supernatural powers for his various sexual crimes. Shaw, on the other hand, is more attracted to the philosophical implications of the Don Juan story. Since Juan, while pursuing his own desires, inadvertently breaks moral, canon, and statute law, Shaw elects him as the agent of revolutionary Shavianism, envisioning him as a kind of Faustian rebel against God. Transformed into a messianic idealist and metaphysical saint, Shaw's Don Juan, therefore, both anticipates and predicts the coming of the God-defying Superman.

By this subtle trick, Shaw manages to ignore the sexual aspect of

Don Juan entirely, for in Shaw's mind this totally unselfconscious libertine takes on the character of a contemplative rebel hero who has progressed past his childish passions to a love of "purpose and principles." Though he manages to extract the amoral, promiscuous element from the legend, however, he does not totally extract its sexual quality, for he transfers Don Juan's amorousness to "Doña Juana," the husband-hunting female. Changing a legend of rape and seduction into a story of courtship and marriage, therefore, Shaw has the opportunity to reflect on a subject close to his heart — the character of the modern "unwomanly woman." Observing that "Man is no longer, like Don Juan, victor in the duel of sex," Shaw adds:

Woman must marry because the race must perish without her travail. . . . It is assumed that the woman must wait, motionless, until she is wooed. Nay, she often does wait motionless. That is how the spider waits for the fly. But the spider spins her web. And if the fly, like my hero, shews a strength that promises to extricate him, how swiftly does she abandon her pretense of passiveness, and openly fling coil after coil about him until he is secured for ever!

All this talk about the spider-woman, treacherously lying in wait for a male quarry and imprisoning him for her own purposes, sounds dangerous. And in the work of Schopenhauer and Nietzsche, where it was first formulated, and Strindberg, where it was first dramatized, the idea *is* dangerous. But Shaw swiftly takes the horror out of the perception. His spider-woman is not the dominating, amoral, and conscienceless *belle dame sans merci* of the Romantic agony, but rather the independent, intelligent, and well-mannered gentlewoman of the Victorian imagination, whose "unwomanliness" consists mainly in her active pursuit of a husband. Thus, Shaw adapts the Don Juan legend to the legend of Venus and Adonis, examining not the ruthless exploitation of the woman by the libertine seducer but rather "the tragi-comic love chase of the man by the woman." Lest the reader suspect that this purely Romantic subject is to be treated in a purely Romantic manner, Shaw adapts both legends to Shavianism, arguing that the whole comedy is played out for a higher purpose, the eventual evolution of the Superman through eugenic breeding. The marriage of John Tanner and Ann Whitefield, therefore — though a perfectly conventional conclusion of Romantic comedy — becomes another myth of the Life Force. Through such marriages man will breed that political capacity which will save him from the ruinous failures of democracy.

In his Epistle Dedicatory, in short, Shaw is single-mindedly devoted to advancing the gospel of Shavianism, elevating his comedy into a "play for a pit of philosophers." The Don Juan in Hell sequence — inserted into Act IV as the dream of Tanner and Mendoza — serves a similar function in a more double-minded way. By turning the Conan Doyle brigand, Mendoza, into the wily, hedonistic Devil, and Tanner into a contemplative Don Juan, Shaw initiates a debate on the virtues of Shavianism, elaborating on the various issues raised in his preface — reality and the ideal, man and woman, reason and emotion, man and Superman. The central device of the sequence is a Blakean inversion of the traditional concepts of Heaven and Hell. But where Blake used this device to express his diabolism and sensualism, concluding that "the tigers of wrath are wiser than the horses of instruction," Shaw imagines his hero trying to escape the sensual pleasures of the Devil's palace into a paradise of pure thought. The difference between the Devil and Don Juan rests mainly in their divergent interpretations of the universe. The Devil — assuming a universe without mind or purpose — holds that emotions rule men's lives and that history takes the form of an eternal recurrence. Ruling out progress, therefore, he has become a "romantic idealist," who posits physical pleasure and the cultivation of the arts as the highest goods. Don Juan, on the other hand, believes in a purposeful universe ruled by the Life Force: "That is, the working within me of Life's incessant aspirations to higher organization, wider, deeper, intenser self-consciousness, and clearer self-understanding." Like the "masters of reality" in Heaven, therefore, he has become a confirmed Shavian, one who believes in free will, the power of the mind, and the capacity of man to transform himself and his environment. If the Devil is right, then evolution is an illusion, marriage serves no particular purpose, and man's essentially destructive nature will climax in his self-destruction. If Don Juan is right, then evolution is a fact, marriage is an instrument of the Life Force, and man's malleable nature will eventually respond to reason. Because of Don Juan's concern with what will be and the Devil's concern with what is, we are not always sure who is the master of reality and who the Romantic idealist. But though Shaw uses loaded terms to suggest his own sympathies, he does not resolve the debate; and the Devil's diagnosis is made just as persuasive as Don Juan's hopes for the future. At the end, Don Juan — asserting his belief that "To be in hell is to drift, to be in heaven is to steer" — goes off to join the other heavenly pilots in their contemplation of a higher life, while the Devil returns to his duties. But while each antagonist remains unconvinced by the other, one person is converted to the "Life to come" — Doña Ana. Echoing Nietzsche's admonition to women ("Let your hope say: 'May I bear the Superman' "), she goes off to seek a father for the Higher Man.

If one were only to read the Epistle Dedicatory and the dream debate — not to mention *The Revolutionist's Handbook,* with its Nietzschean apothegms, Wildean epigrams, and Marxist admonitions — one might easily assume that the play proper was simply a dramatic illustration of these Shavian questions. Almost the opposite, however, is true. Since the play is concrete, contemporary, and ironic, rather than discursive, visionary, and abstract, it has a different quality altogether than the imposing material that surrounds it. The banter of Shaw's comedy, and its exuberant lightheartedness, contrast strongly with the more earnest tone of his prose; and many of the characters are peripheral to his central philosophical theme, being stock Shavian comic types. Roebuck Ramsden, for example, embodies Shaw's perennial satire on the Liberal Briton, the personification of dead conventions and outmoded ideals; 'Enry Straker, the class-conscious automobile mechanic, is a satire on the engineering hero of H. G. Wells; Mendoza, the lovelorn brigand, who turns to Socialism out of unrequited passion, is a satire on amoristic idealists; and Hector Malone, Sr., is a satire on the Irish-American millionaire, revenging himself on the English by buying up their hereditary titles and stately mansions. As for the Violet-Malone, Jr., subplot, this, as Eric Bentley tells us, has a structural function, being an inversion of the main plot (Violet begins with her man and must acquire her fortune; Ann begins with her fortune and must acquire her man) — meanwhile permitting Shaw to recapitulate his old idea (first advanced in *Widowers' Houses*) that a sound marriage must rest on a practical economic foundation.

The central action does develop some of Shaw's philosophical themes, but in a highly circumscribed and limited manner. John Tanner, though based on the gentleman Marxist, H. M. Hyndman, is much more occupied with the doctrine of the Life Force than with Marxist politics, and so he is the prime agent of revolutionary Shavianism. Still, as a rebel, he seems very tame. Considering Shaw's attitude towards libertinage, we are hardly surprised to find that his Don Juan is not only indifferent to women, but actively afraid of them. But if Tanner is no Don Juan, then neither is he that Faustian insurgent and God-killer whom Shaw speaks of in his preface. Shaw concedes as much when he tells Walkley that he has not bothered to put all the "tub-thumping" of the Epistle Dedicatory into the play: "I have only made my Don Juan a political pamphleteer, and given you his pamphlet by way of appendix." Shaw's dramatic instinct is quite sound. The atmosphere of the play proper is much too frothy to bear much "tub-thumping." And while Tanner's ideas may seem revolutionary in the appendix, the most radical thing he is capable of in the play is a willingness to tolerate premarital pregnancy — something designed to shock only the most conventional Victorian figures like Ramsden and Octavius.

Actually, Shaw is less occupied with advancing the cause of Shavianism, in *Man and Superman,* than with etching ironic contrasts between idea and character. "I shatter creeds and demolish idols," boasts Tanner, but he is, at heart, an eminently respectable gentleman of the upper middle class, differing from Ramsden in degree rather than in kind. Tanner implies as much when, defending his character against slander, he cries: "Thief, liar, forger, adulterer, perjurer, glutton, drunkard? Not one of these names fits me. You have to fall back on my deficiency in shame" — which is to say, his only rebellious characteristic is his intellectual impudence. Yet, this impudence remains strictly verbal; even Tanner is easy to shock. For all his talk about the predatory instincts of women — so glibly communicated to that cardboard lover, Octavius — Tanner behaves according to the strictest Victorian sexual standards. Though he is inclined to describe Ann's designs in the language of Schopenhauer and Strindberg (he is always commenting on her hypocrisy, bullying, lies, coquetry, and amorality, besides comparing her with such male-devouring insects as the spider and the bee), he is continually surprised when she does not act like the most conventional Victorian maiden.

Ann, too, seems unconventional only by contrast with an extremely outmoded ideal of feminine behavior. She is hardly the "dutiful" daughter that Ramsden thinks her, but neither is she that "Lady Mephistopheles" that Tanner speaks of. One has only to compare this charming coquette with Strindberg's Laura or Ibsen's Hedda or Chekhov's Arkadina to see that she has been created not by an antifeminist or a realist or a "natural historian," but rather by an archfeminist with a powerful admiration for women. Certainly, Ann's "unwomanliness" is not a fault but a virtue: she tells lies merely in order to win the man she loves. Despite the countless speeches in the play about the ruthlessness of sexual relations, therefore, *Man and Superman* confronts us not with a tragic combat between "the artist-man and the mother-woman" but rather with a classical opposition between two gifted sex antagonists who, like Benedict and Beatrice or Mirabel and Millamant, are ideally suited for the marriage which inevitably will come. Shaw lets his characters discuss the one action, but actually dramatizes the other. This gives the play intellectual depth and makes for ironic contrasts as well.

Reduced to its action, then, *Man and Superman* is too lightweight to support Shaw's doctrines. Rather than "a play for a pit of philosophers," it is a Classical comedy on the order of *Much Ado About Nothing* or *The Way of the World*. The presence of Shavianism in the play, however, does account for the wit inversions and satiric humor. Obviously, John Tanner functions not only as a mouthpiece for Shaw's theory of the Life Force, but also as an independent character with foibles of his own. While Octavius, worshiping women as the living embodiments of the Romantic ideal, is Tanner's butt, Tanner, worshiping life in its perpetual struggle upwards, is Shaw's. The doctrine of the Life Force is another form of Romantic idealization, and one of Shaw's purposes in the play is to show how all ideals are invariably mocked by life. The joke on Tanner, of course, is that all the time he is theorizing about the Life Force, he is being ensnared by it, until he is finally enmeshed in that machinery whose cogs and screws he has so accurately described. Thus, Shaw demonstrates how the self-conscious theoretician is caught up, against his will, by an unconscious, irrational force. Tanner's understanding of the transcendent principles of the universe is not defense against their actual workings. His "romantic imagination" is surprised by "real life."

Shaw is actually playing a practical joke on his own "romantic imagination" here. By distancing himself from the Shavian Tanner, he can demonstrate how Shavianism, being mainly intellectual and theoretical, is really inadequate to the thing it describes. For while Jack preaches Vitalism, it is Ann who personifies the Vitalist truths, precisely because she is motivated by instincts and unconscious will. As she tells Tanner, "You seem to understand all the things that I don't understand; but you are a perfect baby in the things I do understand" — one has the intelligence of the head, the other of the heart. And like the Reverend Morell in *Candida*, this windy preacher must be taught the lesson of life. For this reason, Tanner is always being punctured by Ann during his rhetorical flights, a deflation Shaw suggests through his use, in stage directions, of images of escaping air (Tanner "collapses like a pricked balloon," he falls "in ruins," he is "heavily let down," et cetera).[21] At the conclusion of the play,

[21] The puncturing of the rhetorical male by the unwomanly female is a favorite device of Shaw's, as the author admits in the parenthetical remarks with which he concludes *Too True to Be Good:* "The author, though himself a professional talk maker, does not believe that the world can be saved by talk alone. He has given the rascal the last word; but his own favorite is the woman of action, who begins by knocking the wind out of the rascal, and ends

when Tanner, having yielded to the inevitable, is trying to regain control of his fate by making a stump speech on the evils of bourgeois marriage, Ann contributes Shaw's final satiric thrust with her famous "Go on talking, Jack," and the sound of a punctured gasbag is smothered in "universal laughter." Shavianism, too, has been partly smothered in this laughter. For if Shaw, like Tanner, lacks a "negative capability" before the mystery of existence, he is too much of an artist not to satirize himself for it. His aim in *Man and Superman* is not so much to affirm or deny the principles of Shavianism as to show them in collision with reality — to confront a principle of change with the unchanging principle of life.

Unlike *Back to Methuselah,* then, *Man and Superman* has a double function: the prose portions of the work vindicate Shaw's philosophical ideals, while the drama places these ideals in the way of a gentle, mocking humor. The Don Juan in Hell sequence may take the form of a "consoling myth" (Shaw is later to call this section "a dramatic parable of Creative Evolution"), but his command of dialectic is sure enough to let him credit the arguments of the opposition. At this point in his career, Shaw is still able to control his rebellion, keeping the desperate illusions of his Utopian imagination under strong creative restraint.

The joyous exuberance of *Man and Superman* suggests Shaw's confidence at the time it was written. But when he sits down to compose *Heartbreak House* in 1913, England is on the verge of war, and when he completes it, in 1916, the English are committing suicide on the battlefields of France. Unnerved by the war hysteria at home and abroad, and shaking with frustrated bitterness towards pugnacious jingo patriots, Shaw is now inclined to examine human qualities that he had scanted before. Still not prepared to believe in evil, he is no longer so sanguine about man's philanthropic nature; and the brutality, barbarism, and bloodlust emerging from the war have made his distinction between human cowardice and human malevolence a little academic. Undoubtedly, the Devil's arguments — that all of

---

with a cheerful conviction that the lost dogs always find their way home. So they will, perhaps, if the women go out and look for them."

man's ingenuity issues only in instruments of greater destructiveness — are ringing in his ears with more force; and there is real danger that man will exterminate himself before the Superman is able to evolve. For the first time in his career, Shaw is half-inclined to say, Let it come down.

For *Heartbreak House* is permeated with a powerful prophetic fury: the pessimistic tone of the Preface and the black mood of the play suggest that Shaw has come as close as he will ever come to discouragement and despair. In the face of the reality of war, Shaw's Romantic imagination has momentarily been balked; and his Utopianism is in real danger of disappearing altogether. Still, he has not repudiated Shavianism, for he is still urging political responsibility on the upper classes, who have been wasting their rightful inheritance in the pursuit of pleasure and amorous dalliance.

It is this group, the leisured, cultured amorists, which Shaw identifies with Heartbreak House — a palace of inertia, built on the stones of deterministic science and loss of will:

Heartbreak House was far too lazy and shallow to extricate itself from this palace of evil enchantment. It rhapsodized about love; but it believed in cruelty. It was afraid of cruel people; and it saw that cruelty was at least effective. . . . Heartbreak House, in short, did not know how to live, at which point all that was left to it was the boast that at least it knew how to die; a melancholy accomplishment which the outbreak of war presently gave it practically unlimited opportunities of displaying.

The war, in fact, has come about as a consequence of this irresponsibility, for the Heartbreakers, while engaging in useless private amusements, have permitted "power and culture" to fall into "separate compartments." Born to rule, educated and sophisticated (their libraries contain works by all the latest authors, including Wells, Galsworthy, and Shaw), they have handed the government over to the incompetents and the marauders: the Horsebackers (which is to say, the stupid imperialist classes) and the Practical Businessmen (which is to say, those "who become rich by placing their personal interests before those of the country"). The result, according to Shaw, has been an orgy of blood, pugnacity, and lunacy.

Shaw's response to this is to withdraw, partially, from his public concerns into a more personal, private, and poetic form of expression: in certain passages of the play, the existential roots of his rebellion are finally exposed. Certainly, the work seems peculiarly unplanned, as if it had been snatched from the top of the author's unconscious without much effort at order or organization. The plot is crammed with implausible things, proceeding by fits and starts — new entrances, abrupt reversals, and the most peculiar recognition scenes — almost as if in a dream. The characters, too, possess a dreamlike quality — sometimes they lose their individuality in allegory — and occasionally the atmosphere turns mystical, even phantasmagoric, as at the end of the first act, when Shotover and his family gather together for a weird ritual chant (a foretaste of the kind of choral technique T.S. Eliot will use in *The Family Reunion*) on the loss of heroism in life. Frustrations and resentments fill the air, mingled with a general feeling of aimlessness. As Shaw told Archibald Henderson, *Heartbreak House* "began with an atmosphere and does not contain a word that was foreseen before it was written." Certainly the haunted, almost tortured atmosphere of the play — where, instead of the expected Shavian wit, the dialogue is heavily charged with overtones, breaking out of the usual rhetorical balances and Latinate antitheses into an ambiguous, highly charged dramatic poetry — is something totally new to the Shavian drama.

The new mood, the new structure, and the new techniques of *Heartbreak House* owe something to Shaw's new models: turning away from the rationally ordered Ibsenite drama and the compact problem play, Shaw, as he announces in the first paragraph of his Preface, has adopted the more open forms of the Russians. Shaw feels certain intellectual affinities with Tolstoi, who took a moral attitude towards Heartbreak House, and who "was not disposed to leave the house standing if he could bring it down about the ears of its pretty and amiable voluptuaries." Shaw's Tolstoyan moral judgments on his characters are often apparent in his play; and his cataclysmic conclusion shows a similar desire to raze the walls of the house. Still, Shaw could have found Tolstoi's moral and apocalyptic tendencies in Ibsen. The really new element in the play comes from Chekhov — the "fatalist" who "had no faith in these charming people extricating themselves." Growing disillusioned with long-range Shavianism, Shaw is losing faith in his usual forms of revolt. And instead of a consoling myth, revolving around characters with a high sense of purpose, he is here providing a Chekhovian myth of fatalism, revolving around characters with no sense of direction at all — with the result that we are no longer quite so certain of Shaw's convictions about the possibilities of ethical reform.

In short, Shaw remains Shavian insofar as he still continues to judge his characters; but he is also Chekhovian insofar as he is now permitting them an independent life of their own, while "exploiting and even flattering" their charm. Shaw's subtitle — "A Fantasia in the Russian Manner on English Themes" — suggests a certain misunderstanding of Chekhov's technique. For while the "fantasia" (defined by the *Oxford English Dictionary* as "an instrumental composition having the appearance of being extemporaneous . . . in which form is subservient to fancy") describes the structure of *Heartbreak House* and Shaw's later disquisitory plays, it is not an accurate way to characterize Chekhov's carefully hidden plotting. Nevertheless, Shaw has successfully imitated a number of the more superficial Chekhovian characteristics. His new concentration on the group picture, for example, recalls Chekhov's method of discouraging audience identification with a single hero; and like Chekhov, Shaw is now permitting the exposition of plot and character to proceed at a very leisurely tempo. The scene in the garden, at the beginning of Act III, where the pace is retarded by the sleepy reflections of the characters, recalls the second-act opening of *The Cherry Orchard,* permeated with yawns, coughs, and guitar sounds; Ellie Dunn frequently reminds us of Chekhov's young and innocent heroines; and the relationship between Hector and Ariadne — two bored and unloving creatures toying with each other's emotions — is reminiscent of the relationship between Astrov and Yelena in *Uncle Vanya.* Finally, of course, the weird drumming in the air, variously interpreted by Shaw's characters, is very similar to the ominous sound of the broken string in *The Cherry*

Orchard; and in both cases, the noise embodies a feeling of doom and finality.

On the other hand, Shaw's moralism remains much more dominant than Chekhov's; and his characters are infinitely more self-conscious and self-aware — so much so, in fact, that they frequently pass judgment on themselves. One could not imagine Astrov saying, as Hector Hushabye says: "We are useless, dangerous, and ought to be abolished." Still unable to suppress his subjective revolt, Shaw is still unable to suppress his comment. For the same reason Shaw includes a quite un-Chekhovian author's surrogate in the person of Captain Shotover — superficially similar to such clownish old men as Sorin and Serebryakov, but really indigenous to the Shavian world. Through Shotover, Shaw is able to express his personal feelings about the wastefulness, idleness, and irresponsibility of his characters, while exhorting them to learn their business as Englishmen and navigate the ship of state. Through Shotover, too, Shaw can communicate his anger at the vileness of the contemporary world and at destructive mankind — the dynamite hoarded by Shotover is meant "to blow up the human race if it goes too far." On the other hand, Shotover is not Shaw, for he is also drifting, vainly trying to stave off his terrible fatigue with life. Stranded between memories of the past and illusions of the future, this half-demented old man takes refuge from the present in idle dreams. Seeking the seventh level of concentration, he can find it only in rum, and drinks in order to build his resistance to the seductive pleasure of pure passivity.

As for the play, it is an extended nautical metaphor in three acts. Built in the shape of a vessel, Heartbreak House represents the ship of state; the ship is foundering, and about to go on the rocks. The Captain is a drunken old man with a dissolute crew who have not yet learned to navigate: England is drifting into a destructive and futile war. Aside from its allegorical meaning, Heartbreak House also suggests the Bohemianism of the cultured classes of England, wallowing in a disorder of their own making. While breaking each other's hearts, they have permitted their house to tumble down — the masters are eccentric, the servants are spoiled, and even the burglars act unnaturally. Actually, Heartbreak House is another version of the Shavian Hell. But unlike the Hell of *Man and Superman,* whose inhabitants at least enjoyed themselves, the Hell of *Heartbreak House* is peopled with will-less, exhausted sensualists. Hector Hushabye, for example, might be Don Juan before he has reached the philosophical stage of evolution. Unlike John Tanner, who has developed "moral passion," Hector has not yet progressed beyond eroticism; and he is floating, against his will, in a sea of vacuity and discontent. A lover without conviction, a husband who stays at home, he is the victim of the slavery of men to women, moping about like "a damned soul in hell."

Towards Hector and his seductive wife, Hesione, Shaw is alternately indignant and indulgent. Towards those who have usurped their political prerogatives, however, he shows little sympathy at all. If nobody recognizes that upright equestrian, Ariadne Utterword, then this is because she does not exist. Incapable of any strong emotion except a passion for respectability, she lacks even the self-awareness of the Heartbreakers; and as a member of the Horsebackers, she is dedicated to that imperialist approach to government that Shaw abhors. As for Boss Mangan, the practical businessman, he is one of the most unredeemable characters that Shaw ever created. Vulgar, greedy, sentimental, selfish, and faceless (Shaw provides him with "features so commonplace it is impossible to describe them"), Mangan personifies everything that is vile about the commercial world. Shotover, reflecting on Mangan's type says, "There is enmity between our seed and their seed," and announces that the purpose of his dynamite hoard is "to kill fellows like Mangan." Shaw's instinct, too, is to annihilate Mangan, an impulse so murderously strong that he must continually remind himself that Mangan is also human: "It comes to me suddenly," says Hesione, "that you are a real person; that you had a mother, like anyone else." Most of the time, however, Mangan is not a man but a "Boss." And for those who think that Shaw capitulated to capitalism in *Major Barbara,* this character stands as proof of his abiding distaste for the self-seeking businessman.

The existential quality of Shaw's revolt in *Heartbreak House* is mainly expressed through the gradual disenchantment of Ellie Dunn, who is divested of her illusions one by one through a kind of spiritual striptease, until she stands naked and defenseless against the terrors of reality. Having been brought up on Shakespeare by her romantic father, she is ripe for a broken heart at the very beginning of the play. And when Hector proceeds to break her heart, she decides on a practical marriage of convenience with Boss Mangan. Although, in his earlier work, Shaw might have supported such a marriage, here it is insupportable; and Mangan's money turns out to be as much an illusion as Hector's romantic fabrications. When she contracts a spiritual marriage with Captain Shotover, and learns that his wisdom and purpose proceed primarily from the rum bottle, she can protect herself against total despair only through the vision of "life with a blessing." Since this is a vision of the future, however, the only thing that sustains her now is her expectation of Armageddon from the skies.

Armageddon is about to come, for driven to fury by the failure of men, Shaw, dropping all pretense at comedy in the last act, prepares for that total conflagration which Ibsen envisioned: the torpedoing of the entire Ark. Hector had warned, earlier in the play, "I tell you, one of two things must happen. Either out of that darkness some new creation will come to supplant us as we have supplanted the animals, or the heavens will fall in thunder and destroy us." But now the Superman seems a long way off, and Shavianism just another of Ellie's illusions. The drumming in the air proves to be the sound of approaching enemy bombers; and "the smash of the drunken skipper's ship on the rocks" is heard in the explosion of enemy bombs. Having lived badly, the Heartbreakers prepare to die well. Hesione, comparing the noise to Beethoven, finds the prospect of destruction glorious; Hector turns on all the lights to guide the bombers on their way; and Shotover prepares for the Last Judgment. Yet, at the last moment, Shaw relents in his fury. The two pirates — Billy Dunn, the water-thief, and Boss Mangan, the land-thief — are blown up while seeking safety; and the rectory has been turned into "nothing but a heap of bricks." But the Heartbreakers are still alive to take advantage of the warning. By killing off capitalism and the Church, Shaw demonstrates that his hopeful Utopianism is still more powerful than his existential fatalism; and the play ends with his "romantic imagination" once more dominating his despairing sense of "real life." Still, the bombers will return. And Ellie awaits them with such radiant expectation that, if only for a moment, Shaw's revolt is absolute, finding its consummation in a flaming vision of total destruction.

The negative power of Shaw's rebellion in *Heartbreak House* brings the play closer to an authentic art of revolt than anything in the Shavian canon. Yeats has defined rhetoric as proceeding from the quarrel with others, poetry from the quarrel with ourselves — in this sense, *Heartbreak House* breaks out of rhetoric into genuine dramatic poetry, since there Shaw is disputing the entire philosophical basis of his work. There, too, it is possible to see that when Shaw drops the cheerful mask of the ethical reformer, the sorrow, bitterness, and strength of the existential rebel is deeply etched in his features. But he dropped his public mask too seldom; and if he is fading from us today, then this is because he stubbornly refused to examine, more than fitfully, those illusions he held in common with all men. Shavianism was that "mighty purpose" which kept Shaw writing when his heart said no; and though he continued to say no with wit and vigor, he could never quite sacrifice his delusionary yes. As a writer of high comedy, Shaw has no peers among modern dramatists; but his ambitions are larger; and he lacks, as a rebel artist, the stature of the men he admired and wished to join. If Strindberg thought he failed to be the man he longed to be, then Shaw's failure is the opposite: pursuing his ideal role, he failed to face the man he actually was. Yet, we measure this failure only by the highest standards, and it is because of his generous mind and talents that these standards continue to be applied to his art.

VI

BERTOLT BRECHT

Of all the great modern dramatists, Bertolt Brecht is the most enigmatic — at once both direct and hidden, at once both simple and complex. The great bulk of his work is designed to be an impersonal and schematic contribution to Marxist myth-making. Yet, despite his unambiguous commitment to the Communist cause throughout most of his career, Brecht is an extremely divided artist, whose works, for all their ideological intentions, remain peculiarly enticing and elusive. This reminds us of another Marxist dramatist, Bernard Shaw, and, superficially, Shaw would seem to be Brecht's closest companion in the theatre of revolt. Both support a "non-Aristotelian" theatre, characterized not by cathartic emotional effects but by preachment, protest, and persuasion. Both are absorbed with the materialistic motives behind human ideals. Outwardly, both are social rebels, attempting the salvation of mankind through a change in the external environment. And both involuntarily overcome the narrow utilitarian limitations they impose on their art. Still, for all their surface similarities, Brecht is even further removed from Shaw, temperamentally, than Strindberg is from Ibsen. Whereas Shaw's revolt is modified by the geniality of his character and the meliorism of his social philosophy, Brecht's is intensified by his savage indignation and his harrowing vision of life. Shaw is a suppressed poet who rarely breaks the skin of the unconscious; and though he calls himself a Puritan, he cannot bring himself to contemplate evil in the soul of man. But Brecht is a lyrical, dramatic, and satiric poet of fierce intensity; and few Puritan

[231]

theologians have been more fascinated than he with the brutal, the Satanic, and the irrational aspects of human nature.

Brecht's obsession with the darker side of man stems from his struggles with his own character, and so does his relationship to ideology. While Shaw's Fabianism is the extension of his cheerful, rationalistic personality, Brecht's Communism is a discipline imposed, by a mighty effort of will, on a self which is essentially morbid, sensual, and anarchical. Beginning his career as an existential rebel, abnormally preoccupied with crime, blind instinctualism, and decay, Brecht becomes a social revolutionary only after he has investigated all the blind alleys of his early nihilism. The Communist ideology helps him to objectify his feelings and rationalize his art; and it encourages him to attribute an external cause to the cruelty, greed, and lust that he finds in life; but it is never fully adequate to Brecht's metaphysical *Angst*. Brecht may try to convince us that man's aggressive instincts are an outgrowth of the capitalist system, but he never seems wholly convinced himself, especially when his own aggressive instincts are so difficult to control. Even at his most scientifically objective, Brecht continues to introduce a subjective note; even at his most social and political, he remains an essentially moral and religious poet. In his relentless attacks on the inconsistencies and incongruities of Christianity (invariably phrased in Christian imagery), he generally seems more heretic than unbeliever. And though he supports a political orthodoxy which promises social order and benevolence through revolutionary change, he never quite suppresses his sense of the fixed malevolence of nature as reflected in the voracious appetites of man. Brecht's revolt, therefore, is double-layered. On the surface, it is directed against the hypocrisy, avarice, and injustice of bourgeois society; in the depths, against the disorder of the universe and the chaos in the human soul. Brecht's social revolt is objective, active, remedial, realistic; his existential revolt is subjective, passive, irremediable, and Romantic. The conflict between these two modes of rebellion issues in the dialectic of Brecht's plays; and the conflict is not fully resolved until the very end of his career. Part monk, part sensualist; part moralist, part diabolist; part fanatical idealist, part cynical compromiser, Brecht is a compound of many different simples; but he combines the discords and uncertainties of our time into a product which, being dramatic poetry, is always more than the sum of its parts.

The existential aspect of Brecht's revolt, while present in most of his writings, can be most clearly detected in his early work — the poems and plays which precede *The Threepenny Opera*. Here Brecht reveals affinities with two other German dramatists, separated in time but not in temperament, Georg Büchner and Frank Wedekind.[1] Together with the plays of these two dramatists, Brecht's early plays comprise what we might call a German Neo-Romantic movement — a tradition defined by its opposition to the lofty moral postures and messianic stances of the early German Romantics. (Even late in his career, Brecht, like Büchner, seems to be writing his work in reaction to the Olympian idealism of playwrights like Schiller.) Negative and ironic, scrupulously antiheroic, anti-individualist, and anti-idealist, Brecht shares with this movement a determinedly low opinion of human nature, fastening on the criminal or abnormal side of life, and charting these subterranean avenues in searing, distended images. In contrast with Titanic Supermen of German Romanticism, the central characters of his early plays are usually figures from the lower depths of society, caught in a scene of bondage and frustration, or imposing these conditions themselves.

For if the German Romantic exalts the natural man as an instinctive aristocrat, the German Neo-Romantic invariably finds him to be a much darker and more conditioned character — at best, a helpless thrall, victimized by an inhuman world; at worst, a brutal animal, rampaging through the fragile restraints imposed by civilization. Nature may be a paradise to the *Stürmer-und-Dränger,* but to Brecht, it is a jungle — and man is the cruelest of the beasts. Not that this is the stimulus of humanitarian concern. It is the pride of the Neo-

---

[1] Herbert Luethy, in his essay "Of Poor B.B.," traces Brecht's metaphysical attitudes back to German baroque theatre and the *Trauerspiel* (sorrow play). Although these are indirect sources, however, the literary influences on Brecht can be found much closer at hand.

Romantic that he can regard the predatory nature of man without flinching or moralizing. Brecht's mentor, Wedekind — like *his* mentor, Strindberg — for example, finds the joy of life in the cruel struggles of mankind, declaring in the preface to *Pandora's Box:* "If human morality wishes to stand higher than bourgeois morality, then it must be founded on a profounder knowledge of man and of the world." It is as a tough-minded natural historian that Wedekind turns his gaze on creatures from the underworld — swindlers, whores, pimps, white slavers, beggars, lesbians — those "who have never read a book in their lives [and] whose actions are dictated by the simplest animal instincts." And it is as a disciple of this "ugly, brutal, dangerous" man[2] that Brecht investigates the underside of life, exploiting — also like Wedekind, and like Büchner, too — the popular entertainments, culture, and expressions of the lower classes: proverbs, vernacular poetry, idiomatic speech, the variety theatre, the circus, the cabaret, and the streetsinger's ballad, the *Moritat*.

Despite the studied indifference with which Brecht affects to examine life in this period, however, he cannot disguise his sense of horror at it. To adapt Joyce's phrase about Stephen Dedalus's Jesuit conditioning, he has the cursed Lutheran strain in him, injected the wrong way. Like Büchner, whose disgust and hatred are clear enough — and like Wedekind, whose fixation on the more perverse sexual appetites shows a revolt against bourgeois morality chaneled through a diseased Christian consciousness — Brecht exposes, through his exaggerated view of human nature, a strain of disappointed Romanticism — the identifying mark of the Neo-Romantic. This strain is particularly evident in the obsessive concern of all three with deliquescence, isolation, and the weakness of the human will. Apparently agonized by the failure of Romantic ideals of unlimited human freedom, the Neo-Romantic is inclined to see man as wholly determined by external and internal forces, his aspiration mocked by animal instincts and physical decay. Images of rot, stench, and decomposition pervade this drama;

2 This is Brecht's own phrase, which he uses in his appreciation of Wedekind, "An Expression of Faith in Frank Wedekind," written in 1918 after the German dramatist's death.

characters deteriorate under a peeling shell of flesh. Under the spell of this Augustinian vision, Büchner perceives the "horrible fatalism of all history," [3] a horror which Brecht introduces into his early drama, where man is merely an excremental object of no value, a "creature eating on a latrine."

The typical development of the Neo-Romantic drama, then, follows the progress of human deterioration — the gradual stripping away of morals, ideals, individualization, and civilized veneer until the human being is revealed in all his naked cruelty or insignificance — accompanied by sex nausea, hatred of the flesh, and ill-disguised sado-masochistic feelings. The masterpiece of the genre is Büchner's *Woyzeck* — at once the most typical and the most original of Neo-Romantic plays — and one which exercised a powerful influence on all of Brecht's early writings. In this series of fragments — written in 1837 but not deciphered and published until 1879 — Büchner takes up an actual historical case; that of a regimental Leipzig barber who had murdered his mistress in a fit of jealousy. At the time, a debate had ensued over whether the barber was mad; Büchner handles the problem by ignoring it completely. Woyzeck is certainly mad, but then so is the entire world. Manipulated by a cold, unfeeling environment, and buffeted by his own uncontrollable impulses, Woyzeck seems human only in his ability to suffer; but in comparison with the brute beasts who make him suffer, Woyzeck is very human indeed. Frustrated and inarticulate, Woyzeck represents humanity in its crudest form; he is the natural man, untaught, unmoral, incorrigible. Lectured by his condescending Captain on the need for virtue, Woyzeck replies: "People like us can't be holy in this world — or the next. If we ever did get into heaven, they'd put us to work on the thunder."

[3] The phrase, taken from a letter written by Büchner to his fiancée, is followed by some remarks which also seem appropriate to Brecht: "I feel as though I have been crushed beneath the horrible fatalism of all history. I find in human nature an awful sameness, and in the human condition an inexorable force, given to all and none. The individual is no more than foam on a wave, greatness mere chance, the mastery of genius a puppet play, a ludicrous struggle against an iron-clad law, which to acknowledge is the highest achievement, which to master is impossible."

To such born victims, morality is an extravagance and virtue a luxury — or as Brecht will put it a hundred years later, *Erst kommt das Fressen, dann kommt die Moral.*

Like Brecht's, however, Büchner's social judgment has a metaphysical foundation; it is not just the social system but life itself which inspires Woyzeck's misery. To Büchner, society is merely another form of nature; and in the state of nature, man is simply another one of the beasts. At the fairgrounds, Woyzeck observes his natural cousins in a monkey dressed as a man, and a trained horse who "puts society to shame." When he becomes the experimental object of a proto-Nazi Doctor who holds that natural man is superior to the animals because he can control his urine, Woyzeck urinates against a wall — like a dog. Even the Doctor's Pelagian view of human freedom, limited though it is, is contradicted by Woyzeck's wayward flesh. The natural man is without control, and nature itself is chaos, madness, and disorder: "When Nature gives way," observes Woyzeck, "the world gets dark, and you have to feel around with your hands, and everything keeps slipping, like in a spider's web." Büchner further evokes this sense of dislocation through the accidental, unconnected form of the play — Woyzeck moves blindly from episode to episode like the prey of the spider being dragged down its web. His frenzy increasing over his mistress's infidelity, Woyzeck falls into a "beautiful *aberratio*" (as the Doctor gleefully calls it), and in the grip of a lucid, Shakespearean madness, he begins to visualize the sexual act — the act of nature — in images of bestiality, foulness, and defilement: "Why doesn't God blow out the sun so they can roll on top of each other in filth. Male and Female. Man and Beast. They'll do it in broad daylight. They'll do it on your hands, like flies." It is the language of Shakespeare's Lear perceiving the whole of life dominated by unrestrained appetite. It is the form of nature (anarchy and madness) discovering the essence of nature (lust and frenzy). And acting on this terrible perception, Woyzeck cuts his mistress's throat. Later, trying to wash the blood from his hands, he is drowned himself; and as some children heartlessly fling the news ("Hey, your mother's dead") to the woman's orphaned child, the cycle of inhumanity begins anew.

[236]

Much the same inflamed vision of man in nature burns through Wedekind's *Erdgeist* where — this time with the author's energetic approval — domestic animals are transformed into wild beasts, degenerating under the influence of Lulu, an amoral spirit of the Earth; it permeates the film *The Blue Angel*, where a highly respectable teacher is totally dehumanized through a sordid relationship with a cabaret singer; and it accounts for the lurid horrors and ghastly rot in so much Expressionist painting. It is this vision which inspires the caricatures of Brecht's frequent collaborator in the Weimar days, George Grosz, who describes, in his autobiography, *A Little Yes and a Big No,* the excremental quality of his early drawings:

My drawings expressed my despair, hate, and disillusionment. I had utter contempt for mankind in general. I drew drunkards; puking men; men with clenched fists cursing at the moon; men who had murdered women, sitting on their coffins playing *skat,* while within the coffins could be seen their bloody victims. . . . I drew a cross-section of a tenement house; through one window could be seen a man attacking his wife with a broom; through another, two people making love; from a third hung a suicide with body covered by swarming flies.

In these drawings, as in all Neo-Romantic art, human flesh takes on the quality of pork and beef, and all the natural instincts seem vile, gruesome, and ugly. It is a vision which the Nazis were to actualize and the photographs from Belsen and Buchenwald were to illustrate — the underground art peculiar to a country where purity and idealism have alternated with the most atrocious barbarism, and strong appetites have been brutalized by a repressive authoritarianism.

German Neo-Romanticism culminates in the early work of Brecht, where it takes the form of extreme antipathy to the social and natural world. As Herbert Ihering observed of Brecht when the poet was only twenty-four, "Brecht is impregnated with the horror of this age in his nerves, in his blood. . . . Brecht physically feels the chaos and putrid decay of the times." Much of this physical revulsion pervades Brecht's early poems, collected in his volume *Hauspostille* (*The Domestic Breviary,* 1927), where he deals obsessively with such Neo-Romantic themes as the meaninglessness of individualism, the inescapable isolation of the natural man, and the vileness of the natural functions, besides displaying a typically Germanic interest in decay and death. Putrefying corpses, drowned girls, dead soldiers, and murdered infants populate the balladic structures of these verses. "There are hardly two or three out of these fifty poems . . . in which something is not rotting," notes a hostile critic, Herbert Luethy. And in his moving autobiographical poem, "Concerning Poor B.B.," Brecht openly reveals his conviction that human beings (and he includes himself) are "strangely stinking animals," while proceeding to describe the beauties of nature in these rhapsodic images: "Towards morning the fir trees piss in the gray light/ And their vermin, the birds, begin to cheep."

This obsession with man and nature in a state of putrefaction is also central to Brecht's early drama, where he deals with lower forms of humanity, deteriorating in a terrible environment. In *Baal*, for example, Brecht — employing the ecstatic imagery of Büchner and the cynical indifference of Wedekind — follows the career of a ruthless, bisexual poet, who satisfies his instincts without conscience, and finally dies in swinish degradation amidst offal and urine, declaring that the world is merely "the excrement of God." [4] In *Drums in the Night,* he dramatizes the anarchy and isolation of the central character, a returning soldier named Kragler, who rejects the heroic demands of the Spartakus revolution in order to follow the safest and most comfortable way: "I am a swine, and the swine go home." Brecht's *In the Jungle of Cities* illustrates the disorder of the universe and the gratuitous cruelty of mankind, also concluding with the passive acceptance of evil. And in *A Man's a Man,* he demonstrates the insignificance of the individual by showing how the meek, Woyzeck-like water carrier, Galy Gay, is transformed into a "human fighting machine" by three brutal soldiers — meanwhile illustrating the violence of human instinct in the martinet sergeant, Bloody Five, who can discipline his sexual appetite only by castrating himself.

---

[4] A comparison of Baal, who is Brecht's Don Juan, with John Tanner, who is Shaw's, would sufficiently establish the severe temperamental differences between these two playwrights.

Much of this savagery and cynicism is deliberately designed to shock; and John Willett has ably described how Brecht — along with Joachim Ringelnatz, Walter Mehring, and the Berlin Dadaists — was eager to outrage the maddening complacency of the Weimar bourgeoisie. Nevertheless, Brecht's mordant attitudes are deeply rooted in his own nature — so deeply, in fact, that he feared this *Bitterkeit* would affect his creative powers. In "Concerning Poor B.B." he writes: "In the earthquakes to come it is to be hoped/ I shan't allow bitterness to quench my cigar's glow." Like Strindberg, whom he so much resembles in this period, Brecht tries to deal with his own desperation by turning it into art: Baal, Kragler, Garga, Shlink, Bloody Five, Galy Gay, almost all his early characters are aspects of himself, projected into semiautobiographical form. These characters can be roughly divided into two main types: the active and the passive, those who create violence and those who seek to avoid it — but whether victimizers or victims, almost all of Brecht's characters find themselves repelled by their own instincts, and seek to achieve a state of calm beyond the turmoil of the appetitive life. Brecht, who is remembered as an incorrigible womanizer, almost invariably associates some dire penalty with the indulgence of the appetites; for him, physical satisfaction leads directly to catastrophe — which may explain why Bloody Five in *A Man's a Man,* and, later, Lauffer in *The Tutor,* resort to such desperate expedients as self-castration in order to control themselves. Not only sex but passions of any uncontrolled kind seem to be a source of anxiety to Brecht: anger, outrage, panic, revenge, violence, all are vital elements of his work, and all stand condemned.

Brecht is probably trying to master these emotions in himself, for his work exposes his desire for absolute submission, a state of being in which he can conquer his unbridled feelings, and, instead of engaging himself with the external world, merge with it. Brecht's favorite symbol for this passionless state is the condition of the child in its mother's womb. In "Concerning Poor B.B.," he speaks of how "My mother carried me to town while in her womb I lay," and he refers repeatedly to the pleasant passivity of this kind of prenatal transportation. A recurrent image in Brecht's writings, as Martin Esslin has observed, is that of drifting helplessly with the tide — and water, we should note, is very often associated with the mother's womb:

> You must, of course, lie on your back quietly
> As is usual and let yourself go on drifting.
> You must not swim, no, but only act as if
> You were a mass of flotsam slowly shifting.
> You must look up at the sky and act as if
> A woman carried you, and it is so.
> ("Of Swimming in Lakes and Rivers")

To lie still in this water is to give oneself up to existence; to flail about in it is to involve oneself — sexually, socially, actively — with the external world. What Brecht really desires is the Buddhist Nirvana — but his own physical needs and his rebellious spirit continually press him back into material life. Brecht's unremitting attempts to control his rebellious instincts by surrendering to a discipline outside himself are to issue, later, in his submission to the Communist orthodoxy, and, still later, in his aspiration towards Oriental impassivity, where one becomes a vessel of the universe — acquiescent, will-less, and obedient. But whatever form it finds, Brecht's desire for impersonality and control reflects his need to escape from the pulls of the flesh, to subjugate the instincts which force him into unwilling participation in life.

At this point in his career, Brecht openly reveals his existential horror of life and loathing of the instincts. Like his Neo-Romantic predecessors, he fastens on a world of total bondage and total cruelty. In such a world, self-indulgence is equated with sadism and self-realization with death, and Romantic individualism is a sentimental illusion: "What's all this bother about people," asks one of the soldiers in *A Man's a Man*. "One is the same as none at all. You can't even speak of less than two hundred at a time." As for personality, how can one believe in that when Copernicus has shown "that Man is not in the middle of the universe?" Though Brecht shares Nietzsche's assumption that Copernicus banished the gods from the heavens, he sings not the *Übermensch* but the *Untermensch,* the man without possibilities.

And his concentration on the more insuperable human limitations, the source of his quarrel with existence, leads him to attack not only the God of the Christians but the God of the Romantics as well: "The good god," as he puts it in *Baal*, "who so distinguished himself by joining the urinary passage with the sex organ" — in short, the God of nature. Choking on the same bone that stuck in the throat of Strindberg, Brecht cannot swallow the fact that man is born *inter faeces et urinas;* and his pronounced excrementalism makes him fiercely antagonistic to all Romantic aspiration. GLOTZT NICHT SO ROMANTISCH ("Don't goggle so romantically") reads the placard hanging over the action of *Drums in the Night,* accompanied by another affirming that JEDER MANN IST DER BESTE IN SEINER HAUT ("Each man feels best in his own skin"). In this stage of his career, and probably throughout it, Brecht cannot convince himself that this "strangely stinking animal" is capable of heroism, morality, freedom, or anything more than the cynical pursuit of his own advantage and survival. In short, he leaves open no avenues of idealism; his is a negative assault of thundering aggressiveness. Yet, for all his scorn of Romanticism in its more positive forms, his own Romantic temperament can still be glimpsed in his subjective poetic attack, in his ferocious bitterness and disillusionment, and, especially, in his unremitting rebellion against the straitened conditions of modern existence.

Brecht's existential revolt is best illustrated in *In the Jungle of Cities (Im Dickicht der Städte)*, his third play, completed in 1923 when he was barely twenty-five. Extremely puzzling and sometimes incoherent, this work is often hastily dismissed as an obscure experiment; but for all its difficulty, it is clearly a major achievement of a poet genius which batters at the nerves even when it is baffling the mind. Here Brecht is at his most frenzied and diabolical, displaying that "prodigious and rational disordering of all the senses" which Rimbaud held to be the special attainment of the visionary and seer. Rimbaud's influence, in fact, is unmistakable throughout the play, which embodies long quotations from *Une Saison en Enfer,* and even a central conflict recalling Rimbaud's relationship with Verlaine. In its ecstatic, strained, audacious imagery, however, the play is more reminiscent of Büchner's *Woyzeck,* which also influences its philosophy, its tone, and, especially, its form: *In the Jungle of Cities* consists of eleven scenes, some extremely brief, essentially disconnected, but held together by a single sustained action. Characters act upon each other with no apparent cause-and-effect motivation, as in a dream. Its atmosphere, dreamlike also, is permeated with a thick, harsh, oppressive glow — the hot tones and fiery illuminations of a feverish hallucination.

The general location of the play is Chicago, during the period from 1912 to 1915. With each scene identified by a brief legend (in his early work, Brecht uses legends primarily to fix locales), the action moves from the business section to the slums to Chinatown to the shores of Lake Michigan. Yet, all the settings are mythical; Brecht's Chicago, for example, is a seaport, and his seedy Chinese bars and hotels seem to have come out of Anna May Wong movies or Charlie Chan novels.[5] Brecht is fascinated by Chicago because it strikes him as the archetypical "city of iron and dirt" — Upton Sinclair's *The Jungle* is undoubtedly influential here — the source of those predatory images which the concrete metropolis always evokes in his imagination. Brecht's interest in American cities is also inspired by the coarser texture of American society, its mixtures of racial types, its shameless materialism, its idiomatic speech and jazz culture, and, especially, its love of sport. The central image of the play, in fact (if we

---

[5] This technique is typical of most of Brecht's plays. His sense of place is completely imaginative. Indeed, his indifference to external verisimilitude makes him almost as cavalier about geography as Shakespeare, who also put a seaport in an inland country (the Bohemia of *The Winter's Tale*). John Willett, in his valuable compendium, *The Theatre of Bertolt Brecht,* has traced Brecht's sources for his English and American settings — noting, by the way, that the author's interest in Anglo-Saxon mythology is gradually superseded, as his career progresses, by an interest in Oriental mythology. Whether Brecht sets his plays in Louisiana, Soho, Finland, Chicago, Setzuan, India, or the Caucasus, however, his sense of place is usually guided less by the gazetteer than by penny novels, movies, and newspapers. Brecht himself is unconcerned about errors in external probability, being more interested in the truths evoked by the action. And to criticize this, therefore, as Ronald Gray does in his monograph, *Bertolt Brecht,* is to miss out on one of the more valuable functions of the *Verfremdungseffekt* — what Brecht calls "making the familiar strange."

discount the numerous jungle images), is a metaphor from the world of sport: "The inexplicable boxing match between two men." [6] And the eleven scenes of the play represent the ten rounds of the combat, with an extra scene devoted to the victor, after the other combatant has been "knocked out."

The motives of this seemingly gratuitous conflict have been the subject of some speculation. Martin Esslin, noting the Rimbaud-Verlaine parallels, assumes a homosexual relationship between Brecht's two antagonists; and Eric Bentley, detailing Brecht's borrowings from *The Wheel,* J. V. Jensen's Danish novel of homosexual murder and struggle, agrees — though he emphasizes the sado-masochistic nature of the combat. Brecht, himself, is elusive. In his foreword, he tries to discourage speculation about motives, urging the spectator to concentrate on other matters: "Don't rack your brains over the motives for this fight but note the human stakes, judge without prejudice the style of each contestant, and direct your interest to the finish." And towards the conclusion of the play, one of the antagonists also appears to rule out a purely sexual basis for his behavior: "I wanted the boxing match. Not the physical contest but the spiritual." There are, undoubtedly, strong homoerotic overtones in the play, and, as usual with Brecht, sadism and masochism play their part. But more important than the psychological aspects of the work are the philosophical ones; and in my discussion, I shall assume that the conflict between the central characters is less physical than metaphysical. The theme of *In the Jungle of Cities* is the impossibility of establishing permanent contact between human beings — not only sexual contact, but social, oral, and spiritual contact, too.

Before discussing this theme, however, the play itself needs some exposition and interpretation, for it is extremely devious and highly assumptive. The opening scene, which takes place in a rental library, initiates the conflict — between the fifty-one-year-old Malayan merchant, called Shlink, and the young librarian, George Garga. Under

[6] Brecht's word is *Ringkampf,* which could mean either boxing or wrestling. The word seems to have both meanings for Brecht, since the image shifts throughout the play.

the pretense of buying a book, Shlink offers money to Garga for his opinion of a mystery story. But though Garga is willing to give his opinions freely — or to sell Shlink the opinions of "Mr. J. V. Jensen and Mr. Arthur Rimbaud" [7] — he absolutely refuses to make his own intelligence an object of barter. Actually, Shlink's offer has been carefully calculated to lead to combat. Garga is penniless, and his family is starving; but he has somehow preserved his Romantic insistence on personal freedom. Like Brecht, who moved from "the black forests" to "the concrete cities," Garga has come to Chicago from the spacious prairies; his love of freedom is intimately associated with his natural origins. To sell an opinion is to become a bought thing; and thus, as Shlink continually raises his offer, Garga becomes increasingly incensed and humiliated.

Since Brecht already assumes the total determination of modern city life by economic necessity, Garga's Romantic idealism is his Achilles heel — and Shlink proceeds to goad and prod it. When Garga announces that "I can afford opinions," Shlink asks caustically, "You come from a family of transatlantic millionaires?" "That you go on having opinions shows your failure to understand life," affirms Shlink's henchman, Skinny, and Shlink adds, "Please observe the way things are on this planet, and sell." Garga finds himself helpless before Shlink's "aggressions." Though he recognizes the vulnerability of the Romantic idealist in the city jungle ("We grew up on the plains. . . . Here we're up for auction"), he stubbornly refuses to be a "prostitute." And Shlink, cheered to have found a real "fighting man," begins the match by "rocking the ring." First, he arranges to have Garga's girlfriend, Jane Larry, turned into a prostitute by another of his henchmen. And then he has Garga fired: "Your economic security! Watch the boxing ring! It's shaking!" Forced into action

---

[7] This is the way Brecht slyly insinuates his source materials for the play. Brecht, who was accused of plagiarism after *The Threepenny Opera*, steals a good deal, like all great poets, adapting his thefts to his own purposes. But he usually manages to cite his source at some point in his drama. A typical example is *Arturo Ui* where the prologue compares the protagonist with Richard III, apparently in preparation for a later scene between Arturo and Betty Dullfeet which Brecht adapted from Richard's wooing of Lady Anne.

against his will, Garga begins quoting from Rimbaud, rips off his clothes, and runs into the streets, still begging for his freedom. He is prepared to sacrifice everything to defend his personal independence. And the fight is on.

For in order to recover his freedom, Garga must destroy his opponent — a turn which Shlink, who desires to be destroyed, had shrewdly foreseen. "When I heard of your habits," he tells Garga, "I thought: a good fighter" — for Shlink knows that Garga is a man without limits, a Romantic who will go all the way to keep his self inviolate. To aid in his own destruction, and to equalize the odds, Shlink becomes Garga's thrall: "From today on, Mr. Garga, I place my fate in your hands. . . . From today on, I am your creature. . . . My feelings will be dedicated to you alone, and you will be evil." Garga plays on this advantage to plot Shlink's downfall, first haphazardly, then more cunningly: pouring ink over his ledgers, making him contract a fraudulent lumber deal, firing his employees, shutting up his business. When a Salvation Army man enters for a handout, Garga gives him Shlink's property — on the proviso that he permit the Malayan to spit in his face. Brutality and violence are beginning to enter the combat — "You wanted prairie life," Garga tells his opponent, "you can have it." But just when the match is beginning to get warm, Garga decides to leave the ring and embark for Tahiti.

Garga's decision — soon to be reversed — is based on his growing awareness that the freedom he is fighting for is a chimera:

We are not free. It starts with the coffee in the mornings, and with whippings if one acts like a fool, and the tears of the mother salt the soup of the children, her sweat washes their shirts, and one is secure until the iceage sets in, and the root sits in the heart. And when a man is grown, and wants to do something and give it everything, he finds that he is already paid for, initiated, certified, sold at a high price. And he is not free to go under.

Garga's realization that all human actions are limited and determined — by childhood conditioning, economic necessity, metaphysical bondage, and the desire for filial security — is not enough to make him abandon the struggle. But it does make him resort to less heroic tactics. When Shlink comes to work like a coolie for Garga's family and Garga's sister, Marie, falls in love with him, Garga changes the course of the conflict by forcing her on the unwilling Malayan. And this act, in turn, forces Marie, made desperate by Shlink's indifference, into a life of prostitution.

It is in the cold, loveless scenes between Shlink and Marie that the Malayan's motivations begin to emerge. Shlink's masochistic desire for pain, and ultimately for annihilation, are the result of a "disease" which he contracted during his youth on the Yangtze junks, where the rule of life was torture, and man's skin grew so thick that only the most violent probes could pierce it. Garga has been hired to be his executioner, "to stuff a bit of disgust or decay in my mouth so I'd have the taste of death on my tongue." For only through torture, disgust, and death will Shlink be able to feel. Garga fights blindly. But he, too, is learning "how hard it is to injure a man! And to destroy him, quite impossible! . . . Graze up and down this world of ours. You will find ten bad people but not one bad deed. Man is destroyed by trivial causes alone." In his efforts to perpetrate a really bad deed — to penetrate the armored hide of Shlink — Garga uses increasingly desperate devices. Having prostituted his sister, he marries Jane Larry, now a drunkard and a whore herself. And finally, when Shlink's lumber fraud is discovered, Garga decides to take the blame on himself, and go to jail.

Garga's three-year imprisonment results in the utter downfall of his family. But every blow is a blow against his "hellish husband," Shlink. For on the day of his release, the police open a letter from Garga, accusing Shlink of the various crimes which Garga had forced him to commit: the seduction of his sister, the pursuit of his wife, the destruction of his family, the insult to the Salvationist, and, finally, his own unjust imprisonment. Instead of executing Shlink himself, Garga has thus handed the yellow man over to the white lynch mob. In the metaphor of the match, this is a very low blow; Chicago is throwing in the towel; and Shlink's associates begin to count him out. But another of Shlink's henchmen, Worm, soon reminds us of the horrible durability of human life: "A man is not finished all at once but at least a hundred times over. Each man has all too many possibilities." Further evidence of this comes in the comic suicide attempt of the Salvationist — now disgraced and consumed with self-disgust. After reading a whisky list while a nickelodeon plays the "Ave Maria" (a perfect example of Brecht's blasphemous irony), he shoots himself in the neck, uttering the famous last words of Frederick the Great. But the bullet is wide of the mark and causes only a slight flesh wound. He, too, "has too thick a skin" for a clean and satisfactory end.

Shlink, hanging on the ropes, demands that Garga fulfill his pledge and finish him personally. And the tenth scene (the last round of the match) takes place in an abandoned railroad tent where Garga, like Judas, spends three last weeks with his sacrificial victim.[8] Here Shlink expresses his love for Garga, and filled with the darkest despair, explains the symptoms of his "disease," the dreadful loneliness he had suffered for forty years. Now at the end, he has fallen victim to "the black mania of this planet — the mania for contact," to be reached "through enmity," the Romantic form of love. But even this final will-to-life has failed:

The endless isolation of man makes even enmity an unattainable goal. Even with the animals it is impossible to come to an understanding. . . . I have watched animals. Love — warmth from bodily proximity — is our only grace in the darkness. But the union of the organs is the only union and it can never bridge the gap of speech. Still, they come together to beget new beings who can stand at their side in their inconsolable isolation. And the generations look coldly into each other's eyes. . . . The jungle! That's where mankind comes from. Hairy, with the teeth of an ape, good beasts who knew how to live, everything was so easy, they simply tore each other to bits.

[8] Brecht, in fact, has studded this play with a number of ironic Christian parallels. Shlink, the Oriental lumber dealer, for example, is meant to recall Jesus Christ, the Nazarene carpenter; Marie is a latter-day Mary Magdalene; and Worm, who repudiates Shlink when the lynch mob arrives, is, of course, Peter denying Christ. Religious imagery occurs with extreme frequency throughout Brecht's work — in *The Threepenny Opera,* the Christ-Judas relationship is exploited again, for there Ginny Jenny betrays Macheath with a kiss on a Thursday.

In this beautiful and appalling speech, Brecht combines Büchner's sense of the anarchy, chaos, and isolation of nature with Wedekind's and Strindberg's perception of man as a wild beast. But Brecht denies even that possibility of a clean kill that one finds in *Woyzeck*, denies even that ecstasy through cruelty that informs *Erdgeist* and *Miss Julie*. In the jungle of cities, man's hide has accumulated so many layers of defensive skin that even the contact between clawing, ferocious beasts is no longer achievable: "Yes, so terrible is the isolation that there isn't even a fight." [9]

Garga, however, averts his face from this nihilistic abyss. Having lost interest in Shlink's "metaphysical action," he has determined to escape with his "naked life." For him, survival has become the *summum bonum* — "a naked life is better than any other life." The course of the combat has taught him that the end of such struggles is always the same: "The younger man wins . . . the old yields to the young, such is natural selection. . . . It is not important to be the stronger one, but to be the living one." This Darwinist conclusion signifies that the last bubble of Garga's idealism has evaporated. Accepting determinism, abandoning his belief in freedom, he has turned into a cynical compromiser, taking the nearest way. And he engenders Shlink's instantaneous scorn: "That gesture shows you are unworthy to be my opponent. . . . You a hired boxer! A drunken salesman! . . . An idealist who couldn't tell his legs apart, a nothing!" But Garga is unmoved. Idealism, heroism, individualism, freedom, significant combat — all are "words, on a planet which is not even in the middle." And leaving the ring, he carries his "raw flesh into the icy rains," as Shlink — kayoed — falls to the floor. For Shlink, it only remains to finish himself; and he commits hari-kari, the howl of the lynch mob in his ears, after a burst of surrealist prose. As for Garga, he survives. In the last scene, he has sold Shlink's business — along

[9] There are beautiful similarities between this speech and the opening lines of Büchner's *Danton's Death*, where Danton says to his wife: "We know little enough about one another. We're thick-skinned creatures who reach out our hands towards one another, but it means nothing — leather rubbing against leather — we're very lonely. . . . Know one another? We'd have to crack open our skulls and drag each other's thoughts out by the tails."

with his own father and sister — and with the proceeds, is preparing to enter the jungle of New York. Accepting the consequences of living on a second-rate planet, he has turned his back forever on prairie Romanticism. He has repudiated his combative need for personal opinions; his passion is spent; he will fight no more. But even as he holds the prize money in his hand, he reflects, with a little nostalgia, on the conflicts of the past: "To be alone is a good thing. The chaos is used up now. It was the best time."

The philosophical conclusions of this work are much too bleak to sustain an artist for long — there is nothing in the suicidal nihilism of Shlink to inspire the process of creation — and so it is not surprising that, a few years later in 1927 or 1928, Brecht begins to take instruction at the Marxist Worker's College in Berlin. Brecht's decision is clearly foreshadowed in the development of Garga. For like his semiautobiographical hero, Brecht has repudiated the quest for identity and the need for personal opinions; like Garga, he is pursuing, though somewhat less cynically, the path of his own survival. If subjective individualism leads to chaos, then the subjective consciousness must be expunged; if personal rebellion leads to madness, then one must learn to conform. For him, the way out of existential despair lies along the ideological path of Communism: "Not madness," as Brecht characterizes it in *Die Mutter*, "but the end of madness . . . not chaos but order."

In the Jungle of Cities powerfully suggests the madness Brecht perceives in nature and the chaos he senses in the universe; and it is certainly true, as Martin Esslin observes, that Communism "dissolved the nightmare of absurdity" for the dramatist, and "dispelled the oppressive feeling that life was ruled by vast and impersonal forces." On the other hand, the play also suggests that the anarchy he describes is projected from inside, and the aggressions of his central characters are a crucial element of his own nature. His attraction to Communism, therefore, can also be ascribed to the fact that it offers a system of regimentation, a form of rational control over his frightening individualism and terrifying subjectivity. Brecht's desire for passivity, in short, stems from his fear of activity. And his rage for order is really an extension of his desire to drift with the tide, for Communism represents a tide with a meaningful direction. As Lion Feuchtwanger has observed in a fictionalized biography of the author, Brecht "really suffered from his personality. He wanted to escape from it, he wanted to be only one atom among many," later adding the interesting reflection that he was "singularly deficient in social instincts." For such a one, Communism could be the ideal creed, because it couples antisocial rebellion with the promise of true community — and more important, because it encourages the escape from personality, offering the most impersonal and selfless discipline since primitive Christianity.

What I am suggesting is that Brecht responded as eagerly to the Communist discipline as to the Communist dogma; there is something almost religious about his attachment to his new creed. Like most new converts, his fanaticism begins to exceed that of the orthodox; using "science" and "reason" as ritualistic passwords, he turns to ideology as if it were theology, and enters politics as if he were joining a monastic order. Brecht's monkishness is expressed not only in the new simplicity of his poetry, which grows more functional and clipped, but in almost every aspect of his behavior. He begins to wear a simple worker's uniform as if it were a monk's habit; he crops his hair short; his surroundings become more stark and austere; and his private life more ascetic. Most important, he begins to urge the complete extinction of the personality, accompanied by total obedience to a higher order. As Esslin has noted, the word *Einverständnis* (acquiescence or consent) begins to run like a leitmotiv through his work, especially through those five *Lehrstücke* he writes in quick succession from 1928 to 1930. A few of these plays, in fact, are wholly concerned with the teaching of acquiescence to a rebellious individual, climaxing at the moment when the central figure renounces his personal feelings, denounces his insubordination, and accepts the death sentence imposed by his judges. In *The Measures Taken* (*Die Massnahme*), for example, a sympathetic Young Comrade, having permitted his hatred of injustice to jeopardize the mission of his fellow agitators, is taught the dangers of individual rebellion and instinctual reactions, and consents to his own liquidation. It has been observed that the rigid orthodoxy of such a play is probably more of an embarrassment than a service to the Communist cause; and under pressure from the party, Brecht withdrew *The Measures Taken* from performance, commenting that nobody could learn anything from it except the actor who plays the Young Comrade. On the other hand, one begins to suspect that Brecht writes such works less for the enlightenment of other ideologues than as a self-disciplinary measure. The Young Comrade is probably himself; the subjective, instinctual, and individual qualities he is trying to punish are his own. Even in the act of celebrating impersonality and obedience, Brecht is likely to betray his personal conflicts, inadvertently remaining the hero of his own work. In their harsh, incantatory quality, Brecht's agitprop plays seem like the "Aves" of a novitiate, paying penance for a recurrent sin. In his efforts to renounce this sin, Brecht tries to apply the hairshirt of reason and control to the disobedient passions. But his subjective anarchy is never quite subdued, and his probationary period never really comes to an end.

Brecht's Communism, then, is less a substitute for his early Neo-Romanticism than a layer superimposed on top of it — his rational ideology emerges as the dialectical counterpart of his irrationalism and despair. Brecht's new commitment permits him to function as an artist, but his political solutions are fashioned for essentially metaphysical problems. To be sure, Brecht's assumptions are now more hopeful and optimistic. Where he once identified evil with fate and assumed it to be fixed, he now identifies it with bourgeois society and assumes it to be changeable. "According to the ancients," he writes in his notes to an adaptation of Sophocles's *Antigone* (1948), "man is powerless before the workings of fate. In the adaptation of Bertolt Brecht, man's fate is in the hands of man himself." His despairing belief in Darwinist science (natural selection and determinism) has been replaced by an affirmative belief in Marxist science (class war and revolution) — his despondent feelings about the future of the individual have given way to more cheerful feelings about the future of the collective. Sociological interpretations have grown more important than biological ones; materialistic explanations prevail; and instead of finding everything ruled by blind instinct, Brecht begins to reveal more faith in reason and will. Whatever his expectations of the future, however, Brecht continues to focus on the bleaker aspects of present-day reality. While he refuses to reach tragic conclusions, he is still primarily occupied with tragic conditions. Human deterioration may now be attributed to the social system, but rot still catches his eye, even if it is now called by the name of Capitalism.[10] As for the natural environment, Brecht now believes that "science is able to change nature to an extent that makes the world appear almost habitable" (the "almost" is good); but he still finds man victimized by the external world — still lost in the emptiness of the Copernican universe.[11]

Brecht's characters, however, are also victimized now by a cruel society. As we might expect, his Marxist orientation puts social-economic concerns at the center of his art. The rebel against the chaos of nature has turned into a rebel against the social system. And while his existential revolt found its literary roots in a German Neo-Romantic tradition, his social revolt is influenced by a more international group of writers — I refer not only to the Communist dialecticians but also to pre- and post-Marxist dramatists in a Jonsonian tradition; Ben Jonson, William Wycherly, John Gay, Henri Becque, Henrik Ibsen, and (to a lesser degree) Bernard Shaw.

Even here, however, we can see that Brecht has not so much changed his old assumptions as assimilated them within a new intellectual structure. For between the Neo-Romantic dramatist and the Jonsonian satirist there is one important point of agreement — that man (to use a Renaissance adage) is a wolf to man. If nature is a

10 Max Frisch — Brecht's friend and disciple — inadvertently shows, in his "Recollections of Brecht," how decay and politics now connect in Brecht's mind: "Brecht . . . supports himself against the somewhat rotting balustrade, while he smokes a cigar. It is the rot which interests him most: he makes a joke about Capitalism" (*Tulane Drama Review,* Autumn 1961, p. 35).

11 This cosmic emptiness is still obsessing Brecht as late as 1939. In *Galileo,* a monk tries to bring the astronomer to some realization of how his invention is going to affect mankind: "How could they take it, were I to tell them that they are on a lump of stone ceaselessly spinning in empty space, circling around a second-rate star?"

jungle to Büchner, Wedekind, and the early Brecht, then to Jonson, Becque, Ibsen and the later Brecht, it is society which harbors the wild beasts — *Volpone* and *The Vultures*, in fact, each use animal imagery to suggest the kinship of human beings with such rapacious creatures as the buzzard, the crow, the raven, the fly, and the fox, all picking each other's bones in an orgy of greed and acquisitiveness. "Lions, wolves, and vultures don't live together in herds, droves, and flocks," observes Lockit in an important Brechtian source work, *The Beggar's Opera*. "Of all animals of prey, man is the only sociable one." John Gay takes us on a tour of this social jungle, cheerfully exposing the universality of human venality; Wycherly and the Restoration dramatists depict man as a Hobbesian marauder, plundering and seducing without ever breaking the rules of the social contract; and Ibsen's social plays contrast the selfish motives of power-minded, avaricious men with their pretensions to altruism and lofty moral ideals. These authors generally resemble Marx in their *negative* critique of society. For if they are silent about the perfectability of man, the class struggle, and the classless society, they all visualize a world dominated by economic determinism, where the true god of man is Plutus, the god of gold.

Brecht himself seems to be more responsive to the critical than to the Utopian side of Marx — at least, in his plays. Interpreting life as dominated by the search for food and the lust for money (he wanted money and food to replace sex and power as the central subjects of the drama), he also conceives of man as an aggressive beast of prey who grows fat by battening on the flesh of his victims. "What keeps a man alive," asks Peachum, in a song from *The Threepenny Opera*, "he lives on others — by grinding, sweating, defeating, beating, cheating, eating some other man." "Man does not help man," concludes the Chorus in the *Baden Didactic Play: On Consent*. And in *The Rise and Fall of the City of Mahagonny*, the hero, Jimmy Mahoney, is forced to learn that the only capital crime is the lack of money. In *Saint Joan of the Stockyards*, human beings are sold on the exchange like so many cattle: "Oh, everlasting slaughter," cries the sentimental plutocrat, Mauler. "Nowadays/ Things are no different from prehis-

toric times/ When they bloodied each other's heads with iron bars!"
Life proceeds by "one man coldly stripping off another's skin," and
even the virtuous person must turn "wolf," suppressing all kindly impulses in order to survive. Brecht's inexhaustible gallery of thieves,
swindlers, soldiers, whores, brothel madams, gangsters, landowners,
Nazis, and businessmen form the population of a human bestiary,
concealing behind their charming smiles the razor teeth of the shark.
For whether like the brute beasts of Neo-Romantic drama, or like the
opportunistic cheaters of Jonsonian satire, they are largely dominated by animal appetite, their world regulated only by a jungle morality.

On the other hand, Brecht's Communist orientation does make him
ambivalent about which human faculty creates evil — for here the
views of his double inheritance are in conflict. The characters of Neo-
Romantic drama — Büchner's Woyzeck, Wedekind's Lulu, Strindberg's Laura — are usually driven by the unconscious, while those
of satiric drama — Jonson's Volpone, Gay's Macheath, Becque's
Monsieur Tessier — generally follow the path of their "rational" self-
interest, impervious to all drives besides greed and lust. Brecht's early
characters, as we have seen, are clearly at the mercy of anarchical
impulses, but his later characters seem to alternate between emotional chaos and rational control, intermittently dominated by and
dominating the instinctual pulls of their natures. Many critics, and
most notably Esslin, have commented on the omnipresent Brechtian
conflict between reason and instinct as personified in split characters:
Shen Te and Shui Ta in *The Good Woman of Setzuan,* the two
Annas in *The Seven Deadly Sins,* Puntila drunk and Puntila sober in
Herr Puntila and His Servant, Matti. But, in a sense, all of Brecht's
later characters are split, vacillating between reason and instinct as
dizzily as Classical heroes vacillate between love and duty. These
conflicts suggest some of the contradictions inherent in Brecht's
double revolt. As a Marxist, Brecht is convinced that society is based
on rational self-interest, and believes that a more unselfish use of
reason will bring about a more perfect man and a more benevolent
world. As an existential rebel, however, he is more dubious about

the power of human reason; and his own vestigial anarchism forces him to deal with the wildness of the instincts and the irrationality of life — in short, with *im*perfectability.

Consider his ambivalent treatment of his central conflict. On the social-objective level of his plays, Brecht is drawing a clear-cut moral: Man's instincts are healthy, compassionate, kindly, and courteous, but in a competitive society, he must suppress these natural feelings, exercising selfish reason in order to survive. The emotional Anna of *The Seven Deadly Sins,* for example, can build her *kleine haus' im Louisiana* only by squelching her impulsive decency and charity (identified with Christian "sins"), and following the practical advice of her rational sister; the kindly Shen Te is saved from bankruptcy only by the intervention of her cold-hearted alter ego, Shui Ta. Since unselfishness comes naturally and instinctually, selfishness is an extremely difficult discipline. "Terrible is the temptation to goodness," notes the Storyteller in *The Caucasian Chalk Circle,* while Brecht, in a poem, observing the swollen veins of a Japanese demon, reflects: "What a strain it is to be evil." Nevertheless, the nature of the system demands that man suppress his brotherly feelings, and realistically look after himself. "For when feet are bare and bellies empty," goes a verse in "The Invigorating Effect of Money," "Love of virtue always turns to greed." Or as Peachum puts it: "We would be good, not coarse and crude/ It's just that circumstance won't have it so." Man is good, the system bad; ergo, conform to the system, or change the world.[12]

This is the Marxist Brecht speaking — but the Lutheran Brecht is much less sanguine about the healthiness of human instinct. For though Brecht may insist that man must eat before he can become a

[12] Brecht tries very hard to keep his position consistent ideologically, even at the cost of making his most hated enemy, Hitler, better, than he actually was. In *Arturo Ui* (1941), Hitler is characterized as a broken-down, comical gangster put into power by businessmen in order to protect their financial interests. Because of this relentlessly economic interpretation of the rise of totalitarianism, Brecht neglects to deal with Hitler's madness, cruelty, or evil, and makes no reference whatsoever to his virulent antisemitism. It is remarkable that a writer who was able to imagine the Nazi mentality before it was created was so inadequate before the real thing.

moral being, he cannot always disguise the fact that the process of ingestion fills him with a little disgust. *Das Fressen,* one of the most important activities in Brechtian drama, invariably seems singularly unappealing on his stage. (Eric Bentley, who notices this, also notices that "Brecht's word both for commercial entertainment and for the sensuous, thought-inhibiting, action-inhibiting high art of our era was: culinary.") Certainly, Anna's gluttony, her craving for crabmeat, pork chops, sweet corn, and chicken, is depicted as the least attractive of her "healthy" instincts; Galileo's wolfish appetite, as Brecht tells us in *The Little Organon,* is the key to his moral flabbiness; and Jakob Schmidt of *Mahagonny,* so gluttonous that he wants to devour himself, expires after stuffing his stomach with three whole calves. Not only *das Fressen* is accompanied by a hint of nausea, but *die Liebe* as well — more often than not, Brecht's lovers are merely lechers and whores. Objectively, Brecht may associate instinct with virtue; subjectively, he identifies it with appetite — and appetite, generally, of a debased kind. A fetid hothouse sensuality runs through most of Brecht's work. And instead of positive Marxist heroes, amoral, appetitive types like Baal continue to dominate his plays, still seen through the hideous focus of the excremental vision. In short, Brecht remains unconsciously convinced that man is a creature eating on a latrine. And just as often as instinct issues in economic bankruptcy, it issues in spiritual bankruptcy — decay and death. In *Mahagonny,* for example, Jimmy Mahoney opens the city to total license after a typhoon. His motto (like that of Rabelais's Abbey of Thélème) becomes *Du Darfst* (Do What Thou Wilt). But after abandoning himself to the greedy consumption of food, sex, sport, and whisky, Mahoney discovers that his appetites have led to ruin. Politically Brecht can condemn unbridled instincts as an antisocial trait ("The sexual life," he writes in his notes to *The Threepenny Opera,* "stands in contradiction to the social life"); psychologically, it probably represents his own unredeemable flaw, the main constituent of his continuingly anarchical nature.[13]

[13] In his chapter on Brecht in *Metatheatre,* Lionel Abel tries to find some "definite, unequivocal conviction" in the dramatist, and discovers it in his "ado-

Brecht's ambivalence accounts for the dialectical power and texture of his work. Through the clash of opposites, his *Widersprüchsgeist* (contradictory spirit), as he liked to call it, is able to find its complicated expression. Unable to resolve his contradictions, Brecht fails to create unambiguous political ideology, a lapse for which he is, curiously, chided by Herbert Luethy ("Never has Brecht been able to indicate by even the simplest poetic image or symbol what the world for which he is agitating should really look like"). Yet, his failure to be a Utopian ideologist is his triumph as a dramatic poet; like all the great rebel dramatists, he draws his power from the clash of thesis and antithesis, always skirting a fake harmonious synthesis. Whether Brecht is examining the conflict of reason and instinct, vice and virtue, cowardice and heroism, adaptation and revolt, science and religion, Marxism and Neo-Romanticism, he almost invariably concentrates on the opposition rather than the resolution of his terms; and he even suggests, as in these concluding verses from *Saint Joan of the Stockyards,* that life is good *because* it is unresolved:

> Humanity! Two souls abide
> Within thy breast!
> Do not set either one aside:
> To live with both is best!
> Be torn apart with constant care!
> Be two in one! Be here, be there!
> Hold the low one, hold the high one —
> Hold the straight one, hold the sly one —
> Hold the pair!

Even here, the content of the statement is being dissolved by its tone — the passage is a burlesque of Goethe's *Faust.* Brecht seems constitutionally incapable of creating a positive idea without somehow

---

ration of the body": "What Brecht affirmed was the body, the human body in all its warmth, its weakness, its susceptibility, its appetites, the human body in its longing and its thought." There is just enough surface truth in this remark to disguise its essential inaccuracy. But at what a cost does Brecht acquire that "consistency" which Mr. Abel demands of the dramatic poet. Abel clears away the debris of Brechtian ambiguity by ignoring the entire subterranean movement of his thought.

undermining it. Making parody a crucial element of his art, he finds his function in ridiculing the positive ideas of others — and himself; playing on incongruities, he invariably hedges his own commitment with a mocking, derisory, deflating irony.

Now irony, of course, is the literary device not of the political ideologue but of the free artist. And Brecht's derisive tone may explain why he has never been wholly accepted in Communist countries — and for that matter, in the democracies either. He is very rarely able to make those warm affirmations so beloved by the manipulators of culture on both sides of the iron curtain. Just as he mocks the sentimentality, humanitarianism, and idealism of the liberal West, so is he curiously reluctant to celebrate the "brighter side" of Communism, to create a "positive hero," or even to follow his own declared intention to depict man "as he might become." Brecht's theoretical writings are frequently characterized by optimism about the future of man under Communism; but his plays remain concerned with flawed, imperfect, and unchanging human beings, and even his theory is by no means unqualifiedly sanguine, since he often takes a strong stand against "prettification and complacency" and "facile optimism" (the ship that goes down in *The Threepenny Novel* is, in fact, called *The Optimist*). Brecht is more comfortable as a sceptic. "Scepticism moves mountains," he declares, and "Of all things certain, the most certain is doubt." For Brecht, wariness and mistrust are scientific attitudes, essential to an impartial examination of the world. But they are also the qualities of a Socratic temperament, suspicious from the very beginning:

> I gather some fellows around me towards evening:
> We address each other as "gentlemen."
> They put their feet up on my table
> And say: things will improve. And I don't ask when.
> ("Concerning Poor B.B.")

How Brecht manages to maintain his scepticism, detachment, and irony while declaring his unquestioning allegiance to the Communist cause is one of the most skillful accomplishments of dramatic literature. But it is the achievement of a man who is split in half. Committed and alienated, active and passive, hopeful and cynical, Brecht often seems much like the Poet in Strindberg's *Dream Play,* torn between the purity of the ideal and the mud of the earthly reality, between a vision of the changing tomorrow and a vision of the unchanging today.

Few plays demonstrate this delicate equilibrium as well as *The Threepenny Opera* (*Die Dreigroschenoper*), that inspired collaboration between Brecht and the composer Kurt Weill. Written in 1928 when Brecht's Marxism had already invaded his art, this music drama is the most social, objective, and concrete work he has yet created, and is, in fact, the first complete actualization of Brecht's theory of the *Verfremdungseffekt.* The theory is too well-known to be discussed again at length. Suffice it to say that, on the surface at least, its techniques are designed to create an atmosphere of scientific impartiality. Identification is discouraged. Empathy is forbidden. A more presentational style of acting increases the distance between audience and stage. And various visual devices — including projected screen titles, visible lights, exposed organ pipes, curtain wires, and placards, and blown-up Grosz caricatures — keep one always aware of being in a theatre. Scornful of the hypnotized trance induced by the "bourgeois narcotics factory," Brecht tries to keep the spectator's mind awake for instruction. His plays have one function —"to teach the spectator to reach a verdict." The theatre is a courtroom (a large portion of Brecht's plays now begin to climax with a trial scene) and the dramatic action represents the objective evidence. Brecht's use of the jury metaphor recalls Chekhov's manner of describing his artistic function; and though Brecht scorns the "scientifically exact representations" of Darwinian Naturalism (he calls them "empty visual or spiritual palliatives"), and prefers to call himself a Marxist Realist, he does aspire to that strict impersonality achieved by more Naturalistic playwrights like Chekhov.

Needless to say, he does not always achieve it. If Brecht's theatre is a courtroom, then the author functions as judge, jury, and prosecuting attorney. For all his pretense at objectivity, the subjective note still sounds. Brecht's characters are still, if more secretly, autobiographical; and Brecht himself has now entered his work as a voice and a presence — shaping opinions, manipulating the action, selecting events, heightening and distorting and exaggerating. Among the formal innovations of epic theatre is the permission it gives the author to introduce his own ideas into his work, much as a novelist uses a narrative to shape the reader's responses to action and character. And Brecht takes full advantage of this opportunity, using narrative devices to influence the spectator's mind. This influence leads the spectator more towards an attitude than towards a conclusion — an attitude of ironic disengagement. And *Verfremdung* (literally *making strange*) is really an instrument of the ironic mood, since it removes the observer from the thing observed, functioning, as the German critic Döblin correctly observed in 1929, when "the coldness of the author's feelings stops him from associating himself intimately with the fate of his characters or the development of his plot." In Brecht's theatre, "the generations look coldly into each other's eyes"; the metaphysical isolation of his early characters has now become the basis of his dramatic method.

The Threepenny Opera cogently demonstrates the ironic uses of the *Verfremdungseffekt,* since it creates an atmosphere of distance and withdrawal through the use of sharp satiric contrasts. Peachum's religious placards, for example, like his canting dialogue, are incongruously juxtaposed with his ruthless criminal activities, just as Brecht's rhetorical, often biblical, titles are contrasted with the argot of thieves and whores. The music serves a similar function, being either satiric in itself (Weill shares Brecht's gift for parody) or achieving satire through the conjunction of the composer's lyrical, nostalgic melodies with the author's gritty, insinuating lyrics. The score features melodious forms like the tango, the *Moritat,* the popular ballad, and even one English air from *The Beggar's Opera* (Peachum's "Morning Hymn" is based on the traditional song "An old woman cloathed in gray," reworked by Gay as "Through All the Employments of Life")— but whatever sweetness there is in the tunes is totally dissipated by croaking vocal deliveries and brassy, reedy, percussive jazz orchestrations. The main purpose of these contrasts is to throw a harsh glare on the shadow that lies between romance and reality, between sentimental affirmations and the actualities of human endeavor, or between what Wedekind called "bourgeois morality" and "human morality." The primary target of the play, in short, is hypocrisy, exposed through a burst of dissonance, brutal indignation, and controlled anger.

Brecht's technique of satiric inversion is borrowed, of course, from Gay's eighteenth-century ballad opera, a remarkable work which attacks many things (including opera, politics, marriage, theatrical conventions, and the English prison system), but which is mainly concerned with the manners and morals of the aristocracy. By providing a highwayman with the dash of a courtier, and whores with the graces of fine ladies, Gay suggests the vices of the upper classes without bringing a single upper-class character on stage. Brecht takes over most of Gay's characters, some of his scenes, and even a number of his jokes (particularly those on marriage); and he preserves the Anglo-Saxon setting of the original work, updated and transformed, in Brecht's usual fashion, into a strange and exotic locale (the play, taking place during the coronation of an unnamed Queen, moves from "Soho" to "Wapping" to "Turnbridge," but Brecht's England is more a compound of Villon's Paris, Kipling's India, and his own Berlin). Brecht's most important borrowing — the ironic inversion of high and low life — has also been adapted to his contemporary vision. The underworld of *The Threepenny Opera* is a particularly savage and degenerate place, more akin to Wedekind's world than to Gay's: the thieves have lost their manners, the whores their graces, the delicate Polly Peachum has been coarsened into a gun moll, and instead of the cavalier Macheath, a post-Restoration rogue, Brecht creates in Mackie Messer an unmannerly, cynical ruffian, much like Baal, Kragler, Garga and the British soldiers in *A Man's a Man*. As a result of these adjustments, Gay's cheerfulness has given way to a bitter mordancy, his light wit to gallows humor, and his highly literate dialogue to vernacular thrusts of speech, generously spiced with obscenities — just as the traditional airs from Dr.

Pepusch's score have been replaced by the rasping style Weill lifted from the Berlin cabarets.

The shift in tone signifies a shift in satiric object. Brecht's work is an assault not on the aristocracy but on the bourgeoisie. Instead of being a highwayman with the manners of a gentleman, Mack the Knife is a thief, arsonist, rapist, and murderer with the habits of a burgher — an aging, balding entrepreneur with a paunch.[14] Mackie, like Al Capone, is a gangster who always prefers to call himself a "businessman"; indeed, he keeps books, worships efficiency, and puts great store by effective organization. If he dislikes blood (he is always washing his hands), then this is because wanton violence debases the dignity of his calling: "The very thought of blood makes me sick" he tells his henchmen, after they have unnecessarily broken a few heads. "You'll never make businessmen. Cannibals — but never businessmen." In his notes to the play, Brecht observes that the only difference between the gangster and the businessman is that the former "is often no coward"; and in *The Threepenny Novel,* he goes so far as to turn Mackie into a prosperous banker with a lucrative chain of stores. In the play, however, Mackie never enters legitimate enterprise, though he has very practical reasons for going straight: "Between ourselves," he confides to Polly, "it's only a question of weeks before I switch to banking exclusively. It's safer as well as more profitable." The thieves are in competition with big business and the banks — and free enterprise is edging them out. Mackie laments, in his farewell speech, that he is "the vanishing representative of a vanishing class," being swallowed up by those with larger appetites:

We artisans of the lower middle class who work with honest jemmies on the cash boxes of small shopkeepers, are being ruined by large concerns backed by banks. What is a picklock to a bank share? What is the burgling of a bank to the founding of a bank? What is the murder of a man to the employment of a man?

[14] In his notes to the play, Brecht calls attention to the original English drawings of Macheath, which show "a squat but thickset man in his forties with a head like a radish, already somewhat bald, but not without dignity." Mackie, in short, should never be cast as a swashbuckling Romantic rogue.

These rhetorical questions suggest the Marxist animus of the play: a number of critics have called it a dramatic illustration of Proudhon's "Property is theft." But Brecht cuts below the politico-economic implications of this theorem to its moral-religious implications. Making crime merely a left-handed form of human endeavor, he stigmatizes the religious hypocrisy which accompanies the right-handed forms.

The moral character of Brecht's attack can be seen more clearly in the person of Jonathan Peachum, another small businessman engaged in criminal endeavor. An unromanticized version of Hugo's Beggar King in *Notre Dame de Paris,* Peachum transforms healthy men into deformed, mutilated, and pitiful creatures through the application of artificial limbs, boils, plaster joints, and eye patches, all carefully designed to evoke the maximum of sentimentality along with the minimum of disgust. In short, he thrives by playing on the charitable impulses (which is to say, the guilt) of the rich — those who "create misery but cannot bear to see it." Thus, if Mackie illustrates the relationship between crime and business, Peachum highlights the relationship between the self-seeking Capitalist ethic and the self-abnegating morality of Christianity. Christian brotherhood, in Peachum's view, is simply a superfluous piety in the harsh bourgeois reality: "Your brother may be fond of you," he sings, "But when the food's too short for two/ He'll go and kick you in the bum"— first comes eating, then morality. But the moral rules, as Peachum demonstrates, can also be highly profitable in a competitive society, if exploited properly. For him, a homily such as "It is better to give than to receive" suggests the path to an effective source of income. The Church, in short, is actually another "large concern backed by the banks"; Christianity and Capitalism are really in league. And like the legal system, the moral system is a hypocritical justification for greed, designed "for the exploitation of those who do not understand it or for those who, for naked need, cannot obey it." [15]

[15] One begins to suspect that *The Threepenny Opera* was influenced not only by Villon's poetry and Gay's ballad opera, but also by Max Weber's discourse on the relationship between the Protestant ethic and the rise of Capitalism. In

Brecht's moral satire on the bourgeoisie extends beyond its business dealings and religious ethics to all its conventions and institutions, including marriage, romantic love, and male friendship. Mack's wedding to Polly, for example, is a typical middle-class banquet, replete with toasts, gifts, dirty jokes, and gorging guests — except that it takes place in a stable and all the furnishings are stolen. And the prostitutes in Wapping brothel sit about in their undergarments, washing themselves, playing games, chatting, etc. — a scene which Brecht, in a stage direction, calls a "middle-class idyll." As for romantic love, this is reduced to its most sordid equivalent. In "The Ballad of the Fancy Man," Mackie and Ginny Jenny sing of their past amour, an interlude which featured abortion, pimping, whoredom, and venereal disease — and Jenny proves her love for Mackie by betraying him, twice, for a few dollars.

Betrayal, in fact, is almost a structural element of the play, because the action proceeds through a complicated series of double crosses, climaxing in the betrayal of Mackie by his erstwhile friend, the police chief, Tiger Brown. The relationship between Brown and Mackie, which Brecht added to Gay's plot, is designed to expose the sentiment and hypocrisy Brecht finds at the root of bourgeois friendship. Both are inclined to slobber whenever they recall their army days in India; and neither can speak of the other without invoking the accents of the Romantic novel: "We were boyhood friends," reflects Mackie, "and though the swirling tides of life have swept us asunder, although our professional interests are so different . . . our friendship has survived it all." Actually, the survival of the friendship is based on commercial advantage: Mackie informs on other criminals, while Brown, collecting a third of the reward, reciprocates by providing him with police protection. Brown, Brecht tells us in his notes, has "genuine affection" for Mackie, and suffers from the conflict between his two selves — the "private individual" and the "official" — but the selves are united in a common pursuit of gain. Therefore, when Peachum threatens Brown with an embarrassing riot by the poor if

---

Happy End and *Saint Joan of the Stockyards,* Brecht makes the same connection between Christianity and finance.

he does not arrest Mackie, there is no doubt what decision he will make. After weeping over their broken friendship — and settling their business accounts — he sadly turns Mackie over to the hangman.

Brown's inner conflict — a gibe at the Classical conflict between love and honor — is less satirically recapitulated in Mackie; and here the Neo-Romantic aspect of the play forces its way to the surface. For if Brown must choose between his irrational friendship and his rational self-interest, then Mackie is suspended between his reasonable desire for survival and his unreasonable appetite for women. Brown is able to choose. But Mackie's sexual instincts, like Bloody Five's, are compulsive and irrational; he cannot resist whores and twice is captured in the arms of a trollop. Unlike Brown, he goes *against* himself. In anatomizing Mackie's blind instinctualism, Brecht permits his subjective view of human nature to contradict his Marxist convictions: Man should follow the path of his greatest economic advantage, but he cannot overcome his animal nature. This existential theme is accented in "The Ballad of Sexual Submissiveness," where Mrs. Peachum sings of the slavery of men to their appetites, and the defeat of all spiritual, intellectual, and political ambitions by sensual desire:

> Some read the Bible; others take a Law degree;
> Some join the Church and some attack the State;
> While some remove the celery from their plate
> And then devise a theory.
> By evening all are busy moralizing
> But when the night is falling, they are rising.

The monk in Brecht knows full well how difficult it is to discipline the womanizer, even by abstaining from celery. And in "The Song of Solomon," Jenny confirms this melancholy *aperçu* by telling how all the great of history were brought low by their dominant trait: Solomon by wisdom, Cleopatra by beauty, Caesar by courage — and Macheath by lechery. Whether good or evil, heroic or base, the irrational element in man is the destructive one. The ideal remains out of reach. The flaw is in human nature; and human nature remains the same.

Mackie, therefore, functions in two distinct ways, being both the agent of the author's rebellion and the thing rebelled against. As an underworld figure, he is, by implication, a rebel against society. And by identifying his own activities with those of businessmen, he satirizes the criminal side of legitimate enterprise, exposing the reality behind bourgeois respectability. On the other hand, Mackie is not simply an alienated man, forced into a life by crime by a competitive system. He is also a particularly brutal hood, subject to savage impulses — and not only sexual ones. The Streetsinger's *Moritat*, "Mack the Knife," tells of his complicity in a number of violent crimes, many of them gratuitous; and, like Jenny the Pirate, whose fantasy of revenge is such that she would exterminate the entire world, Mackie is animated by powerful aggressions: "Oh how I wish that I could get them," he signs of his captors, "and smash them with an iron maul. . . ." [16] Mackie's sadistic nature, in other words, has very little to do with the economic system under which he lives, and it suggests that Brecht's indictment involuntarily cuts across class lines.

So does the very ingenuity of Brecht's technique. For while the Capitalist is unquestionably the villain of the play, no wealthy bourgeois ever appears on the stage: here, as in so many Brechtian works, the capitalist is merely a lumpenproletarian or petit bourgeois with money. This ideological "error," a sore point to Communist critics like Ernst Schumacher, suggests the various ambiguities which Brecht has not bothered to resolve. Does human evil stem from the evils of the system? Or do the system's evils reflect the murder in the hu-

---

[16] Eric Bentley has correctly emphasized the fierce aggression found in Brecht's plays. It is a quality especially apparent in *Saint Joan of the Stockyards*, which concludes with the heroine's conversion to a doctrine of force, phrased in language like this:

> Therefore, anyone down here who says there is a God
> When none can be seen,
> A God who can be invisible and yet help them,
> Should have his head knocked on the pavement
> Until he croaks.

man heart? Will man's greed, lust, and cruelty disappear in a less commercial society? Or are they fundamental defects of nature, much like original sin? An answer to these questions would commit Brecht irrevocably to Communism or Neo-Romanticism, to the social or the religious vision, to free will or determinism — but he does not answer. His point is that the world must be changed; his counterpoint is that "the world will always be the same."

This irresolution is exaggerated by the ferocious irony of the conclusion — the famous Mounted Messenger scene — where, in order that "mercy may prevail over justice once a year," the Queen pardons Mackie from the gallows, elevates him to the peerage, heaps him down with gifts, and extends her "royal and cordial felicitations." Brecht's satire on the facile endings of Classical comedy is clear enough — the Messenger comes from the last act of Molière's *Tartuffe*. But the symbolic significance of the Messenger himself is more obscure. He could be the benevolent agent of a future society where justice prevails and life is benign and humane; he could also be the bright angel of that dead God who once presided over an ordered and coherent universe. Again, Brecht's commitment is kept in shadows; only his negative comment is unclouded. For whatever reasons, the world is bad, "Mounted Messengers from the Queen come far too seldom, and if you kick a man he kicks you back again. Therefore never be too ready to oppose injustice." The "Valedictory Hymn" echoes Peachum's warning against facile indignation, adding a note from *Ecclesiastes* about the everlasting bleakness and woe of life. With the whole play inverted, and the whole world seen from its underside, even Brecht's positive affirmations seem to come out backwards. And one finally comes away from *The Threepenny Opera* unbalanced by contrasts, dislocated by contradictions, foundering in the shifting perspective — secure only in the author's unrelenting revolt as transmitted through his negative, ironic tone.

Much the same doubleness of vision and unity of tone can be found in *Mother Courage and her Children* (*Mutter Courage und Ihre Kinder*), Brecht's masterpiece and, without doubt, one of the finest works of the modern theatre. Completed in 1939, when World War

II was just beginning and Brecht was in exile in Scandinavia, *Mother Courage* ostensibly deals with the Thirty Years War, that seventeenth-century feast of death, fire, and pestilence. But its real subject is all wars, as seen from the perspective of one who loathes military heroism. Inspired to some extent by Grimmelshausen's picaresque novel *Simplicissimus,* this play, according to Bentley, can be partly construed as a reply to Schiller's *Wallenstein.* It is also a reply to Shakespeare's *Henry V,* Corneille's *Le Cid,* Dryden's *Conquest of Granada* — in short, to all works which glorify heroism or eulogize national ideals. Brecht has finally made the passive side of his nature the source of a positive position: that of a belligerent pacifism. He observes the exploits of war, like those of peace, from the underside, examining what Edmund Wilson has called "the self-assertive sounds" which man "utters when he is fighting and swallowing others." To achieve his satire on the morality of the military life, Brecht concentrates not on the battles but on the commonplace activities of day-to-day living, as performed by the war's orphans, truants, and subordinates.[17] In the background of *Mother Courage* pass the victories, defeats, reversals, sieges, assaults, retreats, and advances which form the substance of history. In the foreground, the private lives of the noncombatants provide a non-heroic contrast. The external course of the conflict is narrated, like newspaper headlines, in the legends preceding each scene, but it interests Brecht only insofar as it influences local commerce: "General Tilley's victory at Leipzig," the title informs us, "costs Mother Courage four shirts."

For the real struggle is over money, food, and clothing. Brecht, still examining the relationship between Capitalism and crime, is now applying his Marxist perceptions to the crimes of history itself. If the businessman is identified with the gangster in *The Threepenny Opera,* then he is identified with the warmaker in *Mother Courage.* Property is not only theft, but murder, rape, and pillage; war may be the extension of diplomacy but it is also an extension of free enterprise. Locked

---

[17] In his poem, "A Worker Reads History," Brecht underlines his conviction that history is made not by emperors, kings, and generals, but rather by their soldiers, cooks, and slaves.

BERTOLT BRECHT

in endless combat, the Protestant Swedes and the Catholic Germans are told they are fighting for religious ideals, but like the Swedish King Gustavus, whose zeal was so great that he not only liberated Poland from the Germans but offered to liberate Germany as well, the crusading warlords usually make "quite a profit on the deal." The Chaplain may believe that the war "is a religious war, and therefore pleasing to God," but to the Cook, it is just like any other war in "all the cheating, plunder, rape, and so forth." The God it is supposed to please is not around to help the participants; and so when it comes to a real test of the Protestant Chaplain's religious enthusiasm, he switches sides: "God bless our Catholic flag." Obviously, Brecht is again attacking Christian hypocrisy rather than Christianity itself; once again, he is measuring how far mankind falls short of its ideals. Religious piety, jingo patriotism, bourgeois respectability, all are merely synonyms for greed, acquisition, and self-advancement. And since war is "just the same as trading," the morality which justifies it must be considered an evil sanction. Brecht, in short, quarrels with Christianity because its morality has been exploited, its prophecies unfulfilled. The age of miracles is past. Man must now find his own loaves and fishes, and attend to his earthly survival.

Seen from this perspective, heroism looks like a ghastly skeleton, rattling its bones in the wind; and in *Mother Courage,* heroic actions invariably stem either from stupidity, insanity, brutality, or simple human error. The spokesman for Brecht's antiheroic point of view is Anna Fierling, the canteen woman known more familiarly as Mother Courage. Like so many of Brecht's rascally characters, this salty, cunning, self-serving woman has much in common with Falstaff; and like Falstaff, she functions as a satirical commentator and comic deflator. To her, the only quality worthy of respect is cowardice; and she commands respect herself because of her consistency — she invariably chooses the most selfish, ignominious, and profitable course. Even her nickname is ironic: her "courageous" breach of the lines during the bombardment at Riga was made to keep some loaves from going moldy. As the supreme advocate of adaptation and acquiescence, Courage is extremely cynical about the motives of others. She attributes the death of General Tilley, for example, to the fact that he got lost in a fog and strayed to the front by mistake. She is probably right; in Brecht's world, as in our own, there are no more authentic heroes. Brecht, in other words, gives us a Falstaff without a Hal or Hotspur. Courage's unhesitating assumption about the baseness of human motives belongs to the author; and it is not modified by any contrasting ideal.

Yet Brecht's all-embracing cynicism implies an ideal, for he is rebelling against a reality he despises. "The Song of the Great Capitulation" — possibly the most moving lyric in the entire Brechtian canon — reveals the history behind Brecht's cynical attitudes. For here Mother Courage, trying to discourage an indignant soldier from endangering his safety, sings of the degeneration of her own rage against injustice. Beginning as a Romantic individualist — "All or nothing. Anyway never take second best. I am the master of my fate. I'll take no orders from no one" — she eventually becomes the cautious compromiser, marching in time with the band: "You must get in with people. If you scratch my back, I'll scratch yours. Don't stick your neck out!" It is the story of how George Garga is eventually forced to repudiate his belief in freedom. And it may very well be the story of how Brecht abandoned his early Romantic idealism under the pressure of internal passions and external constraints:

> Our plans are big, our hopes colossal.
> We hitch our wagon to a star.
> (Where there's a will, there's a way. You can't
> hold a good man down.)
> "We can lift mountains," says the apostle.
> And yet: how heavy one cigar!

Lifting that cigar has become the whole ambition of Brecht's heroine: her sole purpose is to keep herself and her family safe and alive. In the fulfillment of this difficult and ultimately fruitless task, she employs ruthlessness, charm, bribery, guile, and simple horse sense, always true to her coward's creed that discretion is the better part of valor.[18]

[18] The Brecht character whom Courage most resembles is Galileo, a figure who also identifies cowardice with ease and relaxation, and heroism with death.

Mother Courage's bitter hostility to heroism has made her, paradoxically, a heroic figure to audiences — an image of the "little people," beleaguered by forces beyond their control, yet resiliently continuing to make their way. Bentley observes that the alienation apparatus of the Berliner Ensemble must be "called into action *as a fire brigade"* to douse the natural flow of sympathy which streams toward such characters; and Esslin — noting that Brecht originally designed Courage as a "negative, villainous character" — concludes that the author was unable to control his own affection for her. There is no question that Mother Courage — like Falstaff, who was meant to be a Vice figure (Sloth and Vanity) but who somehow transcended his morality play role — got away from the author. And like the rejection of Falstaff, the pathos of Courage does begin to take on larger dimensions. Nevertheless, one must also realize that Brecht *does* realize his conscious intentions with the character, and that the tragedy he unintentially created coexists with the morality play he designed. The responses evoked by Brecht's heroine are a good deal more complicated than those evoked, say, by the pathetic Nora Clitheroe, the heroine of another antiwar play, O'Casey's *Plough and the Stars:* Courage is not just a passive sufferer, playing on the sentiment of the audience, but also an active source of suffering. She may be a victim of the war, but she is also an instrument of the war, and the embodiment of its evils. Brecht's revolt, in short, remains double. Like Macheath, Mother Courage is both the agent of the author's rebellion, and the thing rebelled against. Her determination to play it safe makes her the enemy of hypocrisy, but it also makes her cold and grasping. And though her single-minded devotion to survival is sympathetic in relation to her three children, it becomes mere aggrandizement in relation to her fourth child — the wagon. This almost human prop is a constant visual reminder that for Courage the war is "just the same as trading." Like a stockmarket investor, she builds up profits on the fluctuating fortunes of war, buying and selling on the lives of men.

"Unhappy is the land that *needs* a hero," cries Galileo, while Courage remarks, "In a good country, such virtues wouldn't be needed — we could all be cowards and relax."

Thus, Mother Courage is no Niobe, all tears, but the author of her own destruction. One of those lower-class Capitalists whom Brecht was always creating, she is, as the Chaplain tells her, a "hyena of the battlefield," and those who live by the war must die by it.

Mother Courage haggles while her children die — this is the spine of the play. For while Courage is pursuing commercial advantage, her family is sacrificed, one by one, to the war. Eric Bentley has already commented on the tripartite structure of the work where, at the end of three discrete sections, another child is laid on the war's altar. The offspring of three different fathers, Finnish Eilif, Swiss Cheese, and German Kattrin are an international brigade of victims, their fates foretold in the initial scene. The episode of the black crosses, like many of the songs in the play, is prophetic. But it is not a supernatural agent which strikes the children down; it is the cruel hand of man, abetted by their own self-destroying instincts. Brecht's emphasis on the destructive power of the instincts reminds us of *The Threepenny Opera;* and indeed "The Song of the Wise and the Good" is a reprise of "The Song of Solomon," adapted, as Bentley has observed, to the instincts and "virtues" of Courage and her offspring. Caesar's bravery is identified with Eilif's heroism, Socrates's honesty with Swiss Cheese's incorruptibility, St. Martin's unselfishness with Kattrin's kindness, and Solomon's wisdom with Courage's shrewdness. The dominant qualities of both the great and the common lay them low; virtue doesn't pay: "God's Ten Commandments" have not "done us any good."

Brecht, however, cannot refrain from giving an ironic twist to his already ironic statement — for the "virtues" he describes are all, with the exception of Kattrin's kindness, highly dubious qualities. Eilif's bravery, for example, is, at best, impulsive foolishness. While the Sergeant is cunningly distracting Courage's attention by bargaining with her over a belt, Eilif is off with the Recruiting Officer, pressed into war by his lust for glory. Eilif's song, "The Fishwife and the Soldier," predicts the outcome of such rashness, for it tells how a headstrong son is killed by his own bravery, despite all his mother's cautious warnings. Impulsiveness leads to death: "The lad is swept out by the tide:/ He floats with the ice to the sea." The song, with its typically Brechtian water images, is obviously influenced by Synge's *Riders to the Sea;*[19] and like Marya's Bartley, Courage's Eilif soon drifts with the tide of death because he ignored his mother's advice to drift with the tide of life. Having "played the hero in God's own war" by slaughtering a number of innocent peasants who wished only to protect their cattle (here bravery turns into sadistic brutality), Eilif repeats this heroic exploit during an interlude of peace — and is led off to be shot. Like Chaplain's Verdoux, he discovers that virtues in wartime are considered crimes in peacetime, and that law and morality shift their ground to accommodate a nation's needs.

Swiss Cheese, the "honest child," is another victim of a dubious virtue. As paymaster of a Protestant regiment, he is entrusted with the cashbox; and when he is captured by the Catholics, he refuses to surrender it up. This kind of honesty, as Courage observes, is sheer stupidity: Swiss Cheese is too simpleminded to provide for his own safety. Here, however, Courage is in a position to save her child through the exercise of her Solomon-like wisdom: "They're not wolves," she observes of his Catholic captors, "they're human and after money. God is merciful and men are bribable." Her analysis of motive is perfectly accurate, but it is precisely because of her excessive shrewdness that the device does not work. Forced to pawn her wagon to obtain sufficient bribe money, Courage is anxious to reserve enough for her own security. But the Catholics are in a hurry, and her prolonged bargaining is climaxed by the terrible realization, "I believe — I haggled too long." Swiss Cheese, the significance of his name finally clear, is carried in on a stretcher riddled by eleven bullets — to be thrown on a garbage heap because his mother is afraid to claim the body. Torn between the contradictory demands of self-survival and mother love, Courage has, in effect, killed her own child. And she suffers the consequence in terror and remorse, looking on the corpse in dumb agony, and choking back the scream which rises in her throat lest she give some sign of recognition.

[19] The play which precedes *Mother Courage* is *Senora Carrar's Rifles,* a reworking of *Riders to the Sea,* given an activist ending, and set not in Ireland but in Civil War Spain. Synge is very much in Brecht's mind at this time.

Kattrin is Courage's only truly virtuous child, the soul of kindness and the most positive figure in the play. It is a characteristic of Brecht's attitude towards positive values that she is a mute; but through her expressive gestures and responses, the cruelty and horror of the war are most eloquently told. Even her dumbness is related to these terrors — "a soldier stuck something in her mouth when she was little" — and when she is attacked and mutilated by some vicious marauders, the war has killed her hopes for a home, a husband, and children, whom she especially loves. Because of her muteness, her serenity, and her love of children, Kattrin sometimes achieves allegorical stature — she is much like Aristophanes's Peace, blinded, gagged, raped, and buried by war. But Brecht's war is endless; and, unlike Aristophanes's mute figure, Kattrin is led to enjoy no hymeneal banquet at the end. Instead of being pulled out of the pit, she is hurled into one: the war buries Kattrin for all time. Courtesans like the camp follower, Yvette, may thrive on conflict, for Yvette accepts the whore's barrenness, so much like that of the war. But Kattrin is *Kinderknarr,* children-crazy, and it is her consuming love for these fruits of Peace that finally destroys her.

Once again, the death occurs because the mother is haggling. Having successfully resisted the temptation to leave Kattrin behind and find a secure berth with her lover, the Cook, Courage is, nevertheless, still looking after her profits: she has left Kattrin with the wagon while she buys stocks cheap from the frightened townspeople. While she is gone, the Catholics capture a farmhouse, preparing for an ambush of the town. The farmers, afraid for their family in the town, appeal to God to save their four grandchildren. But, to their horror, their prayers, for once, are answered. Moved by the mention of children in danger, Kattrin has climbed to the roof of the farmhouse, where she begins to beat her drum. At last, Peace has found a tongue, rhythmically commenting on its ancient, invincible enemy. To smother the sounds of this alarum, the soldiers and peasants try to create their own noises — peaceful ones, they begin to chop wood. Yet Kattrin's drumming mounts in intensity, and in desperation. When a lieutenant offers to spare her mother if she descends from the roof, Kattrin drums more heatedly; when he backs his promise with his word of honor, she drums most furiously of all. The smashing of the wagon, the knifing of a sympathetic peasant, the threat to her own life — nothing stops this desperate tattoo. She is finally shot off the roof by a hail of musketry; but the town is saved.

The episode is simple, startling, magnificent, with a mounting emotional crescendo created primarily through the use of drumbeats. But the catharsis it accomplishes, so rare in Brecht's drama, is followed almost immediately by grim, cooling irony. Kattrin's sacrifice has really been in vain. The town is saved, but the sound which signifies this is the explosion of a cannon. The war will continue for another twelve years; and after this war is finished, three hundred more years of killing will follow.

Brought on stage for the *threnos,* Courage witnesses the utter desolation of her hopes. The fault, again, has partially been hers ("If you hadn't gone off to get your cut," says an Old Peasant, "maybe it wouldn't have happened"), but she is too dazed now to know it. Thinking that Kattrin is only asleep, she sings her a lullaby; even the lullaby concerns the need for clothing and food. Her sustaining illusion is that Eilif may still be alive. Without this illusion, only nothingness confronts her — the inconsolable blankness of life, induced by a malignant universe, inhuman men, and her own flawed nature. We are out of the world of Falstaffian comedy and into the desolate world of *King Lear;* but unlike Lear, Brecht's heroine is denied even the release of death. When the armies move by, singing her song about the certainty of the seasons and the certainty of man's mortality — the coming of the springtime of life before the winter of death — she cries to them: "Hey, take me with you" — and straps herself to the wagon. She is pulling it alone now, but it is no longer very heavy: supplies and passengers have all been destroyed. Courage and the wagon merge — both bruised and battered by war, both somehow still durable. Courage has dragged it over half of Europe, learning nothing. She will drag it a good deal further before she stops, animated only by that basic life instinct: the need to survive. The smallness and the greatness of this woman are clear at the end, as they are clear throughout this monumental work, where Brecht so angrily takes away from the human race — and gives it back so much.

Mother Courage is the culminating work of Brecht's career, but it is hardly the end of it. During the war and after, in exile and back in East Berlin, Brecht continues to create a profusion of plays — including at least one masterpiece, *The Caucasion Chalk Circle*. But after *Mother Courage,* Brecht's savage indignation begins to leave him, his rebellion progressively cools. Even as his plays become more openly Communistic in subject matter, his approach grows more sweet and even-tempered. Virtuous, maternal women like Kattrin — Shen Te, Simone Machard, Grusha — move in to the center of the action, while his secondary characters develop deeper dimensions, and more complex motivations than simple greed and lust. Instead of castigating humanity, Brecht is beginning to celebrate it; instead of illustrating his themes through ironic comparisons, he is beginning to employ moral allegories and parables. Brecht's later approach to character and his use of less exaggerated comparisons suggest how he is losing his need to rebel against reality; as further proof, Nature has returned to his work — no longer hostile and ugly, but calm, serene, and even beautiful. Less sardonic, more relaxed, Brecht grows more lyrical and carefree: in fact, if Brecht's first period is Büchnerian, and his second Jonsonian, then his third is clearly Shakespearean — some of his plays have an atmosphere akin to Shakespeare's Romantic comedies.[20] Even Brecht's theory is loosening up from the rigid didacticism of his early days. In that latter-day *Poetics, The Little Organon for the Theatre*

---

[20] *The Caucasian Chalk Circle,* for example, is not only permeated with the mood and atmosphere of Shakespearean comedy, but also with some of its dramatic conventions. The prologue to the play functions as a Shakespearean induction; the main plot turns on suspense, misunderstanding, and intrigue. Grusha, like Rosalind in *As You Like It,* must flee the city in disguise as a result of usurpation and revolution. And Azdak, like so many of Shakespeare's clowns, is a Lord of Misrule: Toby Belch out of Charlie Chaplin by Groucho Marx. The Storyteller is a kind of Shakespearean chorus in his manipulation of time and space; and the songs of the play, like Shakespeare's songs, function as lyrical breaks in the action. Finally, the reconciliations at the conclusion of the work remind one of Shakespeare's way of tying off a Romantic plot — and like *Much Ado About Nothing,* the play ends with a dance.

(1948), Brecht finally permits himself to speak of "entertainment" in the drama, an element he used to scorn as hypnotic and culinary; and he even expresses the ideological heresy that "the easiest form of existence is in art."

"A contemplative attitude," notes Ronald Gray, "is thus yoked with the revolutionary one that Brecht still maintained." And this contemplative attitude, we should add, is the final development of Brecht's existential revolt. While Brecht has remained a Marxist, he has finally transcended his Neo-Romantic horror at life. Brecht's contemplative interests are underlined by his increasing interest in Oriental forms, characters, and subject matter — a large proportion of his poems and plays are now inspired by the East. It is true that Brecht is attracted to the Noh play, the Chinese drama, and the Kabuki theatre because of their alienation techniques; and like Yeats, he uses such conventions as masks, mime, dance, and gesture in order to restore that naïveté and simplicity that the oversophisticated Western theatre has lost. Still, Brecht has a very special philosophical affinity with the drama of the Orient, for it is a drama of submission, in which the characters recognize a universal intelligence and try to merge with it, freeing themselves of worldly desire.[21]

As proof, Brecht's interest in the Oriental drama is accompanied, during this last period, by an interest in the Eastern religious thinkers — Confucius, Buddha, Lao-Tse, the philosophers of obedience through the annihilation of the physical self. It is probable that, with the advance of age, Brecht had finally subdued his troublesome passions. No longer harried by appetite, he gives himself up to that drifting and merging which he desired all his life. Like Strindberg, in short, Brecht works his way through, after a career of fierce rebellion, to a position of resignation; at last, he achieves that security and se-

---

[21] Cf. Makoto Ueda, "The Implications of the Noh Drama," *Sewanee Review*, Summer 1961, p. 368, where the author affirms that the characters of the Noh play "lack the masculine courage and overpowering energy of the heroes of Western tragedies; they do not fight, they submit. . . . Thus the Noh drama is primarily religious — in the sense that it depicts man's coming to recognize an absolute power in the universe and his learning to submit himself to it." This might be a description of Brecht's ambitions throughout his life.

renity he associates with the mother's womb. In a late poem, "Buddha's Parable of the Burning House," Brecht returns to his recurrent image of passive suspension in water. Buddha has preached the doctrine of the wheel of desire, and advised "That we shed all craving and thus/ Undesiring enter the nothingness that he called Nirvana"; and a student, trying to understand the doctrine, has compared Nirvana with floating in water, wondering whether the sensation is pleasing or *"kalt, leer, und bedeutungslos"* (cold, empty, and meaningless). Buddha replies with his famous parable of those who, while their house was burning, wondered what the weather was like outside; and Brecht, at the end of the poem, applies this lesson to those who would resist Communist revolution, wondering whether it was good. Brecht's desire for revolt is still satisfied by his identification with Communism; but his desire for peace is now expressed through images of Oriental calm. Brecht, therefore, comes to terms with life only by continuing to reject it — by drifting with a political tide, he overcomes his spiritual horror and nausea. And this is the only synthesis of Brecht's double revolt. Only by merging with evil did he feel he could still function for good; only by embracing the destroyers could he still join the ranks of the creators. The chicanery and compromises Brecht accepted for the sake of the survival of himself and his art are not always very attractive. And no modern playwright better exemplifies the dwindling possibilities of revolt in an age of totalitarianism, war, and the mass state. But if Brecht sometimes sacrificed his personal integrity to a collective falsehood, then this was in order that his individualism could still be secretly expressed. His drama remains the final measurement of this achievement — acts of bitterness which did not quench his cigar but rather kept it aglow.

VII

LUIGI PIRANDELLO

In 1933, three years before his death, Luigi Pirandello completed an autobiographical play entitled *When One Is Somebody* (*Quando si è qualcuno*). The unnamed hero of the work, whose speeches are preceded only by three asterisks, is an aging writer of great prominence who finds himself imprisoned in a role defined by his public: "I must not move from a certain concept, every detail of which they have decided upon. There I am motionless, forever!" Chafing against the restrictions of his fame, he takes on a "mask of youth," escaping into temporary freedom by writing lyrics under the pseudonym of a young, unknown poet. For a while, the subterfuge is successful: the new poet is hailed as a "living voice." But the ruse is finally discovered, and the hero must return to his unpleasant public duties — being stared at, lionized, and applauded by uncomprehending admirers. Urged by a sympathetic friend to commit some spontaneous, even outrageous act in order to prove that he is still alive, the hero finds he cannot budge. Only when one is nobody, he learns, can one exist in time; when one is somebody, one is petrified, immobile, dead. In the midst of making a commemorative speech on his fiftieth birthday, he begins to turn into a statue of himself, while his spoken words are engraved on the facade of a house behind him.

The play is flawed by traces of vanity and self-pity, but its final image is a stunning consummation of Pirandello's views about the individual's relationship to his life, and the artist's relationship to his art — two subjects which are really the same subject, and which continue to obsess him throughout his career. Pirandello knows that he is alive and changing, but, against his will, he has hardened into the stiff postures of the stereotyped public man, while his words, though formed in the mind of a living being, are etched in marble as soon as they are uttered. To accept a definition — to become a *somebody* — is to be frozen in time, just as art, the defined world of the artist, rigidifies in its prison of form. The typical Pirandellian drama is a drama of frustration which has at its core an irreconcilable conflict between time and timelessness or life and form; and whether the author is reflecting on human identity or (his other major subject) the identity of art, the terms of the conflict remain essentially the same.

Typical in this sense, *When One Is Somebody* is unusual in another: Pirandello very rarely wrote autobiographical plays. Yet, he is one of the most subjective dramatists in the modern theatre, and certainly the most self-conscious. Pirandello is a peculiarity of the theatre of revolt — an imperious messianic artist who writes compassionate existential plays. In him, the Romantic ego is strong, though usually sublimated. When the mood strikes him, he can be as personally vain and pompous as his hated rival D'Annunzio: "The only thing I have been able to do," he writes to Marta Abba, "is to think beautiful and lofty things." About an inferior quasi-religious drama, *Lazarus,* he boasts that it "would put the modern conscience at peace on the religious question," and about the unfinished *Mountain Giants,* he crows: "The triumph of the imagination! The triumph of poetry, and at the same time the tragedy of poetry forced to exist in the midst of the brutal, modern world." [1]

Pirandello, furthermore, often complains about being misunderstood and unappreciated, though he was heaped with honors in his lifetime. When *Lazarus* is unfavorably reviewed, he declares that Italy will "have to live down the shame of having misunderstood" his plays "and of having treated me unjustly." Deciding to open *Tonight We Improvise* in Germany, he remarks, "I have become a stranger to my own country and . . . I shall therefore have to win another home

[1] To remarks like these, one is tempted to reply with Nietzsche's admonitory words: "Life is hard to bear: but do not affect to be so delicate!"

for my art." But when the opening is the occasion of a riot: "Everywhere I am pursued by hatred." Finally, he takes refuge in a bitter, self-pitying misanthropy: "Mankind does not deserve anything, stubborn as it is in its constantly growing stupidity, in its brutal quarrelsomeness. Time is against me; mankind adverse." In the mouth of Ibsen, such sentiments could be noble and courageous; in the mouth of Pirandello, they sound merely egotistical.

But it is rare when such personal egotism informs his work. As a dramatist, Pirandello is a stern, uncompromising ironist, but his plays are full of pity for the fate of suffering mankind. It is true that the only playwright mentioned in Pirandello's theatre is Pirandello himself (his name is occasionally on the tongues of his characters). But the references are always ironic, and he always resists the temptation to glorify himself, like D'Annunzio, through the agency of superhuman heroes. Pirandello's messianic impulse, on the other hand, is channeled into a personal philosophical vision. If not present as a character, the author is always present as a hovering reflective intelligence — commenting, expostulating, conceptualizing. In this, he reminds us of Shaw, and he certainly fits Shaw's definition of the "artist-philosopher." Pirandello, in fact, provides his own definition of the type in the preface to *Six Characters in Search of an Author*. There he distinguishes between what he calls "historical writers," those who "narrate a particular affair, lively or sad, simply for the pleasure of narrating it," and what he calls "philosophical writers," those who "feel a more profound spiritual need on whose account they admit only figures, affairs, landscapes which have been soaked, so to speak, in a particular sense of life and acquire from it a universal value." He adds, "I have the misfortune to belong to these last."

Pirandello's philosophy, however, is quite different than Shaw's, since it is pessimistic in the extreme, and based on the conviction that the problems of life are insoluble. Because of this conviction, Pirandello sees no possibility of salvation through social or community life. In fact, he is vigorously opposed to all forms of social engineering, and extremely contemptuous of Utopian ideals and idealists (he satirizes them, rather clumsily, in *The New Colony*). Pirandello, furthermore, considers the social use of art to be a betrayal of art: "One must choose between the objectives of art and those of propaganda," he says in a speech before the Italian Academy. "When art becomes the instrument of definite action and of practical utility, it is condemned and sacrificed." This would seem to put Pirandello at opposite poles from Shaw; but in one sense, they are very much alike. Both create plays in which plot and character are largely subordinate to theme; and both lean towards tendentious argumentation in enunciating their ideas. Indeed, Pirandello's weakness for ideas lays him open to the charge that his plays are too cerebral. This charge he does not deny, but he denies that cerebral plays have to be undramatic: "One of the novelties I have given to the modern drama," he declares, with characteristic bravado, "consists in converting the intellect into passion." After Ibsen and (if we define "passion" loosely) Shaw, this is hardly a novelty. But Pirandello is certainly the first to convert *abstract thought* into passion — to formulate an expository philosophy in theatrical terms.

It must be conceded, however, that these terms are not always very satisfactory. Pirandello is exceedingly interested in the *idea* of form, but rather indifferent to form itself. One tends to think of him as an experimental dramatist, but only his theatre trilogy can be called a formal breakthrough. The rest of his forty-four plays are relatively conventional in their use of dramatic materials. As a twentieth-century Italian dramatist, Pirandello had three possible traditions to tap: the *verismo* of Giovanni Verga, the rhetorical Romanticism of D'Annunzio, and the bourgeois drama of the French boulevard. Though Pirandello tried to dissociate himself from Verga's Naturalism and D'Annunzio's bombast, both influenced his work; but the greatest influence on his dramatic writing is that of the French *pièce bien faite*. After writing a series of Sicilian folk plays whch have a peasant earthiness reminiscent of Synge and Lorca, Pirandello devotes himself largely to dramas of the urban middle class. And unlike most of the dramatists in the theatre of revolt, who manage to transform mundane reality into poetic images through symbolic action, character, or atmosphere, Pirandello — despite occasional assaults on the fourth wall — generally keeps us confined amidst the ugly paraphernalia of the cluttered drawing room. Pirandello is not an artist who really develops; as an Italian critic observed, his drama is a single play in a hundred acts.[2] Not until the end of his life, when it is already too late, does he begin to explore the possibilities of poetic myths, in flawed works like *Lazarus, The New Colony,* and *The Mountain Giants.*

As for his dramatic structure, it is extremely conventional, when not downright haphazard. Almost all of his plays are crammed into three acts, "whether they fit or not." Whenever the action flags, Pirandello contrives a new entrance or a new revelation; and each curtain comes down on a not always credible crisis. In the act of converting intellect into passion, Pirandello often tears the passion to tatters. His plots are bursting with operatic feelings and melodramatic climaxes in an exaggerated Sicilian vein. Hyperbolic expressions of grief, rage, and jealousy alternate with murders, suicides, and mortal accidents; wronged wives, maddened husbands, and bestial lovers foment adultery, incest, illegitimacy, plots, and duels. At times, his monologues turn into arias, and would be more appropriate set to Verdi's music.

The characters, furthermore, seem to lose psychological depth as they gain philosophical eloquence — occasionally, their identity is wholly swallowed up in the author's ideas. Pirandello is even more loquacious than Shaw, and has, therefore, less resistance to the *raisonneur.* Shaw is able to preserve aesthetic distance from a character like John Tanner, but Laudisi in *It Is So!* (*If You Think So*) and Diego Cinci in *Each in His Own Way* are hardly detached from their author at all. Shaw's drama is a drama of ideas, in which the ideas change from play to play, and the author can support two positions at the same time. Pirandello's drama is a drama of ideas based on a single underlying concept, consistent throughout his career and enjoying the author's wholehearted endorsement. Still, the basic Pirandellian concept is itself dialectical, and subject to endless combinations

[2] Pirandello is very much aware of such strictures, and signals his awareness through his plays. In his theatre trilogy, for example, the characters comment frequently on the author's limitations, particularly his obscurity and his thematic single-mindedness. As a spectator in *Each in His Own Way* remarks about Pirandello: "Why is he always harping on this illusion and reality string?"

and permutations. The terms of the dialectic may not change, but the author's point of attack alternates from play to play, from thesis to antithesis, depending on the situation being considered.

The basic Pirandellian concept is borrowed from Bergson, and, briefly stated, it is this. Life (or reality or time) is fluid, mobile, evanescent, and indeterminate. It lies beyond the reach of reason, and is reflected only through spontaneous action, or instinct. Yet man, endowed with reason, cannot live instinctually like the beasts, nor can he accept an existence which constantly changes. In consequence, he uses reason to fix life through ordering definitions. Since life is indefinable, such concepts are illusions. Man is occasionally aware of the illusionary nature of his concepts; but to be human is to desire form; anything formless fills man with dread and uncertainty. "Humankind cannot bear very much reality" — T. S. Eliot's perception in *Burnt Norton* (and *Murder in the Cathedral*) is the spine of Pirandello's philosophy.

The way humankind evades reality is by stopping time, for, as Eliot goes on to say, "To be conscious is not to be in time." Through the exercise of consciousness, or reason, man temporarily achieves the timeless. Existence is chaotic, irrational, in flux; man essentializes for the sake of order and form. To quote Eliot once more, "Except for the point, the still point, there would be no dance, and there is only the dance." For Pirandello's characters, too, there is only the dance, and so each one labors to find his still point in the turning world.

The drama Pirandello distills from this concept is usually described through reference to the face and the mask — a conflict he borrowed from the *teatro del grotesco*. The authors who constitute the grotesque movement — Chiarelli, Martini, Antonelli — use this conflict as the basis for bizarre situations, presented in a ludicrous way. The face represents the suffering individual in all his complexity; the mask reflects external forms and social laws. The individual yields to instinct, but he is also ruled by the demands of a rigid code, and the conflict pulls him in opposite directions. This seems like a modern version of the heroic conflict of love and honor, except that, in the *teatro del grotesco,* the central character tries to accommodate both demands at the same time. He is, as a result, not heroic but absurd — and the effect of the play is neither tragic nor comic but grotesque. In Luigi Chiarelli's *The Mask and the Face* (*La maschera ed il volto,* 1916), for example, a passionate Italian announces in public that he will kill his wife if she is unfaithful to him. When he finds her in the arms of another, he is reluctant to exact vengeance, so he exiles her, pretends she has been killed, and goes to trial for her murder. The mask of honor and the face of love have both been preserved. But in order to achieve this, the Italian has had to turn actor, playing his role to the limits of his endurance.

Pirandello takes over this antinomy intact, and proceeds to work manifold variations on it, both social and existential. For in his work, the mask of appearances is shaped both by the self and others. The others constitute the social world, a world which owes its existence to the false assumption that its members adhere to narrow definitions. Man, like life, may be unknowable, and the human soul, like time, may be in constant flight, but society demands certainty, and tries to imprison man in its fictitious concepts. To Pirandello, all social institutions and systems of thought — religion, law, government, science, morality, philosophy, sociology, even language itself — are means by which society creates masks, trying to catch the elusive face of man and fix it with a classification. "Basically," writes Pirandello, "I have constantly attempted to show that nothing offends life so much as reducing it to a hollow concept." Concepts are the death of spontaneity, he explains in his essay, *Umorismo* (1908), and reason is inadequate before the mysterious quality of existence. The human mystery remains beyond human comprehension; and those who would pluck it out will come away baffled and in tears.

On the other hand, the mind of man, being stuffed with concepts, has no defense against these social definitions. Because he is uncertain of his identity, he accepts the identity given him by others — sometimes willingly, like the heroine of *As You Desire Me,* sometimes reluctantly, like the hero of *When One Is Somebody.* Looking for the elusive self, he sees it reflected in the eyes of others, and takes the reflection for the original. This acceptance of a superimposed identity is one side of Pirandello's *teatro dello specchio* (theatre of the looking glass) — aptly named, since the image of the mirror occurs in almost every one of his plays. Laudisi, for example, examining his image in a glass, asks: "What are you for other people? What are you in their eyes? An image, dear sir, just an image in the glass! They're all carrying just such a phantom around inside themselves, and here they are racking their brains about the phantoms in other people. . . ." Knowledge, facts, opinions, all are phantasms, and even conscience is "nothing but other people inside you." As Diego Cinci puts it, in *Each in His Own Way:* "We have of each other reciprocally, and each has of himself, knowledge of some small, insignificant certainty of to-day, which is not the certainty it was yesterday, and will not be the certainty of tomorrow." In this sliding world, the human personality dissolves and changes, and like the hero of Pirandello's novel, *The Late Mattia Pascal,* who awoke one morning holding on to this one positive fact, the only thing you can be certain of is your name.

These are the social implications of Pirandello's treatment of masks. The author — always identifying with the suffering individual in opposition to the collective mind — is in revolt against the social world, and all its theoretical, conceptual, institutional extensions. As he said in an interview with Domenico Vittorini: "Society is necessarily formal, and in this sense I am antisocial, but only in the sense that I am opposed to social hypocrisies and conventions. My art teaches each individual to accept his lot with candor and humility, and with full consciousness of the imperfections that are inherent in it." The stoical sound of this qualification, however, suggests that Pirandello's social revolt has existential roots. Indeed it has because, in Pirandello's view, the adoption of the mask is the inevitable consequence of being human. If the mask is sometimes imposed on the face by the external world, it is more often the construct of internal demands. Hamlet says, "I know not seems" — but Pirandello's characters know almost nothing else.

For whether they know it or not, they are all devoted to appearances, as a defense against the agony of the changing personality. "Continually I hide my face from myself," says a character in *Each in*

His Own Way, "so ashamed am I at seeing myself change." The shame is increased by time, for old age etches change, irremediably, on the human features. "Age," observes a character in *Diana and Tuda,* "which is time reduced to human dimensions — time when it is painful — and we are made of flesh." Or, as the aging writer in *When One Is Somebody* complains, "You don't know what an atrocious thing happens to an old man, to see himself all of a sudden in a mirror, when the sorrow of seeing himself is greater than the astonishment of no longer remembering. You don't know the obscene shame of feeling a young and hotblooded heart within an old body." The body is form, but form which changes under the hungry eye of the cormorant, time. To stop time, to achieve stasis, to locate the still point, Pirandello's characters put on their masks, hoping to hide their shameful faces by playing a role.

This is what Pirandello means by *costruirsi,* building yourself up. Man begins as nothing definite, and becomes a *costruzione,* creating himself according to predetermined patterns or roles. Thus, he plays family roles (husband, wife, father, mother), religious roles (saint, blasphemer, priest, atheist), psychological roles (madman, neurotic, normal man), and social roles (mayor, citizen, socialist, revolutionary). No matter how well these roles are played, however, none of them reveals the face of the actor. They are disguises, designed to give purpose and form to a meaningless existence — masks in an infinite comedy of illusion. The true self is revealed only in a moment of blind instinct, which has the power to break down all codes and concepts.[3] But even then, the self is on the point of changing. Thus, Pirandello refuses to idealize the personality in the manner of the messianic rebels; for him, personality remains a fictional construct. Instead, he concentrates on the disintegration of personality in a scene of bond-

[3] Since Pirandello believed so firmly in the power of the sexual instinct, he was compared — by an adoring disciple, Domenico Vittorini — to his rival D'Annunzio. Pirandello's reply is instructive: "No, no. D'Annunzio is immoral in order to proclaim the glory of instinct. I present this individual case to add another proof of the tragedy of being human. D'Annunzio is exultant over evil; I grieve over it." Or, in the terminology of revolt, D'Annunzio is messianic, Pirandello is existential.

age and frustration — existential revolt in the ironic mode. Pirandellian man has freedom, but his freedom is unbearable; it beckons him towards the waste and void. Though he sometimes plunges into reality through spontaneous, instinctual action, he more often takes refuge from reality in a beneficial illusion. "The greater the struggle for life," as Pirandello phrases it in *Umorismo,* "the greater the need for mutual deceit."

The histrionic implications of this are tremendous — the Pirandellian hero is an actor, a character in disguise. But Pirandello broadens these implications even further. For if his hero is an actor, he is also a critic who cruelly judges his own performance. "Yes I laugh sometimes," says Leone Gala in *The Rules of the Game,* "as I watch myself playing this self-imposed role. . . ." In Elizabethan drama, the disguised character is anxious to protect his disguise from others; in Pirandello, he is also anxious to protect it from himself. Yet, reason, which created the mask, exposes its illusionary nature. In the *teatro dello specchio,* the reflecting mirror is not only the eye of the world but the inner eye as well:

When a man lives [writes Pirandello], he lives and does not see himself. Well, put a mirror before him and make him see himself in the act of living. Either he is astonished at his own appearance, or else he turns away his eyes so as not to see himself, or else in disgust he spits at his image, or, again, clenches his fist to break it. In a word, there arises a crisis, and that crisis is my theatre.

In another place, he adds: "If we present ourselves to others as artificial constructions in relation to what we really are, it is logical that upon looking at ourselves in a mirror we see our falseness reflected there, made galling and unbearable by its fixity." It is for this reason that a character like Baldovino, in *The Pleasures of Honesty,* experiences "an unspeakable nausea for the self that I am compelled to build up and display in the relations I must assume with my fellow men." If Pirandello's characters want to be fixed, they also want to move.

The conflict between appearance and reality, or Art and Nature, has been a traditional subject of Western literature since its beginnings, with Anglo-Saxon writers generally supporting reality and Latin writers generally supporting appearances. The blunt, plainspoken man, who will not hide his true feelings, is a crucial figure in a certain strain of English drama and satire, while French, Spanish, and Italian literature is often more tolerant of the courteous man, who knows how to moderate his temper and disguise his desires. When the Italian Iago goes into disguise, he assumes the appearance of a gruff, honest soldier; when Molière's "misanthrope" enters English drama, he becomes Wycherly's "plaindealer." In Pirandello's drama, on the other hand, the conflict between Art and Nature is translated into a conflict between life and form, while appearances become illusions; but with him, the conflict becomes a real dialectic. Pirandello evokes sympathy for the man who tries to hide from reality and sympathy for the man who tries to plunge back into it. Life and form — reality and illusion — are opposed, but they are the twin poles of human existence.

Pirandello is similarly ambivalent about the faculty of reason. His philosophy, founded as it is on the belief that real knowledge is unattainable, is profoundly anti-intellectual; yet, it is through the intellect that he reaches his conclusions. Such paradoxes proliferate in Pirandello's drama. Reason is both man's consolation and his curse; it creates a false identity which it can also destroy; it applies the masks to the face, and then rips them off. Under the cold eye of reason, the human ego expands and contracts; the *costruzione* is erected, and then demolished. The disguised character in Pirandello is a creature of appearances, whose intellect has created his illusion, but he also has the capacity, through the agency of intellect, to penetrate to a deeper reality. He escapes from life into form, and from form into life. Or, put into the metaphor of the theatre, the improvising actor struts and frets his hour on the stage before the ruthless critic sends him back to his dressing-room mirror, weeping over the inauthenticity of his performance.

This probably sounds impossibly abstruse, an exercise in epistemology rather than drama, but the wonder is the number of effective situations Pirandello is able to create out of such reflections. For Pirandello's concept always takes the form of conflict, and conflict remains the heart of his drama. These conflicts take an internal and external form, depending on which aspect of Pirandello's revolt is in the ascendant. As an existential rebel, Pirandello explores the roles men play in order to escape from life — revolt turns inward against the elusiveness of human existence. As a social rebel, he attacks the busybodies, gossips, and scandalmongers who think they can understand the unknowable mystery of man — revolt turns outwards against the intruding social world. The two levels of Pirandello's revolt generally run parallel in each of his plays; and, as a result, his drama has a "spatial design," in Eric Bentley's words, which consists of "a center of suffering within a periphery of busybodies — the pattern of the Sicilian village."

Extending this description a little further, let us call those in the outer circle *alazōnes* (impostors or buffoons) and those in the center *eirones* (self-deprecators) — terms by which I mean to suggest the affinities of Pirandello's characters with the stock masks of Aristophanic comedy and the *commedia dell'arte*.[4] In traditional comedy, as Northrup Frye tells us, the *alazōn* is typified as "the *miles gloriosus* and the learned crank or obsessed philosopher." In Pirandello's drama, the *alazōn* is an agent of organized society, and is usually identified with one of its institutions — science, bureaucracy, or the state. He is sometimes a doctor, sometimes a petty official, sometimes a magistrate, sometimes a policeman — always a pretender, whose pretense lies in thinking himself a wise man when he is really a fool. The *eiron,* on the other hand, is a suffering individual who has hidden some private secret under a mask of appearances. Sometimes, he is unaware he is wearing a mask, in which case he is merely a pathetic sufferer — a *pharmakos,* or scapegoat. More often, he is a man of superior wisdom, because, like Socrates (the original *eiron*), he *knows* he knows nothing. Hounded and tormented by his persecutors, the buffoonish

---

[4] F. L. Cornford was the first to apply these terms to Aristophanes in his book *The Origins of Attic Comedy;* Northrup Frye, in *The Anatomy of Criticism,* applies them to literature as a whole. Pirandello, who was familiar with the stock masks of traditional comedy, uses them, I think, in a much more conscious way than other Western writers.

alazōnes, he replies with the dry mock: ironic laughter is his only weapon. As Diego Cinci puts it, in *Each in His Own Way:* "I laugh because I have reasoned my heart dry. . . . I laugh in my own way, and my ridicule falls upon myself sooner than on anyone else!" He is thus ironic in the original Greek sense of *dissimulation* — of ignorance purposely affected.

The clash between the two groups occurs when the *alazōnes* try to peel off the masks of the *eirones* — an action which has both tragic and comic consequences. On the one hand, this impertinent invasion of another's privacy may be dangerous, since the *eiron's* illusion is necessary to his life; on the other, the attempt to discover another's secret self is ludicrously impossible, since the face beneath the mask cannot be known. The comic action, then, proceeds along the social level of the play where the *alazōnes* are frustrated in their curiosity, their state changing from knowledge to ignorance, from smug complacency to stupefied bafflement. The tragic action proceeds along the existential level of the play where the *eirones* are dragged under a painfully blinding spotlight which causes them terrible discomfort and suffering. As for the author, his literary endeavors identify him as an *alazōn,* since by writing about the *eirones,* he is meddling in their private affairs.[5] But his tone is that of an *eiron,* since, in his sympathetic identification with the sufferers, he expresses ironic contempt for the social busybodies.

One of the most famous, if not the most artful, of the plays in this mode is *It Is So! (If You Think So)* — *Cosi è (se vi pare)* — which Pirandello wrote in 1917. Here the leader of the *alazōnes* is Commendatore Agazzi, a small-town bureaucrat, who is supported in his buffoonery by members of his and another family, by the Prefect, and by the Police Commissioner. The sufferers are their neighbors:

---

[5] Pirandello suggests this role for himself in *Each in His Own Way* — a *commedia a chiave,* or comedy with a key. This play, which is based on living personages, is interrupted in the middle by some of the figures being represented on the stage; and it is rumored that they have slapped Pirandello's face in the lobby. "It's a disgrace," one of them cries. "Two people pilloried in public! The private affairs of two people exposed to public ridicule!" In this *roman à clef,* therefore, Pirandello clearly assigns himself the function of the meddling *alazōn.*

Signor Ponza, his wife, and his mother-in-law, Signora Frola. The un-usual behavior of this family has been arousing curiosity. Why is Signora Frola never permitted to visit with her own daughter? The neighbors are particularly incensed, because they have also been re-fused admittance to Ponza's house, even though Ponza is Agazzi's subordinate.

As the play proceeds, and Ponza and Signora Frola are cross-exam-ined about their behavior, the mystery thickens. Ponza maintains that he has barred his mother-in-law from his door in order to protect her peace of mind. According to his testimony, her daughter has died in an earthquake and Ponza had married a second time; but when Sig-nora Frola became deranged and refused to believe these facts, Ponza humored her by letting her think her daughter was still alive. Signora Frola, on the other hand, maintains that it is Ponza who is mad. He has convinced himself that his first wife is dead and, to hu-mor him, she let him marry her daughter twice. To compound the con-fusion, each witness is aware of the other's version of the events, but compassionately labors to preserve the other's illusion.

Meanwhile the Agazzi family and their allies are busy trying to get to the bottom of things. Representing themselves as "pilgrims athirst for truth," they are really "a pack of gossips" — prying into secrets, ferreting out facts, forcing painful confrontations. Only Agazzi's brother-in-law, Lamberto Laudisi, disapproves of this meddling in the lives of others. The Ponza family is a *pharmakos* group — passive, victimized, unaware — so Laudisi becomes their spokesman; he is the *eiron* of the play, and it is on his derisive laughter that each curtain falls. To Laudisi, the truth is something perpetually out of reach, while reality is a movable feast which each man samples from his own table. As the buffoons proceed with their interrogations and investiga-tions, turning up documents and official papers, yet continuing to be baffled, Laudisi affirms that facts contribute nothing to the matter, since they leave things just as ambiguous as before. "Oh, I grant you," he concedes, "if you could get a death certificate or a marriage certifi-cate or something of the kind, you might be able to satisfy that stupid curiosity of yours. Unfortunately, you can't get it. And the result is that you are in the extraordinary fix of having before you, on the one hand, a world of fancy, and on the other, a world of reality, and you, for the life of you, are not able to distinguish one from the other."

Finally, the only person who can explain the mystery — Signora Ponza — is brought in to testify. She is "dressed in deep mourning . . . her face concealed with a thick, black impenetrable veil." The veil is her mask — but the veil remains down, the mask continues to conceal the face. For Signora Ponza thereupon announces that she is the daughter of Signora Frola, and also the second wife of Signor Ponza. She has become a construction, built up by the demands of others: "I am she whom you believe me to be" — and in herself, "I am nothing." Externally imposed, the mask changes according to the eye of the beholder, while the face remains an imponderable mystery.

As Eric Bentley observes, there is nothing in the play to suggest that there is not a correct version of the story. Rather, the play is a protest against the "scandalmonger, the prying reporter, and the amateur psychoanalyst" — and we might add, the sob sister, the candid cameraman, and the Congressional investigator — those who recklessly probe the secrets of others. In *It Is So!*, these secrets can only be protected through concealment. "There is a misfortune here, as you see, which must stay hidden," remarks Signora Ponza, "otherwise, the remedy which our compassion has found cannot avail." Professor Bentley concludes from this that Pirandello *does* believe in the existence of objective truth. This may be — but he will show again and again, in later plays, how this truth cannot be grasped by the inquiring mind, since it is in a continual state of flux and varies with each individual. This existential complaint is only suggested in *It Is So!*, then buried under a barrage of social satire. Instead of developing the deeper implications of his philosophy, Pirandello exercises the animus of his social revolt; and the tragedy which threatens is averted at the end. Their right to privacy affirmed, their secret still hidden from the gossips and the busybodies, the *pharmakoi* depart into darkness, while the *alazōnes* stand lost in amazement, whipped by the savage laughter of the *eiron*.

It Is So! (*If You Think So*) is a fairly conventional exercise in the mode of the grotesque. As an expression of social revolt, it has its power and relevance, but the split between the *pharmakoi* and the *eiron* — between the sufferers and their spokesman — shows that Pirandello has not yet perfected his structure. Furthermore, the prominence of Laudisi, the *raisonneur,* suggests that, at this early point, Pirandello is less interested in dramatizing his themes than in stating them flatly. In *Henry IV* (*Enrico IV,* 1922), however, Pirandello dispenses with the *raisonneur* entirely, embodying his ideas in a brilliant theatrical metaphor, and concentrating not so much on the social world of the dumbfounded buffoons as on the existential world of the chief sufferer. And now this world is wonderfully rich and varied. The central character of the play is both *pharmakos* and *eiron,* both a living person and an articulate personification, both the mechanism of the action and the source of the ideas. In Henry's character, Pirandello's reflections on the conflict between life and form, on the elusiveness of identity, and on man's revolt against time, achieve their consummation in a powerfully eerie manner. Henry is the culmination of Pirandello's concept of the mask and the face, as well as embodying Pirandello's notions (developed more elaborately in his theatre plays) about the timeless world of art. In trying to fix his changing life in significant form, Henry emerges as Actor, Artist, and Madman, and, besides this, possesses an extraordinary intellect, reflecting on all three.

The structure of the play, a structure that is to become basic to Pirandello's work, consists of an "historical" story within a "philosophical" framework. The historical line is this: Henry IV (as he is called throughout the play) is an Italian nobleman on whom life has played a cruel trick. Twenty years before, indulging his taste for playacting, he had appeared in a pageant, costumed as the medieval Holy Roman Emperor who had been excommunicated by Gregory VII and forced to walk barefoot to Canossa to do penance. His horse had stumbled — pricked from behind, as we later learn, by his rival, Tito Belcredi — and Henry had fallen, hitting his head on a rock. Henry awoke with the delusion that he actually was Henry IV; the pageant had become his reality. "I shall never forget that scene," recalls his former mistress, Donna Matilda, "all our masked faces hideous and gazing at him, at that terrible mask of his face, which was no longer a mask, but madness, madness personified!" The mask had usurped the face; the actor had turned madman, losing all distance from his role. When this delirium persisted, Henry's nephew, Charles di Nolli, hired men to play his retainers and counsellors. For the next twenty years, they performed their supporting roles in a drama which Henry, the chief actor, had unwittingly substituted for his life.

For only twelve of those twenty years, however, was Henry really mad; after that, his consciousness returned. But he regained his sanity with the terrible realization that he had been cheated of his youth. He had slept away his life in a long dream, and now he had awakened, gray inside and out, about to "arrive, hungry as a wolf, at a banquet which had already been cleared away." His hunger persisting, unappeased, he determined to revenge himself on time by refusing to return to time. He would play his role again, maintain his mask, and live his madness "with the most lucid consciousness." This consciousness is likened to a mirror which he always keeps before him, invisible to everybody else. The actor had turned madman; now the madman would turn actor, in revolt against existence itself.

Henry managed to escape from time by entering history, which is frozen time. He followed the outlines of a plot already written, foreordained, predetermined, seeking — like Yeats in "Sailing to Byzantium" — a corridor into the world of eternity. Yeats's answer to the agonizing flux of life is to contemplate a golden bird upon a golden bough, in a legendary country where time is suspended; Henry finds consolation for his melancholy and despair by constructing himself into a historical figure, fixed and immutable. By remaining Henry IV at the age of twenty-six, "everything determined, everything settled," Henry never suffers the horrors of age. He is held as firmly in an eternal moment as that youthful portrait of himself in costume, which hangs in the throne room beside a portrait of the young Donna Matilda. And now, as he enacts a masquerade, yet remains outside the masquerade — possessing the weird clarity of his lucid madness — Henry moves through life with the supreme confidence of one who knows what came before — and what comes after. Chance, accident, happenstance, the tricks of time, afflict him no more. Freely suspending his freedom of action, he has moved from time into timelessness, into that still point where the dance proceeds.

Henry's narrative is woven skillfully in the play, and its threads are unraveled through the plucking and pulling of another group of Pirandellian busybodies. Playing *alazōnes* to Henry's *eiron* are a number of interested parties who have come to observe this "madman" in the hope of curing him: Donna Matilda, his old mistress; Tito Belcredi, her present lover; Charles di Nolli, Henry's nephew; Frida, Matilda's beautiful daughter; and an alienist named Doctor Dionysius Genoni. These characters are subjected to Henry's, and Pirandello's, scorn, but the alienist is a special object of satire. A "learned crank" with total confidence in his curative powers, Genoni is a jargon-ridden quack — a caricature of a professional man — *il dottore* from the *commedia dell'arte*. To him, Henry is merely a case — a conceptual object rather than a complex human being. But, as always in Pirandello, this kind of labeling becomes an insult to the human soul: "Words, words which anyone can interpret in his own manner!" cries Henry. "That's the way public opinion is formed! And it's a bad look out for a man who finds himself labeled one day with one of these words which everyone repeats: for example 'madman,' or 'imbecile.' "

Having so labeled Henry, Genoni suggests that he and the others enter his madness for the purpose of observing him more closely. Since Henry "pays more attention to the dress than to the person," they put on period costumes, assuming a madness of clothes. Each pretends to be some figure in the life of the historical Henry: a Benedictine monk (Belcredi), the Abbot of Cluny (Genoni), and the Duchess Adelaide, mother of Henry's Queen (Matilda). During the audience which follows, Matilda and Belcredi suspect that Henry has recognized them; and indeed he has; but he continues to play his role to perfection. "Madness has made a superb actor of him," Di Nolli has observed, but none of them is aware how brilliant Henry's performance actually is. For Henry is not only playing Henry IV; he is

[298]

also playing the elderly Henry IV playing the young Henry of the portrait, from which he begs to be freed. His hair dyed, his cheeks roughed, Henry enacts a masquerade within a masquerade. The masks proliferate in defense against the changing shape of life:

A woman wants to be a man . . . an old man would be young again [says Henry to his visitors]. . . . We're all fixed in good faith in a certain concept of ourselves. However, Monsignor, while you keep your self in order, holding on with both hands to your holy habit, there slips down from your sleeves, there peels off from you like . . . like a serpent . . . something you don't notice: life, Monsignor! Has it never happened to you, my Lady, to find a different self in yourself? Have you always been the same?

Shifting skillfully from one self to another, speaking ambiguously about real and imagined conspiracies, Henry confuses the interlopers, and turns the mirror back on them: "Buffoons, buffoons!" he spits, contemptuously. "One can play any tune on them!" For while the *alazōnes* are observing the *eiron*, the *eiron* is observing the *alazōnes*, and with a much more highly trained eye. "And you," he says to his Valets, "are amazed that I tear off their ridiculous masks now, just as if it wasn't I who made them mask themselves to satisfy this taste of mine for playing the madman!" The *eiron*'s superiority is clearly established. The *alazōnes* are acting out Henry's masquerade, lacking the wit to create their own; and Henry's advantage over them is his knowledge that life itself is mad, that the so-called sane live their madness "without knowing it or seeing it." Thus, Pirandello reverses accepted notions of sanity and madness with a paradox taken from the heart of his philosophy. To live in a world where nothing is stable and man grows old is lunacy itself, while Henry's "conscious madness" is the highest form of wisdom: "This is my life!" cries Henry. "Quite a different thing from your life! Your life, the life in which you have grown old. . . ."

When the *alazōnes* attempt to bring Henry back into their world from his refuge in history, their meddling, as usual, issues in painful consequences. The Doctor, comparing Henry to a watch that has stopped at a certain hour, prepares to get the mechanism going again through a "violent trick." He will dress up Frida, who bears an un-canny resemblance to her mother as a young woman, in the costume of the portrait, and place her moving, speaking figure in the frame. Belcredi warns that the shock of pulling Henry across an abyss of eight hundred years might prove so strong that "you'll have to pick him up in pieces with a basket!" But Genoni, his implacable confidence unruffled, proceeds with his dangerous plan.

At the beginning of the last act, the throne room has been dark-ened, and the actors are in place: the living figures of Frida and Charles di Nolli have been substituted for the portraits of Matilda and Henry. When Henry enters the room, and Frida calls to him softly in the darkness, the shock is so great that Henry almost faints. The alien-ist thinks himself vindicated, since Henry is "cured." But Henry quickly reveals that he has been "cured" for eight years, and that this "violent trick" was a foolish and reckless blunder: "Do you know, Doctor, that for a moment you ran the risk of making me mad again? By God, to make the portraits speak. . . ." Henry, meditating a ter-rible revenge, tells his visitors about his decision to play the madman in order to abdicate from life, "that continuous, everlasting masquer-ade, of which we are the involuntary puppets, when, without knowing it, we mask ourselves with that which we appear to be. . . ."

But life draws him back again, against his will, in the form of un-controllable instinct. In Frida, he finds his old love, Matilda, still young and fresh. Time has destroyed, but time, too, has miraculously resurrected what it destroyed. His passion returning, he finds all the treacheries and betrayals of the last twenty years have vanished in an instant. "Oh miracle of miracles! Prodigy of prodigies! The dream alive in you! More than alive in you! It was an image that wavered there and they've made you come to life!" Matilda is old and decayed, but Frida is the realization of the timeless dream. Losing control of himself for the first time, Henry goes to take Frida in his arms, "laughing like a madman." The violent trick proves violent indeed, and the conclusion is melodramatic. Belcredi intervenes, shouting that Henry is not mad, and Henry runs him through the body with a sword. When the *alazōnes* flee in panic, and Belcredi expires off stage, Henry is left alone with his retainers to meditate on the "life of the masquerade which has driven him to crime." Forced back into the role of madman by this act, he is locked in it now. The mask has obliterated the face. The mantle of Henry IV has become a shirt of Nessus. Drawing his Valets around him for protection, he realizes that history has become his prison, and he is now lost for all eternity in its cunning passages: "here we are . . . together . . . for ever!"

Henry IV is unquestionably Pirandello's masterpiece, a complex artwork in which the themes arise naturally from the action — neither discursive nor superfluous, yet, at the same time, eloquently and coherently stated. In the figure of Henry, moreover, Pirandello has found his perfect *eiron-pharmakos,* one who acts and suffers, murders and creates, and one who can enunciate the author's ideas about the need for privacy from interfering busybodies, the vanity of learning, and the way man takes refuge from a harsh reality in beneficial illusions. In Henry, too, Pirandello has dramatized the dreadful loneliness of human beings, encased in shells of steel, never able to know or communicate with another. Pirandello's Henry, like Brecht's Shlink in *In the Jungle of Cities,* watches the hungry generations stare coldly into each other's eyes:

I would never wish you to think, as I have done [he tells his retainers], on this horrible thing which really drives one mad; that if you were beside another and looking into his eyes — as I one day looked into somebody's eyes — you might as well be a beggar before a door never to be opened to you; for he who does enter there will never be you, but someone unknown to you, within his different and impenetrable world. . . .

This "misery which is not only his, but everybody's," as the author describes it in a stage direction, is Pirandello's finest expression of his rage against existence, the source both of his philosophy and his drama. And in *Henry IV,* Pirandello has finally converted intellect into genuine passion, making his existential rebellion the occasion for a rewarding and absorbing play.

Henry IV is also significant for the hints it throws out about Pirandello's view of art — views which form the basis for another important group of his plays. For while Henry suggests certain characteristics of the actor and the artist, a good many of Pirandello's characters actually *are* actors and artists, reflecting self-consciously on the implications of their roles. Pirandello's attention is fixed not on the act but rather on the *process* of the act, as analyzed by the one who commits it. In his more conventional plays, Pirandello imagines men watching themselves live. In his more experimental drama, Pirandello imagines performers watching themselves perform and artists watching themselves create — the mirror remains the central prop of his theatre. Actually, Pirandello's views of art are an extension of his concept of the face and the mask. When man becomes a *costruzione,* placing a mask over his changing features, he stands in the same relationship to his new identity as the artist does to his art — for art is the artist's *costruzione,* the form he imposes on chaotic life. The construction, in each case, is built up by the human demand for order.

In each case, too, Pirandello's attitudes towards the product are split. Like the mask, the work of art is both a limiting and a liberating creation. Art is superior to life, because it has purpose, meaning, and organization — the illusion is deeper than the reality. But art is inferior to life because it can never capture the transitory, formless quality of existence. The work of art is thus a beneficial illusion, an ordered fiction — more harmonious than life, yet still a lie. When Pirandello finds the temporal world unbearable, he takes refuge in the timeless world of art; but when he finds the fixity of art unbearable, he longs to break out into spontaneous life. The author, in consequence, alternates between aestheticism and realism, between nostalgia for permanence and desire for change; and this peculiar ambivalence is never resolved in his work.[6] But Pirandello continues to build his drama not on the affirmation of concepts but rather on the conflict between them — "the inherent tragic conflict," as he phrases it in the

[6] Pirandello's frantic desire for form may account for his attraction to Fascism (he had his Nobel prize melted down for use in Mussolini's Abyssinian campaign!). Like all authoritarian ideologies, Fascism represents a rigid order, providing certainty and definition. Still, considering Pirandello's accompanying desire for flux, and his distaste for propagandistic art, I cannot believe his political position was very serious.

preface to *Six Characters,* "between life (which is always moving and changing) and form (which fixes it, immutable)."

Here we can clearly see the existential consequences of Pirandello's sublimated messianic revolt. For the conflict between life and form is really a conflict between life and death. Pirandello's demand for form is literally a death wish, since, as he tells us, whatever is fixed in form is really dead; like his philosophy, his art is a negation of life. On the other hand, his discontent with art stems from an affirmation of life, since he wants to capture the elusive quality of existence. Only one artist was ever able to create living things, and that was God; and "God alone," as he says in *Lazarus,* "can recall the dead to life." The messianic impulse in Pirandello makes him long to be a god, and create a work of art that lives; but the existential recoil fills him with depair over the impossibility of divine creation.

Thus, the agony of the artist in Pirandello's drama is that, for all his ingenuity, he cannot really create life — to make an artistic form is to deaden and kill. In *Diana and Tuda,* for example, the older sculptor, Giuncano, has destroyed all his statues because, as he grew old and changed, they remained perpetually the same. He urges his younger colleague, Sirio Dossi, to undertake a statue of his young and marvelously beautiful model, Tuda, "the way she is now! When she's quivering with life, in perpetual change from moment to moment!" But Sirio argues that art is not the same as life. He is transforming Tuda, a nobody, into *somebody,* a statue — *"that one* there. . . . That's the function of art." But the melancholy Giuncano feels compelled to add, "And of death too! Death will make statues of both of us when we lie stiff and cold in our beds or in the ground." Death, indeed, makes a statue of the aging writer in *When One Is Somebody,* who is petrified before our eyes, his words hardening into marble — the artwork, like the "somebody," is a thing of stone.

When Pirandello's messianism is the ascendant, however, he argues the opposite point — that the artist's work is superior to God's, because art, unlike man, is immortal: "All that lives, by the fact of living, has a form and by the same token must die — except the work of art which lives forever in so far as it *is* form." Pirandello is playing with semantics, since he has already identified the rigidity of form with the rigidity of death; but he is trying to apostrophize his function, and claim a sanctity for artists. In a more modest mood, however, he will simply suggest that artists are superior to ordinary people because they understand themselves better; they, too, are *eirones*. In *Trovarsi* (*To Find Oneself*), for example, another kind of artist — this time an actress — looking for her essential personality, discovers it lies in her art. An actress *lives* before her mirror, and accepts the various reflections which are thrown back. In the theatrical masks that she wears before an audience her true identity is found: "It is true only that one must create oneself, create! And only then does one find oneself." In short, the artist is superior because he *knows* he uses masks. And the very act of creation — like Henry's recreation of history — becomes a lofty, noble act of rebellion.

The contradictions multiply, and so do the Pirandellian paradoxes; only the basic conflict remains constant. Life and form are irretrievably at odds, and man suffers from his failure to reconcile them. Pirandello's desire to reconcile them explains, I think, his attraction to the theatre, because of all the literary forms, only theatrical art combines the spontaneous and accidental with the ordered and predetermined. In the interplay between actors, audience, and script, life and form merge. The living nature of theatrical art is further exemplified by its immediacy. The novel, with its "he saids" and "she saids" — speeches already spoken — is a tale of past time; the drama takes place in the present, with nothing separating the speaker from the speech. If anything written is fixed and dead, and literary characters are like the figures in Yeats's *Purgatory* — doomed to eternal repetition of their torments[7] — then anything staged is subject to accident, whim, and change, the actor insuring that it will always be new.

[7] Pirandello observes, in the preface to *Six Characters,* how literary characters are forced to repeat their actions forever, always as if for the first time: "Hence, always, as we open the book, we shall find Francesca alive and confessing to Dante her sweet sin, and if we turn to the passage a hundred thousand times in succession, a hundred thousand times in succession Francesca will speak her words, never repeating them mechanically, but saying them with such living passion that Dante every time will turn faint." In Yeats's play, the dead live out

In Pirandello's view, in fact, dramatic characters are not alive at all until they have been bodied forth by actors; the action waits to burst into life, and passion to receive its cue. "We want to live," says the Father to the actors in *Six Characters,* "only for a moment . . . in you." Because the actor is only impersonating the character (*i.e.,* wearing his mask), the theatre performance cannot help but travesty the author's written conception; and much of the comedy in *Six Characters* is based on the disparity between the reality of Pirandello's six and the artificiality of the performers. Still, if the actor distorts his role, he is nevertheless essential to it — only he can make it live. This passion for life in art explains Pirandello's fondness for the idea of improvisation. In contrast with the author's writing, the actor's improvisation is vital, immediate, and spontaneous. And theatre, theoretically, reaches its ideal consummation when it springs, unprepared, from the imagination of the performer.

Thus, in *Tonight We Improvise,* the director, Hinkfuss, is pleased to announce that he has eliminated the author entirely: "In the theatre, the work of the writer no longer exists." Borrowing from Pirandello only a brief and sketchy scenario, his actors will improvise their parts in the tradition of the *commedia dell'arte,* substituting for the old stock masks the masks of their own creation. Hinkfuss, a three-foot tyrant with a huge head of hair, is a caricature of the overbearing Reinhardtian *regisseur;* but he also functions as a Pirandellian *raisonneur* in outlining the author's theories. Repeating Pirandello's obsessive conviction that "a finished work of art is fixed forever in immutable form," and that, on the other hand, "life must both move and be still," Hinkfuss goes on to declare that "only on this condition, Ladies and Gentlemen, can that which art has fixed in the immutability of form be brought to life, and turn, and move — on the condition that this form have again its movement from us who are alive." And this essentializes the difference between the theatre and all other forms of literary creation: "Art it is indeed — but life as well. Creation

---

their purgatory by continually reenacting their fates, though conscious now of the consequences of their deeds.

it is indeed — but not enduring creation. A thing of the moment. A miracle. A statue that moves."

On the basis of this theory, the living actors proceed to improvise a drama, pulling in and out of character, commenting on their roles, expressing dissatisfaction with the director ("No one directs life") — until finally they are caught up entirely in their parts and play them to an unexpected conclusion. In the theatre, anything can happen, and the pattern of art is disturbed by the accidents of life. Thus, in *Each in His Own Way,* the play is not even completed, because among the spectators are the real-life counterparts of the characters on the stage; and angered by being represented in this *commedia a chiave,* they attack the author and the actors, and bring the curtain down. For Pirandello, plot and character are now totally subordinated to the theatrical process itself, for that process is life itself. The theory is courageous — but Pirandello is not courageous enough to put it into practice. In Pirandello's theatre, the playwright still exists. The "improvisations" of the actors are all composed beforehand, and the spectators are planted, their lines written too. Only through the disappearance of the author can the conflict between life and art be resolved, but Pirandello is unable to relinquish control over his work. Still dominated by his messianic obsession to create an organic art — changing from moment to moment, yet still formed by the hand of man — Pirandello refuses to complete his godlike function by withdrawing from the scene.

In his frustration over forming a statue that moves, Giuncano destroyed his art; Pirandello, frustrated but undaunted, continues to create, and the result is his "trilogy of the theatre in the theatre." *Six Characters in Search of an Author (Sei personaggi in cerca d'autore,* 1921), *Each in His Own Way (Ciascuno a suo modo,* 1924), and *Tonight We Improvise (Questa sera si recita a soggetto,* 1930) were all written at different stages of the author's career, but all are unified by a common purpose. Probing the complex relationships between the stage, the work of art, and reality itself, Pirandello attempts, in these plays, to forge out of the old theatrical artifacts a living theatre, destroying the traditional conventions of the stage by crossing the boundaries which separate art from life. In these plays, the illusions of the realistic theatre — where actors pretend to be real people, canvas and lumber pass for actual locations, and forged events are designed to seem real — no longer apply. Now the stage is a stage, actors are actors, and even the audience, formerly silent and half invisible in its willing suspension of disbelief, has been drawn into the action and implicated in the theatrical proceedings. As for the fourth wall, this fiction has been destroyed entirely — nothing separates the spectator from the stage except space, and even this space occasionally evaporates when the actors enter the audience, and the spectators come on stage. Having disintegrated reality in his more conventional plays, Pirandello is now disintegrating stage reality. Having scourged the peeping and prying of the social community, he is now attacking the community's peek-hole pastime, the theatre. For Pirandello, the fourth wall, designed for the entertainment of Peeping Toms, is an avenue that must be blocked.

Pirandello's experimental plays proceed logically from his theory. He had always been dissatisfied with the mere representation of reality on the stage, a function he assigned, with some condescension, to "historical writers." Since reality was a dense and perhaps impenetrable forest, Aristotelian *mimesis,* or imitation, seemed to him futile and presumptuous. How could anyone presume to know, much less to recreate, the unknowable? It was better to be a "philosophical writer," affirming a personal sense of reality and soaking the work of art in a "particular sense of life." This sounds Platonic; and indeed, Pirandello rejects representational art for Platonic reasons. Since reality lies not in material objects but in the Idea, such art can only be *an imitation of an imitation,* two degrees removed. Pirandello's apprehension of the shadows in the cave, however, is intensely subjective. As he said in an interview with Domenico Vittorini: "In imitating a preceding model, one denies one's own identity and remains of necessity behind the pattern. The best is to affirm one's own sentiments, one's own life." Pirandello's desire to affirm his personal identity, to come out from behind the pattern, is not compatible with his desire to let the pattern create itself in the autonomous shape of life. But he is too subjective, too Romantic, too messianic a writer to relax his control over events and let them happen.

We have already seen how this compels him to write out the improvisations of the actors. For the same reason, Pirandello is unable to dispense with stage illusion, despite his angry attacks on it. The actors in the theatre trilogy are no longer pretending to be characters, but they *are* pretending to be actors — actors created in the imagination of Pirandello. And though the stage is now strictly a stage, it is still, to some extent, an illusionistic stage. In *Six Characters,* for example, the action takes place during a rehearsal in an empty theatre, but the rehearsal is really a performance, the "empty theatre" filled with paying spectators. Actually, whatever spontaneity occurs in these theatre plays is carefully planned by the author. As is often the case in these matters, Pirandello has destroyed one convention — and substituted another.

This convention is borrowed, probably unwittingly, from the Elizabethan theatre, for Pirandello's experimental drama is constructed on the pattern of the play-within-the-play. The inner action is "historical," the outer action, "philosophical," but both are products of the author's imagination. Pirandello was tending towards this structure in his more conventional drama: Henry's masquerade, for example, is a play-within-a-play. But now he tries to create the illusion that the outer action is improvised by actors, directors, and spectators, while only the inner action is an anecdote composed in advance. Pirandello goes further than any of his predecessors in breaking down the barriers between the inner and the outer plays; but he uses the convention for the same purpose as the Elizabethans — for commentary, criticism, and extradramatic remarks. Thus, Pirandello has not destroyed illusions; he has merely multiplied illusions. Contemptuous of imitation, he is unable to do without it. In his experimental drama, theory and practice fail to merge; idea and action fail to cohere. Unlike his companions in the theatre of revolt, Pirandello is never able to decide just to what extent he should enter his own work. Torn between messianic and existential demands, his Romantic ego is split wide open by its own contradictions.

Still, Pirandello's attacks on the deceptions of conventional realism and the narcotized stupor of the passive spectator had a revolutionary influence on the experimental theatre which followed. And if he does not ever solve the problem of life and form, he does open up a totally new side of it in each of his three plays. *Six Characters* examines the conflict between fictional characters and the actors who play their roles; *Each in His Own Way,* the conflict between stage characters and actual characters on whom they are based; and *Tonight We Improvise,* the conflict between actors who want to live their parts and the director who is always interrupting them. In each case, Pirandello preserves the pattern of the play within the play, preserving, besides, his earlier pattern of suffering *eirones* or *pharmakoi* surrounded by meddling *alazōnes.* In *Each in His Own Way,* the relationships are consistent with his past work. The real characters (*pharmakoi*) are mortified by their stage counterparts (*alazōnes*), who, by assuming their masks, are dragging their painful secrets into light.[8] In the accompanying two plays, however, the relationships are reversed — there the suffering characters are *eager* to have their secrets exposed, and the *alazōnes* are an obstacle to this end. Thus, in *Six Characters,* the six (*eirones-pharmakoi*) try to persuade the actors and their manager (*alazōnes*) to publicize their fictional private lives; and in *Tonight We Improvise,* the actors (*eirones*) are finally forced to throw the director (*alazōn*) out of the theatre in order to expose the inner souls of their characters (*pharmakoi*). In the theatre trilogy, the conflict between the *eirones, pharmakoi,* and *alazōnes* no longer serves to make a social point, but rather to illustrate the different levels of reality which the stage encloses.

[8] The pattern of this particular play is extremely complicated, because there are *pharmakoi* in the inner as well as the outer action. In the play-within-the-play, Delia Moreno and Michele Rocca are being probed and analyzed by the other characters, and suffer from it. In the action which takes place in the lobby, Signora Moreno and Baron Nuti — on whom the fictional characters are based — feel that they are being travestied on the stage, and suffer from it. In the ironic conclusion, however, the real characters find themselves behaving towards each other in precisely the same way as their stage counterparts, and are horrified at seeing themselves reflected in an accurate mirror.

The initial play in the trilogy, *Six Characters in Search of an Author*, is also the most effective, since its intricate structure permits an elaborate system of ideas to coexist with a striking theatricality. Like the other two plays, this famous work is constructed of a "philosophical" outer action around an "historical" inner action, but while the total play is unified, the play-within-the-play is incomplete — *Six Characters* is subtitled "A Comedy in the Making." As Pirandello informs us in his preface, he had sketched out six members of a family as subjects for a "magnificent novel," but no longer capable of telling a straightforward "historical" tale in a narrative vein, he decided to abandon them. The six, however, refused to accept their fate: "Born alive, they wished to live." And now they have appeared independent of the author's will — some dressed in mourning, all bathed in an eerie, luminescent light — to a group of actors and their manager who are rehearsing, in an empty theatre, Pirandello's *Rules of the Game*. Fragmented and incomplete — part alive in the world of fiction and part still in the womb of Pirandello's conception — they seek another author to complete them. And for this purpose, they offer themselves to the Manager and his cast. What follows is designed to have the quality of an impromptu performance — a play without acts or scenes in which intermissions are provided apparently at random, once when the Manager withdraws to confer with the characters, once when the curtain falls by mistake.

The relationships between the fictional characters and the living actors become exceedingly complex; and the conflict of the play, as Francis Fergusson has perceived, proceeds on several planes of discourse. On the one hand, the characters create friction with the theatre people who first disbelieve their story, then find it too squalid for the stage, and finally travesty it in the act of imitation. On the other hand, the characters struggle among themselves, for they detest each other, and are bound together in mutual hatred. As the drama of the characters is interrupted by the comedy of the actors, and the two parallel conflicts begin to grate, the tragi-comic alternations create an atmosphere of the grotesque. The characters, furthermore, quarrel among themselves over the details of their story. And the first act is almost entirely taken up with trying to determine the vague outlines of this "historical" narrative.

For the author has only completed two scenes of the drama: one in Madame Pace's dress shop, the other in the Father's garden. The rest, conceived but never written down, is therefore open to interpretation by the characters. In brief, the written scenes are form (fixed and immutable), while the unwritten background material is life (fluid and changing). Together, these elements constitute the "book," both form and life, which are the constituents of the characters themselves, and can only be learned from them. Here, in Pirandello's mind, is a statue that moves; his fictional creations have developed an existence of their own. Except for the Mother, who is unaware she is a "character," and the Boy and the Child, both of whom are mute, the characters possess a reflective life beyond the form their author gave them. In typical Pirandellian manner, they both suffer and think about their suffering; they both perform and see themselves performing, as in a mirror. Immobilized in written roles, caught up in an action which is "renewed, alive, and present, always!" they are also cursed with hindsight and, therefore, know exactly what form their purgatory will take.

The most reflective of the six is the Father, who, indeed, acts as Pirandello's philosophical *raisonneur*. It is his function in the first act to narrate "historical" past events — to provide, in other words, the exposition. Reconstructed from the Father's narrative and the Stepdaughter's angry emendations, the story goes like this. The Father had married beneath him — to a humble, ignorant woman by whom he had the Son. Her simplicity attracted him at first, but soon she began to bore him. And when he noticed that his secretary was in love with her and she seemed to respond, he sent them off together — prodded, he says, by the "Demon of Experiment," an urge to transcend ordinary moral conventions. The Father understands that this is only a phrase, a consoling illusion by which he disguised his real motive, and the Stepdaughter has no use for the Father's rationalizing which "uncovers the beast in man and then seeks to save him, excuse him." But whatever the motive, the Father forced the Mother to abandon her two-year-old Son and, deprived of maternal warmth, the Son grew up loveless, supercilious, disdainful.

When the Mother bore to her lover three illegitimate children — the Stepdaughter, the Boy, and the Child — the Father began to take an interest in this family, and visited their city to observe the Stepdaughter as a child. Years went by, and the Father lost sight of them; unknown to him, they returned to his city. When her lover died, leaving the Mother destitute, she desperately cast around for work, finally finding a place as a seamstress in Madame Pace's dress shop. Madame Pace, secretly a brothel madam, employed the Mother because of her interest in the Stepdaughter, whom she wished to add to her stable. Without the Mother's knowledge, she succeeded. And when the Father comes to visit the brothel, he is unwittingly introduced to his own Stepdaughter. With a scream, the Mother interrupts their lovemaking "just in time" (according to the Father) or "almost in time" (according to the Stepdaughter); and this is one of the two scenes to be played. The second scene occurs after the Father has brought the Mother's family into his house, against the wishes of his Son. The Mother is agonized by the Son's disdain; the Stepdaughter is contemptuous of the Father's guilt; the Boy is humiliated at becoming an object of charity. These feelings produce a crisis, and the scene is to conclude with "the death of the little girl, the tragedy of the boy, and the flight of the elder daughter." Neither of these scenes, however, is performed in the first act; they are merely outlined; and the act concludes with the Manager determined to turn this story into a play.

The second act is devoted to the scene in Madame Pace's dress shop, which is performed by the characters involved, and then by the actors who take their parts. For the actors, who "play at being serious," the performance is a game, but for the characters, who are in deadly earnest, it is a compulsion: their drama is their lives. Thus, while the Father and the Stepdaughter *want* to play the scene, the one to expunge his guilt and remorse, the other to shame the Father, the Mother adamantly refuses to play it, in order to protect their privacy and hide their disgrace. But none of them really has a choice — the scene is already determined. When the Manager puts together some

makeshift scenery, and a seventh character, Madame Pace, material-
izes, "attracted by the very articles of her trade" and whispering instructions to the Stepdaughter, the Father and the Stepdaughter thereupon proceed to reenact the origin of their shame and torment.

It is this scene which is altered, censored, and parodied by the actors in a manner which reverberates with Pirandello's shrill animus
against the stage. The function of the actors, according to the Father,
is to lend their shapes "to living beings more alive than those who
breathe and wear clothes: being less real perhaps, but truer!" But although these "living beings" cannot breathe without the theatre, the
theatre makes them even less real than they are, and much less true.
"Truth up to a certain point, but no further," cries the Manager, when
confronted with a scene too violent and strong. He is concerned over
the sensibilities of the critics and the audience: the limitations of the
theatre are those of a society which will not face an unpleasant reality.
The vanity of the star performer, the expediency of the designer, the
commercial-mindedness of the director, the timidity of the spectator
— all throw a vast shadow between the author's intention and the
theatre's execution, a shadow which lengthens in the artificiality of the
theatrical occasion.

Still, it is not just that the theatre scants its possibilities; in a deeper
sense, it is incapable of realizing the author's vision or capturing the
feel of reality. Madam Pace's whispers are inaudible, because "these
aren't matters which can be shouted at the top of one's voice" — private conversations are none of the spectator's business. Similarly, the
actor is unable to penetrate the secret heart of a character, because it
is as elusive as a human being's identity. And dialogue is an added
block to understanding:

But don't you see that the whole trouble lies here. In words, words [cries
the Father]. Each one of us has within him a whole world of things, each
man of us his own special world. And how can we ever come to an understanding if I put in the words I utter the sense and value of things as I
see them; while you who listen to me must inevitably translate them according to the conception of things each one of you has within himself.
We think we understand each other, but we never do.

Like Henry IV, each man stands like a beggar before the locked door of others, and words make the lock secure. Both unwilling and unable to overcome this obstacle, the Manager transforms the sordid, semi-incestuous happening in the dress shop into a romantic and sentimental love scene between the Leading Man and the Leading Lady. And it is at this point that the Father understands how the author came to abandon them — in a fit of disgust over the conventional theatre.

Still, if the second act embodies Pirandello's satire on the stage, the third act embodies his conviction that theatrical art is more "real" than life. The Father has already accused the Manager of trying to destroy "in the name of a vulgar, commonplace sense of truth, this reality which comes to birth attracted and formed by the magic of the stage itself." Now he proceeds to show how the reality of the characters is not only deeper than that of actors, but also deeper than that of living persons. As the Father tells the skeptical Manager, a character in fiction knows who he is; he possesses a "life of his own"; his world is fixed — and for these reasons, he is "somebody." But a human being — the Manager, for example — "may very well be 'nobody.'"

Our reality doesn't change! It can't change! It can't be other than what it is, because it is fixed forever. It's terrible. Ours is an immutable reality which should make you shudder when you approach us if you are really conscious of the fact that your reality is a mere transitory and fleeting illusion, taking this form today and that tomorrow, according to your conditions, according to your will, your sentiments, which in turn are controlled by an intellect that shows them to you today in one manner and tomorrow . . . who knows how? . . . Illusions of reality represented in this fatuous comedy of life that never ends. . . .

The arguments are by now familiar and it is difficult not to share some of the Manager's impatience with the Father's perpetual, and rather windy, "philosophizing." But the cerebrations of the character have been carefully motivated, and it is the Father himself who justifies them: "For man never reasons so much or becomes so introspective as when he suffers; since he is anxious to get at the cause of his sufferings, to learn who produced them, and whether it is just or unjust that he should have to bear them." The Father's sufferings have, Hamlet-like, intensified his introspective tendencies, just as the historical line of the play has intensified its philosophical ramifications. The staple of the argument tends towards verbosity, but it opens the play out of the theatre, and into the theatre of existence itself.

Six Characters concludes in a burst of melodrama, which leaves its various paradoxes unresolved. The garden setting has been arranged, after a fashion, and now the less verbal characters must play their parts. The Mother has overcome her reluctance to perform in order to be near her Son, but the Son refuses absolutely to participate. Horrified with shame, and tortured at having to "live in front of a mirror which not only freezes us with the image of ourselves, but throws our likeness back at us with a horrible grimace," he claims to be an "unrealized character" in an unfinished drama and, identifying with the will of the author in this, refuses to play his part. And yet, as before, the play inexorably proceeds. While the Boy watches in horror, the Child falls into the fountain and drowns, whereupon the Boy draws a revolver and shoots himself. According to the scenario, this is the cue for the Stepdaughter to flee, leaving the original family — Father, Mother, Son — united in "mortal desolation," though still strangers to one another.

But the suicide has created pandemonium in the theatre. The Boy is lying lifeless on the ground. Is he really dead, or is the suicide merely pretence? "Reality, sir, reality," insists the Father, as the actors carry the Boy's body off the stage. Bewildered by this crosspatch of apparent realities and real appearances, the Manager can only throw up his hands in disgust, and on this note of dissonance and irresolution, the curtain falls. The ending of the play, however, suggests another reason why Pirandello left the "historical" action unfinished: it is too operatic to be convincing. But by enclosing this action within the frame of the theatre, he has created a probing philosophical drama about the artifice of the stage, the artifice of art, and the artifice of reality in generally suspenseful and exciting rhythms.

Pirandello's most original achievement in his experimental plays, then, is the dramatization of the very act of creation. If he has not made a statue that moves, he has made a statue which is the living signature of the artist, being both his product and his process. The concept of the face and the mask has become the basis for a totally new relationship between the artist and his work. Thus, Pirandello completes that process of Romantic internalizing begun by Ibsen and Strindberg. Ibsen, for all his idealization of personality, still believed in an external reality available to all, and so did Chekhov, Brecht, and Shaw. Strindberg had more doubts about this reality, but believed it could be partially perceived by the inspired poet and seer. For Pirandello, however, objective reality has become virtually inaccessible, and all one can be sure of is the illusion-making faculty of the subjective mind. After Pirandello, no dramatist has been able to write with quite the same certainty as before. In Pirandello's plays, the messianic impulse spends itself, before it even fully develops, in doubts, uncertainties, and confusions.

The playwrights who follow Pirandello are frequently better artists, but none would have been the same without him: Pirandello's influence on the drama of the twentieth century is immeasurable. In his agony over the nature of existence, he anticipates Sartre and Camus; in his insights into the disintegration of personality and the isolation of man, he anticipates Samuel Beckett; in his unremitting war on language, theory, concepts, and the collective mind, he anticipates Eugene Ionesco; in his approach to the conflict of truth and illusion, he anticipates Eugene O'Neill (and later, Harold Pinter and Edward Albee); in his experiments with the theatre, he anticipates a host of experimental dramatists, including Thornton Wilder and Jack Gelber; in his use of the interplay between actors and characters, he anticipates Jean Anouilh; in his view of the tension between public mask and private face, he anticipates Jean Giraudoux; and in his concept of man as a role-playing animal, he anticipates Jean Genet. The extent of even this partial list of influences marks Pirandello as the most seminal dramatist of our time; and it may be that he will ultimately be remembered more as a great theoretician than as a great practitioner. Still, he has left some extraordinary plays, which continue to live with the same urgency as when they were first written. And the melancholy of his existential revolt still sounds its elegiac music. "A man," he wrote about himself, "I have tried to tell something to other men, without any ambition except perhaps that of revenging myself for having been born."

VIII

EUGENE O'NEILL

As some of the dust begins to settle over the controversial reputation of Eugene O'Neill, and our interest shifts from the man to art, it becomes increasingly clear that O'Neill will be primarily remembered for his last plays. The earlier ones are not all without value, though none is thoroughly satisfying. Some contain powerful scenes; some have interesting themes; and some are sustained by the sheer force of the author's will. Still, the bulk of O'Neill dramatic writings before *Ah Wilderness!* are like the groping preparatory sketches of one who had to write badly in order to write well; and in comparison with the late O'Neill even intermittently effective dramas like *The Hairy Ape, All God's Chillun Got Wings,* and *Desire Under the Elms* are riddled with fakery, incoherence, and clumsy experimental devices. No major dramatist, with the possible exception of Shaw, has written so many second-rate plays.

An important task of the O'Neill critic, therefore, is to account for the extraordinary disparity in style and quality between the earlier and later work; and one might well begin by exploring the external conditions in which O'Neill's talents began to bud. For if the playwright's early blossoms were sere, the cultural climate which helped to nurture them was (and is) peculiarly uncongenial to the development of a serious artist. O'Neill came to prominence in the second and third decades of the century, when America was just beginning to relinquish its philistinism in order to genuflect before the shrine of Culture. The American culture craze was largely directed towards the outsides of the literature, which is to say towards the personality of the artist rather than the content of his art; and the novelists and poets inducted into this hollow ritual found themselves engaged in an activity more priestly than creative. O'Neill's role was especially hieratic, however, since he had the misfortune to be the first dramatist with serious aspirations to appear on the national scene. As George Jean Nathan noted, O'Neill "singlehanded waded through the dismal swamplands of American drama, bleak, squashy, and oozing sticky goo, and alone and singlehanded bore out the water lily that no American had found there before him." That the water lily sometimes resembled a cauliflower, Mr. Nathan was occasionally willing to concede. But to a large body of hungry critics and cultural consumers, who were indifferent to the quality of the product so long as it was Big, O'Neill was a homegrown dramatic champion to be enlisted not only against Ibsen, Strindberg, and Shaw, but against Aeschylus, Euripides, and Shakespeare as well.

In every superficial way, O'Neill certainly looked the role he was expected to fill. A dark, brooding figure with a strain of misfortune in his life, he combined the delicate constitution of a sensitive poet with the robust pugnacity of a barroom Achilles; and his youthful adventures as a seaman, gold prospector, and tramp had a rotogravure appeal to a nation already convinced by the Sunday supplements that an artist needed Vast Experience in order to write about Real Life. O'Neill, in addition, possessed the kind of aspiring mind which F. Scott Fitzgerald assigned to Jay Gatsby; he "sprang from his Platonic conception of himself." Afflicted with the American disease of gigantism, O'Neill developed ambitions which were not only large, they were monstrous; he was determined to be nothing if not a world-historical figure of fantastic proportion. Trying to compress within his own career the whole development of dramatic literature since the Greeks, he set himself to imitate the most ambitious writers who ever lived — and the more epic their scope, the more they stimulated his competitive instinct. The scope of his own intentions is suggested by the growing length of his plays and the presumptuousness of his public utterances. *Mourning Becomes Electra,* which took three days to perform, he called "an idea and a dramatic conception that has the possibilities of being the biggest thing modern drama has attempted — by far the biggest!" And his unfinished eleven-play "Big Grand Opus," as he called it, was designed to have "greater scope than any novel I know of . . . something in the style of *War and Peace.*" At this point in his career, O'Neill, like his public, is attracted to the outsides of literature, and he wrestles with the reputation of another writer in order to boost his own. But to O'Neill's public, ambitions were almost indistinguishable from achievements; and the playwright was ranked with the world's greatest dramatists before he had had an opportunity to master his craft or sophisticate his art.

It was inevitable, therefore, that the next generation of critics — Francis Fergusson, Lionel Trilling, Eric Bentley — should harp on O'Neill's substantial failings as a thinker, artist, and Broadway hero. Subjected to closer scrutiny, the very qualities which had inspired so much enthusiasm in O'Neill's partisans now seemed the marks of a pretentious writer and a second-rate mind. Pushed about by this critical storm, the winds of literary fashion shifted, and O'Neill's reputation was blown out to sea. Although the playwright was awarded the Nobel prize in 1936, obscurity had already settled in upon him, and it deepened more and more until his death in 1953. During these dark years, ironically, O'Neill's real development began. Before, he had prided himself on having "the guts to shoot at something big and risk failure"; now, he had the guts not to bother himself about questions of success and failure at all. Maturing in silence, stimulated only by an obsessive urge to write and a profound artistic honesty, he commenced to create plays which were genuine masterpieces of the modern theatre. Most of these were not published or produced until after his death, some by the playwright's order. In proscribing *A Long Day's Journey into Night,* O'Neill was trying to hide his family's secrets from the public eye; but O'Neill's desire to keep his works off the stage was undoubtedly influenced, too, by the hostile reception accorded to *The Iceman Cometh* and *A Moon for the Misbegotten,* the first of which failed on Broadway, the second, before even reaching New York. The public and the reviewers, having found new idols to worship (the Critic's prize the year of *The Iceman Cometh* went to a conventional social protest play by Arthur Miller called *All My Sons*), began to treat O'Neill with condescension — when they thought of him at all. And he was not to be seriously reconsidered until 1956, when a successful revival of *The Iceman Cometh* and the first Broadway production of *A Long Day's Journey* brought him so much posthumous recognition that his inferior work was soon dragged out of storage for some more unthinking praise.

O'Neill's career, then, can be split into two distinct stages, which are separated not only by his changing position in the official culture, but by changes in style, subject matter, form, and posture as well. The first stage, beginning with the *S.S. Glencairn* plays (1913-1916) and ending with *Days Without End* (1932-1933) is of historical rather than artistic interest: I shall discuss these plays in a general way, as illustrations of O'Neill's early links with the theatre of revolt. The second stage is preceded by a transitional play, *Ah Wilderness!* (1932), and contains *A Touch of the Poet* (1935-1942) the unfinished *More Stately Mansions* (1935-1941), both from the cycle, *The Iceman Cometh* (1939), *A Long Day's Journey into Night* (1939-1941), and *A Moon for the Misbegotten* (1943). All of these works have artistic interest, but *The Iceman Cometh* and *A Long Day's Journey* are, in my opinion, great works of art; these two I shall examine in some detail, as examples of the highly personal revolt which O'Neill pulled out of his own suffering. By contrasting the two stages in O'Neill's drama, I hope to illustrate O'Neill's development from a self-conscious and imitative pseudo-artist into a genuine tragic dramatist with a uniquely probing vision.

Aside from the one-act sea plays, which are modest in scope and relatively conventional in form, O'Neill's early drama tends to be Expressionist in its symbolic structure and messianic in its artistic stance. Both O'Neill's Expressionism and messianism, I hasten to add, are borrowed, ill-fitting robes. By the time O'Neill begins to write, the theatre of revolt is an established movement in every country except America, where the theatre has produced nothing more exhilarating than the fabricated fantasies of Fitch, Boucicault, and Belasco. Thus, the drama of the continent constitutes an untapped mine of material, and O'Neill, recognizing its potentialities, becomes the first dramatist to exploit it; with the aid of the Provincetown Players, he does for the American awareness of European drama what Shaw and the Independent Theatre did for the English.

Although O'Neill is originally considered a wild, untutored genius, therefore, his early work is clearly the offshoot of a very intellectualistic mind, attuned more to literature than to life. Aligning himself with the more radical of the rebel dramatists, he is soon impersonating their postures, imitating their doctrines, and copying their techniques. One can detect the influence of Ibsen, Toller, Shaw, Gorky, Pirandello, Wedekind, Synge, Andreyev, and others in the early plays of O'Neill, but chief among his dramatic models in this period is August Strindberg, whom O'Neill, in his Nobel prize acceptance speech, called "the greatest of all modern dramatists." Nor is he reluctant to acknowledge Strindberg as his master:

It was reading his plays when I first started to write, back in the winter of 1913-1914, that, above all, first gave me the vision of what modern drama could be, and first inspired me with the urge to write for the theatre myself. If there is anything of lasting worth in my work, it is due to that original impulse from him, which has continued as my inspiration down all the years since then — to the ambition I received then to follow in the footsteps of his genius as worthily as my talent might permit, and with the same integrity of purpose.

If the rebel dramatists are inclined to revolt against each other as well as against the external world, O'Neill is similar only to Shaw in his willingness to set himself to school in the composition of his plays.

O'Neill's partiality for Strindberg (like Shaw's partiality for Ibsen) can be partly explained by similarities of temperament: the lives of the two dramatists, as well as their careers, move along closely parallel lines. Like Strindberg, O'Neill was deeply involved with his mother, as an object both of love and hate, and similarly ambivalent towards his father.[1] And he was — again like Strindberg — married three times to domineering women, and perpetually rebellious towards authority. O'Neill's relation to his plays, furthermore, is very Strindbergian: he is almost always the hero of his work, trying to work out his personal difficulties through the medium of his art.

In their biography of O'Neill, Arthur and Barbara Gelb have observed that his plays contain a "long gallery of conscious and unconscious portraits,"

ranging from the land-locked dreamer, Robert Mayo, in *Beyond the Horizon,* through the tubercular newspaper reporter, Stephen Murray, in *The Straw,* the semi-incestuous Eben Cabot, in *Desire Under the Elms,* the possessive Michael Cape in *Welded,* and the defeated idealist, Dion Anthony, in *The Great God Brown,* the suicidal Reuben Light in *Dynamo,* the rebellious adolescent, Richard Miller, in *Ah Wilderness!* to the religion-seeking John Loving in *Days Without End.*

And O'Neill's early self-portraits usually show him striking histrionic attitudes of pride, cynicism, or sensitivity — "sardonic," "mocking," "sneering," and "Mephistophelean," are the adjectives by which he describes the speeches and deportment of his autobiographical characters, when they are not "dark," "spiritual," "poetic," and "suffering." In his later plays, O'Neill will turn back on his past life, honestly remembered, ruthlessly examined, rigorously presented; but in his earlier ones, he is posing for immortality, and rushing his current problems onto the stage before they have had a chance to cool—

[1] In their biography *O'Neill,* Arthur and Barbara Gelb quote a psychoanalyst friend of the dramatist who had concluded that O'Neill's plays "all show an antagonism toward women, which indicated to me that he had a deep antagonism toward his mother. I believe that O'Neill hated his mother and loved his father. He duplicated his father's profession, the theatre, which is one indication. . . . His antagonism toward his mother carried over to his relationships with women; because his mother had failed him, all women would fail him, and he had to take revenge on them. . . . ." Like most vestpocket analyses, this one seems very glib, and fails to take into account the obvious incestuous aspects of the plays. O'Neill's feelings toward both parents were divided between love and hate.

which may explain why Hugo von Hofmannsthal complained that "O'Neill's characters are not sufficiently fixed in the past." This preoccupation with satanic stances, melodramatic suffering, and immediate emotions can again be partially ascribed to O'Neill's fondness for Strindberg. In fact, his identification with the Swedish dramatist is so strong that it sometimes ushers him into crass imitation. *Welded*, for example, is a feeble representation of the sex war, a slavish exercise in the embattled mode of *Comrades, The Father,* and *The Dance of Death;* and *Days Without End* recapitulates, in a very fumbling manner, the spiritual questing of *The Road to Damascus.*

As an experimental dramatist, O'Neill would naturally be attracted to the greatest innovator in the modern theatre; and O'Neill's Expressionism is certainly indebted to Strindberg's dream techniques. The difference is that Strindberg's formal experiments grow out of his material, while O'Neill's seem grafted onto his, and thus give the impression of being gratuitous and excessive. As a British critic correctly observes, "Anything that might be called Expressionism encourages in O'Neill all his faults." Strindberg, in his dream plays, is attempting to evoke the forces behind life, which are essentially nonverbal and nonconceptual. But O'Neill, who at this stage remains on the surface of life, is obsessed with concepts, and defines Expressionism as something which "strives to get the author talking directly to the audience," or, at best, puts "an idea . . . over to an audience . . . through characters." Thus, O'Neill uses Expressionistic devices to communicate ideas which he is either too inarticulate or too undisciplined to express through speech and action. And his masks, asides, soliloquies, choruses, split characters and the like are really substitutes for dramatic writing (most of these conventions are borrowed from the novel), provoked not by a new vision but rather by a need to disguise the banality of the original material. Thus, instead of opening up uncharted territory, O'Neill's devices invariably fog up already familiar ground, as for example the interminable soliloquizing of *Strange Interlude* which, instead of going deeper into the unconscious mind, merely compounds the verbalized trivialities of the characters with their trivial unspoken thoughts. Moving from monodramas to miracle plays to historical dramas to mob plays to Greek tragedies, O'Neill appears to experiment largely for the sake of novelty without ever staying with a form long enough to perfect it. As Ludwig Lewisohn puts it, he "gives the impression not so much of developing as of making a series of excursions into various provinces of the drama's domain and of returning from each of these excursions a little dissatisfied, a little disillusioned, and a little hopeful that his next experiment will result in something not quite so fragmentary and unfinished from within."

Still, O'Neill is very much like Strindberg in giving us a sense of constant process arising out of perpetual dissatisfaction; and this is reflected in another quality they share in common — their restless quest for new absolutes. Throughout the first stage of his career, O'Neill is a Romantic in love with the very notion of rebellion, and the face of his revolt is forever changing. For a short time, during his youth, it takes a social-political form. In a poem printed in 1917, O'Neill imagines his soul to be a submarine and his aspirations as torpedoes directed towards "the grimy galleons of commerce"; and his boss on the *New London Telegraph* remembers him, during his Socialist-Anarchist days, as "the most stubborn and irreconcilable social rebel that I had ever met." O'Neill, however, soon loses interest in social-political programs, and by 1922, he is looking back on this period of his life with ironic bemusement: "Time was when I was an active socialist, and after that, a philosophical anarchist. But today I can't feel anything like that really matters." Later he adds, in something like the apocalyptic tone of Ibsen, "The one reform worth cheering for is the Second Flood. . . ." [2] Lionel Trilling has observed how the political aspect of O'Neill's revolt continues to assert itself dramatically in the recurrent conflict between the creative and the possessive instinct as embodied in the Poet and the Businessman.

[2] O'Neill's frame of mind was often cataclysmic. To Barrett Clark, he wrote: "I am sure that Man has definitely decided to destroy himself, and this seems to me the only truly wise decision he has ever made"; and O'Neill remarked to Lawrence Langner that the atomic bomb was a wonderful invention because it might annihilate the whole human race. See Gelb, *O'Neill*, pp. 824, 861.

But O'Neill's Socialism is a youthful phase, which is soon replaced by more extreme forms of rebellion, structured in religious-philosophical terms, and embodied in messianic plays like *The Hairy Ape, The Great God Brown, Dynamo, Lazarus Laughed,* and *Days Without End.*

O'Neill's messianic revolt centers on the dilemma of modern man in a world without God; and it is informed by the spirit of a philosopher who was also important in Strindberg's life — Frederick Nietzsche. O'Neill's concept of tragedy is obviously influenced by *The Birth of Tragedy,* and his religious ideas are almost all culled from *Thus Spake Zarathustra,* a work which O'Neill discovered when he was eighteen and which, twenty years later, he said "has influenced me more than any book I've ever read." Reared in a relatively orthodox Irish-Catholic household, O'Neill is early persuaded by his readings in *Zarathustra* to reject the God of his parents;[3] but throughout his life, he is seeking some new orthodoxy to which to attach his remaining oceanic feelings. Indeed, he eventually declares his own loss of faith to be the primary subject of modern dramatic art: "The playwright today," he writes in a famous letter to George Jean Nathan, "must dig at the roots of the sickness of today as he feels it — the death of the Old God and the failure of science and materialism to give any satisfying new One for the surviving primitive religious instinct to find a meaning of life in, and to comfort his fears of death with." Less clumsily stated, this could be the definitive credo of the messianic dramatist. It is merely one step further to the formulation of a positive messianic doctrine. By the time of *Days Without End,* O'Neill is calling for "a new Savior . . . who will reveal to us how we can be saved from ourselves"; and though by this time O'Neill has developed a little more humility, the plays that precede this work show O'Neill applying for the position himself. In *Lazarus Laughed,*

---

[3] This development is perfectly clear in *A Long Day's Journey into Night,* where Edmund's (Eugene's) conflict with his father partially stems from their divergent religious views: "Then Nietzsche must be right," shouts Edmund in Act I, "God is dead: of his pity for man hath God died."

for example, O'Neill is solving the problem of death through the Laughter of his biblical Superman. The resurrected Lazarus, functioning as O'Neill's lifeless megaphone, affirms: "It is my pride as God to become Man. Then let it be my pride as Man to recreate the God in me!" And again: "The greatness of Man is that no god can save him — until he becomes a god!" In announcing the coming of the messianic Man-God, however, the playwright is never quite certain whether to put Man (man) or God (god) into upper case.

For O'Neill's messianism is an uneasy compound of pride and guilt. Like Strindberg's, his readings in Nietzsche sit on his stomach like rich food on a man with chronic ulcers. As a salvationist, O'Neill is an extremely timid and tentative figure, and the heady Dionysian wind he offers is invariably diluted with conventional Christian soda water. Consequently, as the doctrinal element becomes more central in his drama, the plays become more and more garbled, until O'Neill's messianic works can compete with any as the most confused writings in dramatic literature. What O'Neill seems to get all mixed up is the fierce, amoral toughness of the pagan tradition and the moralism and compassion of Christianity: rapturous amoral cries alternate with pleas for universal brotherhood. In *The Great God Brown,* for example, the hero is a compound of Dionysius and Saint Anthony, with Mephistopheles and Christ thrown into the bargain (his compassionate, maternal confidante, a prostitute, is called by the name of the cruel Phrygian Aphrodite, Cybel). In *Lazarus Laughed,* O'Neill announces that "Death is dead. . . . There is only life! There is only laughter"; but these tongue-tied Zarathustrian ravings, in which the yea-saying is all about Life and Laughter, are contradicted by other affirmations to the effect that "Love is man's hope — hope for his life on earth, a noble love above suspicion and distrust!"

O'Neill is similarly confused about the face of God in the modern world. In *Dynamo,* God is whirring machinery. In *Strange Interlude,* He presents himself through an "electrical display." In *The Fountain,* God is in the biological inheritance passed on through the family. In *Marco Millions,* He is "an infinite, insane energy which creates and destroys." [4] This constant redefinition of God, O'Neill finds to be his primary function as a dramatist: "Most modern plays," he explains to Joseph Wood Krutch, "are concerned with the relation of man to man, but this does not concern me at all. I am interested only in the relation of man and God." The purpose is Miltonic — but it is difficult to follow Milton's path when you have already declared the death of God, and postulated a purely mechanistic universe. O'Neill's problem is the problem of the modern drama as a whole: how to bring a religious vision to bear on a totally secular world. But instead of working this problem out, O'Neill merely repeats, with almost automatic regularity, that the problem exists — that is, when he is not trying to close the gap between the human and the divine through gaseous assertions. Thus, O'Neill's doctrinal dramas grow increasingly verbose and generalized until the art is finally suffocated in a cloud of abstract vapors.

O'Neill's messianic phase culminates in the last play of this period, *Days Without End,* a semiautobiographical account of the author's spiritual confusions. Like all of O'Neill's messianic plays, *Days Without End* is without literary value, but it is more interesting than the plays which precede it because it exposes the author's growing doubts about his own capacities as a modern Evangelist. The central character — or characters, since John Loving is John and Loving, a split personality like Dion Anthony — is another portrait of the artist, showing him torn between Nietzschean mockery and Christian compassion. In this play, however, O'Neill attempts to heal the breach by uniting John and Loving at the foot of the cross, as "Life laughs with God's love again!" Fortunately, O'Neill does not elaborate further on this unlikely union of paganism and Christianity;[5] but in the course of the play, he does reflect on the fickle religiosity of his past, when he

---

[4] For a good discussion of O'Neill's changing religious views, see Edd Winfield Parks, "Eugene O'Neill's Quest," *Tulane Drama Review,* Spring 1960.

[5] O'Neill's attempt to synthesize paganism and Christianity, by the way, recalls Ibsen's concept of the Third Empire in *Emperor and Galilean,* a play which O'Neill most certainly read. In an unpublished play of his own called *Servitude,* O'Neill even cites some of Ibsen's terms when a character announces, "Logos in Pan, Pan in Logos! That is the great secret. . . ." Needless to say, O'Neill — unlike Ibsen — had a very shaky idea about the content of paganism.

embraced a series of salvationist doctrines in a whirlwind journey through the philosophies of the world. As one character, a priest, ironically describes Loving's (O'Neill's) spiritual Odyssey:

First it was Atheism unadorned. Then it was Atheism wedded to Socialism. But Socialism proved too weak-kneed a mate, and the next I heard Atheism was living in free love with Anarchism, with a curse by Nietzsche to bless the union. And then came the Bolshevik dawn, and he greeted that with unholy howls of glee and wrote me he'd found a congenial home at last in the bosom of Karl Marx. . . . Soon his letters became full of pessimism, and disgust with all sociological nostrums. Then followed a long silence. And what do you think was his next hiding place? Religion, no less — but as far away as he could run from home — in the defeatist mysticism of the East. . . . I enjoyed a long interval of peace from his missionary zeal, until finally he wrote me he was married. That letter was full of more ardent hymns for a mere living woman than he'd ever written before about any of his great spiritual discoveries. . . . The only constant faith I've found in him before was his proud belief in himself as a bold Anti-Christ.

This might be a description of Strindberg, the "world incendiary," seeking ever new forms for his revolt; and the passage certainly sounds like a paraphrase of *Inferno* where Strindberg chides the powers for their cruel manipulation of his destiny.[6] John Loving, pursued by the Hound of Heaven, eventually finds sanctuary in Christianity — a conversion which led Lionel Trilling to conclude that O'Neill had crawled "into the dark womb of Mother Church and pulled the universe in with him." But for O'Neill, as for Strindberg, organized religion is only a way station on a continuing journey, and, within a few months after the play is completed, O'Neill is already regretting the ending and preparing to revise it. The revision never took place, but if it had, O'Neill might very well have echoed the concluding lines of Strindberg's anguished statement: "And supposing I again become religious, I am certain that in another ten years, you will reduce religion to an absurdity. Do not the gods play games with us poor mortals!"

[6] See Chapter III above, p. 93.

Thus, O'Neill exposes the philosophical incertitude of the Strind-bergian rebel — the pain, the doubts, the confusion. But although there are undoubtedly genuine feelings beneath all this, O'Neill's spiritual crises seem very literary, and his expression of them comes to him secondhand. Furthermore, one is never convinced that O'Neill has read very deeply in those philosophies that he affirms and rejects; his works display the intellectual attitudinizing of the self-conscious autodidact. It is this aspect of the early O'Neill, in fact, which most arouses the spleen of the second generation of his critics. "Mr. O'Neill is not a thinker," asserts Francis Fergusson, while Eric Bentley adds, "He is so little a thinker, it is dangerous for him to think." Both critics go on to demonstrate how O'Neill's superficial treatment of fashionable ideas was his main appeal to a superficial and fashion-able audience; and both have shown how emotion and thought fail to cohere in his drama. Certainly, O'Neill, at this stage, is utterly incapable of synthesizing his plots and his themes; to quote from Fer-gusson again, he "is more interested in affirming his ideas than in representing the experience in which they are implied." O'Neill's failure, I would suggest, is not a failure of mind so much as a failure of feeling. It is not that he is incapable of thought but rather that he is incapable of *thinking like a dramatist,* communicating his ideas through significant action. And this may be because all of his ideas, in this period, are borrowed rather than experienced. Thus, we find notions of Tragedy out of Nietzsche, of the Puritan Booboisie out of Mencken and Nathan, of the Racial Unconscious out of Jung, of the Oedipus Complex out of Freud, and of Hereditary Guilt out of Aeschylus and Ibsen — all grafted onto plots which are largely un-convincing, irrelevant, or inconsequential.

In fact, the major components of his plots, in this particular phase, are romantic love and swashbuckling adventure, both treated in a manner more appropriate to the melodramatic stage of his father, James O'Neill, than to the theatre of revolt. Ironically, O'Neill al-ways thinks he is defining himself *against* this kind of theatre: "My early experience with the theatre through my father really made me revolt against it," he once observed. "As a boy I saw so much of the old, ranting, artificial romantic stuff that I always had a sort of contempt for the theatre." [7] O'Neill's attempt to introduce large themes into his work is a sign of his rebellion against the mindless nineteenth-century stage, but he has assimilated more of "the old, ranting, artificial romantic stuff" than he knows. *The Fountain* (1921), for example, is presumably about the conflict between the lust for gain and the contemplation of Beauty, Love, and Life — but it is filled with flashing swords, rodomontade, and the kind of bombast that the man who played Monte Cristo would have adored. In *Marco Millions* (1923-1925) — a play which reads less as if it were written in English than translated from some foreign tongue — O'Neill attempts again to satirize American materialism by contrasting Marco's love of money with his attraction to Kublai Khan's granddaughter, Kukachin. Kukachin, like most of O'Neill's chaste female figures, is a model of incredible virtue and patience; at the climax of a play which indulges in Douglas Fairbanks heroics and bloated praises of the wisdom of the inscrutable East, she pines away and dies for love (Peace!" says her grandfather, in a typical prose passage, "She does not need your prayers. She was a prayer!"). *Lazarus Laughed* (1925-1926) is supposed to be an imaginative philosophical drama with no concessions to popular taste, but its atmosphere is very similar to those silent biblical epics by Cecil B. DeMille, full of frenzied mob scenes and Central Casting Emperors called Tiberius and Caligula.

Even when O'Neill's early plays avoid the devices of melodrama, they fall into the clichés of pulp fiction. *Strange Interlude* (1926-1927) is designed to probe the dark recesses of its characters; but its most profound psychological revelation is that one character has a mother fixation, and what keep the plot going are the barren sexual

---

[7] At another time O'Neill remarked, "I suppose if one accepts the song and dance complete of the psychoanalysts, it is perfectly natural that having been brought up around the old conventional theatre, and having identified it with my father, I should rebel and go in a new direction." Had O'Neill really understood the "song and dance complete of the psychoanalysts," he might have realized that there was a good deal more of the conventional father in the rebellious son than he cared to admit.

adventures of its neurotic soap-opera heroine, Nina Leeds. *Desire Under the Elms* (1924) is presumably fashioned to the dimensions of the Tristan myth; but the myth is self-conscious and external; and for all the symbolic setting (the maternal elms), the phoney elementalism ("Nature — makin' thin's grow — bigger 'n' bigger — burnin' inside ye"), and the staccato New England dialect ("Purty," "Ay-eh"), it is a conventional love triangle, resolved through an outrageously unbelievable plot device. As for *Mourning Becomes Electra* (1929-1931) — a tabloid version of the *Oresteia* in a stereotyped "Puritan" setting — this is a longwinded, overwritten tale of sexual jealousy, each killing motivated not by the will of the gods or by a family curse but rather by romantic love. In O'Neill, everything seems to render down to romance or sex, despite the fact that the author has an extremely naive conception of sexuality. One has only to note his puerile sentimentalization of whores,[8] his Romantic idealization of chaste women — or still worse, his laughable ideas about extramarital affairs, exposed in that fantastic *Strange Interlude* scene where Darrell and Nine cold-bloodedly decide to mate only to produce a child, and discuss the liaison in the third person for the sake of scientific impartiality.

Allied to O'Neill's treatment of sex is his treatment of incest, which is also romanticized in the pulsing accents of *True Confessions* magazine. In *Mourning Becomes Electra,* for example, incest becomes as common as weeds, and equally inevitable. Christine Mannon loves her husband's cousin, Adam Brant; Lavinia Mannon loves her father, Ezra, and also her second cousin, Adam; Orin Mannon loves his mother, Christine, who adores him in return; and when Orin and Lavinia begin, in the final act, to take on the physical characteristics of their father and mother, brother and sister fall in love too! The hero of *Dynamo* identifies the machine with his dead mother, and electrocutes himself with "a moan that is a mingling of pain and loving

---

[8] The Gelbs are very understanding of O'Neill's lifelong attitudes toward whores, observing that "at sixty-three he was still defending the honor of prostitutes" (*O'Neill,* p. 127).

consummation." And in *Desire Under the Elms,* Eben falls in love with his father's wife, Abbie, because she has begun to remind him of his mother:

ABBIE: . . . Tell me about yer Maw, Eben.
EBEN: They hain't nothin' much. She was kind. She was good.
ABBIE: . . . I'll be kind an' good t'ye!
EBEN: Sometimes she used t'sing fur me.
ABBIE: I'll sing fur ye!
EBEN: This was her hum. This was her farm.
ABBIE: This is my hum. This is my farm! . . .
EBEN: . . . An' I love yew, Abbie; — now I kin say it! I been dyin' fur want o' ye — every hour since ye come! I love ye! (*Their lips meet in a fierce, bruising kiss*)

"Fierce, bruising kisses" are called for in almost every one of O'Neill's earlier plays — the more fierce and bruising when they are incestuously motivated — accompanied by bathetic odes to Beauty and jerky apostrophes to Nature. But sex in O'Neill remains without complexity, darkness, or genuine passion, the mentalized fantasy of an adolescent temperament, and totally incompatible with the portentous philosophical attitudes it is meant to support.

In *Ah Wilderness!,* romanticized sex and half-baked philosophy, finally, are the enthusiasms of a character who is an adolescent himself; and, as a result, the play marks a turning point in O'Neill's relation to his material. If *Days Without End* suggests a new detachment towards his religious questing, *Ah Wilderness!* prefigures his transformation into an objective dramatic artist. As his self-awareness grows, O'Neill is beginning to distance himself from dogma and opinions. In the mouth of the seventeen-year-old Romantic, Richard Miller, the author's familiar paeans to Beauty, Love, and Life seem perfectly acceptable, since O'Neill is treating these affirmations with gentle satire and indulgent whimsey. It is the character, not the author, who is now identified with *fin de siècle* pessimism, culled from Swinburne, Nietzsche, and Omar Khayyam, just as it is the character, not the author, who is inclined to sentimentalize prostitutes. The play, in short, has finally become more important than the theme — ideas are effectively subordinated to "the experience in which they are implied." By projecting his literary self-consciousness onto an earlier Self, O'Neill is beginning to free himself from it. And in *Ah Wilderness!*, he exposes previously suppressed talents for depicting the habitual and commonplace side of existence, along with unsuspected gifts for portraying the humorous side of Irish family life.

Ah Wilderness!, to be sure, is an exercise for the left hand — a sentimental piece of Americana written in a holiday mood — but it is less important in itself than for what it portends: O'Neill is preparing to strike out along new paths. The author himself seems perfectly conscious of a new departure in this play, because, in a letter to Lawrence Langner, he couples it with *Days Without End* as evidence of his growing self-understanding: "For, after all, this play [*Days Without End*], like *Ah Wilderness!* but in a much deeper sense, is the paying of an old debt on my part — a gesture toward more comprehensive, unembittered understanding and inner freedom — the breaking away from an old formula that I had enslaved myself with. . . ." What the "old formula" is we have already seen; O'Neill's new approach is to leave all formulae behind, and relax into the role of the artist. Psychologically, O'Neill's bitterness towards authority seems to have left him, along with his restless quest for absolutes; philosophically, he has begun to perceive the hollowness of his messianic pretensions, and to turn towards material which he has pulled out of his being rather than self-consciously adopted; thematically, he has abandoned myths of incest and romantic love for deeper probes of character; formally, he is learning to combine the solipsistic subjectivity of Strindberg with the more detached, ordered, and indirectly biographical approach of Ibsen. Instead of writing about his unassimilated present, O'Neill is beginning to root about in the experiences of his past, and to do so with patience and care. After producing at least one play a year from 1913 to 1933 (in 1920, he wrote four), O'Neill considerably slows his output, completing only four full-length works and one short play in the next twenty years.

Ah Wilderness! is like all the plays which are to follow in being a work of recollection — nostalgic and retrospective. And significantly, it does not contain a trace of Expressionism, being surprisingly conventional in technique and structure. Later, O'Neill is to develop a different kind of realism all his own, built on a centripetal pattern in which a series of repetitions bring us closer and closer to the explosion at the center; but *Ah Wilderness!* is typical of O'Neill's late plays in its avoidance of conspicuous formal experimentation. Masks, split characters, and choruses are gone forever. As a result, O'Neill abandons those ponderous abstractions and inflated generalizations which Expressionism invariably dragged into his plays. If the author once complained, about *The Hairy Ape,* that "the public saw just the stoker, not the symbol, and the symbol makes the play either important or just another play," then he is now able to subordinate symbolism, and sometimes suppress it entirely for the sake of penetrating studies of character.

O'Neill, in short, has finally discovered where his true talents lie. In 1924, in the act of eulogizing Strindberg, he had called Ibsen a "lesser man," attacking Ibsenite realism in these terms: "It represents our Fathers' daring aspirations towards self-recognition by holding the family kodak up to ill-nature . . . we have endured too much from the banality of surfaces." Less embittered towards "our Fathers" nine years later, O'Neill is beginning to create a drama of surface banality himself — beneath which the forces of destruction will proceed with Ibsenite inevitability — and it is precisely the "family kodak" which will be O'Neill's artistic instrument. As John Henry Raleigh has observed about one of these late plays, "Everything pales beside the fact of the *family,* which is the macro-microcosm that blots out the universe. . . ." The family becomes the nucleus of every major work that follows, except the *The Iceman Cometh,* and even there, the characters are thrown together into a kind of accidental family group. As for the unfinished cycle, this was inspired by O'Neill's desire to follow his family further and further into the past: "The Cycle is primarily that," he writes to Langner, "the history of a family. What larger significance I can give my people as extraordinary examples and symbols in the drama of American possessiveness and materialism is something else again." In *Ah Wilderness!,* O'Neill develops a hazy daguerrotype of Irish family life at the turn of the century; but before long, the family kodak will focus on the author's most painful early memories, seen with consuming power and ruthless honesty, yet with compassion, understanding, and love.

O'Neill's retrospective technique is admirably illustrated in *The Iceman Cometh* (1939), where O'Neill closes the door forever on his messianic ambitions, and the suffering artist becomes completely identified with the structured art. *"The Iceman* is a denial of any other experience of faith in my plays," he remarks, soon after completing the play. "In writing it, I felt I had locked myself in with my memories." At first glance, the author's place in these memories is obscure, for the play does not look very autobiographical. Harry Hope's saloon is based on Jimmy-the-Priest's, a West-Side rooming bar that O'Neill used to frequent in his youth — ("Gorky's Night Lodgings," he was later to remark, "was an ice cream parlor in comparison," and the influence of Gorky is certainly evident in the seedy, peeled, splotched setting, and the dissipated characters) [9] and the play contains thinly veiled portraits of some of the derelicts the author used to know there and at another saloon called the Hell Hole. But although the work is set in 1912, the same climacteric year as A *Long Day's Journey,* the author himself is simply a lens through which the characters are seen. Still, if O'Neill is not the central character of the play, romanticized as a mocking, sardonic rebel, he is still present in disguise — partly in two characters, as we shall see, but mostly as a guide through the caverns of his deepest perceptions. O'Neill here is using his "memories" not for personal autobiography in the manner of Strindberg, but in the manner of Ibsen, for spiritual and psychological autobiography. As the author himself says, *The Iceman Cometh* is a repudiation of "any other experience of faith in my plays." In denying his previous philosophical affirmations, he permits a terrible sense of reality to rise to consciousness.

In its repudiation of past faith, *The Iceman Cometh* occupies

[9] For an analysis of Gorky's influence on the play, see Helen Muchnic's article, "The Irrelevancy of Belief: The Iceman and the Lower Depths," in *O'Neill and His Plays,* edited by Oscar Cargill, N. Bryllion Fagin, and William J. Fisher.

much the same place in O'Neill's work as *The Wild Duck* does in Ibsen's; and, indeed, the two plays have more in common even than this positioning. The theme of *The Iceman* — that men cannot live without illusions — is so close to the theme of *The Wild Duck*[10] that some critics have been inclined to dismiss the later play as a mere recapitulation of the earlier one. This is a mistake. O'Neill's play, to my mind, is a greater achievement than Ibsen's, and it certainly has a different emphasis. In *The Wild Duck,* it is morally wrong to rob people of their life-lies; in *The Iceman Cometh,* it is *tragic.* Gregers Werle is a satire on pseudo-Ibsenites who meddle in the lives of others, urging the claim of some impossible ideal, but Theodore Hickman is not a vicarious idealist but a realist, and one who believes he has pragmatically tested the kind of salvation he is pressing on his friends. Although Gregers is misguided, and Hjalmar Ekdal is inadequate to his demands, Ibsen still believes there are heroic individuals (Brand and Stockman, for example) with the courage to face the unclothed truth. But the whole world is inadequate to Hickey's demands, for the truth he offers is a naked, blinding light which kills. Thus, *The Wild Duck* is a savage indictment of some men; *The Iceman Cometh* is a compassionate insight into all. O'Neill is reflecting not ethically, on Right Action or Right Thought, but metaphysically, on the very quality of existence. And, as a result, he is finally working through experientially to that tragic mood so self-consciously imposed on his earlier work.

Because he is universalizing Ibsen's theme, O'Neill has created instead of one antagonist a whole catalogue of them — the deadbeats, alcoholics, pimps, whores, bartenders, and illusionists who inhabit Harry Hope's premises. The proliferation of characters adds greatly to the length of the play, which is bulky and unwieldy in the extreme; and since each character is identified by a single obsession which he continually restates, the play is extremely repetitious as well. Thus, despite the naturalistic setting, the play is much too schematic to

[10] It is also very close to the theme of Pirandello's plays, though O'Neill differs from the Italian dramatist in believing that objective reality can still be reached through the human mind.

qualify as a convincing evocation of reality. Each act offers a single variation on the theme of illusion; the action never bursts into spontaneous life; and the characters rarely transcend their particular functions. A thematic realism rather than an atmospheric realism prevails; O'Neill seems reluctant to let the play escape his rigid control. One must concede that there is some justice in Eric Bentley's objection: "There are ideas in the play, and we have the impression that what should be the real substance of it is mere (not always deft) contrivance to illustrate the ideas." Still, O'Neill's ideas, for once, proceed logically from the action, and, for once, they are totally convincing. I do not think Professor Bentley properly appreciates the depth, sincerity, and relevance of O'Neill's dramatic insights in this play.

Professor Bentley detects padding and recommends cuts; O'Neill's Broadway director, Paul Crabtree, also suggested cuts on the basis that O'Neill has made the same point eighteen times — "I intended to be repeated eighteen times," the playwright said, and refused to tamper with the play. O'Neill was right; cutting would undoubtedly diminish the impact of the work. For once, an O'Neill play is long not because the author knows too little but rather because he knows too much; even the repetitions are an intricate aspect of the total design. O'Neill has multiplied his antagonists in order to illuminate every aspect of his theme, just as he has drawn them from the humblest condition of life in order to show mankind at the extremity of its fate. Dazed by alcohol, isolated from human society, O'Neill's derelicts are stripped of every pretension except the single "pipe dream" that keeps them going, and the sum of these pipe dreams is meant to represent the total content of human illusion.

Thus, Hugo's aristocratic will to power through pretended love of the proleteriat reflects on political illusions; Joe's pugnacious demand for equality with the whites, on racial illusions; Chuck and Cora's fantasy of marriage and a farm, on domestic illusions; the prostitutes' mysterious distinction between "tarts" and "whores," on status illusions; Parritt's false motives for having betrayed his mother, on psychological illusions; Willie Oban's excuse for having discontinued law school, on intellectual illusions; Larry Slade's pretense at disillusionment and detachment, on philosophical illusions — and Hickey's belief that he has found salvation, on religious illusions. All of these dreamers represent a family of men, inextricably bound up with each other. Each is able to see the lie of the other without being able to admit his own, but in this community, the price of mutual toleration is mutual silence. Actually, the community is almost Utopian. Before Hickey comes, the men live in relative harmony together by adhering to a single doctrine — the doctrine of Tomorrow — keeping hope alive through the anticipation of significant action on a day which never comes.

Against the Tomorrow doctrine, Hickey counterposes his doctrine of Today, forcing the derelicts to execute their dreams — and fail them — on the assumption that a life without illusions is a life without guilt. In this conflict of ideologies, Hickey's main antagonist is Larry Slade, the intellectual champion of the Tomorrowmen, who is brought into the lists against his conscious will. Playing the part of the "Old Grandstand Foolosopher," pretending indifference to the fate of his companions, Larry has adopted a mask of total alienation. For him, the essence of mankind is excrement, and life on earth is doomed: "The material the ideal society must be constructed from is men themselves," he observes, explaining his apostasy from Anarchism, "and you can't build a marble temple out of mud and manure." "Old Cemetery," as he is called, is aroused only by the thought of death, and affects to contemplate his own with pleasurable anticipation. But although he pretends "a bitter, cynic philosophy," as Jimmy Tomorrow observes, "in your heart, you are the kindest man among us." Actually, Larry is doomed to inaction by a reflective intelligence which always sees both sides of a question, and he is forever trying to suppress his instinctive compassion. O'Neill describes him as "a pitying but weary old priest." He has heard all the secrets of the confessional, and out of his secret kindness is desperately trying to protect these secrets, including his own, from Hickey's remorseless efforts to bring them into light. Harry Hope's may be "Bedrock Bar, The End of the Line Cafe, The Bottom of the Sea Rathskeller," but it has "a beautiful calm in the atmosphere" which can only be preserved if it is not touched by truth.

Hickey, however, finds this a false calm, and desires to introduce a genuine spiritual peace: "All I want," he says, using a word which ironically concludes every act but the last, "is to see you *happy*." But while Hickey is convinced that only truth brings peace, Larry knows that happiness is based exclusively on mutual deception: "To hell with the truth! As the history of the world proves, the truth has no bearing on anything. . . . The lie of a pipe dream is what gives life to the whole misbegotten mad lot of us, drunk or sober." This tension between truth and illusion reflects, in much stronger dramatic terms, O'Neill's former antithesis of Nietzschean heroism and Christian compassion. But instead of forcing a synthesis, as he does in his messianic plays, O'Neill rejects the heroic teachings of Nietzsche, repudiating superhuman salvation while affirming humanity, pity, and love. Together, Hickey and Larry function in somewhat the same way as the split characters of O'Neill's earlier work; but having relinquished his messianic claims, O'Neill is able to treat both aspects of his personality with a good deal more balance and equanimity. Thus, Larry's facile pessimism, his cynicism, and his fascination with death are all qualities found in O'Neill's earlier "sardonic" heroes, but these are now exposed as mere attitudinizing. And Hickey's evangelism represents the messianic impulse in O'Neill turned back on itself, for his gospel of truth is revealed as the greatest illusion of all.

The Iceman Cometh, then, is about the impossibility of salvation in a world without God, an expression of existential revolt structured in quasi-religious terms. And beneath the realistic surface, O'Neill is developing an ironic Christian parable, in a surprisingly subtle manner. For one thing, Hickey's entrance is delayed so long that — like another long-awaited figure, Beckett's Godot — he begins to accumulate supernatural qualities. "Would that Hickey or Death would come," moans one impatient character — an anticipatory irony, since Hickey will soon be identified with Death. Hickey finally does arrive, but the amiable jester has undergone a startling transformation. "I'm damned sure he's brought death with him," remarks Larry. "I feel the cold touch of it on him." The recurrent iceman motif intensifies these associations. On each of his annual visits, Hickey has joked that his chaste wife, Evelyn, was in the hay with the iceman; and as the derelicts grow more and more tormented by Hickey's penetrating thrusts, their one hope is that the joke has come to roost. And indeed it has, though not in the manner they think. Evelyn is now being held in a frigid embrace; Hickey, we finally learn, has murdered her; "Death was the Iceman Hickey called to his home." Thus, Hickey, Death, and the Iceman are one. The truth doesn't set you free, it kills you dead; the peace which Hickey brings to Harry Hope's saloon is the peace of the grave. Hickey, therefore, is the false Messiah — not the Resurrection and the Life, but the "great Nihilist," starting "a movement which will blow up the world."

To emphasize his anti-messianic point, O'Neill has hidden parallels with another great world movement, Christianity, throughout the play. And Cyrus Day has done us the service of uncovering most of them in his article, "The Iceman and the Bridegroom":

Hickey as savior has twelve disciples. They drink wine at Hope's supper party, and their grouping on the stage, according to O'Neill's directions, is reminiscent of Leonardo da Vinci's painting of the Last Supper. Hickey leaves the party, as Christ does, aware that he is about to be executed. The three whores correspond in number to the three Marys, and sympathize with Hickey as the three Marys sympathize with Christ. . . . One of the derelicts, Parritt, resembles Judas Iscariot in several ways. He is twelfth in the list of dramatis personae; Judas is twelfth in the New Testament of the Disciples. He has betrayed his anarchist mother for a paltry $200; Judas betrayed Christ for thirty pieces of silver. . . .

To this list of striking resemblances, we might add another interesting one. Larry Slade becomes the only real convert to Hickey's religion of Death — he is, like Saint Peter, the rock on which Hickey builds his Church.

The symbolic aspect of the play, however, is not very obtrusive, if indeed it is noticeable at all without the aid of a commentator. On a purely denotative level, the work is still very rich. O'Neill has carefully combined Hickey's symbolic role as a false Messiah with his family background and psychological history, so that Hickey stands as a full-bodied character on his own, and a much more convincing salesman figure than Miller's Willy Loman (at least we know what Hickey sells — hardware). The son of a minister, Hickey has brought an evangelical fervor to the drummer's trade, and the techniques of salesmanship to his evangelism. In a country where everything is bought and sold, O'Neill is suggesting, even a religious vision must be peddled. Bruce Barton's observation that Jesus was a super-salesman may be in the back of O'Neill's mind; Billy Graham's religious "crusades" come immediately to ours. Hickey certainly employs the "hard sell" — cheery, good-humored, loud, brash, and pitiless — bearing down on his victim like Major Barbara bringing God to Bill Walker, or a psychoanalyst unearthing the source of a patient's neurosis. He has an instinctual eye for human weakness, partly because of his own experience ("I've had hell inside me. I can spot it in others"), but partly because he is "The Great Salesman" and can detect the vulnerability of a client in an instant.

As a result of this native shrewdness, Hickey has, by the end of the second act, transformed all the derelicts into caged animals, snarling at each other in their agony: each is beginning to open the other's wounds in order to protect his own, and even the goodnatured Harry Hope has developed an uncharacteristic pugnacity. Torn from the security of their dreams, the derelicts must now confront their Tomorrow, each performing the deed which terrifies him most. The third act takes place in cold, daylight horror. The derelicts are afflicted with the "katzenjammers," their withdrawal symptoms aggravated by a growing apprehensiveness. Harry Hope, symbolizing the communal predicament, prepares at last to walk around the ward — but is unable even to cross the street. His illusion exposed, Harry's hope vanishes, and with it the hope of all his companions: only blank, unstructured reality remains. Having abandoned hope, the men are dwelling in hell; even the alcohol has lost its punch; all escape routes are closed. What results is death-in-life: "Vhat's matter, Harry?" asks Hugo. "You look funny. You look dead." Hugo's babbling, and the growling of the derelicts, turns the atmosphere funereal. Hickey's salvation is failing, and so is Hickey's confidence: "That's what worries me about you, Governor," he says to Harry, as the expected peace fails to come. "It's time you began to feel happy —"

In the last act, the derelicts have turned to stone, their spirits calcified by the death ray of truth. Motivated by growing nervousness over their behavior, Hickey begins his long speech of confession — a confession which is also a discovery — paralleled by an antiphonal speech from Parritt. Both have destroyed a woman; both for reasons that they cannot face. Parritt has informed on his mother not out of patriotism or penury but rather out of hatred; and Hickey has killed Evelyn because she killed his joy of life, filling him with guilt through constant forgiveness of his sins. Thus, Hickey's act was an act of revenge and not of love; he not only hated her illusion, he detested her. As he blurts out, in the unconsidered slip which gives him away, "You know what you can do with your pipe dream now, you damned bitch."

Hickey can admit this feeling to his consciousness only for a moment; then, he immediately pleads insanity. "Good God, I couldn't have said that! If I did, I'd gone insane! Why, I loved Evelyn better than anything in life." It is this plea which leads Eric Bentley to say that "O'Neill's eye was off the subject":

Not being clearly seen, the man is unclearly presented to the audience; O'Neill misleads them for several hours, then asks them to reach back into their memory and re-interpret all Hickey's actions and attitudes from the beginning. Is Hickey the character O'Neill needed as the man who tries to deprive the gang of their illusions? He (as it turns out) is a maniac. But if the attempt to disillude the gang is itself mad, it would have more dramatic point made by a sane idealist (as in *The Wild Duck*).

I cite this passage because it contains a widely shared misunderstanding of the play which has obscured its real profundity. For the fact is, of course, that O'Neill's eye remained steadfastly on the subject: Hickey, consistent in conception from first to last, is not a maniac at all. Actually, he only claims to have been insane at the time of the murder, but even this is a self-deception which he adopts so as not to face his real feelings towards his wife. Such a conclusion is clear enough from the context, and Parritt suggests it even more bluntly in the course of his own confession: *"And I'm not putting up any bluff either, that I was crazy afterwards* when I laughed to myself and thought, 'You know what you can do with your freedom pipe dream now, don't you, you damned old bitch!'"* [My emphasis]. Hickey's plea of insanity, in short, is a bluff — not to escape the chair (he wants to die now) but to escape the truth: he cannot admit that he hated his wife. In a context like this, as a matter of fact, Hickey's mental state is totally irrelevant, since even madness is an escape from an unpleasant reality; the point is that Hickey, who thought he was living the truth, was living another pipe dream. As for the derelicts, they are willing to believe that Hickey was mad, because this means he told them lies; if he will agree to let them have their illusions, they will agree to let him have his. Hickey hesitates because he knows he told them the truth, but for the sake of his own peace, he must agree to the trade. Thus, he enters their community at last: mutual toleration through mutual silence.

Hickey's brand of salvation, in short, has proved of false manufacture: the happiness he discovered after Evelyn's death was merely the happiness of another illusion. Thus, his attempt to "disillude the gang" is not "itself mad," it is simply based on a terrible error; and since his own illusions are directly implicated in the action, Hickey has a good deal *more* dramatic point than Gregers Werle. Hickey, in fact, has some of the dimension of a tragic protagonist, and is brought right up to the brink of a tragic perception; if he does not look over, then Larry Slade does, and what he sees is the bottomless abyss of a totally divested reality:

Be God, there's no hope. I'll never be a success in the grandstand — or anywhere else! Life is too much for me! I'll be a weak fool looking with pity at the two sides of everything till the day I die! (*With an intense bitter sincerity*) May that day come soon! (*He pauses startledly, surprised himself — then with a sardonic grin*) Be God, I'm the only real convert to death Hickey made here. From the bottom of my coward's heart I mean that now!

Hickey has escaped reality by pleading insanity; Parritt by committing suicide; the derelicts by returning to their illusions. But for Larry, too truthful to lie and too cowardly to die, the abyss is constantly before his eyes. Out of compassion for the Judas, Parritt, he has told him to put an end to his miserable existence; and now he must bear responsibility for this and every act until his own life ends: "May that day come soon!" His desire for death is like that of Othello: "For, in my sense, 'tis happiness to die." The play ends in laughter, song, and the drunken babble of Hugo, as Larry stares straight ahead of him, a living corpse, swathed in the winding sheet of truth. Like O'Neill's, his tragic posturing has developed finally into a deeply experienced tragic sense of life.

This extraordinary play, then, is a chronicle of O'Neill's own spiritual metamorphosis from a messianic into an existential rebel, the shallow yea-saying salvationist of the earlier plays having been transformed into a penetrating analyst of human motive rejecting even the pose of disillusionment. O'Neill's "denial of any other experience of faith in my plays" has left him alone, at last, with existence itself; and he has looked at it with a courage which only the greatest tragic dramatists have been able to muster. *The Iceman Cometh*, despite its prosaic language, recreates that existential groan which is heard in Shakespeare's tragedies and in the third choral poem of Sophocles's *Oedipus at Colonus*, as O'Neill makes reality bearable through the metaphysical consolations of art. O'Neill has rejected Hickey's brand of salvation as a way to human happiness, but truth has, nevertheless, become the cornerstone of his drama, truth combined with the compassionate understanding of Larry Slade. Expunging everything false and literary from his work, O'Neill has finally reconciled himself to being the man he really is.

This kind of reconciliation could only have come about through penetrating self-analysis; and it is inevitable, therefore, that the process of self-analysis itself should form the material of one of his plays: *A Long Day's Journey into Night* (1939-1941). Here, combining the retrospective techniques of Ibsen with the exorcistic attack of Strindberg, O'Neill compresses the psychological history of his. family into the events of a single day, and the economy of the work, for all its length, is magnificent. Within this Classical structure, where O'Neill even observes the unities, the play begins to approach a kind of formal perfection. Like most Classical works, *A Long Day's Journey* is set in the past — the summer of 1912, when O'Neill, then twenty-four, was stricken with tuberculosis, a disease which sent him to the sanitarium where he first decided to become a dramatist. And like most Classical works, its impact derives less from physical action (the play has hardly any plot, and only the first act has any suspense) than from psychological revelation, as the characters dredge up their painful memories and half-considered thoughts. O'Neill's model is probably Ibsen's *Ghosts* (even Ibsen's title is singularly appropriate to the later play), because he employs that technique of exhumation which Ibsen borrowed from Sophocles — inching forward and moving backward simultaneously by means of a highly functional dialogue.

O'Neill, however, is not only the author of the play but also a character in it; like Strindberg, he has written "a poem of desperation," composed in rhythms of pain. The author's relation to his material is poignantly suggested in his dedication of the work to his wife, Carlotta, on the occasion of their twelfth anniversary: "I mean it as a tribute to your love and tenderness which gave me the faith in love that enabled me to face my dead at last and write this play — write it with deep pity and understanding and forgiveness for *all* the four haunted Tyrones." O'Neill includes himself in the general amnesty; he has certainly earned the right. The play, written as he tells us "in tears and blood," was composed in a cold sweat, sometimes fifteen hours at a stretch: O'Neill, like all his characters, is confronting his most harrowing memories, and putting his ghosts to rest in a memorial reenactment of their mutual suffering and responsibility.

Because his purpose is partially therapeutic, O'Neill has hardly fictionalized this autobiography at all. The O'Neills have become the Tyrones, his mother Ella is now called Mary, and Eugene takes on the name of his dead brother Edmund (the dead child is called Eugene),[11] but his father and brother retain their own Christian names, and all the dramatic events (with a few minor changes) are true, including the story about the pigs of Tyrone's tenant farmer and the ice pond of the Standard Oil millionaire, an episode to be treated again in *A Moon for the Misbegotten*.

In view of this fidelity to fact, it is a wonder that O'Neill was able to write the play at all, but he is in astonishing control of his material — the work is a masterpiece. While *The Iceman Cometh* has fewer arid stretches and deeper implications, *A Long Day's Journey* contains the finest writing O'Neill ever did — and the fourth act is among the most powerful scenes in all dramatic literature. O'Neill has created a personal play which bears on the condition of all mankind; a bourgeois family drama with universal implications. *A Long Day's Journey* is a study of hereditary guilt which does not even make recourse to arbitrary metaphors, like Ibsen's use of disease in *Ghosts*. Edmund's consumption, unlike Oswald's syphilis, has a bacterial rather than a symbolic source. It is no longer necessary for O'Neill to invent a modern equivalent of Fate, for now he feels it working in his very bones. Thus, O'Neill's characters are suffering from spiritual and psychological ailments rather than biological and social ones (society, for O'Neill, hardly seems to exist), but they are just as deeply ravaged as Oswald and Mrs. Alving. O'Neill's achievement is all the more stunning when we remember that his previous efforts to write this kind of play were dreadfully bungled. In *Mourning Becomes Electra*, for example, the sins of the father are also visited on the sons, but this is illustrated through physical transformations — Orin begins to look like Ezra, Lavinia like Christine — a purely mechanical application of the theme. And the same sort of self-conscious contrivance is apparent in *Desire Under the Elms*, where endless argumentation occurs over whether Eben is more like his "Maw" or his "Paw."

In *A Long Day's Journey*, O'Neill has dismissed such superficial concerns to concentrate on the deeper implications of his theme: what is visited on the sons is a strain of blank misfortune. Here is a

[11] The Gelbs conclude, quite correctly I think, that this exchanging of names indicates a profound death wish on the part of O'Neill. See *O'Neill*, p. 188.

family living in a close symbiotic relationship, a single organism with four branches, where a twitch in one creates a spasm in another. O'Neill was beginning to explore this kind of relationship in *The Iceman Cometh*, where the derelicts aggravate each other's agony and hell is other people, but here he has worked out the nightmare of family relations with relentless precision. No individual character trait is revealed which does not have a bearing on the lives of the entire family; the play is nothing but the truth, but there is nothing irrelevant in the play. Thus, the two major characteristics which define James Tyrone, Sr. — his miserliness and his career as an actor — are directly related to the misery of his wife and children. Tyrone's niggardliness has caused Mary's addiction, because it was a cut-rate quack doctor who first introduced her to drugs; and Tyrone's inability to provide her with a proper home, because he was always on the road, has intensified her bitterness and sense of loss. The miser in Tyrone is also the source of Edmund's resentment, since Tyrone is preparing to send him to a State Farm for treatment instead of to a more expensive rest home. Edmund's tuberculosis, in turn, partially accounts for Mary's resumption of her habit, because she cannot face the fact of his bad health; and Edmund's birth caused the illness which eventually introduced his mother to drugs. Jamie is affected by the very existence of Edmund, since his brother's literary gifts fill him with envy and a sense of failure; and his mother's inability to shake her habit has made him lose faith in his own capacity for regeneration. Even the comic touches are structured along causal lines: Tyrone is too cheap to burn the lights in the parlor, so Edmund bangs his knee on a hatstand, and Jamie stumbles on the steps. Every action has a radiating effect, and characters interlock in the manner which evoked the anguished cry from Strindberg: "Earth, earth is hell. . . . in which I cannot move without injuring the happiness of others, in which others cannot remain happy without hurting me."

The family, in brief, is chained together by resentment, guilt, recrimination; yet, the chains that hold it are those of love as well as hate. Each makes the other suffer through some unwitting act, a breach of love or faith, and reproaches follow furiously in the wake of every revelation. But even at the moment that the truth is being blurted out, an apologetic retraction is being formed. Nobody really desires to hurt. Compassion and understanding alternate with anger and rancor. Even Jamie, who is "forever making sneering fun of somebody" and who calls his mother a "hophead," hates his own bitterness and mockery, and is filled with self-contempt. The four members of the family react to each other with bewildering ambivalence — exposing illusions and sustaining them, striking a blow and hating the hand that strikes. Every torment is self-inflicted, every angry word reverberating in the conscience of the speaker. It is as if the characters existed only to torture each other, while protecting each other, too, against their own resentful tongues.

There is a curse on the blighted house of the Tyrones, and the origin of the curse lies elsewhere, with existence itself. As Mary says, "None of us can help the things life has done to us." In tracing down the origin of this curse, O'Neill has returned to the year 1912; but as the play proceeds, he brings us even further into the past. Implicated in the misfortunes of the house are not only the two generations of Tyrones, but a previous generation as well; Edmund's attempted suicide, before the action begins, is linked to the suicide of Tyrone's father, and Edmund's consumption is the disease by which Mary's father died. Though O'Neill does not mention this, the tainted legacy reaches into the future, too: the playwright's elder son, Eugene Jr., is also to commit suicide, and his younger son, Shane, is to become, like his grandmother, a narcotics addict. The generations merge, and so does Time. "The past is the present, isn't it?" cries Mary. "It's the future too. We all try to lie out of that but life won't let us."

O'Neill, the probing artist, seeks in the past for the origination of guilt and blame; but his characters seek happiness and dreams. All four Tyrones share an intense hatred of the present and its morbid, inescapable reality. All four seek solace from the shocks of life in nostalgic memories, which they reach through different paths. For Mary, the key that turns the lock of the past is morphine. "It kills the pain. You go back until at last you are beyond its reach. Only the past when you were happy is real." The pain she speaks of is in her crippled hands, the constant reminder of her failed dream to be a concert pianist, but even more it is in her crippled, guilty soul. Mary has betrayed all her hopes and dreams. Even her marriage is a betrayal, since she longed to be a nun, wholly dedicated to her namesake, the Blessed Virgin; but her addiction betrays her religion, family, and home. She cannot pray; she is in a state of despair; and the accusations of her family only aggravate her guilt. Mary is subject to a number of illusions — among them, the belief that she married beneath her — but unlike the derelicts of *The Iceman,* who dream of the future, she only dreams of the past. Throughout the action, she is trying to escape the pain of the present entirely; and at the end, with the aid of drugs, she has finally returned to the purity, innocence, and hope of her girlhood. Although the title of the play suggests a progress, therefore, the work moves always backwards. The long journey is a journey into the past.

O'Neill suggests this in many ways, partly through ambiguous images of light and dark, sun and mist. The play begins at 8:30 in the morning with a trace of fog in the air, and concludes sometime after midnight, with the house fogbound — the mood changing from sunny cheer over Mary's apparent recovery to gloomy despair over her new descent into hell. The nighttime scenes occur logically at the end of the day; but subjectively, the night precedes the day, for the play closes on a phantasmagoria of past time. Under the influence of Mary's drugs — and, to some extent, the alcohol of the men — time evaporates and hovers, and disappears: past, present, future become one. Mary drifts blissfully into illusions under cover of the night, which functions like a shroud against the harsh, daylight reality. And so does that fog that Mary loves: "It hides you from the world and the world from you," she says. "You feel that everything has changed, and nothing is what it seemed to be. No one can find or touch you any more." Her love for her husband and children neutralized by her terrible sense of guilt, Mary withdraws more and more into herself. And this, in turn, intensifies the unhappiness of the men: "The hardest thing to take," says Edmund, "is the blank wall she builds around herself. Or it's more like a bank of fog in which she hides and loses herself. . . . It's as if, in spite of loving us, she hated us."

Mary, however, is not alone among the "fog people" — the three men also have their reasons for withdrawing into night. Although less shrouded in illusion than Mary, each, nevertheless, haunts the past like a ghost, seeking consolation for a wasted life. For Tyrone, his youth was a period of artistic promise when he had the potential to be a great actor instead of a commercial hack; his favorite memory is of Booth's praising his Othello, words which he has written down and lost. For Jamie, who might have borne the Tyrone name "in honor and dignity, who showed such brilliant promise," the present is without possibility; he is now a hopeless ne'er-do-well, pursuing oblivion in drink and the arms of fat whores while mocking his own failure in bathetic, self-hating accents: "My name is Might-Have-Been," he remarks, quoting from Rossetti, "I am also called No More, Too Late, Farewell." For Edmund, who is more like his mother than the others, night and fog are a refuge from the curse of living:

The fog was where I wanted to be. . . . That's what I wanted — to be alone with myself in another world where truth is untrue and life can hide from itself. . . . It was like walking on the bottom of the sea. As if I had drowned long ago. As if I was a ghost belonging to the fog, and the fog was the ghost of the sea. It felt damned peaceful to be nothing more than a ghost within a ghost.

Reality, truth, and life plague him like a disease. Ashamed of being human, he finds existence itself detestable: "Who wants to see life as it is, if they can help it? It's the three Gorgons in one. You look in their faces and die. Or it's Pan. You see him and die — that is, inside you — and have to go on living as a ghost."

"We are such stuff as manure is made on, so let's drink up and forget it" — like Strindberg, who developed a similar excremental view of humankind, the young Edmund has elected to withdraw from Time by whatever means available, and one of these is alcohol. Edmund, whose taste in poetry is usually execrable, finally quotes a good poet,

Baudelaire, on the subject of drunkenness:[12] "Be drunken, if you would not be martyred slaves of Time; be drunken continually! With wine, with poetry, or with virtue, as you will." And in order to avoid being enslaved by Time, Edmund contemplates other forms of drunkenness as well. In his fine fourth-act speech, he tells of his experiences at sea, when he discovered Nirvana for a moment, pulling out of Time and dissolving into the infinite:

I belonged, without past or future, within peace and unity and a wild joy, within something greater than my own life, or the life of Man, to Life itself! To God, if you want to put it that way. . . . For a second you see — and seeing the secret, are the secret. For a second there is meaning! Then the hand lets the veil fall and you are alone, lost in the fog again, and you stumble on towards nowhere, for no good reason.

The ecstatic vision of wholeness is only momentary, and Edmund, who "would have been more successful as a sea-gull or a fish," must once again endure the melancholy fate of living in reality: "As it is, I will always be a stranger who never feels at home, who does not really want and is not really wanted, who can never belong, who must always be a little in love with death!" In love with death since death is the ultimate escape from Time, the total descent into night and fog.

There is a fifth Tyrone involved in the play — the older Eugene O'Neill. And although he has superimposed his later on his earlier self (Edmund, described as a socialist and atheist, has many religious-existential attitudes), the author and the character are really separable. Edmund wishes to deny Time, but O'Neill has elected to return to it once again — reliving the past and mingling with his ghosts — in order to find the secret and meaning of their suffering. For the playwright has discovered another escape besides alcohol,

[12] Edmund, like O'Neill, is much too fond of the Yellow Book poets; even the quotation from Baudelaire is in the overly fruity translation of Arthur Symons. O'Neill's literary sources and influences are all enumerated in the stage directions to the play which list the books in the Tyrone library: Balzac, Zola, Stendhal, Schopenhauer, Nietzsche, Ibsen, Strindberg, Shaw, Swinburne, Rossetti, Wilde, Kipling, and Dowson, among many others.

Nirvana, or death from the terrible chaos of life: the escape of art where chaos is ordered and the meaningless made meaningful. The play itself is an act of forgiveness and reconciliation, the artist's life-long resentment disintegrated through complete understanding of the past and total self-honesty.

These qualities dominate the last act, which proceeds through a sequence of confessions and revelations to a harrowing climax. Structurally, the act consists of two long colloquies — the first between Tyrone and Edmund, the second between Edmund and Jamie — followed by a long soliloquy from Mary who, indeed, concludes every act. Tyrone's confession of failure as an actor finally makes him understandable to Edmund who thereupon forgives him all his faults; and Jamie's confession of his ambivalent feelings towards his brother, and his half-conscious desire to make him fail too, is the deepest psychological moment in the play.[18] But the most honest moment of self-revelation occurs at the end of Edmund's speech, after he has tried to explain the origin of his bitterness and despair. Tyrone, as usual, finds his son's musings "morbid," but he has to admit that Edmund has "the makings of a poet." Edmund replies:

The *makings* of a poet. No, I'm afraid I'm like the guy who is always pan-handling for a smoke. He hasn't even got the makings. He's got only the habit. I couldn't touch what I tried to tell you just now. I just stammered. That's the best I'll ever do. . . . Well, it will be faithful realism, at least. Stammering is the native eloquence of us fog people.

In describing his own limitations as a dramatist, O'Neill here rises to real eloquence; speaking the truth has given him a tongue. Having accepted these limitations, and dedicated himself to a "faithful real-ism" seen through the lens of the "family kodak," he has turned into a dramatist of the very first rank.

Mary's last speech is the triumph of his new dramatic method,

[18] This particular scene provides us with interesting insights into the origina-tion of many of O'Neill's early attitudes. It was Jamie, we learn, who "made getting drunk romantic," and it was Jamie who "made whores fascinating vam-pires instead of the poor, stupid, diseased slobs they really are." There is even some possibility that O'Neill assumed his brother's identity when he appeared as the sneering, sardonic hero of the earlier plays.

poetically evoking all the themes of the play; and it is marvelously prepared for. The men are drunk, sleepy, and exhausted after all the wrangling; the lights are very low; the night and fog very thick. Suddenly, a *coup de théâtre*. All the bulbs in the front parlor chandelier are illuminated, and the opening bars of a Chopin waltz are haltingly played, "as if an awkward schoolgirl were practising it for the first time." The men are shocked into consciousness as Mary enters, absentmindedly trailing her wedding dress. She is so completely in the past that even her features have been transfigured: "the uncanny thing is that her face now appears so youthful." What follows is a scene remarkably like Lady Macbeth's sleepwalking scene, or, as Jamie cruelly suggests, Ophelia's mad scene — an audaciously theatrical and, at the same time, profoundly moving expression from the depths of a tormented soul.

While the men look on in horror, Mary reenacts the dreams of her youth, oblivious of her surroundings; and her speeches sum up the utter hopelessness of the entire family. Shy and polite, like a young schoolgirl, astonished at her swollen hands and at the elderly gentleman who gently takes the wedding dress from her grasp, Mary is back in the convent, preparing to become a nun. She is looking for something, "something I need terribly," something that protected her from loneliness and fear: "I can't have lost it forever. I would die if I thought that. Because then there would be no hope." It is her life, and, even more, her faith. She has had a vision of the Blessed Virgin, who had "smiled and blessed me with her consent." But the Mother Superior has asked her to live like other girls before deciding to take her vows, and she reluctantly has agreed:

I said, of course, I would do anything she suggested, but I knew it was simply a waste of time. After I left her, I felt all mixed up, so I went to the shrine and prayed to the Blessed Virgin and found peace again because I knew she heard my prayer and would always love me and see no harm ever came to me so long as I never lost my faith in her.

But the faith has turned yellow, like her wedding dress, and harm has indeed come. On the threshold of the later horror, Mary grows uneasy; then puts one foot over into the vacancy which is to come: "That was in the winter of senior year. Then in the springtime something happened to me. Yes, I remember. I fell in love with James Tyrone and was so happy for a time."

Her mournful speech, which concludes on the key word of the play, spans the years and breaks them, recapitulating all the blighted hopes, the persistent illusions, the emotional ambivalence, and the sense of imprisonment in the fate of others that the family shares. It leaves the central character enveloped in fog, and the others encased in misery, the night deepening around their shameful secrets. But it signalizes O'Neill's journey out of the night and into the daylight — into a perception of his true role as a man and an artist — exorcising his ghosts and "facing my dead at last."

In the plays that follow, O'Neill continues to work the vein he had mined in *The Iceman Cometh* and *A Long Day's Journey:* examining, through the medium of a faithful realism, the people of the fog and their illusionary lives. And in writing these plays, he stammers no more. In the lilting speech of predominantly Irish-Catholic characters, O'Neill finally discovers a language congenial to him, and he even begins to create a music very much like Synge's, while his humor bubbles more and more to the surface. Despite effective comic passages, however, O'Neill's plays remain dark. In *A Touch of the Poet,* for example, he deals with a nineteenth-century Irish-American tavernkeeper, Con Melody, who deludes himself that he is a heroic Byronic aristocrat, proudly isolated from the Yankee merchants and the democratic mob. Cold and imperious towards his wife but full of dash and style, Melody undergoes a startling change when his illusions are exposed, groveling like a cunning and mean-spirited peasant. Poor but proud before, he will now advance himself through any form of chicanery; but he survives as a spiritually dead man, another of O'Neill's living corpses.

In *A Moon for the Misbegotten,* O'Neill follows Jamie O'Neill, the living corpse of *A Long Day's Journey,* into a later stage of his life, after the death of his mother. Whiskey-logged and lacerated by self-hatred, he confesses to an enormous but kindly girl (a virgin

[358]

pretending to be promiscuous) how he stayed with a whore on the train carrying his mother's corpse back East. Sleeping all night on the ample bosom of this symbolic mother, like Jesus in the Pietà, he earns from her the forgiveness and peace that the dead mother can no longer provide.

These two works are minor masterpieces; *The Iceman Cometh* and *A Long Day's Journey* major ones. And in all four plays,[14] O'Neill concentrates a fierce, bullish power into fables of illusion and reality, shot through with flashes of humor, but pervaded by a sense of melancholy over the condition of being human. Like Strindberg, therefore, O'Neill develops from messianic rebellion into existential rebellion, thus demonstrating that beneath his Nietzschean yea-saying and affirmation of life was a profound discontent with the very nature of existence. O'Neill's experiments with form, his flirtations with various philosophies and religions, his attitudinizing and fake poeticizing represent the means by which he tried to smother this perception; but it would not be smothered, and when he finally found the courage to face it through realistic probes of his own past experience, he discovered the only artistic role that really fit him. In power and insight, O'Neill remains unsurpassed among American dramatists, and, of course, it is doubtful if, without him, there would have been an American drama at all. But it is for his last plays that he will be remembered — those extraordinary dramas of revolt which he pulled out of himself in pain and suffering, a sick and tired man in a shuttered room, unable to bear much light.

[14] I have neglected to discuss *More Stately Mansions* because the play is sadly marred and incomplete. Its tedious soliloquies, mother-wife confusions, and Poet-Businessman conflicts suggest that it is a regression, a throwback to an earlier stage of O'Neill's development. O'Neill made notes for completely revising the play in 1941, and, failing this, left instructions for it to be destroyed at his death; it would have been no loss if his instructions had been heeded.

IX

ANTONIN ARTAUD AND JEAN GENET:

The Theatre of Cruelty

The theatre of revolt finds its most apocalyptic expression in *le théâtre de la cruauté,* an approach to the stage most effectively realized by the playwright, Jean Genet, but first conceived in the imagination of the poet and visionary, Antonin Artaud. Artaud's theories of the theatre — expounded in a series of essays, letters, and manifestoes which he wrote in the early nineteen-thirties — were first published together in 1938 under the title *Le Théâtre et son Double (The Theatre and Its Double);* and this work continues to be one of the most influential, as well as one of the most inflammatory, documents of our time. Like the kind of theatre it propagates, *The Theatre and Its Double* has the quality of an exotic and frenzied dream, throwing out flashes of illumination with that hypnotic lucidity which is the hallmark of Artaud's powerful style. A gifted poet himself, Artaud introduces into the theatre the feverish intoxication of the *poètes maudits,* Baudelaire, Rimbaud, Lautréamont. Like theirs, his poetic ecstasy is very close to madness, and his chaotic life is tortured by fits of insanity until his death in 1948. Despite the disordered quality of his career and the fragmentary nature of his contribution, however, Artaud exercises a tremendous impact upon the modern French imagination, belonging, in the words of Jacques Guicharnaud, "to that breed of seers who leave trails of fire behind them as they pass through the world." The most important of these fiery passages leads to the theatre of cruelty, even in its embryonic stage one of the most original movements in the modern drama. Yet, Artaud did not live to see it realized. In this movement, Artaud plays the role of a prophetic Aristotle, writing the *Poetics* of an imaginary theatre which Jean Genet, his posthumous Sophocles, will not begin to execute until after his death.

Before discussing the contributions of these two men, however, some brief preliminary remarks about their predecessors are necessary. For despite Artaud's refusal to serve as a "funnel for everyone else's ideas," the theatre of cruelty is the logical culmination of the avant-garde movement in France. What Artaud achieves, and Genet after him, is to endow this movement with seriousness, depth, and commitment. These are qualities of which it is sorely in need, since, before Artaud, the nihilistic writers of the avant-garde produce works which are relatively sterile. Such writers, aroused by the lifelessness of the Boulevard stage and of the audiences who patronize it, begin with no greater purpose than to annihilate the bourgeoisie and all its works, pursuing this end through two related techniques: Dada and Surrealism. The literary ancestor of the Dada movement is Alfred Jarry, and though the movement doesn't formally begin until the second decade of the twentieth century, no Dada play is more typical or more original than Jarry's *Ubu Roi*, which was written as early as 1897. *Ubu Roi* is basically a Bohemian practical joke on the literary taste of the middle class, being a parody, in nonsensical form, of the best-loved works of Western literature. It is also a savage assault on middle-class man, for it has as its hero a brutal caricature of a *père de famille,* with a head like a turnip and a belly like a balloon. Lustful, venal, and gluttonous, Père Ubu represents what Catulle Mendès calls "the modesty, virtues, patriotism, and ideals of a people who have dined well." And later, Tristan Tzara and his cohorts will continue the attack on this well-fed public in outrageous evenings of mischief, designed primarily to scourge and irritate.[1] The Dada movement, wholly dedicated to incomprehensibility ("Recounting comprehensible things," said Jarry, "only

[1] In a typical entertainment of this sort, Tzara appeared before an audience reading a newspaper while a bell was rung so clamorously that not a word could be heard.

serves to make heavy the spirit and to warp the meaning, whereas the absurd exercises the spirit and makes the memory work"), is one of the foundations of what Martin Esslin calls "the theatre of the absurd," and is particularly influential on the work of Ionesco, whose hatred of middle-class conventions and ideals is channeled into inspired clowning and brutal farce.

Much the same kind of hostility towards the bourgeoisie can be found in Surrealism, just as playful as Dada but somewhat more coherent. The earliest work in this genre, Apollinaire's *Les Mamelles de Tirésias* (written in 1903, but not produced until 1917), is full of Bohemian mischief-making in the style of Jarry, but it does not break so violently with the traditions of Western literature. (It does, however, break with Western traditions of verisimilitude, since it is written in the form of a disjointed dream, with wrenched symbols and abrupt transformations.) Apollinaire's play, in fact, anticipates much of the serious work to be done later in the contemporary novel, painting, music, poetry, and drama, since it employs (very freely, to be sure) a character from Greek myth — Tiresias, stranded in the land of Zanzibar. Under the leadership of André Breton, the Surrealists will later devote themselves exclusively to destroying the values of Christian civilization, declaring the simplest Surrealist act to be the firing of a revolver into a crowded street. But, occasionally, playwrights with Surrealist inclinations — Jean Cocteau, for example — will employ scenic strategies much like Apollinaire's, extending his theatrical ideas by modernizing the Homeric mythology in the manner of Joyce, Eliot, Stravinsky, and Picasso.

Myth drama is quickly assimilated by the Boulevard, and, in the hands of such literary dramatists as Giraudoux and Anouilh, it becomes a highly verbalized form, designed to familiarize the audience with past heroic actions as if they were being performed today. In the hands of a clowning spirit like Cocteau, on the other hand, myth drama is a Surrealist spectacle in which the mythic action is superimposed upon a modern landscape for the sake of ironic contrasts. Cocteau favors "poetry *of* the theatre" over "poetry *in* the theatre" (a poetry visualized rather than heard); to him, the tirades and verbal debates of the Cartel dramatists represent the vestiges of a dead literary tradition. Similarly, since Cocteau is less concerned with flattering the spectator than with satirizing him for his spiritual inadequacy, he takes a much more radical approach to myth. Instead of identifying the heroic past with the unheroic present, he emphasizes their essential disparity; instead of merely updating the Classical protagonist, he minifies and denigrates him. In *La Machine Infernale,* for example, Cocteau presents us with Sophocles's Oedipus as he might be seen by his valet or psychoanalyst — a treacherous, vain, self-conscious bully with a mother fixation. By bringing us inside the palace, and dramatizing his hero's petty household affairs, Cocteau — like Joyce in *Ulysses* and Eliot in his "Sweeney" poems — attempts to highlight the drabness, meanness, and self-consciousness of twentieth-century urban man.

Artaud was associated with both the Dadaists and the Surrealists early in his career, and he shares their loathing of traditional art, of modern industrial life, and of Western civilization. But he turns these negative attitudes into positive acts, transforming the nihilism, sterility, and buffoonery of his predecessors into profoundly revolutionary theory. Artaud's revolt is so radical, and so deadly serious, that it leads him into messianic conclusions. A Romantic who tolerates no boundaries, a prophet of rebellion who preaches "extreme action, pushed beyond all limits," Artaud demands nothing less than a total transformation of the existing structure. And this revolution will begin in the theatre.

For the theatre, to Artaud, is not simply a place where audiences are entertained, instructed, or irritated; it is the very pulse of civilization itself. And one sign that Western civilization is decaying is that its theatre has enshrined such "lazy, unserviceable notions" as "art." In place of these notions, Artaud wants to substitute what he calls *culture.* Western art is essentially divorced from the people and disperses them, but culture brings men together. Art is an excrescence; culture is functional. Art is the expression of one man; culture is the expression of all. For this reason, Artaud is drawn to primitive countries like Mexico, where "things are made for use.

And the world is in perpetual exaltation." Such cultures have not yet buried the instinctual life under layers of sophistication and refinement, and it is in such cultures that Artaud seeks the renewal of his race: "All true culture relies upon the barbaric and primitive means of totemism whose savage, i.e., entirely spontaneous, life I wish to worship."

Thus, Artaud's ideas about the theatre are inseparable from his feelings about the world in which he lives. Behind every theory he advances lies his messianic desire to change the face of the West. Artaud does not merely relax into alienation, like the Dadaist and Surrealists. His revolt is so acute that it has brought him full circle into a vision of communion. And although he declares that "I am not one of those who believe that civilization has to change in order for the theatre to change," he immediately adds, "I do believe that the theatre, utilized in the highest and most difficult sense possible, has the power to influence the aspect and formation of things. . . ." If the theatre can create a cultural community, then the community at large will change.

Artaud's idea of culture is based on primitive ritual which he hopes to reintroduce into civilized life. Like all messianic thinkers, he is trying to bring about change through a revolution in the religious consciousness. The religions of the West, however, are unacceptable, since they have emptied life of its magical content, and killed the instinctual side of man — killed, that is to say, his divinity: "I would even say that it is this infection of the human which contaminates ideas that should have remained divine; for far from believing that man invented the supernatural and divine, I think it is man's age-old intervention which has ultimately corrupted the divine in him." Like D. H. Lawrence, whom he resembles in so many ways, Artaud is attracted by the rituals of the Aztec Indians, where the divine continues to reveal itself in sacrificial frenzy and barbaric joy. Artaud believes this archetypal, pre-logical, primitive spirit still lives in the unconscious of Western man, though deeply submerged under the dead skin of civilization. For it is linked to the sexual instinct itself: "We can say now," Artaud affirms in Lawrentian accents, "that all true freedom is dark, and infallibly identified with sexual freedom which is also dark. . . . And that is why the great Myths are dark, so that one can not imagine, save in an atmosphere of carnage, torture, and bloodshed, all the magnificent Fables which recount to the multitudes the first sexual division and the first carnage of essences that appeared in creation."

Like the Surrealists, then, Artaud would like to build a theatre of myths, "to express life in its immense, universal aspect, and from that life to extract images in which we find pleasure in discovering ourselves." These myths, however, will come neither from the Greco-Roman nor from the Christian tradition, for the traditional myths, though once vital, have now become exhausted and tame, like the civilizations from which they sprang. In the course of his exegesis, Artaud supplies us with the kind of myth he has in mind, in that provocative essay where he compares the effect of his theatre to that of a plague. For Artaud, the beauty of the plague is its destruction of repressive social forms. Order collapses, authority evaporates, anarchy prevails; and man gives vent to all the disordered impulses which lie buried in his soul.[2] It is this delirium — so similar to Rimbaud's "disordering of all the senses" — that Artaud wishes to introduce into the theatre. For like the plague, the theatre has the capacity to upset "important collectivities," to create a "social disaster," to turn an occasion into a conflagration. Artaud's theatre, in short, is designed to have the function of a Dionysian revel, a Bacchanal, a sacrificial rite — relieving the spectator of all the wildness, fierceness, and joy which civilization has made him repress. "If the essential theatre is like the plague," Artaud writes, "it is not because it is contagious, but because like the plague it is the revelation, the

---

[2] Artaud's plague analogy may have been suggested to him through the works of Edgar Allan Poe, of whom he was a great admirer. In a letter to Abel Gance (1927), in which Artaud begged the producer to let him play the leading part in a staged version of *The Fall of the House of Usher,* Artaud wrote: "I do not make many claims for myself, but I do claim to understand Edgar Poe and to be myself the same kind of person as Mr. Usher. If I do not have this person under my skin, *no one in the world has.* . . . My life is that of Usher and his evil house. *I suffer from a plague in my soul and nerves*" (my emphasis).

bringing forth, the exteriorization of latent cruelty by means of which all the perverse possibilities of the mind, whether of an individual or a people, are localized." Thus, the theatre will be able to evoke that lost world of anarchy and danger without which there is neither humor nor poetry, without which freedom is a chimera and delusion prevails. "That is why," declares Artaud, "I propose a theatre of cruelty. . . . We are not free. And the sky can still fall on our heads. And the theatre has been created to teach us that first of all."

Artaud immediately proceeds to explain that by "cruelty" he does not mean "blood." Nevertheless, his proposals have been widely misunderstood, expecially in Anglo-Saxon countries where Artaud has remained a suspect and unwelcome, if not largely unknown, figure. To cultures which prefer their sadism and masochism disguised (for example, in wars, prizefights, gangster movies, and television), the openly sado-masochistic thrust of Artaud's thought has seemed pathological and perverse. Still, Artaud's assumptions are no more unhealthy than Freud's in *Civilization and Its Discontents;* both assume that men created neurosis when they suppressed their sex and aggression to live together in society. Artaud is less stoical than Freud about the sacrifice of these basic freedoms, and less inclined to accept such substitute gratifications as civilization and art; but the Nazi experience suggests that civilization and art are no obstacles to savagery and murder, and may even have helped to turn these impulses into the forms they took in Hitler's Germany.

Artaud himself never advocates perversity, sadism, or violence in daily life. What he proposes is that the theatre serve as a harmless "outlet for repressions," in much the same manner as the analyst's couch: "I propose to bring back into the theatre this elementary magical idea, taken up by modern psychoanalysts, which consists in effecting a patient's cure by making him assume the apparent and exterior attitudes of the desired condition." The theatre of cruelty, then, will evacuate those feelings which are usually expressed in more destructive ways: "I defy that spectator," Artaud asserts, "to give himself up, once outside the theatre, to ideas of war, riot, and blatant murder." The sky is, indeed, preparing to fall on our heads. The world is rapidly moving towards suicide and destruction while continuing to mouth Christian ideals of peace and harmony. Using the theatre as a "beneficial action," Artaud wishes to cut through these lies and deceptions, "for, impelling men to see themselves as they are, it causes the mask to fall, reveals the lie, the slackness, baseness, and hypocrisy of the world. . . ." Thus, Artaud would purge the spectator of those bloody impulses he usually turns on others in the name of patriotism, religion, or love.[3]

The primary function of Artaud's theatre, then, is the exorcism of fantasies. Similar to the Great Mysteries — the Orphic and Eleusinian rites — it is based on sacrifice and revolves around crime; but in exteriorizing the spectator's desire for crime, it acts as a catharsis, and drains his violence. And this is the ultimate meaning of Artaud's plague analogy: "It appears that by means of the plague, a gigantic abscess, as much moral as social, has been collectively drained; and that like the plague, the theatre has been created to drain abscesses collectively." Artaud, in fact, uses this analogy in the same way he would use the theatre — as an image-producing agency instead of as a literal fact. His theatre is a double, because it duplicates not everyday reality but rather "another archetypal and dangerous reality." It is a kind of mirror held up to the unconscious. Elsewhere, Artaud compares his theatre to alchemy, since it arbitrates between real and fictitious worlds; elsewhere, he compares it to a mirage. But the meaning of all these analogies is that the Artaudian theatre will be an outwardly illusory world evoking an inner reality — the kind

[3] The purgative function of Artaud's theatre may become the most controversial feature of his theory, for there are many who hold that, instead of dissipating repressed feelings, a theatre of cruelty would release further violence into the body politic. This opinion is based on the assumed relationship between lurid comic books or television shows and juvenile delinquency. Few critics, however, have considered the idea that violence in the mass media may be a reflection rather than a cause of violence in daily life; and since the mass media invariably moralize cruelty while exploiting its sensationalism, such forms block up a total release of impulses. America is one of the few countries in history to have no socially approved outlets for the wilder instincts; and we are currently paying the consequences in Cold War pugnacity, political paranoia, assassinations, delinquency, and madness. Artaud's theatre has yet to be proved, either way.

of reality usually revealed in dreams. For it is in the cruel content of dreams that Artaud's theatre will find its true material: "The theatre will never find itself again — i.e., constitute a means of true illusion — except by furnishing the spectator with the truthful precipitates of his dreams, in which his taste for crime, his erotic obsessions, his savagery, his chimeras, his utopian sense of life and matter, even his cannibalism, pour out, on a level not counterfeit and illusory, but interior." [4]

Artaud has a blood kinship with Rimbaud, Freud, and Lawrence, but his foster father, indeed the father of them all, is Frederick Nietzsche, who declared in Zarathustra: "Man is the cruellest animal. At tragedies, bull-fights, and crucifixions hath he hitherto been happiest on earth; and when he invented hell, behold, that was his heaven on earth." It is the repression of this cruelty by humanitarian ideals that, according to Nietzsche, has made the world sickly and pallid; and, indeed, even the heroic savagery that Nietzsche looked for soon turned into a bureaucratic, systematic slaughter of the innocent. Like the messianic Nietzsche, the messianic Artaud is concerned with the rediscovery of man, and seeks his metaphysical remains under the rubble of two thousand years of Christianity. Both men are convinced that the soft Christian ideals have drained man's psychic energy; both seek what Artaud calls "the natural and magic equivalent of the dogmas in which we no longer believe." For Nietzsche, the solution lies in a return to the Dionysian ecstasy of the pre-Socratic Greek world. Artaud's nostalgia brings him even further back in history, to that primitive "time of evil" when man was sanguinaire et inhumain. But for each, the purpose of writing is to restore, to a world which has lost its feelings, "a passionate and convulsive sense of life."

[4] Artaud's desire to create a dream theatre illustrates his affinities with Strindberg; and, as we might expect, Artaud admired Strindberg extremely. He drew up a production plan of The Ghost Sonata, remarking, "We have lived and dreamed everything this play reveals, but we have forgotten" — and he was particularly fond of A Dream Play about which he wrote, "In it is found both the interior and exterior of a varied and quivering mind. The loftiest questions are dealt with, evoked in a form that is at once concrete and mystical. . . . The false in the middle of the true — that is the ideal definition of theatrical production."

Artaud, thus, contributes a spirit and a drive to the modern theatre; but his theory has its concrete side as well. Some of his suggestions are positive, many are negative. Taken purely as a polemical document, in fact, *The Theatre and Its Double* is one of the most eloquent attacks on the existing theatre ever penned. What incenses Artaud especially is the theatre of the Boulevard, fit only for "idiots, madmen, inverts, grammarians, grocers, antipoets, and positivists, i.e., Occidentals." For this theatre stinks unbelievably of "provisional, material man. I shall even say *carrion* man." In a state of bloated decay, it imitates a dreary reality, and in producing human interest stories with "intimate scenes from the lives of a few puppets," it turns the public into Peeping Toms.

Artaud is not much kinder to the theatre of the elite, which is to say, the theatre of Molière and Shakespeare.[5] In his essay "No More Masterpieces," he decisively repudiates all the great works of the past — not because they are artistically inadequate, but rather because they are culturally ineffective. Having lost their relevancy and immediacy, they are no longer "understood by the general public." Artaud, therefore, is contemptuous both of highbrows and middlebrows; his "general public" are the great masses at large, without whom no renewal of culture is possible. Appealing primarily to aesthetes and logicians, the existing theatre has alienated these masses, who now frequent the circus, the music hall, and the movies; and the theatre will never find itself until it becomes equally vital and popular. "The public is still greedy for mystery," he proclaims, and

[5] Artaud's letters reveal his profound distaste for the kinds of plays being produced by Jouvet, Dullin, Pitoëff, and, especially, the *Comédie Française*. To the director of the latter, Artaud wrote in 1925: "Your brothel is too greedy. Representatives of a dead art had better stop rattling their bones in our ears. . . . There's enough arrival and departure in your legalized whorehouse. We aim higher than tragedy, cornerstone of your filthy structure, and your Molière is a stupid bastard. . . . The theatre is a Land of Fire, a lagoon of Sky, battle of Dreams. Theatre is a Solemn Ceremony. You crap on a Solemn Ceremony as an Arab does at the foot of a Pyramid. Make way for the theatre, Gentlemen, make way for the theatre of those who will be satisfied only with the unlimited domain of the spirit." It is interesting that Artaud's word for the theatre of masterpieces and the theatre of the marketplace was the same as Brecht's: *culinary*.

with this faith, he demands that dead poets make way for living priests who will speak as truly to their time as Sophocles, Racine, and Shakespeare did to theirs.

Artaud goes on to make some practical suggestions as to how this mystery will be evoked. For one thing, the theatre of cruelty will make war on language, for any theatre based on words is "fixed in forms that no longer correspond to the needs of the time." With Rimbaud, Artaud might cry: *Plus de mots*. Actually, Artaud's dislike of langauge is very Pirandellian, because, like Pirandello, he conceives words to be germs, carrying the diseases of civilization — theories, concepts, definitions, indeed any formulations "which work relentlessly to reduce the unknown to the known." For in this dissipation of mystery lies "the cause of the theatre's abasement and its fearful loss of energy. . . ." Artaud's attack on language is the most radical part of his theory and — some would say — the least influential, since even the most experimental French drama continues, to this day, to be a drama of words. On the other hand, Artaud never proposes suppressing language entirely, but rather "changing its role, and especially reducing its position. . . ." He wants words to be used in a new and shocking manner:

To make metaphysics out of a spoken language is to make the language express what it does not ordinarily express; to make use of it in a new, exceptional, and unaccustomed fashion; to reveal its possibilities for producing physical shock . . . to turn against language and its basely utilitarian, one could say, alimentary sources, against its trapped-beast origins; and finally, to consider language as the form of *Incantation*.

Language, in short, will no longer be used for communicating social or psychological concepts, but rather for its emotional coloring and incantatory tone, as some of the Surrealists have used it. And it is precisely this metaphysical use of language that will distinguish Artaud's great follower, Jean Genet, in whose plays, "language as the form of *Incantation*" finds its most expressive employment.

Along with conceptual language, Artaud jettisons theatre psychology and sociology — his is "an Oriental theatre of metaphysical tendency, as opposed to the Occidental theatre of psychological tendency." This, in turn, alters the whole nature of dramatic characters, as well as the nature of the spectator's response: "Renouncing psychological man, with his well-dissected characters and feelings, and social man, submissive to laws and misshapen by religions and precepts, the Theatre of Cruelty will address itself only to total man." Such an ideal theatre Artaud discovered during a visit to Paris of a group of Balinese actors. Tremendously excited by their "vocabulary of gesture and mime" and by their plastic and physical use of the stage, Artaud himself had responded in the fullness of his being, as a total man. Artaud occasionally experienced this response in the movies also, especially in the films of the Marx Brothers, on whom he wrote a brilliant essay, praising their anarchy, their Surrealist antics, their destruction of language, and their "wholehearted revolt."

As these models suggest, Artaud's idea of theatre is primarily visual. It is a theatre in which character, plot, and diction are subordinated to *mise en scène,* or spectacle. Artaud's *Poetics* eliminates, in consequence, the conceptualizing playwright and substitutes the visualizing director — not the conventional traffic cop or actor's coach of Western theatre but rather a "manager of magic, a master of sacred ceremonies." The director's job is to create a "poetry in space" or, as he sometimes calls it, "a poetry of the senses," quite similar to Cocteau's "poetry of the theatre." As Artaud describes it, "This very difficult and complex poetry assumes many aspects: especially the aspects of all the means of expression utilizable on the stage, such as music, dance, plastic art, pantomime, mimicry, gesticulation, intonation, architecture, scenery, and lighting." In his more specific suggestions for dressing the stage, Artaud is inclined, however, to ignore stage scenery,[6] emphasizing instead properties and accessories, such as "manikins, enormous masks, objects of strange proportions" — a ritual display with an essentially hieroglyphic character.

[6] In an early essay, "The Evolution of Scenery" (1928?), Artaud indicated that he did not think the external paraphernalia of the theatre to be very important: "Stage sets, theatre must be ignored. All the great playwrights thought outside the theatre. Look at Aeschylus, Sophocles, Shakespeare."

Light will be used to evoke delirious emotions; musical instruments will be employed not only as a source of sound but also as visual objects; and the audience will always be surrounded by tumultuous action, and in direct communication with it. Thus, Artaud's "poetry of the senses" is a poetry of ecstasy, designed to induce trance, transport, and paroxysms by distilling the savagery of dreams into the mystery of theatre.

Artaud's proposals include a theatrical program made up of scenarios based on existing works, both dramatic and nondramatic, to be staged in an improvisatory manner without regard to text. Among these are the story of Bluebeard, a tale by the Marquis de Sade, Büchner's *Woyzeck,* and a number of Elizabethan plays stripped down to their bloody action (Ford's *'Tis Pity She's a Whore* exercised an especial fascination for Artaud).[7] In the theatre he founded with Roger Vitrac, in 1927, Artaud mounted the works of Strindberg and Claudel; and in his short-lived *Théâtre de la Cruauté,* founded in 1935, he staged his own adaptation of *The Cenci* — like Ford's play, a tale of incest and murder. In one of his manifestoes, Artaud outlines an original scenario called *The Conquest of Mexico,* a conflict between the armies of Montezuma and Cortez in which the raging, clashing, whirling struggle of men and beasts is described as if it were apocalypse. And elsewhere, he expresses his desire to adapt a theatre to the vision of Goya and El Greco, of Breughel and Hieronymus Bosch. Aside from these suggestions, however, and the few plays Artaud staged before and after writing his essays, he left no practical applications of his theories.[8] His theatre remained in his

[7] Artaud's admiration for the Elizabethan drama was surpassed by his admiration for the Roman dramatist who influenced the Elizabethans so profoundly — Lucius Annaeus Seneca. Artaud called Seneca "the greatest tragic author of history," adding that "One cannot find a better *written* example of what is meant by cruelty in the theatre than *all* the tragedies of Seneca, but above all *Atreus and Thyestes.*" This opinion may seem rather eccentric to us, considering Seneca's fustian diction, but Artaud obviously responded strongly to the external action of his plays, and saw in Seneca's tragedies of blood the "boiling of forces of chaos."

[8] Artaud did leave behind a short play, written in 1924 and called *The Spurt of Blood.* It is a Surrealist work of horror and phantasmagoria, originally in-

[375]

head, a vision he could transcribe only to the written page; and he died before its impact was really felt.[9]

If Artaud never achieved his theatre, then many of his successors partially did. Critics have seen his influence on almost every experimental dramatist after World War II. Artaud's desire to theatricalize "the nightmare of Flemish painting," for example, was realized by the Flemish playwright, Michel de Ghelderode in flamboyant, crowded, baroque plays, studded with Renaissance violence. This connection may be coincidental, but there are indisputable Artaudian influences (most of them mentioned by Guicharnaud) on Camus, Audiberti, Pichette, Vauthier, Ionesco, Beckett, Weingarten, and Adamov. Certainly, Ionesco's disgust with conceptual language ("Oh words," cries a character in *Jack* or *The Submission,* "what crimes are committed in your name") owes something to Artaud; and his Surrealist diction, where one word is monotonously intoned and repeated, monstrous neologisms shake the senses, logic is wrenched, and foreign tongues become interchangeable, achieves Artaud's dream of using language in a "new, exceptional, and unaccustomed fashion."[10] Furthermore, the French avant-garde continues to produce a savagely antisocial and antipsychological theatre, possibly as a result of Artaud's strictures. In Beckett's plays, society hardly exists at all, and man is in a void; in Ionesco's, personality is disintegrated and identity destroyed. The "theatre of the absurd," though not really a

---

cluded in Artaud's *The Umbilicus of Limbo.* Those who are interested can find it translated by Ruby Cohen in the Winter 1963 number of *Tulane Drama Review.*

[9] Summarizing his life, Artaud has left us his own, touching epitaph: "In one of my first theatrical roles, I played a man who appeared in the final scene of an act which was insipid, smug, lifeless, dramatic, overloaded; in two clashing tones, he said: 'Can I come in?' And then the curtain fell."

[10] For a more extended discussion of Artaud's influence on Ionesco's style, see Jean Vannier, "A Theatre of Language," *Tulane Drama Review,* Spring 1963. For a hostile view of Artaud's influence on the modern theatre, see Paul Arnold, "The Artaud Experiment," *Tulane Drama Review,* Winter 1963 ("our avant-garde has learned from Artaud only his vehemence, his scandalous aspect — flinging bile and excrement at all institutions, beliefs, ideas, feelings, without having any substitute ideas or feelings to offer us").

theatre of cruelty, does try to appeal to Artaud's "total man." Fashioning his plays in the shape of a dream, a fantasy, or a nightmare, the absurdist dramatist tries to evoke the metaphysical side of experience, with terror as his recurring motif.

This much can be ascribed to Artaud — but not to him alone. While his impact on the "theatre of the absurd" is strong, he is only one among a host of influences. As a matter of fact, Artaud's central idea of a ritual theatre of cruelty, exorcising fantasies, is not picked up by the absurdists, who never stray too far from the limits laid down by Dada and Surrealism. Though Artaud would have liked his wild humor, a playwright like Ionesco, for example, would probably have seemed to him a little too frivolous, and much too self-conscious, since Ionesco's satire on concepts is itself highly conceptualized, just as his attacks on language and logic are the work of an accomplished linguist and logician. As for the rest of the "theatre of the absurd," Artaud might well have found it too nihilistic in its implications, too special in its appeal, too entrapped in that *huis clos* created by Jarry and his followers. Even the most gifted of these dramatists, Samuel Beckett, might have seemed to him a little too wan and listless for that vital, delirious theatre he envisioned. The messianic element in Artaud's thought never infiltrates the "theatre of the absurd," which remains a ferociously avant-garde movement with an exclusively existential vision.

In Jean Genet, on the other hand, Artaud would unquestionably have seen his most promising heir. Genet has been wrongly classed with the absurdists; yet he goes well beyond the limited boundaries of the avant-garde to create an alchemical, primitive, messianic theatre, embodying many of Artaud's precepts: an Oriental theatre of metaphysical tendency, the modern equivalent of the mystery religions. Genet pulls his myths from the depths of a totally liberated unconscious where morality, inhibition, refinement, and conscience hold no sway; at the basis of his work is that dark sexual freedom which Artaud held to be the root of all great myths. Genet's sexuality, to be sure, is perverse, and his fantasies have been evacuated not only in theatrical myths but also in criminal actions. But while

Artaud might have found Genet a less than healthy manifestation of the diseased Western consciousness, he would surely have admired his capacity to transform pathology into ceremonious drama through a rich, imaginative use of the stage. Genet's plays take the form of liberated dreams, organized into rites. Through the open exaltation of crime, eroticism, and savagery, he hopes to exorcise his own, as well as the spectator's, cruelty.

Genet, the dramatist, in short, is largely created by Artaud.[11] Indeed, their extra-dramatic utterances are sometimes so similar that it is difficult to tell which man is speaking. In his "Notes on the Theatre," for example (published in 1954 as a foreword to *The Maids*), Genet writes of his distaste for the Occidental theatre in marked Artaudian accents: "What I have been told about the Japanese, Chinese, and Balinese revels and the perhaps magnified idea that persists in my brain make the formula of the Western theatre seem to me too coarse. One can only dream of an art that would be a profound web of active symbols capable of speaking to the audience a language in which nothing is said but everything is portended." This dream, which was also Artaud's, can only be effectuated by repudiating all the dramatic traditions of the West: "For even the finest Western plays have something shoddy about them, an air of masquerade and not of ceremony."

No more masterpieces might be Genet's watchword too. The Western masquerade must give way to the Oriental-type ceremony in which character — the psychological aspect of the drama — will dissolve into "remote signs." For Genet, this will not come at once; and his failure with *Les Bonnes* (*The Maids*, 1948), as he tells us,

---

[11] Many critics see the similarities between the two men, but I should mention that Roger Blin, Genet's gifted director, denies them entirely. In an interview with Bettina Knapp, Blin remarks that Genet "read little of Artaud's work," and proceeds to draw the following distinction between them: "Artaud's cruelty resembles in many ways religious cruelty as practiced by the Aztec Indians. Genet's cruelty is more classical and closer to Greek theatre. . . ." This distinction is too precise, since Artaud embraced all primitive religious rites, including the Dionysian; and Genet's theatre does not seem "Greek" to me at all. If Artaud did not exercise a direct and lasting influence on Genet, we must put this down as one of the most extraordinary coincidences in literary history.

stemmed from his inability "to contrive that the characters on the stage would only be metaphors of what they were supposed to represent." For through this use of metaphor comes the Artaudian theatre of doubles, linking the real with the fictitious worlds, disguising and revealing reality. If metaphor and ceremony are the cornerstones of the drama, then for Genet the greatest metaphors and the highest form of ceremony are to be found in the Mass: "Beneath the familiar appearances — a crust of bread — a god is devoured. I know of nothing more theatrically effective than the elevation of the host. . . ."

What the Mass possesses, besides its splendid theatricality and metaphorical magic, is the power of unifying a religious collective in a moment of affirmation and belief. It is precisely this union of spectators that Genet seeks — and cannot find in the Western theatre: "I have spoken of communion. The modern theatre is a diversion. . . . The word somewhat suggests the idea of dispersion. I know no plays that link the spectators, be it only for an hour. Quite the contrary, they isolate them further. . . ." To bring these spectators together, Genet envisions a ritual theatre, drawing not on conventional religious sources but rather on the poet's imagination: he will function, in Artaud's phrase, as "a master of sacred ceremonies." Thus, Genet inherits Artaud's radical messianism. Alienated so completely from the modern world, he will be satisfied with nothing less than a new world, constructed on his own terms. What these unusual terms will be, Genet only hints at in his foreword to *The Maids,* but it is clear enough that his own role will be crucial: "No doubt, one of the functions of art is to substitute the efficacy of beauty for religious faith. At least, this beauty should have the power of a poem, that is, of a crime. But let that go."

In his novels and plays — and especially in his autobiographical work *Journal du Voleur* (*The Thief's Journal,* 1948) — Genet does not let the issue go at all, but rather worries it over and over until beauty, poetry, and crime become the foundations of a new religious faith. Genet is one of those French writers in the rebel tradition of Sade, Lacenaire, Baudelaire, and Rimbaud who extend their dreams of revolt into the waking world, acting out their fantasies, then turning them into literature. But Genet's literary efforts (begun in jail in 1943) are devoted not only to justifying his life but also to sanctifying it. A notorious homosexual and thief, he exalts the underworld, and offers his own criminal experience as the exemplary life. "Saintliness is my goal," he declares in *The Thief's Journal* — though he admits that he is groping towards a definition of what that means: "Unable to arrive at a definition of saintliness — no more than of beauty — I want at every moment to create it . . . so that at every moment I may be guided by a will to saintliness until the time when I am so luminous that people will say, 'He is a saint,' or more likely, 'He was a saint.' "

Saintliness, then, is a condition determined as much by the outer world as by inner qualities — a kind of glory imposed on you by others. Genet is anxious to attract the attention of the world ("I aspire to your recognition," he says, "your consecration"), and it is this desire for glory which originally made him turn his life into literature: "It is what language offers me to evoke it, to talk about it, render it. To achieve legend." Legend, however, lies outside conventional morality. For Genet, it is achieved through rigorous pursuit of the absolute — extreme action, pushed past limits — and may, therefore, derive from an excess of evil as well as from an excess of good. One becomes luminous, for example, through treachery or cruelty or sordidness, as long as they are fiercely pursued. It is for this reason that Genet interprets the scriptural phrase "taking upon Himself the sins of the world" to mean that Christ experienced these sins and subscribed to evil; and for the same reason, he rebukes Saint Vincent de Paul for taking the galley slave's place in irons instead of committing the galley slave's crime.

Genet's idea of the saint, in short, is always coupled, and sometimes identified, with his idea of the criminal: "We shall be that eternal couple, Solange," says Claire in *The Maids,* "the two of us, the eternal couple of the criminal and the saint. We'll be saved, Solange, saved, I swear to you." Said and Leila, for example, form that eternal couple in Genet's most recent play, *Les Paravents* (*The Screens,* 1961) —

the ugly Leila whose extreme fidelity to her indifferent husband sancti-
fies her, and the traitorous Said, made legendary by excessive treachery. What links these two is not the content of their actions, but their
style, for Genet's idea of moral heroism is based exclusively on the
elegant manner in which an action is performed. Like Rimbaud, who
"admired the intractable convict on whom the prison doors are always
closing" because "he had more strength than a saint," Genet sings
the song of the criminal with a religious fervor, attempting to create a
mystique and a liturgy of style.

Genet's morality, then, has only one criterion of value — heroism
— and only one measure of this value — beauty. Genet is fascinated
with pomp, luxury, and vulgarity, and dredges for poetry even in the
foulest sewers of life. But although he is infatuated with evil in its most
excremental aspects, Genet doesn't simply wallow in vileness. He
tries to transform crime, vulgarity, and squalor into something elegant, lyric, and rhapsodic, a transformation he calls "rehabilitating
the ignoble." [12] For him, "the beauty of a moral act depends upon the
beauty of its expression," and "the only criterion of an act is its elegance." This is very close to aestheticism, and the aesthete in Genet
manifests itself even more vividly when he describes his own ambitions:

I want to fulfill myself in the rarest of destinies. I have only a dim notion
of what it will be. I want it to have a graceful curve, slightly bent towards
evening, but a hitherto unseen beauty, lovely because of the danger which
works away at it, overwhelms it, undermines it. Oh let me be only utter
beauty, I shall go quickly or slowly, but I shall dare what must be dared.

Oh let me be only utter beauty — the author could be Keats, demand-
ing for himself the timeless immobility of a poem; but it is this that
Genet means by legend. Much the same need animates Solange, in
The Maids, who visualizes her luminous march to the gallows as if it

---

[12] On this Genet remarked, "To achieve harmony in bad taste is the height
of elegance," and elsewhere, explaining his interest in scatalogical imagery,
"Poetry is the art of using shit and making you eat it." But, as Sartre observes,
"In order to make us eat shit, he has to show it to us, from afar, as rose jam."

were a heroic story; the Chief of Police, in *The Balcony,* who wishes to join the glorious hierarchy of the Nomenclature; Said, in *The Screens,* who becomes embalmed in the emblematic gesture of a traitor. Each discovers "a hitherto unseen beauty" — Genet, like Joyce's Stephen Dedalus, wants to embrace the beauty that has not yet come into the world. Though beauty lurk in the underworld of crime, it can create legends — "the act is beautiful if it provokes, and in our throat reveals, song." Thus, Genet's criminal heroes escape from themselves into poems, emblems, and songs; and thus, beauty, morality, and saintliness become one.

This extraordinary aesthetic is the product of an even more extraordinary life; and Jean Paul Sartre has shown the genesis of these ideas in his exhaustive study of Genet, part biography, part philosophical exegesis, part literary analysis, part psychoanalysis. In this study, appropriately called *Saint Genet: Comédien et Martyr (Saint Genet: Actor and Martyr,* 1952), Sartre recounts how Genet, born a foundling and abandoned to the Assistance Publique, turned homosexual and thief through a combination of childhood events. Genet, according to Sartre, begins as "a good little boy . . . as good as gold" who is taught "an ethic *that condemns him,* for this ethic of ownership casts him doubly into nothingness, as ragamuffin and bastard." Thus, Genet begins his criminal career, playing the games of "saintliness and pilfering," out of inverted veneration for bourgeois laws and virtues: "Our future burglar starts by learning absolute respect for property." Like the two servants in *The Maids,* Genet begins to defile the things he most reveres.

From this point on, Genet's actions are completely regulated by the world from which he is excluded. An illegitimate among the legitimate, he turns to crime in a society of laws. "Abandoned by my family," he writes in *The Thief's Journal,* "I felt it was natural to aggravate this condition by a preference for boys, and this preference by theft, and theft by crime or a complacent attitude in regard to crime. Hence I resolutely rejected a world which had rejected me." Genet, then, turns the world inside out; his life becomes a reversed mirror image of the lives of *les honnêtes hommes*. If the world is good, then Genet will be evil; if men are basically heterosexual, then he will express "a preference for boys." Genet's disposition towards crime is always accompanied by erotic feelings ("I was hot for crime"), as street urchins are aroused by mischief; and throughout his life, Genet, who always remained something of a gypsy, will be sexually stimulated by evil. But Genet's homosexuality, like that of Camus's *Caligula,* is also an extension of his revolt.[13] He lives to discover boundaries and then to exceed them. Thus, Genet needs the lawful world in order to do violence upon it, and though he detests society, he always admires its "perfect coherence," its diversity, and its fearful symmetry. To create his own order, he must reverse the established order, finding his heroic identity through immorality, vice, exile, and total opposition to whatever exists.

Genet is soon to learn that he cannot reach the nothingness he seeks. Nevertheless, he plans a brutal break with "your world" (as he frequently calls respectable society), casting off all civilized restraints and immersing himself in the destructive element: "It is by a long, long road that I choose to go back to primitive life. What I need first is condemnation by my race." Before Genet, Rimbaud had mused: "Misfortune was my God. I laid myself down in the mud. I dried myself in the air of crime." Genet begins to dry himself in the same air, worshiping misfortune, pursuing heroic singularity, following the life of the outlaw. After spending his youth in reformatories, he joins the Foreign Legion, deserts, and wanders through Europe as a thief, derelict, and prostitute. Everywhere, he is met with disappointment. The life of the thief, for example, had seemed to him unique, but he is depressed to discover how common it actually is (his homosexuality is equally common). And in Nazi Germany, he is confronted with "a

---

[13] Sartre explains Genet's homosexuality differently: "Genet, who was born without parents, is preparing to die without descendants. His sexuality will be sterility and abstract tension." This analysis seems to me too cerebral, as does so much of Sartre's book. Trying to prove that man is totally free, Sartre makes out each one of Genet's characteristics to be a self-conscious, philosophical choice.

race of thieves," where evil is institutionalized, and Police and Crime are one. His revolt becomes a travesty: "The outrageous is impossible. I'm stealing in the void."

Genet, in consequence, returns to his home country, thinking "only my love of the French language attaches me to France," but discovering he is also attracted by its coherent laws and regulations. These, he determines to break, along with the bonds of brotherhood and love, always seeking new, more shocking violations of the moral code. He becomes interested in espionage, because it allows him to pollute "through treason, an institution which regards loyalty — or loyalism — as its essential quality." But even espionage can be a positive act, since the spy acts for a nation. Seeking the wholly negative, he decides to inform on his own kind instead, thus betraying evil with evil, for the criminal informer is a man truly alone. Genet desires utter solitude and utter nothingness. But the ultimate break with the outside world is possible only in fantasy: "Murder is not the most effective means of reaching the subterranean world of vileness. . . . Other crimes are more degrading: theft, begging, treason, breach of trust, etc.: These are the ones I chose to commit, though I was always haunted by the idea of a murder which would cut me off irremediably from your world." Though he never commits a murder, Genet, by 1948, has been convicted ten times of theft, and is reprieved from life imprisonment only through a petition of French intellectuals and artists. He had tried to merit the world's contempt by plunging into vileness, but he could not break with the world entirely; and his growing literary reputation was to bring him glory of a quite different kind.

Though he cannot achieve this for himself, then, Genet's ideal is *l'impossible nullité* (the Impossible Nothingness) which rests in the negativity of pure evil. If good is an illusion, then evil is reality — absolute freedom from moral, canon, and statute law. Reality and nothingness, however, remain beyond the reach of man, since most forms of evil are only the reverse of good. Unable to achieve the nonbeing he seeks, Genet determines to achieve the alternatives: legend, martyrdom, and sanctity, which are links with the world of men. "Genet not only wants to will Evil," writes Sartre, "he wants to be the martyr of the impossibility of willing it. . . . When Evil seemed possible, Genet did Evil in order to be wicked; now that Evil is shown to be impossible, Genet does Evil in order to be a saint." *Pecca fortiter* was the injunction of Luther, and Genet, detesting middle ways in good or evil, summons up the great sinner who defies the heavens and steals the crimes of the gods: "If you can't find any more crimes," screams Kadidja in *The Screens,* "steal crimes from heaven, it's bursting with them! Wangle the murders of the gods, their rapes, their fires, their incests, their lies, their butcheries. . . ."

Genet himself occasionally identifies with Lucifer, and struts with Satanic pride: "If pride is the boldest freedom — " he writes in his autobiography, "Lucifer crossing swords with God — if pride is the wondrous cloak wherein my guilt, of which it is woven, stands erect, I want to be guilty." Genet's pride, however, is always derived from his guilt ("My pride," he writes, "has been colored with the purple of my shame"), and, therefore, needs the order which produces it. Like his morality, Genet's theology is inverted, and he cannot do without the idea of God: "It would seem logical to pray to the devil," he remarks in *The Thief's Journal,* "but no thief would dare do so seriously. To come to terms with him would be to commit oneself too deeply. He is too opposed to God, Who, we know, is the final victor." [14] Only the murderer comes close to breaking with God and achieving reality; but although he admires the murderer, Genet cannot follow him to this ultimate destiny. Accepting God, Genet enters God's kingdom backwards, breaking universal laws that he believes in, and thereby toughening the fibers of his integrity. "Will anyone be surprised," he asks, "when I claim that crime can help me insure my moral vigor?" [15] Stealing as an act of moral adventure, seeking misfortune as a sign of grace, Genet plays a game which he knows full well is lost in ad-

[14] Sartre writes: "He might have been able, like certain demoniacs — and like Baudelaire and Lautréamont — to put himself under the protection of Satan. But he is too involved in his situation to fall into Manicheism. The wicked man is not a Manichee: Manicheism defines the thought of the respectable man."

[15] Cocteau, one of those most instrumental in securing Genet's release from prison, wrote: "Sooner or later it will have to be recognized that he is a moralist."

vance. But then he wishes to lose. Only through earning his punishment can he find his identity and merit the martyrdom he seeks.

Genet's desire for martyrdom, as Sartre has shown, has homosexual-masochistic overtones: the world which punishes him is the Male by whom he wishes to be raped and killed. His admiration for murderers ("I want to sing murder, for I love murderers") stems from the same pathological desire: for if Genet sometimes dreams of committing murder, he more often dreams of being the murderer's victim. Genet admires murderers for the same qualities he admires in policemen — for their cruelty, courage, indifference, and virility. But this admiration is not wholly sexual. For Genet, the murderer is not only an aesthetic hero, but also a moral one — not only a beautiful brute, but also a "joyous moral suicide," a true victim of misfortune. Like Lefranc in *Haute Surveillance* (*Deathwatch*, 1949), Genet desires misfortune for himself, but he has learned, as Lefranc must learn, that misfortune cannot be willed. Hoping to join the mystical fraternity of the murderer, Green Eyes, Lefranc kills the young Maurice, but Green Eyes says he "didn't want what happened to me to happen. It was all given to me. A gift from God or the devil, but something I didn't want." Genet awaits the same unwanted gift.

Green Eyes, being illiterate and instinctual, is close to reality and non-being; Lefranc, being conscious and literate, enacts a masquerade. Genet's personal dilemma is similar to Lefranc's. Although he wishes to enter primitive life, he is too self-conscious to refrain from playacting; and his role is determined by the civilized world he is trying to escape. Thus, outrageous as Genet's revolt may seem, it still demands the existence of a traditional social, moral and religious framework. As Sartre puts it, somewhat too strongly: "Rimbaud wanted to change life, and Marx society: Genet doesn't want to change anything. Don't count on him to criticize institutions; he needs them as Prometheus needs his vulture. . . ." Actually, Genet wants to change *everything,* and every word he writes is an implicit criticism of institutions. But he is also aware that even his desire for total change is conditioned by the established order. For Genet to rebel, the Church, the Army, and the Magistracy must remain inviolate. For Genet to commit sacrilege, there must be belief.

Genet, therefore, is compounded of paradoxes and inner conflicts. Seeking nothingness, he is pressed into a quest for legend. Loving anarchy and freedom, he also finds he worships organization and order. Devoted to reality, he cannot escape from illusion. Frustrating in life, such contradictions, however, are the very stuff of drama — and especially of the theatre of revolt, where the conflicts between reality and illusion, being and nonbeing, anarchy and order, have provided the subject matter, and determined the forms, of a large number of superb plays. Like the other rebel dramatists, Genet puts his personal conflicts at the service of his drama, with revolt as the theme, and order as the principle, of his art.[16] And indeed art proves to be his deliverance, for only by creating a world of the imagination can Genet transcend the conflicts of his life.

What also attracts Genet to the theatre, as Sartre informs us, is "the element of fake, of sham, of artificiality" — for him, it is the place of ceremonious masquerade. Genet is frank enough about his love of deception. "What's going to follow," he interjects at one point in *Notre-Dame des Fleurs* (*Our Lady of the Flowers*, 1942) "is false, and you are not to accept it as gospel truth. Truth is not my strong point. But 'one must lie in order to be true.' And even go beyond." External truth is certainly not his strong point. And although he is preoccupied with much the same subjects as the realists and naturalists (crime, murder, prostitution, squalor, etc.), he lacks their interest in the tangible world: "He hates Matter," observes Sartre. "Matter is unintelligible; the insurmountable outrage, it bodies forth the reality of his exile." Scorning external truth and physical reality, Genet, therefore, creates a drama of appearances through which a deeper reality is

---

[16] Genet's ambiguous attitude towards order is expressed in the very shape of his plays. The content is anarchy and freedom; the form is coherence and organization. "Beauty," says Genet, "is the perfection of organization." Genet takes his revenge on the "good" social order by creating his own aesthetic order of "evil."

evoked — an art of being and seeming built around the illusion-making faculty of man.

This sounds Pirandellian, and, indeed, after Artaud, Pirandello is the strongest influence on Genet's theatre. Genet himself, in fact, is what Pirandello would have called a *costruzione*. Like that character in *Our Lady of the Flowers*, who, when asked why he stole, replied, "Because the others thought I was a thief," Genet had built himself up in an image provided by others: *J'ai décidé d'être ce que la crime a fait de moi* ("I decided to be what crime has made of me"). And so it is with his dramatic characters, most of whom play the roles imposed on them by others. Imprisoned in definitions, caught in a reflected mirror-image, they take their parts in an infinite comedy of illusion, chafing against these restrictions at the same time that they submit to them. Thus, Claire, in *The Maids*, hates her sister, Solange, because she is the reflected image of her own servility ("And me, I'm sick of seeing my image thrown back at me by a mirror, like a bad smell"), just as she imagines Madame detesting them both for reflecting her ("You're our distorting mirror, our loathsome vent, our shame, our dregs!").

Genet, therefore, is tortured by illusion, and wishes to annihilate the world which pressed the mask of thief so firmly on his features. He wants to be a man without a mask — in Pirandello's term, a *nobody* — and plunge through appearances into reality, which is the negation of roles. But reality is also *l'impossible nullité;* the nobody invariably finds himself becoming somebody, and acting out a role. Genet idealizes the purity which lies beneath appearances, but it always somehow eludes him: "His initial desire is realistic," writes Sartre. "He wants what exists. But the very object of his desire soon changes into a dream. Genet without ceasing to desire the real embarks into the imaginary." Unlike Pirandello, however, Genet is charmed by impersonation ("I love imposture") and finds the possibilities of heroism in illusion. For if it is impossible to cease from playacting, then the only alternative is to play one's role to its very limits. "If he has courage — please understand," Genet writes, "the guilty man decides to be what crime has made him. Finding a justification is easy; otherwise how would he live? He draws it from his pride." Caught in the act of stealing, and driven by pride and shame, Genet determined to be an ideal thief, pursuing absolute evil. In the same way, Claire and Solange follow their playacting to the point of suicide and martyrdom, and the Negroes in *The Blacks* "persist to the point of madness in what they're condemned to be." The condemnation provides the definition; the condemned provide the moral acts. "We are what they want us to be," observes a character in *The Blacks*. "We shall therefore be it to the very end, absurdly." For in this extreme of role-playing lies Genet's definition of the hero, "the beholding of our own ideal image in an ideal mirror which shows us eternally resplendent."

Genet, in short, conceives of life as a perpetual masquerade, and *les honnêtes hommes,* without knowing it, are playing a game of appearances: "You must go home now," says Madame Irma, dismissing the audience at the end of *The Balcony,* "where everything — you can be quite sure — will be even falser than here. . . ." All of life is a game, and the origin of the masquerade is in Creation itself: "For Genet," writes Sartre, "the origin of the world is in play, and society is organized when the rules of the game are fixed." A nation, therefore, is an entity which has "perpetuated an image" over centuries. The established order consists of roles in a national drama. And "the rules of the game" are a nation's laws and regulations. To break these laws, however, is only to engage in another kind of game, with another set of rules (the "code of the underworld," which Genet finds absurd). Genet's criminals are role-players too, and he is attracted to convicts because they are so much like children in their love of masquerade. Everyone plays his part, policeman and murderer, functionary and rebel, saint and sinner. "My characters are all masks," write Genet. "How do you expect me to tell you whether they are true or false?"

Thus, as Sartre puts it, "In Genet's plays, every character must play the role of a character who plays a role." And thus, the Negroes, in *The Blacks,* are "like guilty persons who play at being guilty," and the customers, in *The Balcony,* impersonate the Great Figures of a nation in a brothel. If this imposture is heroic enough, then the gates of legend are broken, because if all of life is histrionic, then the greatest men are only the greatest actors. And the greatest playwright will be he who reveals and celebrates the imposture of the masquerade. Although Genet continues to feel anguished over his inability to attain reality, he makes marvelous use of his imprisonment in illusion. Like a joyous prestidigitator, he transforms the game of life into a ritual celebration, turning his masked figures into saints, martyrs, and heroes, reflecting back a criminal beauty. "Let the profiles reflect profiles back and forth," says the Lieutenant to his forces in *The Screens,* "and let the image you offer the rebels be of such beauty that the image they have of themselves cannot resist." It is much the same profile that Genet offers the spectator, hoping to make himself irresistible through the image of his art.

Genet creates a drama of transformation — the metamorphosis of one object into another. Nothing is what it seems; everything is in the process of becoming something else. As we have seen, his model for this is the Mass ("Beneath the familiar appearances — a crust of bread — a god is devoured"), which is a ritual based on metaphorical conversions. If the Mass is dedicated to sacred good, however, Genet's ritual is dedicated to sacred evil. His drama, as Sartre has observed, is a kind of Black Mass through which the playwright invokes, not God, but himself. Artaud proposed a theatre of sacrifice and exorcism, and Genet responds. But as Artaud also proposed, Genet transforms these ritual crimes into their magic equivalents. Just as the eating of the Host invokes a primitive act of cannibalism, so the constituent elements of Genet's drama — murder, rape, cannibalism, slaughter, cruelty, suicide, savagery, and eroticism — are transformed into ceremonious acts and hieratic gestures. "Genet cheerfully plays on two levels," writes Sartre. "The greatest crime in the first system will be the most beautiful gesture in the second; the abominable act of the murderer is at the same time the tragic gesture of the sacrificer."

Out of these gestures comes the Artaudian exorcism. Genet purges himself of crime, and purges the spectator too. "By infecting us with his evil," writes Sartre, "Genet delivers us from it. Each of his books is a crisis of cathartic possession, a psychodrama. . . . Ten years of his literature are worth a psychoanalytic cure." It was this "magical idea" that Artaud, too, proposed to borrow from psychiatry: to exorcise the spectator's fantasies by exteriorizing the "truthful precipitates of his dreams." On the other hand, not everyone agrees that Genet's fantasies have this universal quality, and critics have found his exotic dream world, in which everything is possible, too personal to be meaningful. Jacques Guicharnaud, for example, has complained that the universe of his plays is "Jean Genet's private Hollywood," adding that "the spectator's consciousness of a universe in which he does not participate outweighs the communion. Although relatively free in his use of subject matter, Genet is more imprisoned within himself than any of the contemporary playwrights." It is certainly true that Genet's fantasies have been colored by his sado-masochistic imagination; and even his most enthusiastic partisans have been bothered by the homosexual perfume which occasionally hangs over his plays. I cannot agree, on the other hand, that Genet's world is rare or inaccessible. After his early novels, and after *The Maids* and *Deathwatch,* which take place within relatively enclosed scenes, Genet's dreams have become progressively more open until in *The Balcony, The Blacks,* and *The Screens,* he has enlarged his vision to include world politics, racial struggles, history, and religion.

And done so with tremendous verbal and theatrical skill. Genet's love of appearances leads him into dazzling stage effects. Sharing Artaud's taste for theatrical spectacle, Genet prepares a rich visual feast with the aid of settings, properties, and accessories. In *The Screens,* for example, he juxtaposes real objects with objects drawn in *trompe-l'oeil* on mammoth screens, at one point suggesting a giant conflagration through stylized flames painted before the eyes of the audience. And Genet's use, in all his full-length plays, of dummies, masks, tragic boots, and padded costumes realizes Artaud's vision of a theatre equipped with "manikins, enormous masks, objects of strange proportions." Genet, similarly, uses dance, mime, and gesticulation, particularly in *The Blacks,* creating that Artaudian "poetry in space" through "all the means of expression utilizable on the stage."

Genet transforms through verbal poetry as well. It is through language, in fact, that he achieved his own transformation. "My victory is verbal," he writes, "and I owe it to the sumptuousness of the terms." Having ordered his chaotic life by means of language, Genet uses it to order his plays as well. And because it transformed him from a criminal into an artist, language, for Genet, always remains an agency of metamorphosis. Again, this metamorphosis is derived from Christian ritual. For if bread and wine are the magical equivalents of flesh and blood, then words are the magical equivalents of things and can be made to have the same symbolic power. For Genet, the justification of art is "the task of images, that is, of correspondences with the splendors of the physical world." These correspondences, however, are not fixed. Accepting the artificiality of words, Genet wrenches their meanings, somewhat in the manner of the Surrealists. Words lose their function as descriptive symbols and become more like ciphers and heraldic signs, transformed into whatever Genet wants them to mean. "Anything can become a woman," observes Sartre in discussing *The Maids,* "a flower, an animal, an inkwell."

From the dislocation of the thing and its verbal symbol comes Genet's rich, baroque style — often obscure, often the source of stunning effects.[17] For if words can mean anything, then objects, too, can be willfully transformed. In *Deathwatch,* for example, Green Eyes describes the shapes he tried to assume to avoid being a murderer: "Tried to be a dog, a cat, a house, a tiger, a table, a stone! I even tried, me too, to be a rose." In his later plays, Genet actually attempts this varying of shapes on the stage. The Missionary, in *The Blacks,* literally turns into a cow; and Leila and the Mother, in *The Screens,* share a moment as barking dogs. Sartre relates how Genet confided to him that he hated *roses,* but loved the word *rose;* for Genet, therefore, the word is no longer connected to the object. Similarly, in *The Thief's Journal,* Genet tells us "there is a close relationship between flowers

17 Not to be overlooked, either, is Genet's stunning use of French argot, which he partially derives from Céline, partially from his own experience among criminals. About argot, Sartre writes: "To talk argot is to choose Evil, that is, to know being and truth but to reject them in favor of a nontruth which offers itself for what it is. . . . For that very reason argot is, in spite of itself, a poetic language."

and convicts. The fragility and delicacy of the former are of the same nature as the brutal insensitivity of the latter." By the same token, there is a close relationship between steel and spiderwebs — and between all the objects in the animate world. "For Genet," writes Sartre, "poetry reveals nothing." And yet, Genet's rhetoric of transformation is crucial to his art. Through such verbal effects, he creates what Artaud called "a metaphysics of spoken language," considering it, in Artaudian fashion, as "the form of *Incantation.*"

In Genet, then, two strains of the modern theatre converge — the primitive and the self-conscious. In the manner of Artaud, Genet forges a theatre of cruelty, fashioning rites of sacrifice and exorcism designed to bring about that cathartic possession in which the spectator's taste for crime is purged. On the other hand, these primitive rites have been organized by a highly sophisticated mind which provides them with a meaning beyond their surface hieroglyphics. For Genet is not only an instinctual rebel, pouring out criminal fantasies, but also a rebel philosopher, reflecting on rebellion and crime. He not only dreams, like Artaud, but also, like Pirandello, analyzes his dreams.

It is this self-conscious analysis that makes Genet so complicated and ambiguous. His myths invariably revolve around revolt, and reveal the author's anarchistic desire for total liberation. But the rebellion which proceeds throughout his plays is almost always ineffective. Genet wishes to annihilate the established order; at the same time, he knows that order is ineradicable and absolute rebellion impossible. Just as he learned that his own way of life was only a reversed mirror image of existing laws and conventions, so he knows that all rebellions are doomed to take on, if only negatively, the characteristics of the old order. It is for this reason that the established regime, in Genet, usually takes the credit for the revolution: "At least say to them," observes the White Queen in *The Blacks,* "that without us their revolt would be meaningless — and wouldn't even exist," while the Colonials observe of the Arabs in *The Screens,* "What *can* be said with a certain amount of justice is that we were a pretext for their revolting. If not for us . . . they'd have gone under." For it is a tragic fact, in Genet, that even if a rebellion succeeds in the short run, it always fails in the long run; rebellion and order are merely two roles in the same masquerade.

Thus, while Genet always sympathizes with his rebel characters (maids, murderers, anarchists, Negroes, and Arabs), he knows, too, that they are doomed to futility by a love of playacting; their reality is swallowed up by illusion; their sacred negativity ultimately gives way to the positive need for emblems, banners, and heroes. Genet's work, therefore, is not accurately described, as some have described it, as a drama of "social protest." It is a denial, and at the same time an affirmation, of the fundamental conditions of life.[18] Stripping away the lies, deceptions, and impostures of the respectable world, Genet concludes that these are, nevertheless, essential to existence. The Impossible Nothingness remains his ideal, but an ideal never to be realized except in the imagination. Genet thus imposes Pirandellian concepts on Artaudian chimeras. He both rebels and criticizes revolt; and since he loves beauty, he poses his dialectic with elegance, power, and style.

Genet has written two masterpieces of revolt — *Le Balcon* (*The Balcony*, 1956) and *Les Nègres* (*The Blacks*, 1958). *Les Paravents* (*The Screens*, 1961), though theatrically spectacular, is too diffuse to be effective, and adds nothing especially new to the other two plays. Both *The Balcony* and *The Blacks* are interpretations of rebellion, the latter concentrating on the rebels, the former on the established order against which the revolt takes place. Of the two, *The Balcony* is a more coherent work of art, for this probing philosophical drama embodies Genet's most impressive theatricalization of the sham and artificiality on which he finds life to be based. It is, besides, one of the richest and most complex works in the modern theatre, and despite occasional borrowings, one of the most original. Dazzling in its twists and turns of thought, *The Balcony* begins as a piece of theatrical pornography, then enlarges into a theatricalized view of society, and

[18] "The radical criticism which Genet levels against society," remarks the French critic Marc Pierret, "is strictly apolitical, but profoundly disturbing and subversive. It strips bare the foundations of existence."

concludes as a conception of history and religion by a subversive and audacious mind.

The opening scenes of the play seem like an actualization of one of Artaud's scenarios, because — in their unification of power, cruelty, and sex — they owe a good deal to the writings of the Marquis de Sade. The play opens on a sacristy, adorned with a Spanish crucifix. There, a Bishop, in miter and gilded cope, is confessing a half-naked penitent. This Bishop, we are to learn, is an impostor, and the penitent is a whore, confessing make-believe sins. The whole setting, in fact, is sham. The sacristy is merely one studio in a brothel called the Grand Balcony, run by Madame Irma, who presides over the erotic revels and supplies the costumes, props, and supernumeraries, while the customers provide the scenarios.

The "Bishop," then, is not a cleric but a gas man, dressed in an exaggerated version of episcopal garb, with *cothurni* to give him height and padded shoulders to give him authority. And the ritual he conducts with the penitent is merely an elaborate prelude to sexual intercourse. He has chosen a sacred function in order to commit sacrilege against it, defiling the Church through its official costume. "And in order to destroy all function," he says, "I want to cause a scandal and feel you up, you slut, you bitch, you trollop, you tramp. . . ." His sacrilege, however, remains a fantasy; his revolt against function is without real effect. In this house of illusion, there is always something fake amidst the authentic details, and reality never breaks through. "Reality frightens you, doesn't it," says the penitent, to which the Bishop replies, "If your sins were real, they'd be crimes, and I'd be in a fine mess." The atmosphere of evil is titillating as long as it is not wholly genuine. The appearance of crime and sacrilege must never become a reality.

It is much the same for the other customers, who include an Attorney General, judging, condemning, and licking the foot of a fleshly thief; a General, taken on a tour of his battlefield by a pulchritudinous horse; a lice-ridden tramp being whipped by a girl in leather boots; and a leper who is cured by the Virgin Mary. As always in French erotic literature, sex in *The Balcony* is accompanied by some artificial stimulation of a sado-masochistic nature, and also by the desecration of some sacred office. But Genet gives these scenes the distance of ritual (they should be presented, he stipulates, "with the solemnity of a Mass in a most beautiful cathedral"), and they are always a form of fantasy. The brothel is a reflection of the outside world, but the two worlds are kept distinct. "In real life," says Madame Irma, the sacred costumes of the official figures are "the props of a display that they have to drag in the mud of the real and commonplace. Here, Comedy and Appearance remain pure, and the revels intact." Thus, her customers can playact to the limits of their sexual imaginations; and even Christ can be imitated, and defiled, with all his "paraphernalia."

These pornographic scenes, however, are only a prologue to the play proper. Genet soon proceeds beyond the titillations of the erotic masquerade to its philosophical implications. Upon the entrance of the Chief of Police — Irma's failing lover, and Hero of the Republic — we learn that the Grand Balcony is an ally of the established regime, and that the blasphemous revels are not only tolerated by this regime but absolutely essential to its survival. For at the same time that the sacred offices are being desecrated in the brothel, *they are also being preserved there.* To imitate a function, even by defiling it, is to assume its power and accept its authority. Genet, who played a criminal role written by society, remembers the inverted veneration for society which his criminal acts implied. Blasphemy hinges on belief; sacrilege keeps the system in power.

The real threat to the system, in fact, comes not from this whorehouse imposture but rather from a rebellion which is raging in the streets of the city. For the rebellion is dedicated to destroying the whole artifice of government, clergy, magistracy, and army, the masquerades through which the system perseveres. This is the purpose, at any rate, of one of the rebel leaders — the proletarian Roger — who wants the rebellion to adhere to a chaste Puritan ideal and put an end to role-playing. Genet has already discovered this to be *l'impossible nullité,* and he articulates his discovery through the mouth of the Chief of Police: "The rebellion itself is a game. From here you can't see anything of the outside, but every rebel is playing a game. And he loves his game." For the Chief of Police, however, the danger is that the rebels will be carried away by their game, and leap, without realizing it, "into reality."

The leap into reality is Roger's goal, for he knows that if the rebellion does not begin by "despising make-believe," it will soon come to resemble the other side: "Instead of changing the world, all we achieve is a reflection of the one we destroy." To change the world in deed, he wants everything aimed at utility. Skirmishes must be fought without gestures, elegance, or charm. Sexuality is forbidden, along with anger, frenzy, or excitement. Reason must prevail, for only through the cold exercise of the rational faculty can sham and duplicity be expunged from the world. For the same purpose, he orders that when the Great Figures are captured, their costumes are to be ripped off, and neither their names nor their functions are ever to be mentioned again: "If the heavens are studded with such constellations as that of the Archbishop and Hero, then we've got to tear heaven down." Roger desires absolute revolt and total nothingness — the end of compromise, the annihilation of illusion, the conclusion of the masquerade.

But Roger is an impossibilist. Even as he is formulating his ideals, the rebellion is getting out of hand and turning into a carnival. The men are fighting with a sexual pleasure ("one hand on the trigger, the other on the fly"), killing for the fun of it, instead of rationally, earnestly, gravely. As another rebel leader tells Roger: "You're dreaming. Dreaming of an impossible revolution that's carried out reasonably and cold-bloodedly. You're fascinated by it, the way those in the other camp are by other games. But you've got to realize that the most reasonable man always manages, when he pulls the trigger, to become a dispenser of justice." Absolute revolt, then, is a dream, and even Roger is becoming a kind of functionary — a Justicer — engaged, against his will, in playing a game.

The rebellion is entirely doomed when the rebels begin to demand emblems, heroes, and banners. Looking for a legendary figure to worship, they fix on Chantal, whom Roger rescued from the brothel;

she will become the female saint of the revolution, "the glorified whore who sings an anthem and is virginified." Excited by an historical role which only a few women have been permitted to play, Chantal agrees to embody the revolution, becoming "an emblem forever escaping from her womanliness." In the brothel, she had learned "the art of shamming and acting." Now she applies this art to a higher role, while Roger, who wants her to nurse the wounded, begins to realize she has merely reentered the whorehouse ("She's flying into the other camp!"). There is no escape from the masquerade. The revolution is, indeed, reflecting the world it had wanted to destroy.

Genet has modeled this revolt on the French revolution, which also began by despising artifice before developing its own ceremonies; and the Puritan Roger, with his love of Reason and Virtue, is obviously patterned on Robespierre. Genet, however, generalizes his drama to include most of the revolutions of modern history. The impulse to change is subverted by the need to play a role; rebels adjust themselves to limits already defined; and the revolutionary leaders become enshrined as new kings, their chaste and simple dress serving as another kind of costume. Thus, Robespierre introduces a terror far worse than the atrocities of the *ancien régime;* Stalin creates a bureaucracy to rival the feudal hierarchy of the Romanoffs; Castro assumes many of the repressive characteristics of his archenemy, Batista. All progress is a dream, because reality is unattainable. For if real time moves forward, illusory time moves in circles. And men are doomed to an eternal repetition by their love of masquerade.

The scene in the rebel camp is the most "realistic" in the play; but it is also the scene in which "reality" is defeated. From this point on, the dream quality of *The Balcony* intensifies, and its outer logic dissolves. The actual fate of the rebellion, for example, becomes highly ambiguous. It is historically successful, philosophically a failure. The rebels have achieved their immediate goals insofar as the Queen, the Judge, the Bishop, and the General have been killed. But having failed to destroy the ideas these figures represent, or their own love of playacting, they have lost the game. A Queen can die, but the idea of

Queen has not been killed; and the hieratic sanctions of two thousand years of Christianity have kept the Church, the Army, and the Magistracy very much alive. Thus, when the Court Envoy comes to the Grand Balcony to say that the Queen is dead, he can speak only inferentially, through a series of obscure metaphors. The Queen is embroidering a handkerchief which will never be completed. She is engrossed in an infinite meditation. "She makes herself unfindable and thus attains a threatened invisibility." One Queen is threatening invisibility; another must become visible. And so the Envoy suggests that Madame Irma play this role, and that the other brothel impostors assume the parts of Bishop, Judge, and General.

The impersonation of a Queen by an actress is a device used by Yeats in *The Player Queen* and by Ugo Betti in *The Queen and the Rebels*. But in *The Balcony,* Genet transforms this borrowed device into a mocking commentary on the whole nature of function. To him, men not only impersonate the Great Figures in the brothel of their imaginations; the Great Figures are themselves impersonators. Whatever intrinsic qualifications they may possess are immaterial; their function is defined by clothes and gestures, and by an ability to create reverence in the common people. As for the masses, they recognize only outsides and ornaments. And so, when they wear the proper ornamental costumes and make the proper gestures, the four impostors are able to pass before the crowd for the real thing ("No one could have recognized us. We were in the gold and glitter. They were blinded"). Thus, the rebellion is quashed, and Chantal is killed. And thus, Genet attempts to show that all the sacred offices are the manufacture of sham. The artifice of the outside world is identical with that of the brothel. If the whorehouse is a mirror of society, then society, in turn, reflects the whorehouse.

Genet, however, goes beyond even this mordant conclusion. Through the character of the Chief of Police, he delivers a scorching attack on the very structure of the heavens. Unlike Roger, the Chief of Police thrives on make-believe; through artifice, he hopes to attain to immortality. He has already been hailed as a Hero of the Republic, with a gigantic mausoleum being constructed in his honor.[19] But his ambitions are large, and, before long, he is demanding to become a part of the Nomenclature, with greater authority even than the Bishop, Judge, and General. Like Cocteau's Oedipe, the Chief of Police longs for *le gloire classique;* like Genet himself, "He insists on breaking open the gates of legend." His legendary function, however, has yet to be invented. As Madame Irma sympathetically remarks: "In his effort to win renown, he has chosen a more difficult path than ours." For if the Government, Church, Army, and Magistracy are functions of an established order, and draw their sanctions from tradition, the function conceived by the Chief of Police has no precedent in Christian history.

The Chief of Police will know he has achieved legend when he is impersonated in the brothel; for simulation, as we have seen, is the proof of sacredness. In order to develop legendary dimensions, the Chief of Police casts about for a suitable emblem — one adviser suggests that he appear as a bloody executioner, another as a gigantic phallus. Despite these graphic emblems of sex and power, however, glory continues to give him "the cold shoulder." His studio remains vacant and his image relatively small. Irma advises him to keep on killing — perhaps excessive cruelty will make him luminous, as it brought an evil fame to Hitler and Stalin. But the Chief of Police aspires to be much more than a secular dictator. He wants authority not only over the Nomenclature, but even over God: "Well, gentlemen," he says to the Great Figures, "above God are you, without whom God is nothing. And above you shall be I, without whom. . . ." The exhausted functions of the Nomenclature will receive new strength from the Chief of Police. For he will be both secular and divine, "both legendary and human," having created a function that will haunt men's minds.

The Chief of Police, in short, longs to be supreme. And the su-

[19] In his article *"The Balcony* and Parisian Existentialism" (*Tulane Drama Review,* Spring 1963), Benjamin Nelson suggests that Genet got his idea for the Chief's mausoleum from Franco's tomb in the Valley of the Fallen. Mr. Nelson also points out a number of other striking historical parallels in the play.

premacy he imagines for himself, I think, is that of a god — the Man-God, whose life sets a pattern for the multitudes: "I shall not be the hundred-thousandth-reflection-within-a-reflection in a mirror, but the One and Only, into whom a hundred thousand want to merge." In Genet's scheme, even God is an impersonator, with a part in the masquerade. When it is finally announced that he is about to be impersonated, the Chief of Police realizes he has achieved his goal: "Gentlemen, I belong to the Nomenclature." The proof comes in the person of Roger. Mourning the revolution, convinced finally that reality was inaccessible and "no truth was possible," Roger has determined to become an actor in the comedy of illusion, and the chief actor, too: "If the brothel exists and I've a right to go there, then I've a right to lead the character I've chosen to the very limit of his destiny . . . no, of mine . . . of merging his destiny with mine." In the Mausoleum studio, where he has come dressed in a padded replica of the Chief of Police's clothes, Roger proceeds to act out his supreme role: "Everything proclaims me! Everything breathes me and everything worships me! My history was lived so that a glorious page might be written and then read." And he climaxes the impersonation by castrating himself, thus proving the divinity of the Chief of Police — for mutilation is the destiny of the Man-God, whether he be Christ, Osiris, or Dionysus.

Irma screeches about the mess on her rugs, but the Chief of Police, after some momentary terror, accepts the implications of his Godhead: "Though my image be castrated in every brothel in the world, I remain intact." Like his divine predecessors, he has been mutilated and remained whole; like them, he has been imitated, and will continue to be imitated. He achieves his apotheosis, ordering food for the next two thousand years, and descends into his tomb, as the sound of machine guns signifies that a new rebellion is beginning outside. The acts of men continue in their cyclical way, but the Chief of Police has been immobilized in legend. The God of love has been replaced by the God of sex and violence, that rough beast Yeats saw slouching towards Bethlehem to be born; and this God, too, will reign for two thousand years. Irma turns out the lights and sends the audience away. But in the course of this sacrilegious masquerade, religion, revolution, and the cycles of civilization have been redefined as purely erotic phenomena, while the Grand Balcony has become society, the universe, and the entire stage of history as conceived by a cunning and diabolical mind.

In his next play, *The Blacks,* Genet again invokes a theatre of cruelty in a messianic play revolving around revolt. But here the philosophical note is more subdued, and a primitive, ritualistic quality is more accentuated. In *The Balcony,* Genet was occupied with interpreting the past of the West; in *The Blacks,* he is more concerned with predicting its future — and that future is annihilation. *The Blacks,* like Artaud's image of the plague, is pure metaphor — a dream of pandemonium. As such, it is the myth towards which all the previous work of Genet has been pointing. In the foreword to *The Maids,* Genet had tried to imagine "a clandestine theatre, to which one would go in secret, at night, and masked," adding:

It would be sufficient to discover — or create — the common Enemy, then the Homeland which is to be protected or regained. I do not know what the theatre will be like in a socialist world; I can understand better what it could be among the Mau Mau, but in the Western world, which is increasingly marked by death and turned toward it, it can only refine in the "reflecting" of a comedy of a comedy, of a reflection of a reflection which ceremonious performance might render exquisite and close to invisibility. If one has chosen to watch oneself die charmingly, one must rigorously pursue, and array, the funeral symbols.

In *The Blacks,* Genet discovers and creates "the common Enemy," arranging Western funeral symbols in a ceremonious performance which is probably close to his idea of theatre among the Mau Mau. The play is a rite of murder, sacrifice, and revolt, enacted by Negro supremacists, and culminating in the ritual slaughter of the entire white race.

The Blacks, of course, is written by a white man — but one who hates the color white. Genet identifies with Negroes, as he identifies with servants, Arabs, beggars, and thieves, because they are rebels and outcasts. Rimbaud, who loathed his Christian heritage, made the same kind of identification in *Une Saison en Enfer:* "I am a beast and a nigger. But I can be saved. You are sham niggers, you, maniacs, fiends, misers. Merchant, you are a nigger; Judge, you are a nigger; General, you are a nigger; Emperor, old itch, you are a nigger. . . ." And Artaud expressed much the same contempt for the fake superiority of the white race: "If we think Negroes smell bad," he writes, "we are ignorant of the fact that anywhere but in Europe it is we whites who 'smell bad.' I would say we give off an odor as white as the gathering of pus in an infected wound." In *The Blacks,* it is the *absence* of white odor which offends the nostrils of the Negroes ("you, pale and odorless race, race without animal odors, without the pestilence of our swamps"), but the infection of the white race is just as advanced. The whites are exhausted, and paling into invisibility; soon they will vanish from the earth. Genet's purpose is to dramatize, in advance, the obliteration of the color white through the liquidation of the Great White Figures, at the same time defining the color which is to supersede it. *The Blacks* originated in his mind, he tells us in a note, when an actor asked him to write a play for an all-Negro cast — "But what exactly is a black?" he asks. "First of all, what's his color?"

To answer this question, Genet sets up a mortal conflict between black and white; and to refine his play into a "reflection of a reflection," he places these conflicts on a number of parallel planes. The most obvious of these are reminiscent of the inner and outer conflicts in Pirandello's theatre trilogy, for they take place both on the stage and in the audience. The first level of conflict is between the actors (black) and the spectators (white). A group of Europeanized Negroes, who work for whites either as servants, professionals, or prostitutes, appear before the audience in disguise — and in attitudes of open hostility.[20] This hostile confrontation is so essential to the play that Genet stipulates that a symbolic white should always be present in

[20] Ionesco is said to have left a performance of *The Blacks* before it was over, because he felt that he was being attacked, and that the actors were enjoying it.

the audience, even if the work is being performed before Negroes. For the white spectator is "the common Enemy"—a respectable bourgeois who is spotlighted as the potential victim of the blacks. This ominous implication, however, is possible only in the theatre—which is to say, in the world of "play." Outcasts and outlanders among the whites, Negroes are permitted to communicate with them only by playing a role: "They tell us we're grown-up children," says the Negro "master of sacred ceremonies," Archibald. "In that case, what's left for us? The theatre." Like licensed jesters, the Negro performers have certain privileges, denied to other Negroes. Because they appear in the role of subordinates, entertaining paying customers and laboring to gain their approval, they can express certain feelings which are ordinarily suppressed.

For this reason, Genet subtitles his work *Un Clownerie,* which means not only "A Clown Show." but a farce or practical joke; it is not to be taken seriously. The Negroes' anger is sham; their insolence is artificial; the play is just a play. We are soon to learn that, beneath their histrionic disguise, the Negroes are deadly serious, and that what they are enacting is the end of subordination. But in the theatre, their violence is constrained and ritualized, and the audience left serenely undisturbed. As Archibald says:

This evening we will perform for you. But in order that you may remain comfortably settled in your seats in the presence of a drama that is already unfolding here, in order that you may be assured that there is no danger of such a drama's worming its way into your precious lives, we shall have the decency—a decency learned from you—to make communication impossible.

The spectators will be allowed to maintain their sense of supremacy. The anger of the performers is actually genuine, but they will conceal their real feelings in opaque metaphors and obscure ceremonies. Thus, the Negroes appear before the whites in Pirandellian fashion, both as fictional characters and as living people. And to intensify the Pirandellian atmosphere of reality in the midst of artifice, the outer action is presumably improvised, and the play proceeds without act breaks, in one long scene.

The second level of conflict is placed inside the play itself, and it takes the form of a make-believe ceremony in which Negroes enact ritualistic roles. Like the Pirandellian play-within-the-play, this ceremony — though it can be altered slightly if the actors find "a cruel detail to heighten it"— is fixed and rehearsed. And the audience is mute, functioning only as a silent witness. The audience, however, is still implicated in the action, because the audience is impersonated by Negroes — Negroes who have masked their faces "in order to live the loathsome life of the Whites and at the same time to help you sink into shame." These white masks represent the "Court," and include all the Great Figures of European colonialism — Rimbaud's "sham niggers" (Merchant, Judge, General, Emperor) now transformed into Queen, Queen's Valet, Judge, Governor, and Missionary.[21] Caricaturing white attitudes, satirizing white achievements, reviling white paternalism, the Negroes impersonate the postures and manners of the world which has condemned them to servitude, thereby attempting to destroy the idea of white, in conception and in fact. The Court has come to attend its own funeral rites, and the Governor even has his death speech in his pocket.

The destiny of the whites is dramatized in a ritual ceremony; and it begins when a group of Negroes, dressed in the height of fake elegance and bad taste, dance a Mozart minuet around a catafalque covered with flowers. Resting on the catafalque, we are told, is the corpse of a white woman, freshly killed for each performance; the ceremony is a Black Mass, witnessed by the Court. While it reflects reality, however, the ceremony is not real. The corpse doesn't exist, and the ritual celebrants are wholly involved in pretense. Introduced by fictional, melodious names, the actors are careful to keep their true

[21] The resemblance to the Great Figures of *The Balcony* is obvious. In *The Screens,* Genet again puts on stage some representatives of the established order: Judge, Banker, Academician, General, etc. His theatre of revolt is always presided over by images of authority.

identities, as well as their true feelings, concealed. What they portray are not the servile Europeans they have become, but the primitive Africans they wish to be; they will reveal not their individual lives but a collective racial identity.

"The tragedy will lie in the color black," says Archibald. "It's *that* that you'll cherish, *that* that you'll attain and deserve. It's *that* that must be earned." In order to transform their guilt into saintliness, their taboo into totem, the Negroes try to purge themselves of all the emotions and attitudes they learned from whites: tenderness, pity, gratitude, love. If man is an animal who imitates, then their image must be cruel: "I order you to be black to your very veins," shouts Archibald. "Pump black blood through them. Let Africa circulate in them. Let Negroes negrify themselves":

Let them persist to the point of madness in what they're condemned to be, in their ebony, in their odor, in their yellow eyes, in their cannibal tastes. . . . Let them invent a criminal painting and dancing. Negroes, if they change towards us, let it not be out of indulgence, but terror.

To prove themselves worthy of their color, the Negroes must pursue it to its very limits. This, too, is imposture and playacting, for their color is determined not only by their tribal past but also by the white's conception of this past. Nevertheless, this kind of playacting is, at least, heroic, and it has a meaning: the annihilation of the whites. The color black — formerly a source of loathing and contempt — will become a source of beauty, evil, and terror. By choosing their destiny, the Negroes will grow into sacred figures, becoming, in Genet's terminology, saints of savagery.

The stage ritual, then, is a celebration of a future event — a kind of homeopathic magic through which the Negroes hope to achieve their victory. But this future event — the murder of the white race — is symbolized in a past event — the rape and murder of a white woman. The ritual consists of a reenactment of the crime, and the trial of the criminal — the Negro, Deodatus Village. Like the play proper, which is judged by white spectators, Village's crime is judged by the White Court. In each case, the guilty condemn the judges.

Village reenacts his crime in startlingly beautiful imagery, with swagger, arrogance, and pomp, and in this crime lies the meaning of the color black. Despite his studied cruelty, however, Village is unable to prevent his real feelings from breaking through his playacting. He is too infected with white emotions — and especially love, which he feels for the prostitute, Virtue. Yet, it is precisely this emotion, as Archibald tells him, which must be suppressed: "Invent not love, but hatred, and thereby make poetry, since that's the only domain in which we are allowed to operate."

While Village invents his poetry of hatred, the White Court attempts to keep its courage up ("Have confidence, Madame, God is white")— at the same time, covertly admiring the beauty, sexuality, and spontaneity of the criminal it has come to indict. Invoking the past triumphs of the West (the Parthenon, Chartres, Byron, Chopin, Aristotelian principles, heroic couplets), reading stock market quotations, uttering colonial clichés, the Court manages only to expose the bankruptcy of its civilization — a civilization now involved in a "long death struggle" from which nothing can rescue it. One of the Negroes, however, the Clergyman Diouf, is an integrationist, and is disposed towards nonviolence. Having learned brotherhood and kindness from the white religion, he pleads that the ceremony "involve us, not in hatred . . . but in love." But for his pains, he is transformed into a "straight man" (or scapegoat) for Village. Equipped with a blonde wig, a pasty carnival mask, pink knitting, and gloves, he is made to impersonate the woman Village raped and killed. When Diouf gives birth to a number of dolls representing all the Great Figures of the Court, it becomes clear that Village's victim was none other than the Mother of the White Race — and Village's crime, therefore, is symbolic of the massacre of all the whites. "He killed out of hatred," remarks the Court. "Hatred of the color white. That was tantamount to killing our entire race and killing us till doomsday."

Genet extends this black-white combat to a third plane of action, which moves it out of the theatre and into reality. For while Village's crime is being reenacted before the Court, and the entire play before the audience, a serious Negro rebellion is being organized behind the scenes. The theatrical ritual, in fact, exists only to mask the secret preparations for this uprising, which will make the stage events not metaphorical but real: "Our aim is not only to corrode and dissolve the idea they'd like us to have of them, we must also fight them in their actual persons, in their flesh and blood." The ritual, therefore, is designed to disintegrate the white image, the uprising to disintegrate the whites. But the stage events reflect, disguisedly, the events occurring behind the scenes; the illusion of the theatre both conceals and reveals the reality outside.

This third conflict, in fact, is a parallel action, because it also takes the form of a trial, conducted offstage and cryptically reported by a Negro messenger — the condemnation and conviction of a Negro traitor before an all-black Court. Unlike the other trials in the play, therefore, this one is attended exclusively by Negroes, and since they must assume responsibility for the death of one of their own, it is an intensely serious affair. Ritual blood is metaphorical, but the Negro's blood is real: "It's no longer a matter of staging a performance." Negroes can sham before whites, but "we've got to stop acting when we're among ourselves." Again, like Roger's rebellion in *The Balcony,* the revolt will put an end to playacting. But when the traitor is executed, and a new Negro leader is elected to carry on the fight, the actors continue their ritualistic masquerade. The moment for open conflict not having arrived, the Negroes are not yet permitted to plunge into reality, and the artifice proceeds. As Archibald says: "As we could not allow the Whites to be present at a deliberation nor show them a drama that does not concern them, and as, in order to cover up, we have had to fabricate the only one that does concern them, we've got to finish this show and get rid of our judges . . . as planned."

The extermination of the judges on stage, however, predicts the outcome of the actual rebellion; and it constitutes the concluding scenes of the play. The White Court, in order to try the Negroes, has pursued them to Africa. They enter this dread region of "leprosy, sorcery, danger, madness . . . and flowers" drunk and walking backwards, as if retreating dazedly through history into the primitive heart of darkness. The Judge arraigns the Negroes, making them whimper and tremble before him — but the trial quickly turns into combat. In their homeland, the guilty criminals have turned into savage heroes, and, as Genet is to write in *The Screens,* "There are no more judges, there are only thieves, murders, firebrands. . . ." The Negro force is increasing, called to the rescue by the sorceress, Felicity ("Negroes of the docks, of the factories, of the dives, Negroes of the Ford plant, Negroes of General Motors"), and the whites are hugely outnumbered. About to be overrun by the black masses, the Queen invokes Dr. Livingstone, Kipling, the white man's burden — but to no avail. As Felicity tells the Court, "You are pale, but you're becoming transparent. . . . You will vanish utterly." The metamorphosis of color begins; black begins to usurp all the privileges of white. "Everything is changing. Whatever is gentle and kind and good and tender will be black. Milk will be black, sugar, rice, the sky, doves, hope, will be black." Even the color of slavery (despite the Queen's refusal to take any position lower than a governess) will change from black to white.

And the whites do vanish utterly. Each member of the Court makes a rhetorical death speech, and is shot to the accompaniment of crowing cocks and clapping hands — the Missionary being castrated and turned into a cow. The last to be exterminated is the Queen, who declares, as she goes to join the others in hell, that the whites will lie torpid like larvae or moles, to rise again in ten thousand years and renew the struggle for the Homeland. And in Genet's mind, they will, for his geometry of revolt is circular. One cycle of civilization has ended, its conclusion signified, in Vico's images, by the crowing of cocks and ominous thundering. But just as inevitably as night gives way to day, the cycle will repeat itself again, like an Eternal Recurrence, when the blacks become the "common Enemy" against whom the white outcasts will eventually rebel.

Already, in fact, Genet is beginning to suggest that the Negro revolt will fail to achieve its goals; reality will remain elusive; the masquerade will continue till doomsday. For in the last dialogue of the play, Village — trying to make love to Virtue — has not been able to invent a wholly original language of love. Still impersonating the whites, he is still caught in their web. And the negativity of black remains only an inverted image.

VIRTUE: All men are like you: they imitate. Can't you invent something else?

VILLAGE: For you I could invent anything: fruits, brighter words, a two-wheeled wheelbarrow, cherries without pits, a bed for three, a needle that doesn't prick. But gestures of love, that's harder . . . still, if you really want me to . . .

VIRTUE: I'll help you. At least, there's one sure thing: you won't be able to wind your fingers in my long golden hair.

But this is not much consolation. The "criminal painting and dancing" demanded by Archibald has not yet come into existence. And, as Genet is to observe in *The Screens,* "If there's no art, there's no culture. Are they therefore doomed to decay?" The question is barely suggested in *The Blacks;* the play simply ends with the completion of the ritual. The dance around the catafalque is repeated (this time without the White Court, the Negroes having removed their masks) to give cyclical form to this cyclical play. But the absence of the whites signifies that the black prophecy has been fulfilled, and that the ceremony is no longer a forecast of the future but rather a mythic rite in memory of a past historic event.

Like all of Genet's work, then, *The Blacks* is a depth charge of evil which plunges through the placid surface of rational discourse and social benevolence to the dark sea floor of the unconscious, where myths of danger, sado-masochistic fantasies, and primitive sacrificial rites explode on us unaware. Taken as a programmatic essay on relations between the races, it is, of course, intolerable — but Genet's art never functions programmatically. It is, rather, imaginative and metaphorical, creating a world contiguous with our own but not identical with it. Appealing to whatever has remained unconditioned and uncivilized in the spectator's soul, Genet fashions his plays as cruel purgative myths — deeply subversive in their implications, profoundly liberating in their effect.

No art, however, is totally self-contained. And Genet, whose criminality and depravity not only attack but exemplify the degeneration of our culture, may well go down as the dramatic artist who presided over the disintegration of the West. Unlike Artaud, whose theories of cruelty were animated by a robust spirit and a healthy conscience, Genet is sick with evil, impregnated with it, consumed by it. His art, however, is his health, and he has managed to wring from his pathology myths which are beautiful, spontaneous, and profound. If he can cure himself, then he may help to cure us, and the dying civilization he chronicles may again revive.

And, in a sense, this is his purpose. For like Artaud, Genet is profoundly implicated in the world against which he revolts, and earnestly seeks to animate its consciousness. Through sex and cruelty he has tried to still the bleating of the community and give it a strong voice, if only for a moment; through art, he has tried to recreate the collective ecstasy, hitherto granted only to the faithful of a religious sect. Genet's messianic theology is compounded of crime and sacrifice, but then these are the elements found in all primitive religions, and Prometheus himself was really a thief for man. In the works of Artaud and Genet, the theatre of revolt has come full circle; its messianism has been revived and its religious implications made more manifest. Indeed, the drama seems to be returning to its original roots in ritual and belief. The radical solutions each man proposes for a regeneration of Western culture may have come too late — and some would say, may even contribute to its end. But if practical solutions are no longer possible, and we are all imprisoned in our destiny, then our imaginations are still free, and imaginative revolt remains the most creative and most lasting kind. We may not be able to transform our fate, but our fate can still be stirring. And this has been a function of dramatic art — to celebrate our possibilities even in defeat: in Artaud's words, to make us look "like victims burnt at the stake, signaling through the flames."

AFTERWORD

Afterword

I have tried in this book to trace the development of an attitude through a hundred years of modern drama, believing that this attitude gives unity to a number of otherwise diverse and disparate playwrights. Revolt is the energy which drives the modern theatre, just as faith drove the theatre of the past. Revolt, however, is not simply an energy but also a body of ideas, a system of values; and these have both their implicit and explicit aspects. In order to emphasize similarities rather than differences among the various playwrights, I have primarily examined the negative side of their revolt: inclined to disagree about what they are for, these playwrights are generally agreed about what they are against. My emphasis sounds like special pleading — but it is an emphasis very frequently made by the playwrights themselves. The theatre of revolt occasionally houses positive ideas and revolutionary programs — especially, as we have seen, in its messianic phase. But more often, its values are implicit. In its negative critique of existing conventions and institutions, it rarely offers any substitute ideas or ideals.

Such destructive criticism accounts, in part, for the unpopularity of this drama, for the modern world wants affirmations. The man who knocks the props out from under the shaky structure of our beliefs is expected to provide us with a new foundation: it is for this reason, perhaps, that the artist in our time has become the focus of so much expectation, and so much chagrin. Revolt is all very well, but revolt on behalf of what, in support of whom? If all our hopes are illusions, what hopes can he give us in return? Such questions the rebel dramatist is stubbornly disinclined to answer, or proceeds to answer with impossible programs and fantastic demands. To those who labor on behalf of the world, this man is an exasperating figure and a false prophet — radical when the world needs moderation, fanatic when the world needs men of goodwill, acrimonious when the world needs harmony.

But in demanding of him the positive values that they themselves possess, the men of action mistake his function. It is senseless to ask the modern dramatist to be what he is not and cannot be; it is important to recognize what he is. For this raggletail, disreputable impossiblist embodies what may be the last genuine humanist value of our crippled civilization: an abiding, indestructible respect for the truth (he holds this even when he no longer believes the truth is attainable). To be a committed political animal today is to care for something more than truth, to involve oneself in compromise for the sake of the well-being and progress of man. But if politics is the art of the possible, art is the politics of the impossible — the free artist would sooner sacrifice the world than relinquish the integrity of his vision. Thus, art encompasses politics but refuses to affirm it. The artist lives in compromised reality, but he lives in another world as well, the world of the imagination, and there his vision is pure and absolute. The conflict between reality and the imagination is the conflict between the ethical and aesthetic views of life; and it is the pivot of the modern theatre. Politics demands resolution; dramatic art is content to leave us in ambiguity. The consequences are unreconciled opposites, tension, inaction — but also the metaphysical joy which comes from a pure truth, beautifully expressed.

It is, therefore, in the art of the modern dramatist that we must look for his affirmation and find our consolation, even when that art is relentless, inconsolable, bleak. What makes Job's torments bearable to us is the way they are set down; what reconciles us to the horror of Lear is the expressive power of Shakespeare. Terror and torment are too much with us today to make us choose to dwell upon them; but in our sometime capacity to face these feelings lies the hope for our spiritual regeneration. "Dare to be tragic men," wrote Nietzsche, "and ye shall be redeemed." The theatre of revolt is not a tragic theatre, but it teaches us how to be tragic men; and if comfort and happiness are not often found there, strength and courage are. The redemption of which Nietzsche speaks is the redemption of the human spirit in a time when spirit is failing; and it is towards this end that the great modern dramatists forged their revolt in enduring harmonious form.

Sources for Quotations in the Text

I: THE THEATRE OF REVOLT

Eric Bentley, *In Search of Theatre*, Knopf.
Albert Camus, *The Rebel*, trans. Anthony Bower, Vintage Books.
——— *Caligula and Three Other Plays*, trans. Stuart Gilbert, Knopf.
T. S. Eliot, *Complete Poems and Plays*, Harcourt, Brace.
Northrup Frye, *Anatomy of Criticism*, Princeton.
Frederick Nietzsche, *Thus Spake Zarathustra*, trans. Thomas Common, Modern Library.
Arthur Rimbaud, *A Season in Hell*, trans. Louise Varèse, New Directions.
Arthur Schopenhauer, *The World as Will and Representation*, trans. E. E. J. Payne, Falcon's Wing Press.
Lionel Trilling, "The Fate of Pleasure," *Partisan Review*, Summer 1963.
Edmund Wilson, *Axel's Castle*, Scribner's.
W. B. Yeats, *Collected Poems*, Macmillan.

II: HENRIK IBSEN

Henrik Ibsen, *The Collected Works*, ed. William Archer, William Heinemann.
——— *Brand*, trans. Michael Meyer, Doubleday Anchor.
——— *Eleven Plays*, trans. William Archer, Modern Library.
——— *The Oxford Ibsen*, trans. and ed. James Walter McFarlane, Oxford.
——— *Lyrics and Poems*, trans. Fydell Edmund Garrett, E. P. Dutton.
——— *Letters*, trans. John Nilsen Laurvik and Mary Morison, Fox, Duffield & Co.
Janko Lavrin, *Ibsen, An Approach*, Methuen.
Arthur Miller, adapter, *An Enemy of the People*, Viking Press.

[419]

George Bernard Shaw, *The Quintessence of Ibsenism*, Hill and Wang Dramabooks.

III: AUGUST STRINDBERG

Pär Lagerkvist, "Modern Theatre: Points of View and Attack," trans. Thomas R. Buckman, *Tulane Drama Review*, Winter 1961.

F. L. Lucas, *Ibsen and Strindberg*, Cassell.

Elizabeth Sprigge, *The Strange Life of August Strindberg*, Hamish Hamilton.

August Strindberg, *Six Plays*, trans. Elizabeth Sprigge, Doubleday Anchor.

———— *Five Plays*, trans. Elizabeth Sprigge, Doubleday Anchor.

———— *Miss Julie*, trans. Evert Sprinchorn, Chandler Editions.

———— *The Road to Damascus*, trans. Graham Rawson, Grove Press.

———— *Letters to Harriet Bosse*, ed. and trans. Arvid Paulson, Thomas Nelson & Sons.

———— "Notes to the Members of the Intimate Theatre," trans. Evert Sprinchorn, *Tulane Drama Review*, Winter 1961.

———— *Inferno*, Le Griffon d'Or.

IV: ANTON CHEKHOV

Anton Chekhov, *The Plays*, trans. Constance Garnett, Modern Library.

———— *Selected Letters*, ed. Lillian Hellman and trans. Sidonie Lederer.

David Magarshack, *Chekhov the Dramatist*, Hill and Wang Dramabooks.

Ernest Simmons, *Chekhov: A Biography*, Atlantic-Little Brown.

Constantin Stanislavsky, *My Life in Art*, trans. J. J. Robbins, Meridian.

V: BERNARD SHAW

Eric Bentley, *Bernard Shaw*, New Directions.

G. K. Chesterton, *George Bernard Shaw*, Hill and Wang Dramabooks.

Richard B. Ohmann, *Shaw: The Style and the Man*, Wesleyan University Press.

George Bernard Shaw, *Standard Edition*, Constable & Co.

———— *Shaw on Theatre*, ed. E. J. West, Hill and Wang.

Edmund Wilson, "Bernard Shaw at Eighty," in *The Triple Thinkers*, John Lehmann.

VI: BERTOLT BRECHT

Lionel Abel, *Metatheatre*, Hill and Wang.

Bertolt Brecht, "An Expression of Faith in Wedekind," trans. Erich A. Albrecht, *Tulane Drama Review*, Autumn 1961.

———— *Kalendergeschichten*, Rowohlt.

———— *Selected Poems*, trans. H. R. Hays, Grove Press.

———— *Seven Plays*, ed. Eric Bentley, Grove Press.

———— *Stücke*, Suhrkamp.

Georg Büchner, *Woyzeck*, trans. Theodore Hoffman in *The Modern Theatre*, Vol. I, ed. Eric Bentley, Anchor.

Martin Esslin, *Brecht: The Man and His Work*, Doubleday.

Max Frisch, "Recollections of Brecht," trans. Carl R. Müller, *Tulane Drama Review*, Autumn 1961.

Ronald Gray, *Bertolt Brecht*, Grove.

George Grosz, *A Little Yes and a Big No*, trans. Lola Sachs Dorin, Dial Press.

Makoto Ueda, "The Implications of the Noh Drama," *Sewanee Review*, Summer 1961.

John Willett, *The Theatre of Bertolt Brecht*, Methuen.

VII: LUIGI PIRANDELLO

T. S. Eliot, *Complete Poems and Plays*, Harcourt, Brace.

Luigi Pirandello, *Diana and Tuda*, trans. Marta Abba, Samuel French.

———— *Henry IV*, trans. Edward Storer, in *Naked Masks*, ed Eric Bentley, Dutton Everyman.

———— *It is So!* (*If You Think So*), trans. Arthur Livingstone, in *Naked Masks*, ed. Eric Bentley, Dutton Everyman.

———— *Six Characters in Search of An Author*, trans. Edward Storer, in *Naked Masks*, ed. Eric Bentley, Dutton Everyman.

———— *The Mountain Giant and Other Plays*, trans. Marta Abba, Crown.

———— *Tonight We Improvise*, trans. Claude Fredericks.

Domenico Vittorini, *The Drama of Luigi Pirandello*, Dover.

VIII: EUGENE O'NEILL

Eric Bentley, "Trying To Like O'Neill," in *In Search of Theatre*, Knopf.

Cyrus Day, "The Iceman and the Bridegroom," *Modern Drama*, May 1958.

Arthur and Barbara Gelb, *O'Neill*, Harper and Bros.

George Jean Nathan, "Portrait of O'Neill," in *O'Neill and His Plays*, ed. Oscar Cargill, N. Bryllion Fagin, and Wm. J. Fisher, New York University Press.

Eugene O'Neill, *Standard Edition*, Jonathan Cape.

Edd Winfield Parks, "Eugene O'Neill's Quest," *Tulane Drama Review*, Spring 1960.

John Henry Raleigh, "O'Neill and Irish Catholicism," *Partisan Review*, Fall 1959.

Lionel Trilling, "The Genius of O'Neill," in *O'Neill and His Plays*, ed. Gargill, Fagin, and Fisher, New York University Press.

IX: ANTONIN ARTAUD AND JEAN GENET

Paul Arnold, "The Artaud Experiment," trans. Ruby Cohen, *Tulane Drama Review*, Winter 1963.

Antonin Artaud, "States of Mind: 1921-1945," trans. Ruby Cohen, *Tulane Drama Review*, Winter 1963.

—— *The Theatre and Its Double*, trans. Mary Caroline Richards, Grove Press.

Jean Genet, "A Note on Theatre," trans. Bernard Frechtman, *Tulane Drama Review*, Spring 1963.

—— *Oeuvres Complètes*, Gallimard.

—— *Our Lady of the Flowers*, trans. Bernard Frechtman, Olympia Press.

—— *The Balcony*, trans. Bernard Frechtman, Grove.

—— *The Blacks*, trans. Bernard Frechtman, Grove.

—— *The Maids and Deathwatch*, trans. Bernard Frechtman, Grove.

—— *The Screens*, trans. Bernard Frechtman, Grove.

—— *The Thief's Journal*, trans. Bernard Frechtman, Olympia Press.

Jacques Guicharnaud with June Beckelman, *Modern French Theatre*, Yale University Press.

Bettina Knapp, "An Interview With Roger Blin," *Tulane Drama Review*, Spring 1963.

Marc Pierret, "Genet's New Play: *The Screens*," *Tulane Drama Review*, Spring 1963.

Jean Paul Sartre, *St. Genet: Actor and Martyr*, trans. Bernard Frechtman, George Braziller.

INDEX

INDEX

Robert Brustein founded the American Repertory Theatre Company in 1979 and since then has been its artistic director as well as professor of English at Harvard University. Born in New York City, he studied at Amherst College, the Yale Drama School, and Columbia University. He later taught at Columbia and Yale, where he founded the Yale Repertory Theatre and was dean of the Yale School of Drama. Mr. Brustein has served as drama critic for the *New Republic* since 1959. His books include *Seasons of Discontent, The Third Theatre, Revolution as Theatre, The Culture Watch, Critical Moments, Making Scenes,* and *Who Needs Theatre.* His criticism has won him the George Polk Memorial Award and the George Jean Nathan award twice.

ELEPHANT PAPERBACKS

Theatre and Drama
Robert Brustein, *The Theatre of Revolt,* EL407
Plays for Performance:
    Aristophanes, *Lysistrata,* EL405
    Georges Feydeau, *Paradise Hotel,* EL403
    Henrik Ibsen, *Ghosts,* EL401
    Heinrich von Kleist, *The Prince of Homburg,* EL402
    Christopher Marlowe, *Doctor Faustus,* EL404
    Luigi Pirandello, *Six Characters in Search of an Author,* EL406

Literature and Letters
Stephen Vincent Benét, *John Brown's Body,* EL10
Philip Callow, *Son and Lover: The Young D. H. Lawrence,* EL14
James Gould Cozzens, *Castaway,* EL6
James Gould Cozzens, *Men and Brethren,* EL3
Clarence Darrow, *Verdicts Out of Court,* EL2
Floyd Dell, *Intellectual Vagabondage,* EL13
Theodore Dreiser, *Best Short Stories,* EL1
Joseph Epstein, *Ambition,* EL7
André Gide, *Madeleine,* EL8
Sinclair Lewis, *Selected Short Stories,* EL9
William L. O'Neill, ed., *Echoes of Revolt: The Masses,*
    1911–1917, EL5
Ramón J. Sender, *Seven Red Sundays,* EL11
Wilfrid Sheed, *Office Politics,* EL4
Tess Slesinger, *On Being Told That Her Second Husband Has*
    Taken His First Lover, and Other Stories, EL12